LATIN
AMERICAN
IDENTITIES
AFTER
1980

LATIN AMERICAN IDENTITIES AFTER 1980

Gordana Yovanovich
and Amy Huras,
editors

Wilfrid Laurier University Press

We acknowledge the financial support of the Government of Canada through the Book Publishing Industry Development Program for our publishing activities.

Library and Archives Canada Cataloguing in Publication

Latin American identities after 1980 / Gordana Yovanovich and Amy Huras, editors.

Includes bibliographical references and index.
Issued also in electronic formats.
ISBN 978-1-55458-183-2

1. Latin America—History—1980–. 2. Latin America—Politics and government—1980–. 3. Latin America—Social conditions—1982–. 4. Latin America—Civilization—1948–. 5. Latin America—Intellectual life—20th century. 6. Latin America—Intellectual life—21st century. 7. Globalization—Latin America. I. Yovanovich, Gordana, 1956– II. Huras, Amy, 1983–

F1414.3.L38 2010   980.03'3   C2009-904923-6

Latin American identities after 1980 [electronic resource] / Gordana Yovanovich and Amy Huras, editors.

ISBN 978-1-55458-213-6 (PDF).—ISBN 978-1-55458-300-3 (EPUB).
Electronic formats.

F1414.3.L38 2010a   980.03'3   C2009-904924-4

© 2010 Wilfrid Laurier University Press
Waterloo, Ontario, Canada
www.wlupress.wlu.ca

Cover image based on *Harlequin*, by Canadian painter Dragan Sekaric Shex. Cover design by Martyn Schmoll. Text design by Daiva Villa, Chris Rowat Design.

Every reasonable effort has been made to acquire permission for copyright material used in this text and to acknowledge all such indebtedness accurately. Any errors and omissions called to the publisher's attention will be corrected in future printings.

No part of this publication may be reproduced, stored in a retrieval system or transmitted, in any form or by any means, without the prior written consent of the publisher or a licence from The Canadian Copyright Licensing Agency (Access Copyright). For an Access Copyright licence, visit www.accesscopyright.ca or call toll free to 1-800-893-5777.

Contents

vii   Introduction
     Gordana Yovanovich

     PART ONE
3   Latin America and the New Pax Americana
     Jorge Nef and Alejandra Roncallo

27   Cultural Resilience and Political Transformation in Bolivia
     Susan Healey

51   Globalization and *Indígenas*: The Alto Balsas Nahuas
     Frans J. Schryer

79   Language Shift, Maintenance, and Revitalization: Quichua in an Era of Globalization
     Rosario Gómez

97   Afro-Brazilian Women's Identities and Activism: National and Transnational Discourse
     Jessica Franklin

117   Legal Creolization, "Permanent Exceptionalism," and Caribbean Sojourners' Truths
     Adrian Smith

     PART TWO
145   Cuban Culture at the Eye of the Globalizing Hurricane: The Case of *Nueva Trova*
     Norman Cheadle

167 From Pablo Neruda to Luciana Souza: *Latin America* as Poetic-Musical Space
Maria L. Figueredo

197 The Transculturation of *Capoeira*: Brazilian, Canadian, and Caribbean Interpretations of an Afro-Brazilian Martial Art
Janelle Joseph

217 Kcho's *La regata*: Political or Poetic Installation?
Lee L'Clerc

235 Collective Memory of Cultural Trauma in Peru: Efforts to Move from Blame to Reconciliation
Jennifer Martino

PART THREE

257 Individualism and Human Rights in Antonio Skármeta's *Match Ball*
Gordana Yovanovich

273 Collective Memory and the Borderlands in Guillermo Verdecchia's *Fronteras Americanas*
Pablo Ramírez

287 From Exile to the *Pandilla*: The Construction of the Hispanic-Canadian Masculine Subject in *Cobro Revertido* and *Côte-des-Nègres*
Stephen Henighan

301 Contributors

305 Index

Introduction
Gordana Yovanovich

The objective of this collection of articles is to discuss the period from 1980 to the present as a stage in Latin American political, social, and cultural development, a period after violent unrest in which the Latin American continent, inspired by the Cuban Revolution and international communism, attempted to transform its class and social structure. The post-1980 cultural period also follows the Latin American Boom, a cultural phenomenon inspired by a literary movement that made a conscious effort to render continental cohesion, gave Latin American culture a high profile on the international scene, and incorporated internationalism into the modern conception of Latin American identity. Although the links between pre- and post-1980 are not easily explained, it is evident that in both periods local developments have been driven by *mundial* (global or international) cultural and political movements: whereas previously the proletariat of all countries were called to unite in violent class struggle for economic equality, in recent decades, the countries of the world have been called to unite peacefully into a single economy with more individual freedom. In the cultural domain, the integration of the international and the global with the local has been explained as transculturalization (Angel Rama) in the Boom and as hybridization (Néstor García Canclini) in the more recent period. Inspired by European and Anglo-American modernism, the earlier period succeeded in liberating the form, in questioning old traditions and hierarchies and in introducing the idea of equality into Latin American discourses.[1] Employing this new language, the post-1980 period has not so much pursued the idea of class equality, but rather has adopted the idea of universal equal rights which promises greater individual liberty and greater ethnic, cultural and gender equality.

In his study of the relationship between modernism and postmodernism, George Yúdice explains that "the postmodern does not necessarily seek to innovate, as does the modern, but rather to rearticulate alternative traditions in order to desalinate contemporary life" (1992, 15). In the case of Latin American culture, "alternative traditions" were very much a part of the Boom, from the inclusion of African spiritual elements in Alejo Carpentier's *El reino de este mundo* [*The kingdom of this world*] to indigenous, African, and Gallego superstitions found in Gabriel García Márquez's *Cien años de soledad* [*One hundred years of solitude*]. However, these "alternative traditions" have been much more visible in the post-1980 period. In a period when neoliberal globalization is driven by international institutions such as the International Monetary Fund, the World Bank and the World Trade Organization, the credibility of the "grand récits" — such as Christianity, Revolution, the Hegelian Absolute Spirit, and Marxism — as Jean-François Lyotard explains, is lost and hope is placed on practical solutions and international legal justice. The work of non-governmental organizations (NGOs) and international activism supported by the United Nations and financed by private granting agencies, private scholarly foundations, private galleries, and private (music and film) industries becomes particularly important. This change is celebrated by some articles in this collection, particularly those which study indigenous "alternative" cultures. However, several contributors remain skeptical that globalization is bringing significant improvements to Latin America despite the fact that they recognize the attempt made to construct different modern identities.

Previous studies of Latin American identities have largely been written from the point of view of political or cultural theory. In this collection, theoretical issues are used only as heuristic devices in the interpretation of modern Latin American culture and society. Instead of focusing on political and cultural theories and dominant ideologies, the basic framework for this study is the human condition and the attempt to answer a basic question: What does it mean to be Latin American (person or artist) in an age of globalization? Articles in this collection address North–South relationships in the Americas, examine the impact of global movements on indigenous situations, study the effect of globalization on the liberation of women and compare and contrast foreign and local realities, recognize the rise of the new Socialist governments in Latin America, and study the changes that music industries and global markets are bringing to Latin American music and art. Throughout this collection, the authors have demonstrated an awareness of the masterful twist in the development from the preceding (communist) internationalization to the present (capitalist) globalization.

This collection by Canadian scholars has a unique interdisciplinary approach to Latin American social and cultural change. In its broad regional coverage and its focus on Latin American contact with other cultures and nations, its scholarship combines the scientific method of evidence-based case studies with the Latin American tradition of essay writing in areas where the discourse of the establishment does not match the political, social, and cultural realities, where it is not easy to empirically prove something that is purposely covert but where logic and deduction lead to certain conclusions.

This study of the *becoming* and *being* of Latin American cultural and social identities begins with an interpretation of the new Pax Americana designed in the 1980s by the North in agreement with the southern elites. As the agreement ties the hands of national governments and establishes new regional and global strategies, Latin American identity is emphasized over national identities. The multifaceted impacts and effects of globalization in Bolivia, Ecuador, Mexico, Cuba, Brazil, Chile, Peru, and the Caribbean are then examined, with an emphasis on social changes, the transnationalization and commodification of Latin American and Caribbean arts, and the adaptation of cultural identities in a globalized context as understood by Latin American authors writing from transnational perspectives.

Although there is probably as much difference between Bolivia and Argentina as there is between Sweden and Greece, terms such as "Latin American" and "European" have been significant in the past and are also relevant today. In "Who Is Afraid of Identity Politics?" Linda Martín Alcoff indicates that "it makes sense to talk about national [or continental] identity or ethnic identity even while one assumes that there are differences between the individuals who might share such an identity as well as similarities that such individuals may share with those in another identity group" (2000, 318). According to John King, the term "Latin America" is a mid-nineteenth-century European invention, providing a way of differentiating Spanish- and Portuguese-speaking America from the anglo-American world "in particular from the growing power of the United States" (2004, 1). How Latin America has struggled for its own identity in its contact with both Europe and the United States is best explained by Mario Vargas Llosa who argues that the Latin American relationship to dominant political and cultural powers in the twentieth century has not been one of rejection, but of unique incorporation.

> Culturally Latin America is and is not Europe. It cannot be anything other than hermaphrodite.... No radical denial of European influences has always produced in Latin America shoddy pieces of work, with no creative spark; at the same time, servile imitation has led to affected works with no life on their own.... By contrast, everything of lasting value that Latin America has produced in the artistic sphere stands in a curious relationship of both attraction and rejection with respect to Europe: such works make use of the European tradition for other ends or else introduce into that system certain forms, motifs or ideas that question or interrogate it without actually denying it. (Vargas Llosa 2002, 24)

As Latin American transculturation in Boom literature incorporated European modernist formal and philosophical issues with local Latin American cultural realities, the larger cultural development also had to deal with important covert political North American interventions. In the post-1980 period, the US intervention is more evident.

It is interesting to briefly trace the development of the Latin American Boom, a literary period of the 1960s and 1970s produced by writers such as Gabriel García Márquez, Julio Cortázar, Carlos Fuentes and Mario Vargas Llosa because this literary movement made a conscious effort to construct continental Latin American identity which has been extended to other cultural manifestations. Particularly outside the continent, we ask for Latin American books, listen to Latin American music and consume other Latin American cultural goods. "An outstanding feature of the Boom coterie," Irene Rostagno indicates, "was its sense of importance as a group of innovators and their determination to be recognized as Latin American writers in Europe and the U.S." (1997, 90). Rostagno's study of the development of the Boom is relevant for the study of the post-1980 period because it shows that identity is constructed by an interesting literary, political, and marketing interplay, which is active after 1980, but in a different way. Her study also shows that although cultural identities are constructed by institutions of the power establishment, events also develop spontaneously because the power establishment cannot fully control what artists and the public make and understand.

In the latest studies of identity, works of "post-positivist realists," such as *Reclaiming identity: Realist theory and the predicament of postmodernism* edited by Paula Moya and Michael Hames-García, an attempt is made to view the question of personal and cultural identity from a holistic position where the construction of realities is also experienced and perceived from a subjective perspective. In other words, the power establishments are active in shaping the world through their strategies, but individuals and different groups are also in the position not only to subvert the fabricated order, but to turn it into a reality which is their own. "Our conceptions of who we are as social being (our identities)," Paula Moya writes, "influence — and in turn are influenced by — our understandings of how our society is structured and what our particular experiences in that society are likely to be.... Identities are not simply products of structures of power; they are often assumed or chosen for complex subjective reasons that can be objectively evaluated" (2000, 9).

The politicization and strategic intervention in the construction of modern Latin American identity and culture began when Haydée Santa María, the director of the Casa de las Americas, made the dissemination of Boom writing a top priority and created a situation which allowed the intellectual capital of Latin America to shift from Paris to Havana. She also directed the movement and political and artistic thinking to be interpreted within the context of the Revolution. The later director, Cuban poet Roberto Fernández Retamar, carried out further the "Cubanization" of Latin American culture, which would provoke a reaction from the United States. However, this did not occur without an intervention from Europe. The Boom was also supported by the Spanish socialist poet Carlos Barral who befriended many Boom writers during his travels to Cuba and who published their works in Barcelona. The Boom authors became a "boom" when they met Carmen Balcells, an aggressive literary agent who, in the late sixties, helped bring their works to North American markets. The North American interest in the Latin American new novel then became the US camouflaged interest in Latin American politics, as José Donoso argues (Rostagno 1997). The most important effort to disseminate modern Latin American literature in the United States was initiated in 1962 by the Inter-American Foundation for the Arts (IAFA) and later by the Center for Inter-American Relations. According to Rostagno, "Though never overtly stated, the intention behind IAFA was to counteract the impact of Cuba's cultural revolution on Latin intellectuals" (1997, 103). The Center searched for and employed the best translators, such as Gregory Rabassa, influential personalities such as Susan Sontag and John Updike, and prominent critics such as Rodriguez Monegal, who edited the literary journal *Mundo Nuevo*, which represented some of the best South American writing of the 1950s and 1960s. The journal has been linked to the British literary journal *Encounter* which, *The New York Times* wrote, had received CIA funds by the way of the Congress for Cultural Freedom. The US government's justification of this covert funding was to defend pro-Western values in an intellectual milieu dominated by Marxism.

While the CIA support for the new direction of the Boom was covert, the support of the Rockefeller brothers was clear. They also endorsed Kennedy's Alliance for Progress with the intention of making the Center an effective instrument in offsetting what they considered to be leftist propaganda. With this intervention, non-governmental foundations and organizations assumed a political role through cultural intervention and gave a new direction to Latin American cultural production and politics. The point made here is that cultural institutions are not politically neutral, and that they and NGOs can be used for political goals, as the former president of Russia, Vladimir Putin, recently argued in his disagreement and banning of NGO meddling in Russian political developments. This is significant for the study of the post-1980 period because international foundations and NGOs play an important part in the making of the contemporary conception of identity. It is important to keep in mind that they are not apolitical and that they can be tools of the power establishment regardless of good intentions of modern activists.

It is interesting to note that as North American and French critics and readers discovered Jorge Luis Borges, North American institutions tried to undermine thematic issues in the writing of the Boom by emphasizing formal innovation: "After Borges, one reads García Márquez and Fuentes less for what they tell us about Latin American culture than for what they offer as writers of fiction," Rostagno writes (1997, 119). Ironically, but for the same reason, post-1980 Latin American literature became known in the United States for its thematic importance: "If the writer came from Central America, much ado was made of political turmoil there; if from Chile or Argentina, the issue of human rights was the password for rapid recognition" (Rostagno 1997, 137). Argentine Luisa Valenzuela's astounding rise to fame in the early 1980s is said to owe much to the backing of prominent North American women writers like Susan Sontag and Erica Jong. The female Latin American artists who may have benefited the most from North American feminism are Isabel Allende and Frida Kahlo. The support from the North is of great importance for the artists, for the female gender, and for Mexico, Chile, and Argentina. However, as post-1980 identities are constructed, it is important to recognize a change in artistic quality and in ideological emphasis. For example, the North American interpretation of Isabel Allende's novel *La casa de los espíritus* in the popularized Hollywood-style film *The House of Spirits* places a greater emphasis on the exotic love relationship between Esteban Trueba and his wife, daughter, and granddaughter than on the political story and the 1973 US-supported military coup. Likewise, Isabel Allende's recognition of the traditional empowering relationship between women in Latin America is turned into a lesbian love story between Clara and her spinster sister-in-law Ferrula. Similarly, as North American feminism does not emphasize the notion that women are or should be equal *compañeras* to men, but portray women as victims of male-dominant societies, in Frida Kahlo's case, the female artist is no longer portrayed as the wife of progressive Marxist painter Diego Rivera, whom she adored and followed, but as a victim of her macho Latin American husband.

This collection will study some further twists in North American emphasis. For example, the difference between North American feminist discourse and the Latin American reality of marginalized black women will be discussed in this collection in "Afro-Brazilian Women's Identities and Activism: National and Transnational Discourses," by Jessica Franklin, who recognizes the importance of the work of international women's movements but also observes that in the post-1980 period Brazilian black women find the greatest strength in the local tradition of the survival of their race and gender. Franklin also observes that although international movements are able to challenge national oppression, the weakening of national governments and institutions advanced by globalization makes the enforcement of international policies difficult.

The interdisciplinary approach in this collection hopes to present a view of Latin American identity constructed after 1980 in its complexity, and to show that Latin America is again becoming something unique. The question of indigenous rights, women's rights, and human rights in general will be addressed in several articles included in this collection. Articles in the first part of the collection view social changes within various Latin American realities with an amount of skepticism as social security is being eroded. However, they recognize that the United Nations Decade of the World's Indigenous Peoples (1995–2004) has brought positive changes to the indigenous part of Latin America. The declaration of the United Nations supported by work of non-government organizations helped bring about the 2005 election in Bolivia, which brought to power the first indigenous leader, Evo Morales, who was also supported by a rural-based social movement. Various other involvements of NGOs and learning communities around the world will be discussed as the decentralization of politics occurs peacefully, and as new possibilities are opening up. At the same time, arguments are also provided for caution. One wants to share Octavio Paz's optimism expressed in his famous lecture in New York that the modern aesthetics established by experimental Boom writers had prepared the ground for the creation of a new culture which could be multi-centred, where the periphery could be brought to the centre (as Mexican, Cuban, Chilean, indigenous art is brought to New York) and where differences could be translated into similarities. As Octavio Paz repeats the spirit expressed in Rubén Darío's poem "Salutación al águila," written during the third Pan-American conference held in Rio De Janeiro in 1906, "May this grand Union have no end," followed by the Latin proverb "E pluribus unum!" one also cannot help but remember Rubén Darío's later poem "A Roosevelt" and take the optimism for political and cultural unity with some skepticism.

Part I

The United Nations Decade of the World's Indigenous Peoples (1995–2004), the 1992 commemorative celebration of "Discovery of Americas," and the agreement between the Northern and the Southern elites to create a new hemispheric alignment or new Pax Americana are three major events which have defined social and political changes in Latin America since 1980. With indigenous or Native American, Euro-American, and Afro-American populations that are pervasive from Alaska to Tierra del Fuego in multicultural combinations, the new union may be different, but it is still uneasy. This uneasiness, loss of security, and the highlighted emphasis on differences are the subject of the next six articles which make up the first part of this manuscript. The first article, by Jorge Nef and Alejandra Roncallo, provides a comprehensive and deft overview of the current moment in geopolitics, along with its economic and social impact, across the Americas. The following three articles focus on the formation of new ethnic identities of indigenous Latin American peoples and study the cultural, historic, and geographic aspects which interplay with international interventions as they create new conceptions of group being. While Susan Healey celebrates the election of the first *campesino* indigenous president in Bolivia and argues that "alternate" cultures find strength in their tradition, Frans J. Schryer argues that globalization has brought mostly positive changes to the everyday lives of Mexican Indians of the Alto Balsas because they have largely benefited from their experiences of migration and other forms of globalization. This inclusion of subjective experience studied by objective scholarly approaches in the discussion of the question of identity is important despite the fact that improvements themselves may not be great. The last of these three articles, a piece by Rosario Gómez, focuses on changes in indigenous identity by studying the linguistic shifts and linguistic revitalizations that occur as globalization brings linguistic homogenization but also support for differences. Next, Jessica Franklin's article focuses on the question of racial and gender identity as international women's movements confront local government practices. The final article in Part I is a study of the legal system which enables the exploitation of migrant workers from Mexico and the Caribbean. While migration brings some economic and personal satisfaction to seasonal workers, as Frans Schryer shows, Adrian Smith argues that their legal consciousness needs to be raised, as the postcolonial practices are not fundamentally different from colonial ones.

In their article "Latin America and the New Pax Americana," Jorge Nef and Alejandra Roncallo point out that the present-day Latin American and Caribbean realities and identities have been shaped by a new Pax Americana, designed in the 1980s by the North in agreement with Southern elites engaged in a regional and global strategy of accumulation of wealth as well as in the legitimization of new rules of enforcement. While the old Pax Americana constructed "Latin America" as a geo-strategic space in which the perceived and illusive communist threat had to be combated through Northern incentives to local elites in the form of development projects and foreign aid, the new Pax Americana of the 1980s has attempted to "solve" the debt problem through the imposition of structural adjustment and the creation of a transnational legal framework that ties the hands of national governments in favour of transnational capital. The state, instead of providing and securing the reproduction of society, has been transformed into a mere collaborative regulator of the private sector. The weakening of the state has occurred with the promise of democratization and the reduction of poverty and corruption. Although this discourse has become the choice of the day, the reality does not match the rhetoric. Nef and Roncallo also note a significant deterioration of security for most people—not only south of the Rio Grande but also in Canada and the United States.

Borrowing the paradigm of "Eastern Europe" where the political system was a greater defining factor than sovereign entities, Nef and Roncallo discuss Latin American identity in the context of "the Americas" and conclude that "without profound changes in both the South and the North" the region will be defined by limited democratic process, by the widening gap between the rich minority and poor majority, and by profound human insecurity. They observe that in the next period of development Latin America will take the role of leadership because populism and anti-status quo feelings have been on the rise. They cite the series of electoral victories of populism and left-of-centre parties in Argentina, Brazil, Uruguay, Nicaragua, Bolivia, and Venezuela, all of them at odds with Washington's neoconservative politics, and link them to mass mobilizations in 2006 which brought millions of protesters to the streets of Los Angeles, New York and Chicago.

The work by Nef and Roncallo is not a revolutionary piece, but it is a study that recognizes the failures or traps of neoliberalism and observes that the "transition to democracy" is still a long way away from true democracy. Sovereignty and democracy, according to these two authors, are "precariously balanced civilian regimes, based on negotiations with elites" where the popular sectors are kept outside the political arena, and where external economic and military actors have the veto power over state policies. As they observe that instances of torture, disappearances, and blatant state terrorism have become less frequent, they point out that there is a persistence, and even revival, of authoritarian and oligarchic traditions.

In her chapter, "Cultural Resilience and Political Transformation in Bolivia," Susan Healey provides a very insightful and informative overview of the current situation of indigenous movements in Bolivia. She indicates that the supposed 1992 commemorative celebration of the "Discovery of the Americas" became an opportunity for people from indigenous, black, and popular segments of society to rebuild grassroots movements from the bottom up, and that the "Five-Hundred Years of Resistance" campaign marked the beginning of a process that brought indigenous movements from different nations of the Americas together for the first time. Healey also examines the major historical events and conditions which have contributed to the strength of indigenous determination and which continue to drive their struggle to reassert the primacy of indigenous land rights and traditions. She argues that the Andean cosmology or *cosmovisión* was never completely lost and remains a vital part of life in highland communities throughout Bolivia. Such a world view seeks to balance the material needs of an impoverished people with the recognition that the Western-imposed notions of capitalist development are neither spiritually nor ecologically congruent with the overarching, holistic view of the world that directly impacts the daily lives of *campesinos*. Their reality is expressed in a system of social structuring exercised through familial and communal organizational structures. Inspirational indigenous figures from the past, such as Tupac Amaru, are viewed not merely as rebel leaders but rather as persons imbued with divine authority to carry out the prophesied Inca *recuperación* or recovery. These stories, which help to sustain a powerful sentiment that indigenous peoples are "oppressed but not defeated," give strength and inspiration to the indigenous rural-based social movement. However, it remains to be seen how this political alternative will deal with the Western-imposed capitalist notions of development. Healey believes that the election of Evo Morales, who won an absolute majority, marks a fundamental and perhaps irreversible shift in the Bolivian political landscape.

While *campesino* and indigenous movements in Bolivia have had a dramatic turn of events, indigenous groups in Mexico and Ecuador have also been influenced by global politics and, as a result, have a better opportunity to negotiate less-discriminated-against identities. In his study, "Globalization and *Indígenas*: the Alto Balsas Nahuas," Frans J. Schryer examines the transformation of an indigenous Nahuatl-speaking village in the state of Guerrero, Mexico, as a result of the adoption of craft production and the migration of their inhabitants to the United States. In his work, Schryer aims to "debunk a set of misconceptions and simplistic ideas about both globalization and what it means to be indigenous." He observes that the most obvious and widely publicized connection between globalization and Mexico's *indígenas* is the Zapatista uprising in Chiapas following the signing of the North American Free Trade Agreement (NAFTA). He also concludes that "the web-site presence and political activity of the Zapatistas and their sympathizers in Mexico and abroad have become symbols for resistance against globalization and the struggle for indigenous rights." Yet Schryer chooses to examine a different group of indigenous people and argue that the villages of the Alto Balsas have benefited from globalization. First, their situation improved due to the economic boom in North America following World War II as many children received their first exposure to the Spanish language and literacy. Then, in the 1980s, the development of crafts, especially *amate* painting, gave these indigenous people another contact with the outside world and changed their idea of group identity. Most of the *amate* paintings were bought by tourists and middle-class Mexicans. The Mexican state also organized indigenous art exhibitions, and awarded prizes to *amate* painters whose work was outstanding. Finally, *amate* art produced by better-known artists has been exhibited in art galleries and museums in New York and Paris. The participation of indigenous Mexicans from the Alto Balsas region in the international field of arts and crafts was made possible by globalization, Schryer argues.

Migration to the United States is another important factor in the creation of group identity in the region. Schryer shows that from the mid-nineties onward, it became typical for both male and female teenagers from the region to leave and seek their fortunes in "*el Norte.*" By the year 2000, as much as one-third of the households had family members living in Los Angeles, Houston, and Atlanta. These people often save enough money in three or four years to build a house in Mexico and even buy a pickup truck, Schryer indicates. They also hold luxurious weddings and birthday parties in Texas and California, which are recorded and shown to local people. Thus, some residents of Ahuehuepan who have never been outside of Mexico are today more familiar with the apartment buildings, shopping malls, and gardening centres in Lincoln, California, than they are with downtown Mexico City.

With the global attempts to improve the situation of indigenous peoples, changes can be noted not only in the socio-economic and political spheres, but in linguistics as well. In her chapter, "Language Shift, Maintenance, and Revitalization: Quichua in an Era of Globalization," Rosario Gómez studies how, in the second half of the twentieth century, educational reforms in Ecuador which promoted native culture and values, literacy, administrative reforms, and indigenous people's rights have given importance to the Quichua language and have fostered greater contact between Quechua and Spanish. Estimates for the total number of Quechua speakers in South America range from 8 to 10 million. Despite these numbers, from the 1980s onward, intergenerational transmission as well as the domains in which Quechua is spoken have rapidly decreased, clearly indicating that this language is in danger of extinction. One of the factors for the language loss is rapid urbanization promoted by modern technology and the desire for a better life. As indigenous groups move into cities, social networks are disrupted and individuals lose the linguistic support systems in which Quechua is the language of interaction. In recent decades, indigenous individuals have been bound not only toward metropolitan centers within Ecuador but also toward the United States, Canada, and Europe, particularly Spain. The loss is happening not only because of the contact with Spanish but with English and other languages as well. However, technology and increased communication have also empowered some indigenous organizations to maintain their traditional values and languages while being incorporated into the global economy.

An influx of international tourists interested in Ecuador's indigenous cultures initiated a cultural identity-based shift among middle-class Ecuadorians in the 1970s. This paved the way for the significant language policy changes of the 1980s that aimed to reform the Spanish-dominant national education system by adopting bilingual education. The establishment of the first indigenous university in Ecuador in 2004, La Universidad Intercultural de Nacionalidades y Pueblos Indígenas Amawtay Wasi, was an unprecedented and important development in indigenous language education. In 1986 the Confederation of Indigenous Nationalities of Ecuador was established and subsequently recognized by the government in the attempt to guarantee indigenous peoples a political voice. Policy reforms in Ecuador are inextricably linked to the fundamental changes in policies in Peru and Bolivia, which advocate the recognition and appreciation of indigenous cultures and languages while striving toward intercultural bilingual education. In her work, Gómez also examines the contact between Spanish and Quichua in the Highlands of Ecuador and presents some evidence of linguistic change in Spanish produced by the social, political, and cultural interaction of the speakers of these two languages.

The ideals of globalization, and particularly those of the universal human and minority rights movement, give a glimmer of hope not only to marginalized ethnic groups but also to those facing gender discrimination. Through electoral quotas, the modern movement has helped women incorporate themselves into politics in many Latin American countries. However, despite the election of Michelle Bachelet in Chile in 2006 and Cristina Kirchner in Argentina in 2007, the women incorporated into the new political economy are a select group of elite Euro-American women; obviously much more is needed to make real change for women in general. In her chapter, "Afro-Brazilian Women's Identities and Activism: National and Transnational Discourse," Jessica Franklin argues that, despite class and ethnic differences and the lack of solidarity among women, Afro-Brazilian women, the poorest segment of the population, have taken a leadership role in the effort to combat racial and gender discrimination in their country. Their activism has been stimulated and supported by a transnational discourse and the activism of three groups. The specific linkages between Afro-Brazilian women and the African Diaspora have focused on promoting the distinct history and culture of the Afro-Brazilian population. Universal human rights ideologies and legislation have been utilized to challenge the actions of the state. And the global doctrines of black feminism have impacted on identity formation and have mobilized the strategies of Afro-Brazilian women. In the struggle to construct new Afro-American identities, it is necessary to move beyond the negative associations with poverty and weakness and to emphasize the collective identities, complex histories, and recognizable culture of the Afro-American population. Franklin indicates that the World Conferences on Women's Rights and Racism have provided a powerful platform for many Afro-Brazilian activists seeking to challenge the state on issues of human rights, citizenship, and racial and gender equality. Nonetheless, Franklin also observes, as Healey does in her study of the indigenous struggle for change, that a key point of contention is the ability of various forums to translate these transnational discourses into national-policy-oriented actions and to incorporate the voices of excluded populations in law and in practice.

Following the 1948 Universal Declaration of Human Rights, major educational efforts have been made in favour of peaceful, legal means of change over violent struggles against discrimination and exploitation. For example, in recent times, the former Chilean dictator, Augusto Pinochet, was almost brought to justice — together with Slobodan Milosevic and war criminals from Rwanda. However, as Jessica Franklin asserts, the legal practice has yet to live up to the ideals of globalization.

In his study of the legal protection of Caribbean and Central American migrant workers in Canada, "Legal Creolization, 'Permanent Exceptionalism,' and Caribbean Sojourners' Truths," Adrian Smith rejects the notion that the post-colonial ideology of globalization has resulted in a geo-strategic "reconfiguration of space" in the Western Hemisphere. Smith, a law scholar, suggests that there is no transnational legal system which protects migratory workers' rights. He explores the role of Canadian nation-state-based law which shapes the legal consciousness of Caribbean workers. Given that a number of countries regard Canada's temporary labour migration scheme as the prototype of "new" and "managed" migration, Smith recognizes the need to question the role of the Canadian state as a legal imperial force. Over twenty thousand labourers from the Caribbean, Mexico, and Guatemala sojourn in Canada by way of the Seasonal Agricultural Workers Program (SAWP). These mostly male sojourners arrive to pick fruits, vegetables, and tobacco in southwestern Ontario. The regulatory framework of the SAWP mimics that of the H2-A worker program in the United States. Hence, in the current regulatory framework that governs the transnational work performed by migratory workers, there are no new global laws but rather the transferral and adaptation of American legal norms across borders. This "Empire's law," as one socio-legal scholar has recently called it, treats labour migration as a means through which the Canadian state not only facilitates the exploitation of migratory workers but renews the particular conditions of Third World (and in particular, Caribbean, and Latin American) underdevelopment. To confront this situation, Smith develops the idea of "legal creolization" as a way to capture and characterize the transnational development of migrant farm workers' legal consciousness. For him, legal creolization is a potential strategy of resistance through which workers might begin to construct a critical legal consciousness based on Third World political sensibilities.

Part II

While the first part of this collection examines various interactions within Latin America of international and global forces with local social and political realities, Part 2 studies what happens to Latin American music, poetry, and sports as they are exported outside of Latin America, and how Latin American identity is changed as music industries, different audiences, and different realities consume them. There is no doubt that with globalization, translation, and the opening up of borders, Latin American culture and arts are reaching greater audiences and are better known throughout the world. Precisely what is known and how they are understood, however, is a different issue, which depends on aspects such as the capabilities and the sensitivity of the translator, on market profitability, and on the willingness of the centre to accept the periphery. The Miami technology and music industry, led by a new generation of Cuban Americans, has played a particular role in exporting and internationalizing Cuban or Cuban-based music today. However, it is still difficult today to solve the fundamental question of how to supersede binary social and political divisions such as: for or against the Cuban Revolution, political or poetic, true Latin American or North Americanized adaptation, truly artistic or popular and exotic, etc. There is no doubt that as Latin American music dance and sports cross borders, they are not merely adopted but also adapted by the receiving cultures. The best example is that of the tango, which originated as an erotic dance performed by African slaves in Argentina and Uruguay but was turned into an elegant dance in European salons. More recently, *capoeira*, a spontaneous Brazilian sport/dance/martial art which incorporates free movement, instrumental and vocal music, martial combat, and Afro-Brazilian dance, has been flattened and commodified in the vanguard of fitness cultures in Canada and the United States.

In the first article of this section, Norman Cheadle questions "La caída del muro de Florida," as the 2007 headline of Spain's major newspaper *El País* says. Perhaps as the fall of the Berlin Wall, which marked the end of the Cold War, only promised a new global political, social, and economic improvement, "La caída del muro de Florida" and the forces of globalization bring change mostly when that change is profitable and politically correct. While Cheadle is skeptical, Maria Figueredo believes in border crossings and transculturation in poetry and music because, in the case she examines, Luciana Souza is such a competent and sensitive translator of Neruda's poetry. In the third article, Janelle Joseph shows how identities can be studied through the relationship to sport, in this case Brazilian *capoeira*, which is performed differently in Brazil, in the Caribbean, and in Canada. In the fourth article of this section, Lee L'Clerc discusses how difficult it is for Cuban artists to be viewed not for the political for-or-against-Castro implications in their works but for their artistic merits. Any study of identity in the post-1980 period would be incomplete without reference to the violence and cultural trauma the continent continues to suffer. Jennifer Martino's article addresses the question of collective memory and cultural trauma in Peru produced by the conflict initiated in 1980 by the Sendero Luminoso or the Shining Path.

In his chapter, "Cuban Culture at the Eye of the Globalizing Hurricane: The Case of *Nueva Trova*," Norman Cheadle observes that Miami has established a highly sophisticated infrastructure for servicing the music industry and that it attracts famous recording artists from North America, Latin America, and Europe. Referring to the concept of the new Pax Americana and its "managerialist organizational strategy" for imposing the neoliberal privatization of social welfare and natural resources in Latin America, Cheadle follows George Yúdice in *The expediency of culture* (2003) by suggesting that the same exploitative managerialist strategy is operative in the cultural sector. He argues that culture is no longer merely an ancillary support in the new regime of accumulation established by the neo-liberal globalization of the planet but is, in fact, integral to the process. For Cheadle, as for Yúdice, Miami has become the command-and-control centre from which the culture industries extract value from rich Latin American culture. In his chapter Cheadle analyses the trajectory of *nueva trova*, the song form that arose in Cuba after the Revolution and which stands as a cultural synecdoche of revolutionary Cuba itself. Although an eminently transcultural phenomenon because it draws on a variety of international musical influences, *nueva trova* is, Cheadle argues, distinguishable from the paradoxically "homogenized diversity" which is disseminated by the world-music industry in Miami.

In her article, "From Pablo Neruda to Luciana Souza: *Latin America* as Poetic-Musical Space," Maria Figueredo looks at the global cultural phenomenon which combines traditional Latin American music idioms with progressive technologies and often politicized lyrics. She studies in detail one of the most recent settings of Neruda's poetry, completed in 2004 by Brazilian composer and vocalist Luciana Souza. Her collection uses rhythmic inflections of the original poetry, her own Brazilian-jazz compositions, and classical music by the Catalan composer Federico Mompou. She also transposes the verbal text to a third language, English, problematizing thus the notion of the linguistic and cultural tension. The use of English for the Neruda musical settings may be viewed as a negative aspect of globalization as equal to cultural colonization.

Figueredo favours, however, the use of translation and transculturalization. She explains that as Brazil became an important economic force in the last decades of the twentieth century, its powerful cultural production outside its borders and its opening and cross-cultural and translational interactions with Spanish America gave those who, through exile and migration, established themselves in other areas such as Canada and the United States an association through music to their country of origin which they could also share within their new linguistic community.

Souza's CD focuses on more personal poems and the representation of home and the daily existence of the subject "I" within the larger collective and social project. The music focuses on the multiplicity of the self, seen particularly in "Sonnet 99." As she examines the recordings of Luciana Souza in English translation, Figueredo argues that Souza's lyrical interpretations and musical compositions transpose the Spanish-language poetry into English "without missing a beat of their original meaning or inflection." Souza's musicalization of Neruda's poetry is different from the "homogenized diversity" disseminated by the world-music industries such as the one in Miami which Norman Cheadle examines. It universalizes the human experience inherent in Neruda's poetry, Figueredo argues, and aspires to be a voice for social imperatives which call for the reassigning of an alternative value system that affirms greater equality and social awareness in the distribution of power.

In addition to poetry and music, sports also play a role in the transculturalization of Latin American identity. In her article, "The Transculturation of *Capoeira*: Brazilian, Canadian, and Caribbean Interpretations of an Afro-Brazilian Martial Art," Janelle Joseph traces the migration of *capoeira* from Brazil to Canada via the Caribbean. Using Norman Cheadle's concept of false oppositions, Joseph explains how this "exotic," "underground" or "alternative" cultural form is adopted to be flattened and commodified in Canada. She explains that *capoeira* originated among enslaved Africans in Brazil and that it incorporates free movement, instrumental and vocal music, martial combat, and dance. She then describes how elements of this cultural practice are played and practiced differently in Canada than in Brazil due to age and class differences of the participants, not to mention the nationality of some of the teachers. *Capoeira* has made its way to the vanguard of fitness cultures in Canada in just over a decade. In Canada the game/dance/martial art is taken predominantly by people of Caribbean and European descent in a much different setting, which produces different forms and styles of play, echoing thus José Ortega y Gasset's proverbial definition of one's identity: I am I and my circumstances.

In his analysis of an artistic installation entitled *La regata* (1993–94) by the Cuban artist Alexis Leiva Machado, better known as Kcho, Lee L'Clerc, an academic and a visual artist himself, examines how this work has been identified with an historic event—the Cuban rafter crisis of 1994—and, therefore, placed within the context of a local narrative. In his article, "Kcho's *La regata*: Political or Poetic Installation?," L'Clerc rejects both the politicization of this work of art and the post-colonial critical approach that sees the work as a cultural sign through which notions of identity can be formed. He contends that it can be counterproductive to identify artists according to national or local narratives, particularly when, as in the present day, global and local dimensions are interrelated. Following Gayatri C. Spivak's pronouncement that "when a narrative is constructed, something is left out" (1990, 18), L'Clerc observes how the aesthetic experience and the poetics of the work can be overlooked. He places Kcho's work within the aesthetics of *Arte Povera* and within the theatricality of display and the metaphoric constructs of art installation. By focusing on the work itself and the aesthetic experience, L'Clerc attempts to rescue *La regata* from being reduced to a political narrative centred primarily on the collective consciousness of *los balseros*, a politically disaffected people seen as heroes by the Miami community and as deserters by Cubans on the island. He concludes that the work can be both political and poetic. However, he points out the need to both negotiate between political and artistic boundaries in the face of continuing changes in politics and contemporary art, and to consider also that the continual shifting of art and politics upsets any attempts at the localization of meaning.

Jennifer Martino's chapter, "Collective Memory of Cultural Trauma in Peru: Efforts to Move from Blame to Reconciliation," examines the question of how to move forward in the context of seemingly incompatible interpretations of the past as she explores the role of the Peruvian *Comisión de la Verdad y Reconciliación* and addresses three specific cultural works which have played a role in building a new collective memory of the violence that occurred during Peru's period of greatest internal conflict: Yuyanapaq: para recordar (both phrases mean "to remember," the first in Quechua and the second in Spanish), a memorial titled El ojo que llora (The Eye That Cries) and Santiago Roncagliolo's novel *Abril rojo* (Red April). Peru's Truth and the Reconciliation Commission, modeled after Nelson Mandela's Truth and the Reconciliation Commission in South Africa, is now an international process which has been active in number of Latin American countries which have experienced a tremendous amount of violence.

Another foreign presence in the construction of the traumatized local Peruvian identity is the Dutch sculptor Lika Mutal. After visiting Yuyanapaq, an exhibit of 40 of the 250 photographs brought together by the Truth and Conciliation Commission, and moved by "a compelling look at political violence in Peru," Mutal created a memorial entitled El ojo que llora (The Eye That Cries). Consisting of a large rock in the middle of a pond and surrounded by a labyrinth of circular stones on which the names of tens of thousands of victims are inscribed, Mutal intended the memorial to commemorate the suffering of all sides of Peruvian society; however with the controversy that followed, the commemoration has developed into a larger identity performance than she ever intended.

Martino also examines Santiago Roncaglio's detective novel *Abril rojo* (Red April) because it challenges the categories of victimhood and liability in the context of the conflict between Sendero Luminoso and the Peruvian military, and more importantly because it addresses the myth of the infallible archive. The novel's protagonist, District Fiscal Assistant Félix Chacaltana Saldvídir, is a steadfast believer in the power of the archive and takes great pleasure in composing meticulous reports on the findings of his investigations. He quickly finds his convictions challenged by ever-growing tension between the official position on the status of social and political turmoil in Peru and his own consistent traumatic encounters with remnants of the period of conflict.

It should be noted that the genres examined by Martino, performance art and *novela negra*, as well as artistic installations, discussed also by L'Clerc, are dominant genres in the post-1980 period. Guillermo Gómez-Peña's performances as well as his book *Ethno-techno: Writings on performance, activism and pedagogy* have set the foundation in Latin American studies for the new genre. The notion of the audience as the performer is an extension of the Boom's search for the active reader.

Part III

The essays included in the first part of this manuscript have concentrated on the economic and political impositions of globalization and on the hopes and possibilities of positive changes that NGOs and world ethnic and cultural alliances have brought to minority groups in Latin America and the Caribbean. In turn, Part 2 has analyzed how Latin American identity has been constructed as either exotic or political by the outside world, unless it is received by artists and individuals who are able to share its artistic and humanitarian qualities. Part 3 concentrates on works created by Latin American writers who live in transnational settings, outside Latin America, and who construct characters who form their identities as cultures come in contact. Three of the four writers studied in the third part of this manuscript live and write in Canada, while the fourth lives and works between Chile, Germany, and the United States. Stephen Henighan and Pablo Ramirez concentrate on the Canadian Latino writers and make an important contribution to this undeveloped area of study. Henighan's article also contributes to the study of masculine identity, whereas my article examines the strength of the individual in the era of individual human rights.

In my article "Individualism and Human Rights in Antonio Skármeta's *Match ball*," I study character interactions in *Match ball* (1989), a novel written by a Chilean writer, Antonio Skármeta, while he was living in exile in Berlin. In this novel, each character embodies an ideological position and contributes to our understanding of the contemporary globalized world in a

Bakhtinian polyphonic fashion as the protagonist is pushed to live a more meaningful life. While Canadian writer, historian, and politician Michael Ignatieff celebrates what he calls "the rights revolution" (2000, 1) and reveres the age of individualism, the Chilean novelist suggests that old traditions die slowly, that one must be fit in order to be an individual, and that it is difficult to achieve changes smoothly because, as he says, in order to make a cake one has to break the eggs.

It is difficult to disagree with the dominant ideology of human rights as modern identities firmly establish that the idea of universal rights is a fundamental part of the modern conception of human identity. Historian Lynn Hunt strongly supports the modern political campaigns for human rights in her *Inventing human rights: A history* (2007) as she traces the development of the "rights of man" from the works of famous writers such as Thomas Jefferson, Thomas Paine, and Jean-Jacques Rousseau to the post-1948 period. Hunt demonstrates that the formal declaration of universal rights made it difficult for governing elites to limit the rights of religious minorities, racial minorities, or lower social classes. However, as rights are not natural but are culturally and historically constructed, very few countries are at the rights "revolutionary" stage. Hunt notes that even developed countries such as France, with a long claim of protection of universal human rights, have denied political and legal rights to women and more recently to Muslims. She also notes that although an early advocate of universal rights, the United States has used torture in Iraq.

Regardless of the examples given above, Joel Feinberg is right that the modern attitude is such that, as he insisted in 1966, "rights are not mere gifts or favours" because they are "something that can be demanded without embarrassment or shame" (8). Skármeta implies that the marginalized people share this mentality, but he also suggests that they move up the social scale only partially because they are supported by human rights policies; most of the time their strength comes from their intelligence, alertness, and some traditionally passed down survival skills. As I refer to two studies which focus on the question of the individual, Charles Taylor's *The malaise of modernity* and John Kingdom's *No such thing as society? Individualism and community*, it appears that Latin American individual has a strong sense of survival such as the one Antonio Benítez-Rojo discusses in *La isla que se repite* [The repeating island]. The street skills of Latino males in Montreal that Stephen Henighan refers to in his study seem to come from the same source.

In his chapter, "Collective Memory and the Borderlands in Guillermo Verdecchia's *Fronteras Americanas*," Pablo Ramirez also discusses Latino identity in Canada in Guillermo Verdecchia's widely acclaimed *Fronteras Americanas/ American Borders*, a play that won the prestigious Canadian Governor General's Award for Drama in 1993. The autobiographical play views the relationship between the individual and collective memory and studies what happens to individuals whose memories have no social meaning in the new geographic location or when their histories and memories cannot be contained within a single nation's boundaries. In the play of this Argentinean-Canadian, the character Guillermo Verdecchia is lost and filled with self-doubt because of his national displacement. However, his alter ego Wideload, who embodies Latino stereotypes formed by North American media outlets, not only faces and critiques North American racism on stage but acquires his strength and intelligibility from a long history of contact between Latin America and North America. In other words, by playing the role constructed for Latinos by Anglo world, he redirects Latin stereotypes and asks the Anglo audience to examine their own memories and cultural formations. As he traces the evolution of the main character from a traumatized refugee to a global citizen with a sense of identity placed in his body and self, Ramirez views nationalism as an oppressive force. When he says that "Verdecchia is finally able to subvert the nation's power to impose boundaries on people's histories and memories and give his experience a new coherence," he celebrates displacement as a form of liberation. His last sentence is so optimistic that it is almost utopian. He says: "With the ever-closer ties between Latin America and North America, all North Americans may one day have to call off the border patrol and enter the borderlands to make sense of their own histories and memories." A Latino himself, Ramirez hopes that Guillermo Verdecchia's experience of exile and return, which finds expression and coherence by transforming the borderlands from a Mexican-American dichotomy into a contact zone between North America and Latin America, can become a model for integration. The play certainly allows us to imagine how Latino communities across North America can function as a community and how cultural leaders like Gillermo Verdecchia can be historians and interpreters not only of the Latin culture but of the Americas.

Stephen Henighan's chapter, "From Exile to the *Pandilla*: The Construction of the Hispanic-Canadian Masculine Subject in *Cobro Revertido* and *Côte-des-Nègres*," addresses the question of Latin American identity in relation to Canadian culture. His article studies the instability of Latino-Canadian masculine identity in two novels written in Canada by Chilean-born authors. In José Leandro Urbina's novel *Cobro revertido* (1992), the male protagonist's identity is constructed through a succession of identifications with women: first his mother, then a divorced older lover, then his English-Canadian wife and his Québécoise lover. As an exile, the protagonist attempts to recover the motherland which has been erased by the macho dictatorship of "*tata Dios General Augusto*" (Pinochet). Urbina, born in 1949, writes in Spanish while Mauricio Segura, born in 1969, writes in French. In Segura's novel, *Côte-des-Nègres*, which is about a gang war in Montreal between two groups of teenage boys, one of Latin American origin and the other of Haitian origin, the male characters are uncritical of their acceptance of their fathers' *machista* customs. While Urbina's characters embrace exile as an opportunity for expanding their sexual repertoire, the young men in Segura's novel have Chilean-Canadian girlfriends, spurning young Anglo-Canadian and Québécoise women. The theoretical support for Henighan's study of the paradoxical movement in which the Latin American immigrant male becomes more closed off in the second generation than in the first is Matthew Guttman's *Changing men and masculinities in Latin America*.

This collection brings together an unusual yet not unrelated array of disciplinary perspectives which cluster around the theme of Latin American identity after 1980. It hopes to attract a broad audience, from both undergraduate and graduate students to people interested in current Latin American culture and society. It does not have a single definition of identity, but in general it shares Satya P. Mohanty's view that "identities are theoretical constructions that enable us to read the world in specific ways.... In them and through them, we learn to define and reshape our values and our commitments, we give texture and form to our collective futures" (2000, 43).

Notes

1 As Raymond Williams explains, the Boom writers participated in the international modernist aesthetic and philosophical project mainly to find a freer form which would allow them to seek a more authentic identity, both personal and Latin American: "[They] still believed through the 1960s in the possibility of articulating truth, although they adopted many of the narrative strategies pioneered by First World Modernists" (1992, 7).

References

Benítez-Rojo, A. 1996. *The repeating island*. Trans. James E. Maraniss. Durham, NC: Duke Univ. Press.
Feinberg, J. 1966. Duties, rights and claims. *American Philosophical Quarterly* 3(2): 8.
Garcia Canclini, N. 1995. *Hybrid cultures: Strategies for entering and leaving modernity*. Minneapolis: Univ. of Minnesota Press.
Gómez-Peña, G. 2005. *Ethno-techno: Writings on performance, activism and pedagogy*. London: Routledge.
Guttman, Matthew. 2003. *Changing men and masculinities in Latin America*. Durham, NC: Duke University Press.
Hunt, L. 2007. *Inventing human rights: A history*. Chapel Hill: Univ. of North Carolina.
Ignatieff, M. 2000. *The rights revolution*. Berkeley, CA: Publishers Group West.
King, J. 2004. *The Cambridge companion to modern Latin American culture*. Cambridge, U.K.: Cambridge Univ. Press.

Kingdom, J. 1992. *No such thing as society? Individualism and community.* Buckingham: Open Univ. Press.
Martín Alcoff, L. 2000. Who's afraid of identity politics? In *Reclaiming identity: Realist theory and the predicament of postmodernism,* ed. P. Moya and M. Hames-García, 312–45. Berkeley: Univ. of California Press.
Mohanty, S. P. 2000. The epistemic status of cultural identity: On *Beloved* and the postcolonial condition. In *Reclaiming identity: Realist theory and the predicament of postmodernism,* ed. P. Moya and M. Hames-Garcia, 29–67. Berkeley: Univ. of California Press.
Moya, P. 2000. Introduction: Reclaiming identity. In *Reclaiming identity: Realist theory and the predicament of postmodernism,* ed. P. Moya and M. Hames-Garcia, 1–29. Berkeley: Univ. of California Press.
Rama, Angel. "Los procesos de transculturación en la narrativa latinoamericana." *La novela en América Latina.* 203–29. Bogotá: Instituto colombiano de cultura, 1982.
Rostagno, I. 1997. *Searching for recognition: The promotion of Latin American literature in the United States.* Westport, CT: Greenwood Press.
Spivak, G. C. 1990. *The post-colonial critic: Interviews, strategies, dialogues,* ed. S. Harasym. New York: Routledge.
Taylor, C. 1991. *The malaise of modernity.* CBC Massey lecture series. Concord, ON: Anansi Press.
Vargas Llosa, Mario. 2002. A sumptuous abundance. *Fernando Botero,* ed. D. Elliott (exh. catalogue). Stockholm: Moderna Museet.
Williams, R. 1992. Truth claims, postmodernism, and the Latin American novel. *Profession.* New York: MLA, 92: 6–9.
Yúdice, G., Juan Flores, Jean Franco, eds. 1992. *On the edge: The crisis of contemporary Latin American culture.* Minneapolis: Univ. of Minnesota Press.

PART ONE

Latin America and the New Pax Americana

Jorge Nef and Alejandra Roncallo

Introduction

In the last three decades, the Americas, with the exception of Cuba, have undergone a rapid and multifaceted process of globalization driven by transboundary alliances of elites at both the global centre and its periphery. This order of things is being presently challenged by a reconfiguration of political domestic and regional forces intent in redefining inter-American relations. In the 1980s, northern elites, in agreement with their southern counterparts, imposed structural adjustment policies on Latin American and Caribbean nations in order to "solve" their debt crises. In so doing they created a transnational regime with a legal infrastructure to solidify such structural changes. This Pax Americana tied the hands of national governments in favour of transnational capital and, thus, transformed the state into a mere collaborative regulator of the private sector. The state was weakened with the promise of "low-intensity democratization," uneven and highly inequitable growth, and widespread corruption. Moreover, the much-heralded democratic transition in Latin America has not been synonymous with the entrenchment of participatory practices nor with responsible government, let alone with the enhancement of human dignity. The "safe," "limited," and substantially meaningless democracy brokered and supported by Washington and the famous unilateral Consensus impeded more than facilitated the emergence of a sustainable security community for the Americas, as does the persistence of neoliberal economic dogmatism and the rebirth of national security doctrines designed to fight elusive and perpetual global enemies from terrorism to criminality. De-democratization and authoritarianism throughout the hemisphere are the political corollary of these profoundly reactionary socio-economic processes and alliances. The net result is a significant deterioration of the security of most people and the generation of democratic deficits, not only south of the Rio Grande but also in North America.

The New Pax Americana
Following the explorations initiated in the 1980s by Robert Cox, Stephen Gill, Richard Fagen, and Terry-Lynn Karl, we propose to examine Latin America and the Caribbean in the context of a new hegemonic framework. Going beyond traditional and somewhat disembodied conceptions of realism, regime theory, and dependency, this proposed conceptualization examines complex interactions around military and economic instruments that exhibit both coercion and consensus.

This approach draws on Robert Cox's analysis of historical structures in order to re-examine the changing mechanisms of hegemony developed by the region's transnational elites since the end of World War II. In his *Approaches to world order* (1996) Cox identifies three categories of factors — ideas, material conditions, and institutions — that interact dialectically on three levels: social forces, states, and world orders. He distinguishes two periods germane to our study of the Americas: the Pax Americana proper (1945–1964) and the period of "non-hegemonic condition" which starts in 1964.

Retrospectively, the older version of Pax Americana at the continental scale — what Cox called Pax Americana — originated with the 1947 Rio Treaty. This event signaled the rise to the Cold War in the continent; the political side of the Keynesian World Order. This world order was expressed regionally over a decade later in the Alliance for Progress, a project created as a response to the Cuban Revolution. It was a policy initiative based on development as the soft side of counterinsurgency. Its intellectual foundation was modernization theory and area studies, which constructed "Latin America and the Caribbean" as a contested geo-economic and strategic space. In light of the perceived and illusive communist threat in the hemisphere, hegemony was maintained through concessions and incentives to local elites in the form of development projects and foreign aid. However, this approach always rested on military force and counterinsurgency as instruments of last resort.

By the mid-1960s this regional order gave way to a period that Cox called "non-hegemonic condition," in which the elite was not hegemonic any more but merely dominant. During this period, concessions were ignored — although not totally eliminated — and the mechanisms of control shifted towards support for military dictatorships. This project involved the combination of the internationalization of production and finance with the implementation of Milton Friedman's monetarism, leading to the 1982 debt crisis.

The factors and levels that Cox identified in his examination of world orders are in a state of constant flux and thus, over time, new concepts may be required to explain shifting realities. Re-thinking Cox's periodization from a non-US standpoint, we have identified a third period in inter-American relations: the "new" Pax Americana. Beginning in the 1980s, this revised US strategy attempted to solve the debt problem that had emerged in Latin America and the Caribbean through the imposition of structural adjustment conditionalities and a transnational legal framework that weakened local governments in favor of transnational capital. "Old" social concessions were eliminated while politico-ideological adjustments such as democratization, the elimination of corruption, and poverty reduction became the hegemonic instrumentalities and discourses of choice. During this period there was a geo-economic and strategic reconfiguration of space: from "Latin America and the Caribbean" to "the Americas." This reconfiguration of space included all the nations in the hemisphere, with the conspicuous absence of Cuba, under US leadership. Free trade and foreign investment accelerated the interconnectedness of the system. However, this also increased mutual vulnerability as "the weakness of the periphery increases the exposure of the centre, making the entire configuration, including the centre, more unstable" (Nef 1999, 13).

Examining 'the Americas'
Mirroring the abovementioned geo-economic and strategic reconfiguration of space, our study takes a critical approach to the elite's construction of the Americas. As Karl and Fagen (1986) suggested decades ago, the paradigm developed by experts to analyze Eastern Europe can be applied to the Americas. This conceptual framework posited that Eastern Europe was an integrated region where Soviet elites enjoyed relational control or metapower over its satellites. Thus, the study of individual countries and of the region as a whole began from the premise of penetrated political systems, not sovereign entities.

The relatively permeable borders of the Western Hemisphere continuously experience formal and informal asymmetrical interpenetration. Northern elites, in alliance with their Latin American and Caribbean counterparts, exert relational control or metapower over other subordinate groups in the region. This process is framed within a dominant and messianic economic, ideological, and cultural matrix, which is as dogmatic and compelling as its Soviet equivalent. In this complex exchange system, capital, technology, and ideology flow south, while profits and migrants flow north.[1]

Latin America and the Caribbean are integrated in a hub-and-spokes relationship with the United States. There is a growing asymmetry in the limited free trade arrangements known as NAFTA, CFTA-DR, and the presently paralyzed

FTAA. Military integration under the Rio Treaty—and the letter's structural and ideological mechanisms—has been a fact of life since World War II, much longer in Central America. For contemporary US elites, what lies south of the Rio Grande continues to be simultaneously perceived as a resource-rich El Dorado and as a cultural and political threat. In this sense, almost echoing Theodore Roosevelt's characterization, the South is constructed as a source of evil in the form of narcotics, illegal aliens, and undesirable values. This American-perceived threat has also emerged "indoors" in the form of a growing Hispanic population within the United States (Huntington 2004).

Although the Americas are one of the richest continents on the globe, distributional inequity throughout the region, deeply rooted in powerlessness and exclusion, has not only continued to exist, but has become increasingly more pronounced. The region contains three geopolitical giants: the United States, Canada, and Brazil. Two of these are the most prosperous countries in the world: one of them is a global superpower, and the other has persistently had one of the highest scores in the United Nations Human Development Index. Latin America, in contrast, (including Brazil) continues to be "the region of the planet with the worst [distribution] indicators," according to a 2004 report by the United Nations Economic Commission on Latin America and the Caribbean. The same report estimated that by 2002, forty-four per cent of the population was below the poverty line and over nineteen per cent lived in extreme poverty (ECLAC 2004, 1, 5). This means that two out of every five Latin Americans are poor and survive under precarious circumstances.

To understand this hemisphere as a whole, the notion of rich versus poor countries is misleading: wealthy individuals reside in poor countries and poor people exist in richer countries. The abysmal gap between the rich and poor *within* all of the countries in the Americas continues to expand. By most statistical accounts and with very few exceptions (Haiti, Honduras, Bolivia, and Nicaragua), the nations south of the Rio Grande comprise the upper layer of the Third World.[2] But poverty and exclusion are not just Latin American or Third World traits. For all its wealth and power, the United States has nearly fourteen per cent of its population living in permanent poverty and its income distribution has persistently worsened over the last decades. In 2000, the top one per cent of the US population earned on average 88.5 times as much as the lowest twenty per cent (Hogan 2005, 1). Poverty and income inequality have also risen in Canada where, in 2003, almost sixteen per cent of the population was under the poverty line (CIA 2006).

Above and beyond the differences that exist between the nations of the Americas, what is patently clear is a growing structural interconnectivity between the North and the South of the Western Hemisphere. This realization points towards the need to study the Americas as the elites' social construction of space. In fact, as Boas, Marchand, and Shaw have pointed out, "regionalization can be seen as an integral part of globalization processes, i.e. the transformation of the global political economy (GPE)" (1999, 900).

Dependent Development and Intervention

Historically, structural underdevelopment has been imbedded in the pattern of inter-American relations. The key function of regional and national political systems has been the maintenance of a hemispheric and international order based on inequality and de-development. As a result, Latin American and Caribbean states are caught in a vicious cycle: the more vulnerable and penetrated their states are, the more illegitimate their regimes become. Lack of internal popular support has made them weak and unstable.

Intervention does not occur in a vacuum; most regimes in Latin America and the Caribbean are tied to the export of commodities. They suffer from chronic vulnerability and the fluctuations of international trading. In this context, internal and external factors combine to produce instability. Even in the once-more-institutionalized democracies such as Uruguay and Chile, the economic crises of the 1950s and 1960s led to a breakdown of civic confidence and elite rule. Political conflict and socio-political stalemates eroded the legitimacy and the effectiveness of these regimes. Labour practices inherited from the populist years of the Depression and World War II reproduced and accelerated the "push-up" effect of institutionalized social conflict, resulting in political deadlock and chronic hyperinflation.

The rules of the pluralistic game decomposed in the midst of rapid mass mobilization during the 1960s. In order to maintain the existing domestic and international socio-economic order, several domestic elites, with ostensible US support, resorted to naked and highly bureaucratized repression under a new political alliance. Such alliance involved a coalition between the externally linked corporate elites, which supported conservative economic policies, and the security establishments. The latter had effectively become transnationalized by the ideological professionalism of US-made counterinsurgency doctrines adopted during the Cold War.

The military in the Americas, with few exceptions, are a trained, indoctrinated, and well-financed ultraconservative fraction of the middle class. As armed bureaucrats specializing in coercive and repressive violence, they provided the force required to keep the populace at bay. Their ideological-professional software was—and continues to be—the National Security Doctrine (NSD) developed during the Cold War (Weil et al. 1979; Rojas 2003). South of the Rio Grande, the professional and ideological indoctrination of the security forces, as well as their financing, is often externally generated, which gives the US military an upper hand in controlling their allegiance.

The NSD—also called "Pentagonism" by Juan Bosch (2000, 5–14)—is based on three elements: the existence of an external global enemy, manifested in an apocalyptic ideological conflict between East and West; an internal enemy ("subversion") supported by the external enemy; and the existence of an external friend (the regional security regime ruled by the United States). In the 1950s and 1960s the modernization of the regional military structure and culture gave the local military a new self-justifying mission: fighting subversion—however loosely defined—with Special Forces schooled in "counterinsurgency" and "civic action" (Corbett 1972).[3] In a relatively brief period and irrespective of declared intentions, the local military, now in alignment with police forces, were transformed into the internal operational units of an integrated hemispheric security regime. This reorientation became manifest as early as 1964, with the Johnson administration's promotion of the Brazilian military's counter-revolution of 1964 as a model to be emulated.

The adoption of this professional "software" has eroded, and continues to erode, the national character of local military institutions. More than in the former Communist bloc, this type of regional security regime has decisively transnationalized the states in the region. The most explicit articulation of this strategic ideology was the Nixon Doctrine, outlined in the Rockefeller Report of 1969 (Rockefeller 1969). This report clearly showed a shift in the normative ideal of the US political establishment from pluralist democracy and popular participation to the maintenance of law and order through authoritarian measures. Under this blueprint, the number of military dictatorships in Latin America steadily climbed from ten in 1969 to twelve in 1970, fourteen in 1972, and fifteen in 1973 (Nef 1978).

The National Security Regime and Neoliberalism

The authoritarian conceptions of economic liberalism that unfolded under military rule in the 1970s rejected the nationalist and protectionist premises underlying the import substitution policies of the 1940s, 1950s, and 1960s as well as other Keynesian economic policies. Instead, economic growth was viewed as a function of the re-insertion of Latin American and Caribbean economies into the international division of labour, primarily as exporters of raw materials. This economic policy shift represented a return to the earlier export-based economies of the region's colonial and neo-colonial past. Authoritarian capitalism rejected the demand-side policies that were part of the Alliance for Progress initiated by the Kennedy administration. The neoliberal strategy of development involved the maintenance and expansion of three comparative advantages: a friendly investment climate, cheap natural resources, and, above all, cheap labour. Favourable conditions for foreign investment were created through the deregulation, de-nationalization, and privatization of the national economies and the dismemberment of labour organizations. Additionally, the welfare state and most of the import substitution industrialization and social safety nets developed since the 1930s were minimized. These neo-liberal policies required large amounts of external financing. The latter was available in the 1970s and early 1980s due to the massive deposits of petrodollars in Western private banks, which made them willing to extend large loans to most Latin American and Caribbean governments and business elites. Other than offering economic miracles financed by foreign investment, this approach favored monetarism (later identified with the Chicago School) over the Keynesian doctrine pursued by ECLAC. The combination of repressive policies and the subsequent more hegemonic adjustment recipes pushed through the International Financial Institutions (IFIs) allowed domestic and transnational elites associated with these policies to increase their share of regional wealth and promote a greater degree of regional economic integration. It also attempted to legitimize through market rules Cuba's exclusion and isolation.

The regimes of exception that emerged in South America, patterned on the example of the post-1964 military regime in Brazil, were attempts at economic modernization from the top down, combined with strong external inducements. The benefits of this new order accrued to a small alliance of domestic entrepreneurs and speculators supported by a technocratic-military middle class and their business, political, and military associates in the United States, Canada, Western Europe, and Asia. Its narrow social base created a persistent crisis of legitimacy that was managed by three instruments. The first was the use of military force, which was backed by an alliance between the military officer corps and the domestic socio-economic elites. The second was the inclusion of external, chiefly US, surrogate constituencies — military, business, political and diplomatic — to compensate for the loss of internal support. The third was the political demobilization and exclusion of the bulk of the population from the political system. Thus, military dictatorship became an intrinsic component of the strategy to secure economic freedom for the local elites and the US constituencies associated with these regimes (Letelier 1976, 138, 142). The dictatorships imbedded a set of authoritarian enclaves and mechanisms to control the process of economic liberalization and regulated opening to unfold with the alleged return to democracy.

The authoritarian policies discussed above were far more effective as a shock therapy — in atomizing labour, freezing wages, letting domestic prices float to world levels, and privatizing Latin American economies — than in raising living standards. They were effective in the short run as economic weapons in a socio-political war that benefited the rich and punished the poor, rather than bringing about national development. The social cost for the popular majorities was enormous: living conditions deteriorated and the social gap between the haves and have-nots grew. The long-term economic, social, environmental, and financial consequences have been, by and large, catastrophic for the region. Far from generating stability and prosperity, the combination of dictatorial rule and unrestricted free-market policies created serious governability and corruption problems, paving the way for the debt crisis and recession of the 1980s.

Debt and Regime Crisis
In the mid-1980s, as Latin American and Caribbean governments increased their financial obligations, the failures of production and exports to keep pace with the level of borrowing and with rising interest rates resulted in a debt crisis. This economic crisis underscored the political crisis of dictatorships, as the national security regimes failed to stem the erosion of the political alliances that had permitted them to implement regressive social and economic projects. The failure of US-supported military-civilian dictatorships in Central America revealed that repression had become unviable; a negotiated transition became the only alternative to popular revolution. With the Nixon and Ford alliance in shambles, a new political coalition in Washington concerned about the long-term effects of authoritarian solutions created the conditions for the military's withdrawal from the commanding heights of the state. The Linowitz Report, heavily influenced by the views of the Trilateral Commission (Sklar 1980), outlined a transitional strategy in 1975 (Linowitz 1975). This document constituted the blueprint for the Carter administration's initiative for democratic transition (Siat and Iriarte 1979). However, the substance behind Carter's political and ethical framework vanished with his 1980 electoral defeat. Under Reagan, democratic transition for most of Latin America was largely confined to intra-elite negotiation, mediated and supervised by external actors and geared to preserving the status quo. Rather than regime transition, it was the consolidation of a largely non-democratic socio-economic order under a formal democratic political façade.

The mounting debt and regime crises set the conditions for the emergence throughout the Americas in the mid-1980s of a new political configuration: the "receiver state," blending limited democracy with neo-liberal economics. This type of state acts in partnership with foreign creditors and international financial institutions as the manager, executor, and liquidator of assets in a bankrupt country. The central function of the state is the administration of national and international debts, combined with the implementation of structural adjustment packages (SAPs). Such policies are geared to assure the payment of debts through the privatization of the state's assets and the denationalization of the economy. This state is highly transnationalized, weak and has only narrow spaces for popular political participation. Generally speaking, national economic and fiscal policies, with structuring capacity to set the rules of the game, are effectively excluded from domestic political debate. Meanwhile, SAPs possess the metapower to define such rules, and discipline and impose strict limits on all domestic social and economic policies, including investment, labour, education, health, environment, social security, and other related fields.

This system has perpetuated the economic dependence and underdevelopment of Latin American and Caribbean economies. The SAPs imposed to manage debt have given rise to the institutionalization of the above mentioned vulnerability to external economic and political influences. In a vicious cycle, Latin American and Caribbean states require increasing amounts of external involvement and financial support. This situation is exemplified by the inability of these countries to extricate themselves from their chronic indebtedness: they are caught in a "debt trap" (Martinez 1992; World Bank 1988, 1990, 1992).[4] Debt-management became the number one state function in the regional agenda during the early 1980s. The service of the region's debts, both payments of principal and interest, grew from slightly over 40 per cent of the total value of annual exports in 1979 to over 65 per cent in 1983. Despite the fact that about half of the countries in the region had reduced their debt liabilities by 1990–91, the total debt in the region had grown to $421 billion. By 2001, it reached $740 billion, subsequently expanding at an average annual rate of 5 per cent (ECLAC 2001).[5] Out of the seventeen most indebted countries in the world in 1992, twelve were in Latin America. On an average, the annual interest rate payments fell from 33 per cent of all exports in 1987 to 22 per cent in 1991 as the lost decade of the 1980s came to an end. Between 1992 and 1999, the burden was reduced even further in Brazil and Mexico, which decelerated their rate of indebtedness from triple to double digit annual rates. Even this improvement was unsustainable by any stretch of imagination. Argentina accelerated its rate of indebtedness from a fifteen-year average annual growth of 178 per cent to 256 per cent between 1970 and 2000. Venezuela, in turn, went from a yearly increase of 320 per cent between 1970 and 1985 to 465 per cent between 1970 and 2000.

An analysis of the ratio between exports and debt service shows figures that are equally gloomy. The debt service in relation to the total value of export earnings for Argentina moved from 34 per cent in 1990 to over 71 per cent in 2000. For Brazil, the increase was from 23 to 91 per cent. In 2003, the average annual debt service for Latin America had climbed to 201 per cent of the value of exports (World Bank 2003). So far, despite major economic crises in Mexico (1994), Ecuador (1999), Argentina (2001), Brazil (2002), and Bolivia (2003), most countries in the region have not defaulted outright on their loans. The pursuit of this policy of fiscal responsibility has been extremely hard on the general population, which has had to absorb the full impact of the use of a major portion of their countries' export earnings and revenues for debt payments.[6]

Regime Change and Continuity

Despite the orderly retreat of the national security regimes and irrespective of the elected nature of Latin American and Caribbean governments, the economic agenda of the transition period has a striking resemblance with the agenda imposed under authoritarian rule. This is due to the fact that the restructuring of the regional economy along free-market lines through political repression was so profound as to prevent a return to economic nationalism. Likewise, the restructuring and transnationalization of the security establishment made the pursuit of nationalist and non-aligned foreign policies impossible. In a sense, the repressive states of the 1970s and the more hegemonic receiver states of the 1990s and 2000s are two different political arrangements that protect the interests of a similar cluster of elites. The receiver state expresses the interests of a transnational and conservative coalition, managed by political actors who form moderate right to centre-left governments, but whose policies are conservative. Limited democracy, with narrow opportunities for political participation, provides a thin cushion over the deep structural problems that were formerly controlled by repression. The current modality of conflict management, while reducing the most blatant forms of human rights abuses, has left the most pressing and fundamental socio-economic and political problems largely unresolved. The political regimes that emerged in Latin America as a result of the democratic transition, while possessing the formal trappings of sovereignty and democracy, have been neither truly democratic nor sovereign. They are precariously balanced civilian regimes, based on negotiations among elites, with exclusionary political agendas and narrow internal support. The popular sectors are effectively kept outside of the political arena, while external economic and military actors, chiefly from the United States, enjoy de facto veto power over state policies.

Limited Democracy and Elected Plutocracies

The new model of democracy that has developed in Latin America and the Caribbean following the demise of the national security regimes is at best a plutocracy with limited popular support, which occasionally resorts to electoral rituals and is ultimately backed up by an elaborate security apparatus, engaged in a perpetual state of war. While this low-intensity democracy may appeal to the consumption-intensive, high-income core groups throughout the hemisphere, it is based neither on majority rule nor popular accountability.

It corresponds to the same elitist formula articulated by the Trilateral Commission in the mid-1970s, which considered the root cause of the crisis of democracy at the time to be too much democracy (Chomsky 1977).[7]

Limited democracy is not only a Latin American phenomenon. The region's social and economic systems, from Patagonia to Alaska, are mostly conservative and elitist, with occasional symbolic trappings of populist nationalism, as was the case with the Bush (Jr.) administration. Democratic development in the Americas, with the qualified exceptions of Costa Rica, Canada, and to a much lesser extent contemporary Chile, has been until the turn of the twenty-first century weak and fragile throughout the hemisphere. The Americas as a whole, with few exceptions, have not undergone profound social reforms. The very few attempts at progressive reform have been stunted and reversed. North America, especially the United States, has moved in recent years toward de-democratization and authoritarianism. The prevailing discourse on democracy among the official intelligentsia throughout the Americas involves the equation of a substantially restricted form of participation with neo-liberal economics and the protection of national security (Montecinos and Markoff 1993). It can be argued that securitization and militarization lie at the core of human insecurity in the hemisphere.

Current political developments throughout the hemisphere, while conveying a less repressive picture than in the past, especially in contrast to the sombre record of the 1970s, present at best mixed signals. On one hand, most of the region is currently ruled by governments that have been generated through free and competitive elections. There have also been sporadic yet significant attempts to hold these governments accountable to the electorate. Instances of torture, disappearances, and blatant state terrorism have become less frequent, with notable exceptions such as in Colombia. However, there are also disturbing signs, one of which is the persistence, and even revival, of authoritarian and oligarchic traditions. Political power also remains highly concentrated in small and hardly accountable elites. Fundamental democratic values, such as respect for human rights, honest government, and the reduction of discrimination and official abuse, are neither widely shared nor practiced. Corruption in the entire Western Hemisphere is widespread and growing (Nef 2004b).

Electoral processes, while a common sight throughout the Americas, have become increasingly void of choice and real meaning. Guyana's former President Cheddy Jagan sarcastically called this type of politics "five-minute democracy" (Jagan 1996). Electoral fraud and manipulation still persist. Voters can cast ballots but the choices and policy options are roughly the same. The socio-economic and institutional pillars of the current, limited democratic regimes are similar to those of the national security regimes—agribusiness, financial, and corporate elites, foreign investors and authoritarian elements within the military, the judiciary, and the technocracy. Thus, it is hardly surprising that public apathy and cynicism throughout the hemisphere have been at an all-time high, while governmental legitimacy has been declining (Graham and Sukhatenkar 2003).

Despite the unfolding of formally contested elections during the 1990s and 2000s throughout the Americas and the abundance of constitutional reforms, these formal processes of democracy have provided only limited real democratic alternatives. The above-mentioned alienation of the population from the political process has resulted in extremely high rates of electoral abstention (Robinson 1994, 8). Colombia tops the list of electoral abstention, with only some forty per cent of the eligible voters casting their ballots in 2000. This dismal example is followed closely by the United States.[8] In addition, many of these contests, including the 2000 and 2004 US elections, have been tainted with irregularities.

Apart from the ceremonial transfer of office by electoral means and the absence of direct military rule, democracy in the Americas has not been consolidated in this decade. The transition remains incomplete and in some cases there has been a process of "undoing democracy" (Close 2004). Oligarchies throughout the continent have shown a remarkable ability to prevail. The old practices of executive *continuismo* and dynastic-type succession have resurfaced in unexpected places like Costa Rica and the United States. There is also significant continuity of policy: neo-liberal formulas have become entrenched in the conditionalities attached to debt-alleviation, regional trade agreements (such as NAFTA or MERCOSUR), and the macroeconomic equilibrium policies. These effectively remove fiscal, monetary, and credit policy decisions from national political and democratic control. In addition, the new war against terrorism in the context of US unipolarism, with its pseudo-moralistic and messianic discourse, is undermining genuine progress toward greater democracy, sustainable and equitable development, and human security.

The Continued Militarization of the Americas
With the withering away of the Cold War, the presence of military officers is less conspicuous in Latin American politics than in the recent past, but closer scrutiny reveals a more complex picture. Beneath the civilian mantle, praetorianism has a lingering presence. With the retreat of the national security regimes, what has emerged in their place is not a political system in which the military is subordinate to civilian control. Instead, what can be considered civil-military regimes contain powerful and relatively autonomous security establishments composed of the military and the police and in some cases paramilitary forces.

The end of the civil wars in Central America, the declining insurgency threat in Peru, as well as the effects of structural adjustment packages upon defense budgets, suggest a trend towards demilitarization.[9] Yet, overall budget reductions between the 1980s and the early 2000s have not been matched by comparable personnel reductions. Rather, a small increase in military personnel has taken place. The average figures for the region are deceiving since reductions in countries with large military establishments, such as Argentina, Chile, Nicaragua, and Peru, offset the significant increases in most other countries (IISS 2001). Twelve out of twenty countries actually increased the size of their armed forces between 1985 and 2002. Colombia topped the list with a 76.7 per cent increase, followed by Venezuela (53.1 per cent), Guatemala (40.7 per cent), and Mexico (35.6 per cent). The largest military establishment other than the United States is Brazil, with armed forces totaling nearly 270,000. Its contingent grew 7 per cent between 1988 and 1993, averaging an annual increase of 4 per cent by 2002 (IISS 2001).

In comparison with the G8 nations and the Middle East, the size of the Latin American forces is relatively modest, but the impact, influence, and transnationalization of these security establishments, especially of the officer corps, remain extensive. It is not an exaggeration to suggest that the Latin American military are a branch-plant establishment, heavily dependent on US training, and organizational and ideological hegemony. The current concept of "Hemispheric Security" in fact encourages the militarization of numerous human security issues (Chillier and Freeman 2005). Not including some 760 thousand paramilitaries and an indeterminate number of reserves, Latin America has over 1.3 million individuals under arms and spends close to $9 billion annually on defence (Chillier and Freeman 2005). Given its economic base and geostrategic situation, the Americas remain overly militarized. This constitutes a persistent financial drain, an obstacle to the sovereignty and cooperation among nations in the region, and continues to be the single most serious threat to political stability, sustainable democracy, and human rights. The recent (2008) initiative to create an independent South American Defense Council under the sponsorship of Brazil and Venezuela and in the context of UNASUR has been an attempt to reduce military and security dependence on the United States.

In the United States, the militarization of most spheres of life has been a constant aspect of society since the end of World War II. The United States remains by far the most militarized country in the hemisphere, possessing the only truly global military reach. Its awesome might is combined with a ritualized and extreme patriotism, and a political elite that is ever ready to overplay nationalistic feelings. The George W. Bush administration (2000–2008), like many others, showed a proclivity to militarize hemispheric relations, including unabashed support in 2002 for a failed coup to overthrow the elected government of Hugo Chávez. In the long run, this predisposition presents a clear, persistent, and present danger to democracy both regionally and domestically.

The Impact of Public Policies
Since the 1980s, the Americas have experienced an expanding and converging set of problems whose common denominator is a fiscal crisis of the state, at times vaguely masked in neo-liberal rhetoric and national security diversions. These crises affect employment, purchasing power, housing, the safety of drinking water, and the quality of sanitation and health care. This has occurred at a time when social safety nets and health delivery mechanisms have been drastically reduced as a consequence of neo-liberal recipes and adjustment policies. Elsewhere in the Americas, the combination of poverty-driven diseases, multiplied by the dismantling of the institutional mechanisms for their containment and treatment, have had the effect of multiplying health insecurity across class and national boundaries (Nef 2004a). This convergence of multiple socio-economic problems has also had significant migratory effects.

Environmental threats are another example of policy-driven dysfunctions. These include untreated sewage, air pollution, and climate change, but also encompass a broader complexity and multiplicity of reciprocal problems. Current industrial, mining, and agricultural practices, mixed with uncontrolled urbanization,[10] have created an interwoven pattern of biophysical and social stress upon the ecosystems and human populations of the region. In the midst of the widespread expansion of commercial agricultural production for export, food insecurity has increased even in the statistically richer countries. The pressures to manage the debt and its conditionalities has put a premium upon cash crops instead of food crops for domestic consumption as well as the merciless exploitation of natural and human resources. An earlier study (Nef and Robles 1998) described the broader complexity and multiplicity of these environmental problems: retro-feeding and destructive processes have created a vicious cycle of vulnerabilities. In the United States, these contradictions came to a head in 2005 with Hurricane Katrina's devastating impact on New Orleans, revealing the hitherto hidden dimension of poverty, neglect, and exclusion, combined with inadequate policies and misplaced security priorities (e.g., Homeland Security).

Between the 1980s and the 1990s, those living below the poverty line in Latin America and the Caribbean increased from above 120 million to over 200 million and from forty-one to forty-six per cent of the population (Robinson 1994; Altimir 1994). The most affected have been those already vulnerable: women, children, the elderly, and ethnic minorities. Though extreme conditions of poverty and indigence have decreased to mid-1990s levels in most countries, overall deprivation is still higher than two decades ago, and rural poverty has increased steadily. Even the much-hailed economic "miracles" in the region have not produced sustained development. The combination of entrenched elite interests, extreme deregulation, and structural adjustment policies has left a lasting burden of poverty and despair.

Chile's "success story" does not fare much better under close scrutiny. Between 1970 and 1987, the proportion of Chileans defined as poor increased by an average yearly rate of 7.2 per cent, while real income per capita grew at an annual average rate of 0.3 per cent. This was not the result of unfathomable economic forces but the result of government policy. Since 1990, with a succession of democratic governments and despite the fact that the speed of impoverishment has been arrested and even reversed, widespread privation persists. Despite impressive GNP annual growth rates between 4.5 and 10 per cent and a generally successful poverty alleviation package implemented by the Lagos and Bachelet administration, Chile remains a nation with one of the worst income distributions in the region.

Pauperization and expanding inequity are present all over the hemisphere. Poverty and inequality have significantly expanded in North America, where a similar neo-liberal policy model has been followed, bringing about the worst global recession since the 1930. Although the rural and urban poor are the worst-hit, white-collar, middle-class sectors have seen their economic opportunities and social safety nets dramatically eroded. Throughout the hemisphere, the middle classes are shrinking in the growing gap between the extremities of wealth and poverty (Robinson 1994; Wolff 2003).[11]

Assessing Re-democratization and De-democratization

The politics of limited democratization combined with neo-liberal economics, while an improvement over the human rights abuses of the military dictatorships of the 1970s, imposes built-in constraints that block the realization of a truly stable and sustainable system of democratic politics in the Americas. This has caused a profound structural contradiction to emerge in the region's systems of governance. If elected governments stress democracy, equity, popular rule, and the interests of the general public, they encounter relentless opposition from the domestic and transnational elites who dominate the region's economies. The course taken by most governments in the region is to rule in the interest of the elites, stressing economic liberalism and ignoring the interests of society in general. This is what, in the North American context, Ralph Nader (1992) has labelled a plutocracy. The long-term political cost of this option is high: loss of popular and national sovereignty and the erosion of trust between elected officials and the electorate, a central tenet of both democratic governance and pluralist politics. Moreover, if the neo-liberal economic policies continue to fail to produce better standards of living for the alienated majorities, and should the structural crisis deepen, it is likely that these civilian regimes may be replaced by repressive civil-military regimes once again in the name of national security.

The national security ideology remains the cultural software of the security establishments in most countries of the Americas; it is a staple in the training of the military, police, and paramilitary forces throughout the hemisphere. The communist subversion of yesteryear has been expanded to include new internal enemies: terrorism, anarchy, and drug traffickers, anything that threatens the investment climate or core elites' interests qualifies as a threat to national security. Moreover, the post-9/11 atmosphere has had a deleterious effect on the prospects for democracy in the Americas, having granted the US government the opportunity to assume a hard-line counter-terrorist posture that justifies authoritarian measures and the violation of civil rights.

Given the level of political alienation throughout the region, it is not surprising that there have been popular insurrections by communities that have risen up to confront the growing threats to their livelihood and dignity: Chiapas (1994), Quito (2000), Buenos Aires (2001), and La Paz (2003 and 2005). These popular insurrections have had broad domestic and international implications. They are specific examples of the Latin American variant of the Global Justice Movements. They reveal grassroots attempts to recreate the kind of civil society and popular organizations that were crushed by the double squeeze of military rule in the 1970s and the neo-liberal economic restructuring of the 1980s and 1990s. They also reveal that, in recent years, populism and anti-status quo feelings have been on the rise throughout Latin America.

A more institutional manifestation of this expanding protest movement is the series of electoral victories of populist, nationalist, and left-of-centre parties in Argentina (Néstor and Kirchner), Brazil ("Lula"), Uruguay (Vázquez), Nicaragua (Ortega), Bolivia (Morales), Venezuela (Chávez), and other unprecedented turns to the left in Ecuador (Correa), Paraguay (Lugo), Guatemala (Colom), and El Salvador (Funes), all of them at odds with Washington's neo-conservative politics (Latin Reporters 2004). These developments suggest that popular movements and popular rebellions remain an important element in the new globalized regional order (*LAWR* 1994a, 1994b). Inter-American relations dominated by the US monologue and the Washington Consensus are increasingly being challenged. Leftist groups and platforms have re-emerged as political options and it is likely that we may witness more popular mobilizations in the near future. This has had immediate consequences in reshaping the institutional configuration of the regional system, away from the Washington-centred organizations, including a significant shift within the Organization of American States (OAS) itself.

Instability in the once-hegemonic regional order is increasing despite the illusion of US-driven regional integration characterized by NAFTA and CAFTA. By challenging the legitimacy of the inter-elite and transnational regional arrangements, the new modes of resistance reveal the intrinsic weakness and precarious legitimacy of the post-transition regimes. Even the United States is not exempt from this turmoil and protestation. Two important events deserve special attention. The first was the massive mobilizations in 2006 that, despite growing electoral apathy, securitization, and cynicism in the American body politic, brought millions of protestors to the streets of Los Angeles, New York, and Chicago. These protestors, the majority of which were of Hispanic origin, demonstrated against attempts by right-wing elements in the US government to criminalize the large number of undocumented immigrants in the United States under the rubric of the "War on Terror" and the strengthening of "homeland security" to fight what Samuel Huntington called the "Hispanic Threat" (Huntington 2004). This momentous event indicates that social movements against the status quo are becoming ubiquitous throughout the hemisphere. The second, even more important, event was the victory of Barack Obama in the 2008 presidential election and his platform for change. Recent mild overtures by the new administration in Washington regarding Cuba and the statements made by the president himself in the 2009 Summit of the Americas in Trinidad-Tobago provide a glimmer of hope for a more constructive engagement. This is something not seen since FDR's Good Neighbor Policy in the 1930s.

However, as demonstrated by experience, the past has an ability to persist and reproduce its nastier strains. As the entire region becomes more closely integrated, a potentially dysfunctional system of mutual vulnerability constitutes a real and present danger. Its impact on the life of millions throughout the Americas is potentially catastrophic. The unfolding scenarios, in the context of a world economic meltdown, indicate dysfunctional trends feeding upon each other and transcending national boundaries. These include poverty, growing unemployment, criminality, health hazards, environmental decay, drug addiction, massive population displacements, and repression. Without profound changes in both the South and the North, the possibility of arresting or reversing the existing threats to human security will remain doubtful. Short of a radical reorganization of the pattern of governance throughout the Americas, including decision-making, accountability, and regional cooperation, multiple and critical dysfunctions are likely to increase within these societies.

Table 1
Latin American Foreign Debt, 1990, 1992, 2000, and 2003

Countries	Debt/GDP per Capita				Debt Service as % of Exports			
	1990	1992	1999	2003	1990	1992	2000	2003
Bolivia	94.3	61.2	65.9	38*	39.8	39.0	39.1	166.0
Brazil	28.8	31.2	40.0	54.0	20.8	23.1	90.7	330.0
Chile	74.7	48.9	50.7	67.0	25.9	20.9	26.0	178.0
Colombia	42.4	36.9	44.7	47.0	36.4	38.9	28.6	232.0
Costa Rica	70.9	58.7	33.6	36.0	24.5	20.6	8.2	77.0
Dominican Republic	74.7	57.0	28.7	33.0	10.3	13.5	4.8	71
Ecuador	119.9	99.9	107.3	82.0	33.2	27.1	17.3	296.0
El Salvador	36.9	25.5	17.4	55.0	17.1	13.2	6.7	198.0
Guatemala	33.6	24.2	28.6	21.0	13.3	24.0	9.4	115.0
Haiti	37.0	n/a	30.6	29.0	9.5	n/a	8.0	214.0
Honduras	116.3	92.0	83.3	54.0	40.4	33.7	19.3	134.0
Mexico	44.5	34.1	33.5	25.0	27.8	44.4	30.2	88.0
Nicaragua	199.4	750.3	231.0	40.0	14.7	21.8	23.0	129.0
Panama	152.0	107.2	55.7	93.0	9.7	12.6	10.0	124.0
Paraguay	44.7	24.6	22.6	51.0	11.0	40.3	10.4	112.0
Peru	83.9	92.7	50.9	60.0	11.0	23.0	42.8	335.0
Uruguay	46.7	46.7	40.1	90.0	41.8	23.2	29.2	353.0
Venezuela	66.1	61.1	71.1	42.0	20.7	19.5	15.7	139.0

Source: World Bank, World development report, 1990, 1991 and 1992 passim and 1994, pp. 206 passim. Valuable data is available also in the United Nations PNUD *World Development Report* (1999). Income figures are calculated as purchasing power parity (PPP) = parity equivalent in US dollars; also from the United Nations PNUD *Informe sobre desarrollo humano* (1999, 134–241). Figures were calculated from data contained in The International Bank of Reconstruction and Development/World Bank, World Development Report (1989, 1992) and World Bank (2001). Tables used include Table 1 Basic Indicators, Table 21 Total External Debt, Table 24 Total External Debt Ratios, Table 26 Population Growth and Projections. The 1990 GNP figure for Nicaragua was estimated on the basis of the 1987 figure and an average decline of 2.5 per cent per year. 2000 figures came from the United Nations Development Program, Human Development Report (2002, 203–5).

Other Statistical Sources and References: Gross Domestic Product per capita, GDP (thousands of US dollars) comes from the CIA *World fact book* (2006). Data on corruption is from Transparency International's 2004 Corruption perception index (CPI). United Nations Human Development Index Value (HDI) from US Aid (2003). The IISS figures for the GNP in Latin America and the Caribbean, unlike that of the World Bank used to calculate debt/GNP ratios, are higher than those prepared by UN agencies, like the World Bank and the UNDP.

*Data from debt sustainability analysis, Heavily Indebted Poor Countries initiative (HIPC). Estimates for such countries are for public and publicly guaranteed debt only, http://www.worldbank.org/date/wdi2005/wditex/Section4.htm.

The limited and substantially meaningless democracy designed and supported by Washington is deeply flawed. This model of democratic development, advocated by transition theorists and the neo-authoritarians at the core of the hemispheric order, impedes rather than facilitates the materialization of a sustainable security community and real democracy for the region. So does the persistence of neo-liberal economic dogmatism and the re-emergence of the national security doctrine designed to combat global "enemies." That narrowly defined concept of military security as practised in the Americas is, in fact, flawed with insecurity. This link underpins the insurmountable contradiction between globalization and militarization (Benítez-Manaut 2004, 59). In this context, real regime change throughout the Americas, and especially in the United States, is a necessary condition for human security and the well-being of the vast majority of its peoples.

Notes

1 This sketchy characterization fails to capture the unique dynamic intermeshing taking place in the Americas. For instance, a significant portion of the so-called "Hispanic population" in the United States—such as Mexicans and Puerto Ricans—did not have to cross any border. Like the First Nations, they were already there when the boundary moved. This seemingly amalgamated but not quite "melted" complexity needs to be analyzed as such in its multiple and nuanced manifestations. The current ideographic and comparative paradigms, both realism and complex dependency—as well as classical dependency theories—do not allow for interactive and integrated analysis of this sort. Rather, they obscure the understanding of this complex reality by adopting theoretical assumptions—like the capsular nature of nation states—and class determinism as empirical facts.
2 Unlike most of the Middle East, Africa, and Asia, the ratio and diversity of natural resources to population is highly favourable. In this sense, taken together, Latin America and the Caribbean, beyond their proximity to the overdeveloped North, appear at least statistically to have overcome the worst conditions of poverty (CPRC 2005, 79–82).
3 See Appendix F (1966, 275–76, 217–45); US Army Special Warfare School (1964).
4 See also World Bank, *World development report*, 1990, 1991, 1992; and 1994, 206–7; and World Bank (1988).
5 Calculations made on the basis of ECLAC (2001, table 285 and others).
6 The economic factors that undermined the national security regimes were not exclusively experienced by the dictatorships. The few remaining civilian governments in Latin America during the 1980s, such as Colombia, Venezuela, and Costa Rica, were also severely affected by the debt crisis.
7 It was based upon the Task Force report to the Trilateral Commission prepared for the first plenary meeting of the Commission in Tokyo, in May 1975; for a critique of this report see Wolfe (1975, 559).
8 The rate in the United States for 2002 was 46.6 per cent and roughly 55 per cent in Canada (2000). An examination of voter turnout in parliamentary elections held

in Latin America and North America between 1988 and 1991 and 1998 and 2001 shows that nearly half of the nations experienced higher rates of voter absenteeism than most European democracies (IDEA 2005).
9 Between 1985 and 1991, the region's defence budgets declined on the average 24.6 per cent, or 4.1 per cent per year, and twelve out of twenty countries made cuts ranging between 59 per cent (Chile) and 4.8 per cent (Honduras) to their defence expenditures. On the other hand, two rather large countries, Venezuela and Colombia, dramatically increased such expenditures: 23 per cent and 275 per cent respectively. When the number of troops is examined, the overall trend is a seemingly modest increase of 4.2 per cent for the region, or 0.7 per cent per year (IISS 2001).
10 Urban population has expanded exponentially in the region at nearly twice the average rate of population growth. While in 1950, only one city (Buenos Aires) was among the ten most populated cities in the World, by 2000 there were three Latin American cities among the world's largest, respectively ranking number two, four and ten: Mexico City (18.5 million), São Paulo (17.8 million), and Buenos Aires (12.6 million). While this expansion of mega-cities has been dramatic, even more pronounced is the growth of large metropolitan areas (Santiago, Bogota, Caracas, Lima) and secondary cities (Medellín, Curitiba, Córdoba, Concepción, Guadalajara, etc.). This phenomenon is the tip of the iceberg of a looming urban crisis, resulting from migrations rooted in widespread rural poverty (see Table 1 in text). It has been estimated that by 2050 Latin America will have double the population of North America (US AID 2003).
11 Robinson (1994), citing the 1993 UNDP *Human development report*, notes that the wealthiest 20 per cent of humanity receives 82.7 per cent of the world's income. They also control 80 per cent of world trade, 95 per cent of all loans, 80 per cent of all domestic savings, and 80.5 per cent of world investments. They consume 70 per cent of world energy, 75 per cent of all metals, 85 per cent of its timbers, and 60 per cent of its food supplies. In this context, the middle-classes are shrinking considerably. A US study by the Levy Institute, based on the 1998 Federal Reserve's survey of consumer finances, indicated that while the top 1 per cent of the population controlled 38 per cent of the country's net worth, the poorest 40 per cent controlled 0.26 per cent of it (see Wolff 2003, Tables 2 and 3). All indications are that income concentration has worsened since 1998.

References

Altimir, O. 1994. Income distribution and poverty through crisis and adjustment. *CEPAL Review* 52 (April): passim.
Appendix F: Précis of the counterinsurgency course at the special warfare school Fort Bragg, North Carolina, 1963. 1966. In *Internal security and military power: Counterinsurgency and civic action in Latin America*, ed. W. Barber and N. Ronning, 217–45, 275–76. Columbus: Ohio State Univ. Press.
Benítez-Manaut, R. 2004. *Mexico and the challenges of Hemispheric security*. Washington, DC: Woodrow Wilson International Center for Scholars, Latin American Program.
Boas, M., M. H. Marchand, and T. Shaw. 1999. The weave-world: Regionalisms in the South in the new millennium. *Third World Quarterly* 20(5): 1061–70.

Bosch, J. 2000. *El Pentagonismo sustituto del imperialismo*. 3rd ed. Santo Domingo: Editora Alfa y Omega.
Chillier, G., and L. Freeman. 2005. Potential threat: The new OAS concept of Hemispheric security. *WOLA special report*. Washington, DC: Washington Office on Latin America.
Chomsky, N. 1977. Trilateral commission's RX for crisis: Governability yes, democracy no. *Seven Days*, February 14, 10–11.
CIA (Central Intelligence Agency). 2006. *The world factbook*, December 19. https://www.cia.gov/cia/publications/factbook/geos/ca.html.
Close, D. 2004. Undoing democracy in Nicaragua. In *Undoing democracy: The politics of electoral caudillismo*, ed. D. Close and K. Deonandan, 2–4. Lanham, MD: Lexington Books.
Corbett, C. D. 1972. *The Latin American military as a socio-political force: Case studies of Bolivia and Argentina*. Miami: Center for Advanced International Studies, Univ. of Miami Press.
Cox, R. W. 1996. *Approaches to world order*. Cambridge: Cambridge Univ. Press.
CPRC (Chronic Poverty Research Centre). 2005. *The chronic poverty report 2004–05: Institute for development policy and management*. Manchester: Univ. of Manchester.
ECLAC (Economic Commission on Latin America and the Caribbean). 2001. *Anuario estadístico*. Santiago: ECLAC.
———. 2004. *Panorama económico de América Latina*. Santiago: ECLAC.
Graham, C., and S. Sukhatenkar. 2003. Is economic crisis reducing the support for markets and democracy in Latin America? Some evidence from the economics of happiness. Paper presented at the Brookings Institution.
Hogan, J. 2005. *New Scientist*. Print ed. March 1.
Huntington, S. 2004. The Hispanic threat. *Foreign Policy* (March–April). http://www.keepmedia.com/pubs/ForeignPolicy/2004/03/01/387925.
IDEA (International Institute for Democracy and Electoral Assistance). 2005. *Voter turnout from 1945 to date*, July 25. http://www.idea.int/vt/analysis; http://www.idea.int/ americas/index.cfm.
IISS (International Institute of Strategic Studies). 2001. *The military balance 2000–2001*. London: Oxford Univ. Press.
Jagan, C. 1996. Sustainable development in the Americas. Keynote address to the 27th Annual Congress of the Canadian Association of Latin American and Caribbean Studies (CALACS), York University.
Karl, T., and R. Fagen. 1986. The logic of hegemony: The United States as a superpower in Central America. In *Dominant powers and subordinate states: The United States in Latin America and the Soviet Union in Eastern Europe*, ed. J. Triska, 218–38. Durham, NC: Duke Univ. Press.
Latin Reporters. 2004. Uruguay, Chili et Venezuela votent à gauche; le Brésil se recentre, November 2. http://www.latinreporters.com/uruguaypol02112004.html.
LAWR (Latin America Weekly Report). 1994a. January 13(2).
———. 1994b. February 17: 62.
Letelier, O. 1976. The "Chicago Boys" in Chile: Economic freedom's awful toll. *The Nation*, August 28.
Linowitz, S. 1975. Commission on United States–Latin American relations. In *The Americas in a changing world*. New York: Quadrangle Books.

Martínez, O. 1992. Debt and foreign capital: The origins of the crisis. *Latin American Perspectives* 76.20.1 (Winter): 65.

Montecinos, V., and J. Markoff. 1993. Democrats and technocrats: Professional economists and regime transition in Latin America. *Canadian Journal of Development Studies* 14(1): 7–22.

Nader, R. 1992. Plutocracy and the citizen agenda for '92 and beyond. Speech given to Harvard University Law students, 15 January. http://www.ratical.org/co-globalize/RalphNader/RN01.15.92.html.

Nef, J. 1978. Myths in the study of Latin American politics. In *Canada and the Latin American challenge*, ed. J. Nef, 19–42. Toronto: Ontario Cooperative Program in Latin American and Caribbean Studies (OCPLACS), Canadian Association of Latin America and Caribbean Studies (CALACS).

———. 1999. *Human security and mutual vulnerability: The global political economy of development and underdevelopment*. 2nd ed. Ottawa: IDRC Books.

———. 2004a. Socioeconomic and political factors of health security and insecurity in Latin America and the Caribbean. *Journal of Developing Societies* 19 (Fascicule 2.3): 172–226.

———. 2004b. Structural correlates of government corruption in Latin America: Explaining and understanding empirical findings. In *Governance in Southern Africa and Beyond*, ed. D. Olowu and R. Mukwena, 283–304. Windhoek, Namibia: McMillan-Granberg.

Nef, J., and W. Robles. 1998. Environmental issues, politics, and administration in Latin America: An overview. In *Governmental response to environmental challenges in global perspective*, ed. J. Jabbra and O. Dwivedi, 42–62. Amsterdam: IOS Press.

Robinson, W. 1994. Central America: Which way after the Cold War? *NotiSur* 4(8) (February 25): 1–9.

Rockefeller, N. A. 1969. *The Rockefeller report on the Americas: Report of a United States presidential mission for the Western Hemisphere*. New York: Quadrangle Books, 1969.

Rojas, R. 2003. Notes on the doctrine of national security. http://www.rrojasdatabank.org/natsec1.htm.

Siat, A., and G. Iriarte. 1979. De la seguridad nacional al trilateralismo. *Cuadernos de Cristianismo y Sociedad* May: 23–24.

Sklar, H. 1980. Managing dependence and democracy: An overview. In *Trilateralism: The Trilateral Commission and elite planning for world management*, ed. H. Sklar, 1–55. Cambridge, MA: South End Press.

Transparency International. 2004. Corruption perceptions index (CPI). Berlin: http://www.transparency.org.

United Nations Development Program. 2002. *Human development report 2002*. http://www.worlbank.org/date/wdi2005/wditex/Section4.htm.

United Nations PNUD. 1999. *Informe sobre desarrollo humano*. Madrid: Mundi Prensa Libros.

US Aid—Bureau for Latin America and the Caribbean. 2003. Latin America and the Caribbean: Selected Economic and Social Data. http://qesdb.cdie.org/lac/LACbook/chapter01.pdf.

US Army Special Warfare School. 1964. *Counterinsurgency planning guide: Special text* (May): 31–176.

Weil, J., J. Comblin, and Judge Senese. 1979. The repressive state: The Brazilian national security doctrine and Latin America. *LARU Studies* Doc. No. 3, 36–73. Toronto: LARU.

Wolfe, A. 1980. Capitalism shows its face: Giving up on democracy. In *Trilateralism: The Trilateral Commission and Elite Planning for World Management*, ed. H. Sklar, 295–307. Cambridge, MA: South End Press.

Wolff, E. 2003. Recent trends in wealth ownership: 1983–1998. Levy Institute Working Paper 300.

World Bank. 1988. *World debt tables: External debt of developing countries 1987–1988*. Vol. 2. Country Tables. Washington, DC: World Bank.

———. 1990. *World debt tables: External debt of developing countries 1989–90*. Vol. 2. Country Tables. Washington, DC: World Bank.

———. 1992. *World debt tables: External debt of developing countries 1991–92*. Vol. 2. Country Tables. Washington, DC: World Bank.

———. 2001. *World development indicators* (1999–2001). http://esdb.cdie.org/cgibin2/broker.exe?_service=default&_program=lacprogs.pov_3.sas&sscode=WDI180800+&cty=ALLC&year=2002+&year=2001+&year=2000+&year=1999+&output=1.

———. 2003. *World debt tables: External debt of developing countries*, Vol. 2: Country tables.

World Development Report. 1989, 1992. *Development and the environment*. New York: Oxford Univ. Press.

Cultural Resilience and Political Transformation in Bolivia

Susan Healey

Introduction

In just over two decades, Bolivia has undergone socio-political changes so profound that the year 2006 may be remembered as a defining moment in Bolivia's history, on the scale of the 1952 National Revolution. On 22 January, Evo Morales Ayma was sworn in as President of the Republic, the first indigenous leader of a rural social movement to be elected to a Latin American presidency, and the first Bolivian president to win an absolute majority since electoral democracy was reinstated in 1982.[1]

Against the historical backdrop of a brutal colonial regime, elitist statehood, revolution, and, most recently, the political-economic phenomenon known as globalization, the resilience of Bolivia's original peoples is striking. This chapter explores key events and actors in a protracted struggle through which Bolivia's marginalized, mostly rural indigenous population succeeded in gaining the most powerful voice in the national political arena—a voice that had been silenced for over five hundred years. Based in part on in-depth interviews with *campesino* (peasant) and indigenous leaders, intellectuals, and political activists in Bolivia during the period leading up to the December 2005 election, the chapter identifies critical elements in the evolution from Andean cultural resilience to indigenous political capital, providing a basis for comparison with similar efforts under way in other parts of Latin America.

Bolivia's indigenous peoples make up sixty percent of the country's population. The earlier 2002 presidential election saw the peasant–indigenous coalition known as the Movimiento al Socialismo—Instrumento Político por la Soberanía del Pueblo (Movement toward Socialism—Political Instrument for the Sovereignty of the People, or MAS-IPSP)[2] propelled to national importance as the second most voted-for party in the country. The slim majority won by Washington-raised Bolivian mining heir Gonzalo "Goni" Sánchez de Lozada, bolstered by a sophisticated North American–style election campaign managed by a team of high profile US consultants,[3] could not last long in the face of unpopular economic policies, mounting urban unemployment, acute rural problems, and a generalized crisis of legitimacy of the traditional political parties. After a mere fourteen months, on 17 October 2003, Sánchez de Lozada was forced to resign the presidency and leave the country amidst nation-wide opposition to the government's plan to export gas to the United States via Chile.

When vice-president Carlos Mesa Gisbert subsequently assumed the presidency, he found himself in an untenable position as the clamour for constitutional reform and nationalization of the strategic hydrocarbon (oil and natural gas) sector peaked anew, while rural demands went unattended. Mesa resigned the presidency on 5 June 2005. A caretaker government set the date for early general elections on 18 December 2005. The election took place as planned with one of the highest voter turnout rates in recent history (85 percent of registered voters cast their ballot), and the predictable yet still stunning victory of the predominantly rural-indigenous MAS-IPSN (or MAS) — with 53.7 percent of the popular vote (see Crabtree 2006).

It is important to note that the "political instrument" born of Bolivia's peasant organizations is the relevant subject of analysis. The reconstituted *Movimiento al Socialismo* (MAS), which is the simpler acronym and reflects a political ideology not incongruent with dominant currents within the peasant–indigenous movement, in fact subsumed an existing, legally registered political party in order to participate in the 1999 municipal elections.[4] The MAS proposes the "re-founding" of a multiethnic and pluricultural sovereign state, with far-reaching constitutional reform providing the framework for an ambitious community-based national development project.

What are some of the key factors that explain the emergence and consolidation of the MAS as Bolivia's principal political force? One explanation is found in the opening up of political space at the municipal level through decentralization reforms, which provided fertile ground for cultivating indigenous political leadership. A second set of factors relates to Bolivia's history of working-class militancy, strengthened by and leveraged through a single national labour confederation (the COB — *Central Obrera Boliviana*) that incorporates a wide range of otherwise politically powerless sectors, from domestic workers to university students, peasant farmers, miners, and schoolteachers. Additionally, the profusion of rural livelihood issues — eroded and fragmented plots of land in the highlands, land trafficking and incursion into traditional indigenous territories in the lowlands, and military-police intervention in coca-producing zones — reached a peak following Bolivia's dramatic turn to neo-liberalism in 1985, and combined to form the set of "acute peasant grievances" that have sparked rural uprisings around the world and throughout history (see Wolf 1969). In Bolivia, however, a strategy of resistance more suited to the present conjuncture was already in preparation—the construction of an autonomous political instrument, born of the *campesino* organizations but open to alliances with others who shared the same fundamental goal: sovereignty for Bolivia, and democratic rights for Bolivia's indigenous majority.

This chapter suggests that in addition to the above, the concepts of cultural resilience and ethno-ecological identity—a social identity shaped by the unique human–environment relationships of highland and lowland peoples—are key to understanding the dominant political alliances in Bolivia today and visions for the future. The articulation of diverse indigenous identities linked by a common history of exploitation, marginalization and—perhaps most importantly—resistance led to the unification and mobilization of resources that might otherwise have remained divided. As a central factor in the restructuring of national political power, the cultural resilience of Bolivia's original peoples created ideal conditions for unleashing processes of identify formation and the development of critical alliances between highland *campesino* and lowland indigenous peoples, and their non-indigenous allies.[5]

With the political empowerment of peasant and indigenous organizations, Bolivia's condition as a multilingual, plurinational state will play a critical role in shaping the strategies and outcomes of the escalating conflict over land and natural resources. These conflicts are expressed in the struggles of small-scale farmers against an entrenched agribusiness elite, and in the revival of efforts to defend the national interest by regulating and taxing, if not completely eliminating, the stake in Bolivia's natural gas sector held by transnational corporations.

The Roots of Cultural Resilience

To the dismay—or horror—of many Bolivians who identify with the lowland tropical and subtropical two-thirds of the country, Bolivia is typically perceived as a mountainous Andean nation. Thinly cloaked as regionalism, deep-seated discrimination along easily blurred lines of race, ethnicity, and class is just one sign of the grim history that marks Bolivia, Latin America, and indeed most parts of the world where indigenous peoples were subjugated by superior firepower during Europe's Age of Discovery. The effort to construct "a modern Bolivia, fully national, integrated, and *mestizo*" following the 1952 Revolution did not succeed in establishing the unifying national identity envisioned by its proponents (Sanjinés 2004). Instead, the persistence of colonial-era social relations and encroachment on indigenous lands were factors in the gradual emergence of a new indigenous consciousness, particularly during the final quarter of the twentieth century. The 1994 reform of the constitution (State Political Constitution or CPE), which recognized for the first time Bolivia's condition as a multilingual, plurinational state, signalled the official retreat of the politics of assimilation and made way for an increasingly robust politics of identity.

Interviews conducted with national and regional leaders of the MAS in 2004 reveal the important role that indigenous identity is playing in shaping both contemporary political discourse and visions for the future. An interview with David Choquehuanca, an Aymaran intellectual,[6] popular educator, and later, foreign minister for the MAS, focused on the connections between the human–environment relationships that characterize the indigenous world view or cosmology, and the thinking and political strategy that was evolving at the leadership level of the MAS.

Choquehuanca spent fifteen years as the director of the NINA program, a non-governmental leadership development program for *campesinos* that lately had prioritized two principal areas of education: the recuperation of indigenous culture and values based on the "laws of nature"; and the critical analysis of national legislation, including the 1994 Popular Participation Law and the 1996 agrarian reform legislation. In this way, the NINA program served to create a space where *campesinos* could begin to "question [the current state of affairs] and generate viable alternative proposals" by analyzing contemporary reality through the lens of indigenous knowledge and values (Choquehuanca 2004). In particular, the recuperation of indigenous knowledge, regarded as a valuable repository of age-old dormant capacities, was viewed as one means of moving away from the resistance of old—the reactive development of counter-proposals to laws and programs initiated by the government—and towards a more proactive role that would see the *campesino* and indigenous sectors initiate their own policy proposals. As Choquehuanca made clear, the 1992 "Five Hundred Years of [Indigenous] Resistance to Colonialism" campaign in Latin America had produced a deep and lasting impact on *campesino* and indigenous leaders, fuelling renewed aspirations for political participation.

It is evident that in Bolivia, indigenous identities are not being constructed or portrayed on the basis of ethnicity alone. Rather, beyond the first layer of identity construction as indigenous peoples, identities are closely tied to specific sets of grievances, which in turn vary significantly with the ecological zone in which communities are located, and the consequent mix of livelihood opportunities, constraints, and struggles characteristic of each zone. This can perhaps be understood most easily by considering the coca producers of Cochabamba's Chapare region. A zone with the high heat and humidity characteristic of lowland tropical areas, the Chapare region has, over decades, attracted Quechua and Aymara-speaking colonizers from highland regions across the country. In the political realm, group identity as indigenous *campesinos* engaged in coca production has been reinforced through community-based organizational affiliation to the coca-growers syndicates, and takes precedence over place-of-origin-, language- or religion-based identities. Similarly, the frequent self-referential use of the terms "highlanders" and "lowlanders" is evidence of a profoundly new discourse not readily apparent in oppositional political currents in Bolivia prior to the rise of the MAS.

Thus, the term ethno-ecological identity serves to highlight a principal aspect of identity construction and representation for Bolivia's politicized rural indigenous population, a representation that is key to understanding both the dominant political alliances in rural Bolivia and the ecological realities that will necessarily inform future development planning.

The Contested Realm of Identity, Class, and Social Movements

Identity, specifically collective or group identity, has emerged for some observers as "the central problem of modern societies at the end of the twentieth century" (Eder et al. 2002, 1). Indeed, it is a subject at the very centre of the post-modern–structuralist debate on the nature of contemporary societal issues and the means for understanding and addressing them. Identity connotes a sense of belonging that derives from shared origins or characteristics. Shared origins include the same birthplace, perceived common roots, or a shared history (Bates and Fratkin 1999, 292). Shared characteristics include a common language or livelihood, elements that are frequently (though not always) a function of origin. Because there are so many possible combinations of origin and characteristics on the basis of which identity can be constructed, let us focus here on one form of identity that serves as a foundation for organized collective action aimed at challenging the status quo; namely, ethnic identity.

Max Weber's (1997, 18–19) understanding of ethnic group identity is similarly focused on political agency. While ethnicity is fundamentally a social category "rooted in socially perceived differences in national origin, language and/or religion" (Bates and Fratkin 1999, 457),[7] in Weber's view "ethnic membership does not constitute a group; it only facilitates group formation of any kind, particularly in the political sphere. On the other hand, it is primarily the political community, no matter how artificially organized, that inspires the belief in common ethnicity" (1997, 19).

This perspective on ethnic identity has been taken up and further developed by others who view ethnicity as a phenomenon which is "socially and ideologically constructed, and perhaps even politically manipulated by elites fighting for control over resources and privileges" (Martinussen 1997, 324). By this account, collective identities are what people make them out to be, with "creative history writing [containing] a good deal of inventions and imaginings with added notions of common cultural inheritance, common heroes... and so on" serving as potent unifying forces (ibid.). Along the same lines, Paul Brass proposes that the symbol manipulation necessary for ethnic-based collective mobilization has its origin in elite competition but that its success is dependent on other factors, including the existence of an appropriate mechanism for communicating the selected symbols of identity across the ethnic group as well as the absence of extreme class differences within the group which could otherwise hamper support for leaders (Brass 1991).

Ethnic identity, viewed from this perspective, is a strategic asset cultivated and deployed for political ends. Furthermore, these theories employ class analysis by incorporating the class differential both between and within groups as a key variable in ethnic-based group formation. It is somewhat surprising, therefore, that contemporary research into social movements has tended to posit the relevance of identity and class as an either/or scenario, sparking fervent debates as well as attempts to reconcile two allegedly contradictory positions. One example is Geraldo Otero's theory of political-class formation, which combines the structural analysis of Marxism with new social movements theory's focus on cultural politics. As will be seen, the premise that identity and class are inseparable elements of Indian-peasant mobilization in Latin America (Otero and Jugenitz 2003) proves to be a useful vantage point for understanding the Bolivian experience.

The Geo-physical Environment

Bolivia is a landlocked tropical nation comprised of nine *departamentos* (the largest sub-national political unit) and three main geographic regions, distinguished in the first instance by their extreme variation in altitude and running like three vertical strips from west to east across the country. The three regions are the Andean highlands, comprised of two mountain ranges and the high plateau that lies between them (twenty-eight percent of Bolivia's land surface), the high valley or sub-Andean region on the eastern slopes of the Andes (thirteen percent of the land surface), and the northern and eastern lowlands (fifty-nine percent). The first two zones share more physical and cultural linkages and are often jointly referred to as the highlands, although both are punctuated by swathes of humid, low-lying river valleys.

Within these three broad regions lies an immense array of ecosystems. The Andean highlands alone consist of several hundred ecological micro-zones in varying combinations of precipitation, topography, vegetation, and human influence (Dollfus 1986, 11; see also Luteyn and Churchill 2000). It is the region with the greatest plant diversity per unit area in the tropics and possibly the world (Luteyn and Churchill 2000, 281). The Andes Mountains are also the site of the *altiplano,* the highest, largest, and most level plateau in South America. Bordering the *altiplano* on the east, the Royal Cordillera forms the divide between the highlands and the remainder of Bolivia's territory. As the site of important silver and tin deposits, the zone where the *altiplano* meets the Cordillera formed the economic axis of colonial and republican Bolivia.

The second principal ecological zone, the high (or mesothermic) valleys, is situated on the descending eastern slopes of the Royal Cordillera. With numerous fertile plains and river valleys, this area supplied maize to the highland populations in pre-Columbian times, and wheat to the mining industry after the Spanish conquest, in return for key staples grown on the *altiplano,* including quinoa grain, potatoes, and other root crops (Klein 2003, 5–7). Following Bolivia's National Revolution, most land reform was carried out in this region, and it remains the principal area of intensive small-scale agriculture today. The urban centres of Cochabamba, Sucre, and Tarija are situated in large valleys with temperate climates and forested hills at the lower altitudes.

The high valleys give way to rolling foothills until finally reaching the lowland eastern and northeastern flatlands of the Oriente, the most extensive but least populated region of Bolivia. The Oriente in turn comprises three distinct ecological zones characterized by an even greater number of microclimates. In the northern and central part of the Oriente bordering Brazil, four large rivers together with numerous smaller tributaries form part of the Amazon River system. Directly south of Bolivia's Amazon rainforest lies the Llanos de Moxos (or Mojos), an extensive floodplain with the third-largest complex of grasslands in South America, together with humid forest and associated wetlands (Daly and Mitchell 2000). Towards the southwest, the Oriente landscape becomes a mix of flatlands and scattered ranges of low hills with vegetation ranging from savanna to scrub cover and tropical dry forest. The vast dry plain of the Gran Chaco is the third distinct ecological zone of the eastern lowlands. The Chaco extends across Bolivia's southern border with Paraguay and Argentina, and is one of the few forested (rather than desert) transition areas between a tropical and temperate zone found anywhere (ibid.).

Highland Ethno-ecology

In the late pre-Hispanic era (fifteenth and early-sixteenth centuries), the Bolivian highlands were dominated by two indigenous peoples—the Aymaras and the Quechua-speaking Incas—and included a number of other less populous linguistic groups. Militarily inferior but organizationally stronger than the divided Aymara nations, Inca control of the highlands was achieved under Pachakuti[8] (1438–71) and further consolidated under Tupac Yupanqui (1471–93) (Delgado Burgoa 2002, 89; Klein 2003, 17). The language, religion, and institutions of the Incas spread throughout the Lake Titicaca basin of

Qullasuyu in what is now Bolivia, by then the westernmost of the four provinces that made up the Incan realm of *Tawantinsuyu* (Land of the Four Parts). Nevertheless, Aymara society was not significantly disrupted, and its resilience is reflected in the survival of the Aymara language and community structures, and the twenty-five percent of the population that are identified as ethnically Aymaran.

Essential to the functioning of the Aymara, Inca, and other highland societies were the socio-political and economic relationships maintained with farmer-colonists (*mitmaq* or *mitimaes*) settled on the lower eastern slopes and valleys of the Andes, frequently in close proximity to other ethnic communities. This way of organizing space has come to be known as "vertical integration," uniting ecologically distinct zones at widely varying altitudes into an economy and society built on the principle of complementarity (Delgado Burgoa 2002, 88; Murra and Wachtel 1986, 4). This allowed for production and access to a variety of crops, animal products, and handicrafts through elaborate non-market systems of exchange based on reciprocity, social relations, barter, labour obligations, and shared access to resources. Researchers concur that such an arrangement was essential to the sustainability of human populations in the harsh Andean environment.[9]

Following the arrival of the Spanish in 1532 to present-day Peru, the discovery of Potosí's rich silver veins in 1545 generated serious interest in what is now Bolivia. Three years later, the establishment of the city of La Paz in Aymara territory secured the important transportation route connecting Chuquisaca and Potosí with Cuzco in Lower Peru, facilitating the flow of precious metals to Lima and on to Spain (Klein 2003, 31–33).

In an effort to replicate the Inca system of indirect rule, the Spanish sought to preserve the ayllu structure of social relationships, political leadership, and access to land (Collier, Blakemore, and Skidmore 1985, 182; Klein 2003, 34).[10] So-called free peasant communities were obliged to render goods and services as tribute directly to the Spanish crown. Other communities were organized into districts. Groups of people—and in practice, their lands as well—were subdivided into *encomiendas*, the control over which was granted to prominent colonists (*encomenderos*). The *encomendero* was supposed to bring Christianity and Spanish customs to the indigenous peoples, and he in turn was entitled to peasant labour and production, on the land or in the mines. Under Spanish Viceroy Toledo (1572–76), rural households were relocated or "reduced" into a smaller number of larger communities so that they could be managed and taxed more efficiently (Klein 2003, 35–37). Though the process took over one hundred years to consolidate, the reforms impacted directly on the ayllu form of social organization and settlement. The *reducciones* were permanent settlements that had the effect of grouping people from various ayllus into one indigenous community, at the same time separating them from their *mitmaq* (colonists) in other regions. Settlement sizes increased from an average of 142 people per community to about 2,900 each. Even though the ayllu structure did not completely disappear, and lowland and valley communities remained linked to the highland core ayllus, the nucleated indigenous community structure eventually came to dominate in the Andes.

Lowland Ethno-ecology
The pre-Conquest ecology of lowland Bolivia differed from that of the highlands and is key to understanding subsequent differences in the colonial and post-colonial history of the two regions. The Incas were unable to penetrate and subdue areas not dependent primarily on peasant agriculture, the surplus of which supported the non-food-producing sectors of the population that were essential to the functioning of the Inca state. Thus it was a "complex combination of hunters and gatherers, village agriculturalists, and even multivillage states" (Klein 2003, 20–22), comprising a large but indeterminate number of ethnic groups possibly numbering in the hundreds, that formed a virtual barrier to the eastward expansion of the Pax Incaica. These sedentary, semi-sedentary, and nomadic groups are represented today by, among others, the Guaraní, Chiquitano, Ayoreo, and Guarayo peoples in the southern and central eastern lowlands, and the Mojeños and Sirionó in Bolivia's northeastern Amazon region.

With regard to indigenous politico-economic structures in the lowlands, Temple (2003) argues that reciprocol relationships based on consensual rights and obligations were not limited to Andean peoples but were the foundation of political authority in all New World indigenous societies, without exception.[11] In Temple's view, understanding reciprocity, which was and remains *the* central feature of indigenous social systems, is essential not only to developing a sound interpretation of the past but also to constructing a viable political alternative for the future—one that recognizes and incorporates age-old communal systems of reciprocity.

In the eastern lowlands, contact between indigenous peoples and Spanish explorers seeking gold and a northwest route to Peru dates from as early as 1516 (Temple 2002, 27). Basing her analysis on first-person historical accounts, Temple (2002, 28–35) describes the typical pattern of these early encounters. After first being warmly received, fêted, and fed by their New World hosts, the navigators eventually wore out their welcome and, at times on the brink of starvation, overcame indigenous resistance and took by force what had once been freely given. Entire communities were exterminated or enslaved. Continued efforts by the Spanish to discover mineral resources in the east proved fruitless, although indigenous peoples were captured and transported west to work in the mines.

Over time the eastern lowlands were transformed from hinterland into new frontier as silver production in the core areas entered a period of decline beginning in the mid-1600s (Klein 2003, 58). Increased European contact in the eastern lowlands occurred during the period of the Missions (1682–1767). Jesuit priests from Spain began the process of Catholic evangelizing by grouping together people of different ethnicities, based on the model of the *reducción*. In the missions, people were obliged to adopt the language of whatever ethnic group was numerically predominant, or some variation of it (Parapaino 2002, 38; Sweet 1995, 23). The Jesuits had less success in establishing missions among the Guaraní of southern Bolivia and Paraguay (Temple 2002, 41), considered to be among those native peoples who most fiercely resisted colonization (Albó 2002, 10). Even by the end of the colonial period, the Spanish were unable to exercise direct control over the lowland plains of the Gran Chaco (Klein 2003, 33).

The mission regime was a standard-bearer for Western beliefs of the time that saw women (as well as indigenous men) and nature as wild, brute things (see Merchant 1989). Because native peoples did not differentiate between goods of greater or lesser economic value when engaging in reciprocal exchange, they were considered irrational, inferior beings who, quite possibly, were not human at all (Temple 2003, 32–33). They needed to be tamed or dominated before they could be exploited in the interest of accumulation, expansion, and trade. The once multiple and authority-imbued role of women in community activities and agricultural production was reduced to reproductive, domestic, and artisanal functions. Under the missionaries, nature—once a powerful spiritual force that was revered, tended, and feared—was recast as a commodity to be systematically exploited as efficiently as possible. Indigenous social mores were, then, completely at odds with the interests of the colonizers, whose primary intent was "the accumulation of the value of exchange" (Temple 2003, 24); that is, the generation of profit. According to Sweet (1995, 31), the mission Indians

> lost their sense of membership in nature and became small-time, generally not very successful exploiters of nature. They learned to hunt and fish and harvest more than they needed to feed their families, to waste that which they could neither use nor sell. They learned to plant in rows, to chop down all the trees when clearing a field rather than planting around the stumps of a few. In time... they came to threaten the species that had once fed them, to destroy the forests, to provoke the erosion and hardening of the soil itself by altering landscapes to conform to ill-conceived human designs.

The most significant impact of the missions on lowland indigenous peoples may have been their conversion "from a spirituality of participation to a monotheism of powerlessness and exploitation" (Sweet 1995, 31). This was exacerbated by a process referred to as "infantilization." By subjecting people to a completely foreign and rigid belief system that physically punished the merest transgression while rewarding compliance and passivity, adults were deprived of their dignity and children were moulded to remain childlike as adults (Sweet 1995, 27–28). It may also be inferred that a significant expansion of humankind's ecological footprint in Bolivia's eastern lowlands can be traced to this time. Thus, deculturation combined with the enormous loss of life and commercial exploitation of natural resources significantly altered the ecology of parts of Bolivia's eastern lowlands.

Still, when Bolivia gained independence from Spain in 1825, nearly three-quarters of its estimated 1.1 million population were indigenous. Historians concur that the economic exploitation of native peoples during the republican era was even more extreme than in colonial times (Collier, Blakemore, and Skidmore 1985, 192, 211, 239). The relative political autonomy of free communities was incompatible with the republican vision of national development through the more intensive exploitation of rural land and labour. Even when genuine attempts were made to end the oppression of peasants and servants, the mixed race (*mestizo*) and white *patrones* usually managed to close off livelihood alternatives for their serfs and dependents, in effect resigning them to personal bondage for the rest of their lives (Mayer 2002, 117).

In the southeast, indigenous communities came under increasing attack as the new state "promoted private property rights in the llanos, deprived the nomadic plainsmen of their traditional common usages, and reduced them to the status of rural labourers" (Collier, Blakemore, and Skidmore 1985, 211). In the Bolivian Chaco, hunter-gatherer peoples including the Tobas, Matacos, and Choretes were especially hard hit by republican policies that sought economic and social progress for the region through integration into the national economy. Within a century, the warlike Tobas had been relegated to the annals of Bolivian folklore, with students donning tall headdresses and dancing as "Tobas" in pre-Lenten carnival parades around the country.

Andean Cosmology and Indigenous Resistance
That the subject of ethnic identity has resonance in Bolivia or anywhere else in Latin America today says much about socio-cultural resilience in the face of wave upon wave of ethnocidal onslaught.[12] Nevertheless it is the strength of their determination to re-assert the primacy of indigenous lands and ways, and their resistance to external forces of oppression and exploitation, which are arguably the most important elements of ethno-ecological identity construction and rural political mobilization in Bolivia today. Andean cosmology or *cosmovisión*, never completely lost and still a vital part of life in highland

communities throughout Bolivia, is being "rediscovered" by indigenous political leaders (Choquehuanca 2004) as they seek to balance the material needs of impoverished people with the recognition that Western-imposed notions of capitalist development are neither spiritually nor ecologically congruent with their world view.

Augstburger (1990, 21) describes Andean *cosmovisión* as an overarching, holistic view of the world that directly impacts the daily lives of *campesinos*. It is expressed in a system of social controls exercised through family and communal organizational structures, which also serve to reinforce the belief that virtually all things that touch the life of a *campesino* are interconnected. Reciprocity, wholeness, inclusiveness, and change are central to the Andean worldview (Grillo 1990, 58; Rocha 1990, 68): the fluid, continual transformation or domestication of the environment is not antithetical to these beliefs so long as it for the reciprocal benefit of nature and society. The dual non-market exchange mechanisms of reciprocity and redistribution are portrayed as vital elements of contemporary Andean culture, as a means of regulating relationships among people in society and between society and nature (Grillo 1990, 60). While Andean reciprocity has been described as the act of giving and receiving, and of guaranteeing equity in economic relationships at the communal, inter-communal, and continental level (Rocha 1990, 69), there is considerable evidence that the meanings and practices of reciprocity and redistribution are varied, nuanced, and complex (D'Altroy 2000; Temple, 2003). Nevertheless, of primary interest is the importance that these concepts hold as examples of enduring, more equitable, less accumulative and potentially more sustainable forms of production and consumption.

Andean cosmology is also an agro-centric one (Augstburger 1990, 21). Virtually all components of Andean culture, from modes of social organization through the sciences, arts, philosophy, religion, value systems, language, and technologies, are constructed in relation to agricultural activity (Grillo 1990, 58). For example, the interest in astronomy is not only spiritual but also a function of its relevance to the agricultural production cycle (Grillo 1990, 58; D'Altroy 2000).

Ordered, controlled equilibrium is another current that runs through most treatments of the subject of Andean cosmology. Rocha (1990, 67–68) suggests that this is achieved through the dialectic or "dynamic game" between, on one hand, austerity and, on the other, the sacred and profane religious festival (*festividad sacro-profano*). Austerity is an economic concept based on the hierarchical ordering of goods according to their human and social use value for the purpose of optimizing their use and avoiding excess and waste. The sacred and profane festival is characterized as a function that tempers the rigour of austerity and transcends the physical-biological realm in order to satisfy human psychological and spiritual needs. Among other things, it also serves to redistribute surplus production, reducing the possibility of unnecessary material accumulation, concentrated power, and domination. Together, these two functions serve not only to articulate a hierarchy of priorities but to optimize and justify the use of resources and reduce the natural and man-made risks associated with agricultural activity in the Andean region.

Another defining characteristic of the Andean worldview is the understanding that the future is in the past. It is completely abstract and irrational to do something that is unknown to the *campesino* and, by extension, to his/her ancestors (Augstburger 1990, 21). An option is valid only if history has proven it so (San Martín 1990, 87). Consequently, Andean cosmology infuses the process of knowledge creation and dissemination, resulting in a concept of learning that is very different from Western epistemologies based on discipline-based scientific inquiry. Blanco (1990, 77–78) is candid in his criticism of orthodox, Western-styled learning focused on compartmentalized knowledge and its incongruity with the Andean world view of integration and regard for the whole: "[T]here is the agronomist engineer, the zootechnical engineer, the agricultural economist... the forestry engineer... [A]griculture is totally fragmented. This does not respond to the needs of the family agricultural enterprise that we have in the Andes, because here the family enterprise, with a couple of hectares or less of land, has agriculture, livestock, sometimes a little agroindustry, and sometimes handicrafts."

By now it is apparent that in addition to representing a belief system and a process for regulating behaviour in the family, in the community, and on the land, the concept of Andean cosmology represents nothing less than survival in, and of, an age-old way of life, one which may hold important clues to the forging of a more sustainable future.

Nevertheless, as Karl Polanyi (1944, 8) once noted, "[i]nterests,... like intents, necessarily remain platonic unless they are translated into politics by the means of some social instrumentality." The history of peasant–indigenous resistance in Bolivia has served a fundamental purpose in this regard, and the stories of its heroes and heroines serve as potent symbols of the sacrifices of the past, and the possibilities for the future. Any discussion of the ecological and historical antecedents of identity construction in rural Bolivia would not be complete without considering the more important figures in the history of indigenous resistance. Research suggests that "politically engaged Aymara peoples and their opponents think in terms of memories spanning two centuries' time" (Stern 1987a, 12). The period 1780–82 is known as the Great Rebellion, the events of which posed a genuine threat to the colonial regime and figure prominently in the *campesino*-indigenous political consciousness of Bolivia today.[13] Based on his exploration of the underlying and multiple causes of the insurrection, Stern (1987a, 73) offers the following insight: "It is the moral memory—or myth—of an alternative, Andean-based social order, a cultural memory nurtured and sustained by Andean peoples... that in part explains why economic pillage led not merely to local revolt... but rather to dreams of a great transformation under nativist or neo-Inca auspices."

Campbell (1987, 116–17, 121) concurs, suggesting that the rebellion was part of a "larger effort of cultural recovery" fuelled by a cosmological belief that linked "God, the Spanish King, and the Inca" in a uniquely Andean view of the past and the future. Moreover, Campbell argues that the work of numerous Andean scholars clearly demonstrates that "the concept of Inca recovery through the reappearance of a *messiah* was flourishing by the mid-eighteenth century" (1987, 117; emphasis added). According to this interpretation, then, indigenous heroes of the past were not merely rebel leaders but rather persons imbued with divine authority to carry out the prophesized Inca *recuperación* (recovery).

Two key indigenous leaders from Bolivia emerged during the age of insurrection. The first, Aymara leader Tomás Katari, led a 1777 rebellion from his base in Macha, Chayanta (on the Bolivian *altiplano* in the department of Potosí), actually predating the Great Rebellion by a few years. Able to mobilize "up to 30,000 Indians," Tomás Katari was ultimately betrayed and executed in 1781, but "the people refused to accept that their messiah was dead" (Campbell 1987, 119). Shortly before Katari's death, the Great Rebellion had already begun in the area of Cuzco, Peru, spearheaded by Quechua leader and Inca descendent José Gabriel Condorcanqui, known as Tupac Amaru (Campbell 1987, 112; Stern 1987b, 35).

The second part of the Bolivian story unfolds following the defeat of the Cuzco rebellion and Tupac Amaru's subsequent betrayal and execution in May 1781. At this point the history of the indigenous rebellion moves out of the "tupamarista phase" and into the "katarista phase"[14] (Campbell 1987). Another charismatic leader, a commoner named Julián Apasa (or Apaza), had appeared and quickly filled the leadership void created by the death of Tomás Katari. Through a reincarnation ceremony that served to unite and strengthen the legacies of Tupac Amaru and Tomás Katari, Apasa took the name Tupac Katari. Leveraging his adopted names, he positioned himself as leader of both the Quechua and Aymara-led factions opposed to Spanish rule (Campbell 1987, 127–29). With a rebel force of 40,000, Katari fought for control of the city of La Paz, which remained under siege for six months from March until October of 1781 (Campbell 1987, 129; Echazú Alvarado 2003, 183; Klein 2003, 76). The eventual fall of La Paz to royalist troops, together with a negotiated settlement with Tupac Amaru loyalists who had resisted (and may have betrayed) Tupac Katari, brought the rebellion to a close and Tupac Katari to trial and execution, but "Katarismo" evolved into, and remains, an important political current in Bolivia today. Later indigenous uprisings produced other historical figures, notably Pablo Zárate *"El Temible"* (the feared) Wilka, another legendary Aymara leader, and the Guaraní rebel leader "El Tumpa" Apiaguaiqui (see for example Echazú Alvarado 2003, 183–84, 281). Their stories help to sustain a powerful sentiment within the *campesino*-indigenous movement that they are a people oppressed but not defeated.

Campesino Organization and the Process of Identity Construction
Following Bolivia's National Revolution of 1952, in which *campesinos* played a supportive but not decisive role (see Malloy 1970), Bolivia's Agrarian Reform was initiated (1953), agricultural lands were redistributed, and *campesinos* were organized at the community level into agrarian syndicates. These are frequently a hybrid of trade-union models and traditional indigenous organizations.[15] Local unions are in turn grouped together at increasingly centralized levels of decision-making—the Sub-central, Central, and Federation, generally following the country's geo-political divisions (canton, province, etc.), culminating in a national Confederation of Campesino syndicates (the CSUTCB). These are formally structured organizations with the rights and responsibilities of each agrarian union and its members clearly defined.

While the Agrarian Reform did not significantly alter the extreme poverty and marginalization of indigenous peoples, it did emancipate them from feudal-type labour obligations. The first appearance of an emerging ethnic consciousness in Bolivia occurred during the 1960s, when a group of Aymara students studying in La Paz formed a grouped called the "Cultural Centre 'November 15th'"—the date of Tupac Katari's death (Ticona 1996, 11–14). Influenced by the teachings of Indianist Fausto Reinaga, who had founded the *Partido Indio* in 1962, the group undertook an alternative reading of Bolivian history from an indigenous-indianist perspective, focusing on two principal aspects: the need to resist the continued colonialist oppression of Indian peoples and the notion of the *campesino* syndicate as "a privileged instrument of resistance" (Ticona 1996), albeit one that also served to perpetuate domination by a non-indigenous state. Their analysis revealed the fundamental challenge of melding the "long" pre-hispanic, anti-colonial memory with the "short" revolutionary memory into a collective indigenous identity and political vision. In Ticona's view, the frustrated expectations born of the 1952 revolution wakened the long memory of centuries-old indigenous resistance to the state, giving rise to a new ethnic consciousness and a more sophisticated understanding of the political challenges that lie ahead.

In the late 1960s, the peasant syndicates of the Aymara province of Aroma, department of La Paz, took on the mantle of "katarista-indianism" (Albó

1987; Ticona 1996). After first gaining control of the *campesino* syndicates at the local, provincial, and departmental levels, Katarista leader Jenaro Flores was elected to the maximum post (Executive Secretary) of the then-named National Confederation of Campesino Workers of Bolivia (CNTCB) at the national congress of 1971. Only a few days later, the military coup of Hugo Banzer Suárez took place, driving the newly elected *campesino* leadership underground. It was during this time that the first political platform explicitly linking class and ethno-cultural nation was formulated. The Tiwanaku Manifesto was signed in 1973 by four political organizations, including Flores's MRTK (*Movimiento Revolucionario Tupac Katari*) — "at the foot of the great pre-Inca ruins of Tiwanaku [or Tiahuanaku]" — and clandestinely distributed in Spanish, Quechua, and Aymara (Ticona 1996; see also Dunkerley 1984, 213–15). The restoration of some civil liberties in 1978 led to the re-emergence of opposition political currents and the return of the Kataristas to the leadership of the Campesino Confederation which, not insignificantly, now bore the added descriptor "Tupac Katari" (CNTCB-TK).

Under the Kataristas, *campesinos* won official membership to Bolivia's powerful national labour confederation, the COB. To overcome differences in political currents within the *campesino* sector, a congress of *campesino* unity was convened by the COB on 25 and 26 June 1979, marking the birth of the *Sole* Union Confederation of Campesino Workers of Bolivia (*Confederación Sindical Unica de Trabajadores Campesinos de Bolivia*, or CSUTCB), which for the first time grouped the majority of highland indigenous and *campesino* peoples of Bolivia into a single national confederation. Thus, Katarismo played a fundamental role not only in the consolidation of Bolivia's first autonomous highland indigenous-*campesino* organization but also in the forging of an enduring (though often problematic) alliance with organized labour through membership in the COB. In time, the *campesinos* increased their power and influence within the COB (Ticona 1996, 30), an important achievement, given the COB's capacity to undermine, or sustain, governments in Bolivia. By 1992, the CSUTCB had won a position on the Executive Committee of the COB, gaining one of two General Secretariats, the second position in importance after the Executive Secretariat (a role reserved by statute for the Miners' Federation) in addition to four other Secretariats (Ticona 1996, 32).

The year 1992 also marked the five-hundredth-year anniversary of the arrival of Columbus in the New World. This was supposed to have been a commemorative celebration of the "Discovery of the Americas." Instead, for people from the indigenous, black, and popular segments of society, it became an opportunity to rebuild grassroots movements from the bottom up, and throughout the hemisphere.

Strategic Alliances: The 'Five Hundred Years of Resistance' Campaign

Through a series of massively attended continental meetings starting in Bogota and concluding in Managua, the "Five Hundred Years of Resistance" campaign marked the beginning of a process that brought indigenous movements from different nations of the Americas together for the first time (León, Burch, and Tamayo 2001; Infodesarrollo 2001). The campaign counted with the early participation of the National Organization of Indigenous Peoples of Colombia (ONIC), the Confederation of Indigenous Nations of Ecuador (CONAIE), and the US-based South and Meso American Indian Information Center (SAIIC). Its goals were to develop a coordinated plan of action that would project the theme of "five hundred years of indigenous resistance and struggle against colonialism" onto the world stage, as well as to re-establish intercultural relations and reaffirm the unity of indigenous peoples of the Americas (Native Web 1990, 1991). The campaign marked an important juncture in the process of what Alison Brysk (1996) calls the "internationalization of Indian rights." To be sure, the evolution of a transnational indigenous social movement network, which quickened its pace during the 1970s with the support of key international allies,[16] has played an important role in catalyzing social movements of Latin American indigenous peoples who are "rich in identity but poor in everything else" (Brysk 1996, 39–40).

The Five Hundred Years campaign was a turning point for Bolivia's *campesino*-indigenous movement (Villca 2004; Choquehuanca 2004). Bolivia's highland peasant organizations were already well positioned to actively participate in a hemispheric indigenous rights campaign. A confederation representing Bolivia's lowland indigenous peoples had been organized more recently, in 1982, with the support of some of the same international organizations behind the Five Hundred Years campaign. While the coming together of indigenous peoples from across the Americas served to legitimize the cultural recuperation and quest for territory that were central to lowland indigenous demands, the impact on *campesinos* was arguably even more significant. It appears to have opened the door to nothing less than the beginning of a complete reorientation of the movement in Bolivia that, though historically dominated by political parties and the labour confederation, was about to discover the possibility of greater autonomy by pursuing the path of identity politics. David Choquehuanca (2004) notes that "through the Campaign we learned that in Bolivia the Aymaras and Quechuas were the majority population... that we are the real owners of these lands and territories.... We began to want to participate politically... we said, from now on, let's begin to construct our own proposals, according to our own way of thinking, our feeling, our own ideology."

In addition to benefiting from a solid organizational structure to support active participation in a hemispheric initiative, a small handful of non-indigenous allies of Bolivia's *campesino*-indigenous organizations have played a critical role in strengthening the movement. Men and women in Bolivia who have remained firm in their commitment to social justice, including political activists and legal experts of the left, have rejected careerism and opted instead to work for the social and political transformation of their country. Reflecting Brazilian Paulo Freire's concept and methods of popular education and consciousness-raising, the formation of leaders to guide Bolivia's *campesino*-indigenous movement has been a steady and deliberate process, one that has had to overcome numerous limitations and obstacles, not the least of which is the ever-present risk of leadership co-optation by powerful third parties. In some cases, new organizations have emerged where existing ones were unwilling or unable to defend the interests of those they were supposed to represent, or where critical organizational alliances floundered because of political or personal differences too vast to overcome. In spite of these kinds of difficulties, alliance-building with key supporters and among grassroots organizations themselves at the local, national, and international level has been essential to the strengthening of Bolivia's *campesino*-indigenous movement.

The New Millennarian Challenge: Constitutional Reform and the 'Re-founding' of Bolivia

By the close of the first decade of the new millennium, there is no doubt that Bolivia will have experienced the most profound socio-political changes in its history as a nation-state. On 9 December 2007, a multi-party constituent assembly formed to recommend changes to Bolivia's Constitution brought sixteen long months of deliberation to a close. In a surprise move, President Evo Morales called for a presidential recall referendum that would put his mandate (to the year 2010) to the test, along with that of the country's nine governors, six of whom are staunch opponents of his, and of the proposed constitutional reforms. A victory for Evo Morales in the recall referendum would signal the likelihood of majority support for a new Constitution in the second referendum planned for 2009. As it turned out, Morales won the recall referendum held on 10 August 2008 with 67.4 per cent of the votes (CNE 2008). In the constitutional referendum that followed on 25 January 2009, 61.4 per cent of the electorate voted in favour of the new Constitution (CNE 2009).

Opposition to the MAS government and to the proposed constitutional reforms originates in elite sectors of Bolivian society that are allied with transnational capital. Their presence is strongest in the resource-rich departments of Santa Cruz and Tarija, and in the frontier-like departments of Beni and Pando in Bolivia's Amazon region. After the constitutional recommendations were approved by the necessary two-thirds majority of the assembly, the governors of these four departments declared autonomy from the Bolivian state, though these declarations carry more rhetorical than political weight — at least in the short term.

Several of the new Constitution's 411 articles reflect and legitimize the long process of *campesino*-indigenous identity construction — and reconstruction — described throughout this chapter. Article 30 of the new Constitution accords legal recognition to those *campesino*-indigenous first nations and peoples who "share cultural identity, language, historical tradition, institutions, territory and cosmology, [and] whose existence pre-dates the Spanish colonial invasion" (República de Bolivia 2008). Article 30 also gives first nations the right to implement political, legal, and economic systems derived from their cosmological beliefs and to exercise autonomous management of their territories. They are also given exclusive rights over the management and use of renewable natural resources in those territories. Article 100 further states that "The cosmovisions, myths, oral history, dances, cultural practices, knowledge, and traditional technologies are patrimony of the *campesino*-indigenous first nations and peoples," and they "form part of the expression and identity of the State" (ibid).

The new Constitution thus gives legal voice and authority to the goals of a protracted struggle for human rights and cultural survival in Bolivia that began in the aftermath of the Spanish invasion, and culminated in the rise to power of a movement that became the political instrument of the majority peasant-indigenous population. This historic achievement has been likened to the fulfillment of a prediction made by hero and martyr Tupac Katari just before being drawn and quartered by his Spanish captors over two hundred years ago: "I will return, and I will be millions ..."

Conclusions

The period beginning with the arrival of Europeans in Latin America and continuing to the present has brought about social and environmental change at a scale and intensity "far greater than at any comparable span of time in prehistory" (Erickson 2000, 349).[17] At the same time, particularly in the Andean highlands, some pre-Columbian forms of community organization and exchange, as well as technologies, landscapes, and an array of other knowledge and customs, have proven to be remarkably resilient.

For some forty years now, a process of converting Andean cultural resilience into indigenous political capital has been under way, and is being replicated in the Amazon and eastern lowlands of Bolivia. Leaders of the MAS, the first politically consolidated expression of Bolivia's peasant-indigenous movement, are moving forward towards a new vision of autonomous development by reaching back to elements of their long history — a history in which resilience, reciprocity, and resistance to a world view not of their making figure prominently.

The extent to which strength and unity in diversity makes for a viable and durable political alternative to Western-imposed capitalist notions of development remains to be seen, but there is no doubt that it marks a fundamental and irreversible shift in the Bolivian political landscape.

Notes

I am grateful to the leaders and members of Bolivia's MAS-IPSP for allowing me to draw on their experiences and knowledge throughout my field research in 2004. Special thanks to Hugo Salvatierra Gutiérrez and Edil Mojica Burgos (Santa Cruz, Bolivia). This chapter is based on research funded in part by the Doctoral Fellowships Program of the Social Sciences and Humanities Research Council of Canada. An earlier version of this chapter was presented at the 11th biennial conference of the International Association for the Study of the Commons in Bali, Indonesia, 19–23 June 2006.

1. Between 1964 and 1982, Bolivia's political scene was dominated by a succession of military governments.
2. The MAS-IPSP is usually abbreviated to either MAS or "the Instrument"; the terms are used interchangeably.
3. The documentary film by Rachel Boynton titled *Our Brand Is Crisis* (2005) reveals the "democracy for hire," purely technocratic approach to winning a political leadership race that was employed by Bolivia's neo-liberal MNR party during the 2002 presidential election campaign.
4. The political instrument initially called the Assembly for the Sovereignty of the People (ASP) and later the IPSN was denied political party status (legal personage) by Bolivia's National Electoral Court, obliging the *campesino* organizations to participate in a coalition of the United Left (IU) in the municipal elections of 1995 and the national elections of 1997 before gaining official party status as the MAS in 1999 (see Burgoa 2006).
5. It is useful here to point out that the terms *campesino* and *indígena* to describe Bolivia's native peoples reflect historically ascribed roles and organizational affiliation more than anything else. After the 1952 revolution, *campesino* provided an acceptable substitute for the pejorative *indio* (Indian) for highland peasants, while *indígena* served the strategic need of forging a collective identity for lowland peoples (Healey 2005, 166). *Pueblos originarios* (original peoples) has emerged more recently to describe people in highland communities outside of the agrarian syndicate structure.
6. Choquehuanca's ethnic roots are Quechua, but he was raised in Omasuyos, an Aymara-speaking highland province bordering Lake Titicaca.
7. In much of the scholarly literature as well as contemporary usage, ethnic groups in Bolivia are differentiated primarily on the basis of language. However, studies of the ethnic makeup of pre-Conquest society use terms such as "ethnic group," "people," "nation," or "tribe" (sometimes interchangeably within the same study) to refer to separate groups of people who spoke the same language but who self-identified with a particular name, territory, and maximum authorities (Del Río 1996,

14). Studies of contemporary peoples may refer to a linguistic group as a "nation" comprising various groups that were distinct from one another in pre-Conquest ethnic groups (see for example Bastien 1985).
8   *Pachakuti* (or *pachacuti*) is a term of considerable significance in the Andean world view and indigenous politics. One meaning is provided by Campbell (1987, 115); see also Medina n.d., 132): "Andean time...views temporal change in terms of a series of *pachacutis*, or cataclysms, led by representatives of Wiracocha, the Andean Creator God, who are deemed to have returned to earth to reverse the existing, unjust world order." Similarly, Choquehuanca (2004) defines *pachakuti* as "the return to equilibrium."
9   D'Altroy (2000, 383) notes that verticality as a productive regime is not unique to the Andes, but is also a traditional practice in some parts of Japan, Hawaii, northwestern North America, Nepal, California, and Switzerland, though distances between zones were much greater in the Andes.
10 Ayllus are corporate kin groups with access to communally owned and managed land.
11 Like other leading anthropologists and economic historians studying indigenous reciprocity, Temple draws on the seminal contributions of Marcel Mauss (1872–1950) and Bronislaw Malinowski (1884–1942).
12 In Sweet's (1995, 43) and others' views, what took place in Latin America is best understood not as genocide but as ethnocide. The Spanish never intended to annihilate entire peoples upon whose labour (or souls) the colonial regime depended; rather, the goal was to break their cultural systems. That their cultures proved more resilient than the people themselves (whose numbers declined dramatically), and the ways in which that cultural patrimony might inform present and future generations, is of central interest to social movements today.
13 After Campbell (1987, 110), political consciousness is understood here as "the self-identifications, cultural meaning systems, interpretations of contemporary society, and aspirations for the future which [shape] political behaviour."
14 The "katarista phase" refers to the period of activity of Tupac Katari. Nevertheless, the linear sequence of the two periods was conceivably much less salient to the protagonists of the time (and their descendants today), as meaning was more likely construed within the context of the cyclical *pachakutis*, or cataclysms, that characterize the Andean concept of time (see Campbell 1987, 115–16).
15 In much of highland Bolivia, agrarian *sindicatos* coexist with *ayllus* but fulfill different functions (Kohl 2003, 157), while in other parts of the country traditional organizations were melded into *sindicatos*. In the eastern lowlands, the community-based *Central Indígena* is typical, while the Guaranís have continued a long-existing organizational form known as *Capitanías*.
16 Brysk (1996) lists a number of organizations and people that have played key roles in the social movement network supporting indigenous rights in Latin America, including the International Work Group on Indigenous Affairs (IWGIA), Cultural Survival, the World Council of Churches, OXFAM America, the Inter-American Foundation, and the South and Meso-American Indian Information Centre, among others.
17 Erickson is referring specifically to environmental change in the Andes, a conclusion that has been extended here to socio-cultural change in all of Bolivia.

References

Albó, X. 1987. From MNRistas to Kataristas to Katari. In *Resistance, rebellion and consciousness in the Andean peasant world, 18th to 20th centuries,* ed. S. J. Stern. Madison: Univ. of Wisconsin Press.

———. 2002. La identidad "Chiriguana." In *Ñande Reko: La comprensión Guaraní de la vida buena,* ed. J. Medina. La Paz: FAM Bolivia, PADEP/ Componente Qamana.

Augstburger, F. 1990. Agroecología andina: El concepto y las experiencias de AGRUCO. In *Agroecología y saber andino,* ed. AGRUCO (Proyecto de Agrobiología de la Universidad de Cochabamba)—PRATEC (Proyecto Andino de Tecnologías Campesinas). Cochabamba and Lima: AGRUCO-PRATEC.

Bastien, J. W. 1985. *Mountain of the condor: Metaphor and ritual in an Andean ayllu.* Prospect Heights, IL: Waveland Press.

Bates, D. G., and E. M. Fratkin. 1999. *Cultural anthropology.* 2nd ed. Boston: Allyn and Bacon.

Blanco, O. 1990. Enfoque andino de desarrollo. In *Agroecología y saber andino,* ed. AGRUCO (Proyecto de Agrobiología de la Universidad de Cochabamba)—PRATEC (Proyecto Andino de Tecnologías Campesinas). Cochabamba and Lima: AGRUCO-PRATEC.

Brass, P. 1991. *Ethnicity and nationalism: Theory and comparison.* New Delhi and Newbury Park, CA: Sage.

Brysk, A. 1996. Turning weakness into strength: The internationalization of Indian rights. *Latin American Perspectives* 23(2): 38–57.

Burgoa M. C. 2006. El MAS en la incursión de la historia de Bolivia. *Rebelión.* http://www.rebelion.org/noticia.php?id=27257.

Campbell, L. G. 1987. Ideology and factionalism during the Great Rebellion, 1780–1782. In *Resistance, rebellion and consciousness in the Andean peasant world, 18th to 20th centuries,* ed. S. J. Stern. Madison: Univ. of Wisconsin Press.

Choquehuanca, D. 2004. Personal interview. June 23.

CNE (Corte Nacional Electoral). 2008. *Referéndum revocatorio: resultados.* La Paz: República de Bolivia.

———. 2009. *Referéndum nacional constituyente: resultados.* La Paz: República de Bolivia.

Collier, S., H. Blakemore, and T. E. Skidmore, eds. 1985. *The Cambridge encyclopedia of Latin America and the Caribbean.* Cambridge: Cambridge Univ. Press.

Crabtree, J. 2006. Evo Morales's challenge. *Open Democracy.* http://www.opendemocracy.net/democracy-protest/morales_3210.jsp.

D'Altroy, T. N. 2000. Andean land use at the cusp of history. In *Imperfect balance: Landscape transformations in the Precolumbian Americas,* ed. D. L. Lentz. New York: Columbia Univ. Press.

Daly, D. C., and J. D. Mitchell. 2000. Lowland vegetation of tropical South America: An overview. In *Imperfect balance: Landscape transformations in the Precolumbian Americas,* ed. D. L. Lentz. New York: Columbia Univ. Press.

Del Río, M. 1996. *Relaciones interétnicas y control de recursos entre los aymaras del macizo de Charcas. Los soras del repartimiento de Paria: Estrategias de acceso al tierras. Siglos XVI–XVII.* Doctoral thesis, Univ. de Buenos Aires, Buenos Aires, Argentina. Ms.

Delgado Burgoa, J. M. F. 2002. *Estrategias de autodesarrollo y gestión sostenible del territorio en ecosistemas de montaña.* La Paz: AGRUCO/Plural Editores.

Dollfus, O. 1986 [1978]. The tropical Andes: A changing mosaic. In *Anthropological history of Andean polities*, ed. J. V. Murra, N. Wachtel, and J. Revel. Cambridge: Cambridge Univ. Press.
Dunkerley, J. 1984. *Rebellion in the veins: Political struggle in Bolivia, 1952–82*. London: Verso Editions.
Echazú Alvarado, J. 2003. *El desafió de las naciones: Naciones y nacionalidades oprimidas en Bolivia*. La Paz: Editorial Liberación.
Eder, K., B. Giesen, O. Schmidtke, and D. Tambini. 2002. *Collective identities in action: A sociological approach to ethnicity*. Aldershot, Hampshire: Ashgate Publishing.
Erickson, C. L. 2000. The Lake Titicaca basin: A Precolumbian built landscape. In *Imperfect balance: Landscape transformations in the Precolumbian Americas*, ed. D. L. Lentz. New York: Columbia Univ. Press.
Grillo F. E. 1990. Cultura y agricultura andina. In *Agroecología y saber andino*, ed. AGRUCO (Proyecto de Agrobiología de la Universidad de Cochabamba) — PRATEC (Proyecto Andino de Tecnologías Campesinas). Cochabamba and Lima: AGRUCO-PRATEC.
Healey, S. 2005. Rural social movements and the prospects for sustainable rural communities. *Canadian Journal of Development Studies* 26(1): 151–73.
Infodesarrollo: Tercer Congreso CLOC. 2001. *III congreso coordinadora latinoamericana de organizaciones del campo (CLOC)*. listas.ecuanex.net.ec/pipermail/infodesarrollo/2001-August/000312.html.
Klein, H. S. 2003. *A concise history of Bolivia*. Cambridge: Cambridge Univ. Press.
Kohl, B. 2003. Democratizing decentralization in Bolivia: The law of popular participation. *Journal of Planning Education and Research* 23: 153–64.
León, O., S. Burch, and E. Tamayo. 2001. *Social movements on the net: Chapter 3, exclusion and resistance in Latin America*. http://www.alainet.org/publica/msred/en/chapter3.html.
Luteyn, J. L., and S. P. Churchill. 2000. Vegetation of the tropical Andes: An overview. In *Imperfect balance: Landscape transformations in the Precolumbian Americas*, ed. D. L. Lentz. New York: Columbia Univ. Press.
Malloy, J. M. 1970. *Bolivia: The uncompleted revolution*. Pittsburgh: Univ. of Pittsburgh Press.
Martinussen, J. 1997. *Society, state and market: A guide to competing theories of development*. London and New York: Zed Books.
Mayer, E. 2002. *The articulated peasant: Household economies in the Andes*. Boulder, CO: Westview Press.
Medina, J., ed. n.d. *La comprensión indígena de la buena vida*. La Paz: GTZ (Proyecto de Apoyo a la Planificación y Gestión Participativa Municipal), FAM Bolivia.
Merchant, C. 1989 [1980]. *The death of nature: Women, ecology and the scientific revolution*. New York: HarperCollins Publishers.
Murra, J. V., and N. Wachtel. 1986 [1978]. Introduction. In *Anthropological history of Andean polities*, ed. J. V. Murra, N. Wachtel, and J. Revel. Cambridge: Cambridge Univ. Press.
Native Web. 1990. *500 years of Indian resistance: Call to action on the first continental meeting of Indigenous Peoples*. http://www.nativeweb.org/papers/statements/quincentennial/firstcont.php.

———. 1991. Resolutions of the Continental Indigenous Coordinating Commission on 500 Years of Indian Resistance. http://www.nativeweb.org/papers/statements/quincentennial/resolutions500.php.

Otero, G. and H. A. Jugenitz. 2003. Challenging national borders from within: The political-class formation of indigenous peasants in Latin America. *Canadian Review of Sociology and Anthropology* 40(5): 503–24.

Parapaino, P. 2002. Identidad cultural y desarrollo indígena chiquitano. In *Identidad cultural y desarrollo de los pueblos indígenas de Santa Cruz: Memoria de los foros debates*, ed. CPESC, APAC, and SNV, 25–26 April, Santa Cruz de la Sierra and San Ignacio de Velasco.

Polanyi, K. 1944. *The great transformation*. Boston: Beacon Press.

República de Bolivia. 2008. *Nueva Constitución Política del Estado*. http://www.presidencia.gob.bo/download/constitucion.pdf.

Rocha, E. 1990. Visión cósmica del mundo andino tradicional. In *Agroecología y saber andino*, ed. AGRUCO (Proyecto de Agrobiología de la Universidad de Cochabamba)—PRATEC (Proyecto Andino de Tecnologías Campesinas). Cochabamba and Lima: AGRUCO-PRATEC.

Sanjinés C. J. 2004. *Mestizaje upside-down*. Pittsburgh: Univ. of Pittsburgh Press.

San Martín, J. 1990. El nayra pacha: Aproximaciones metodológicas para el desarrollo andino. In *Agroecología y saber andino*, ed. AGRUCO (Proyecto de Agrobiología de la Universidad de Cochabamba)—PRATEC (Proyecto Andino de Tecnologías Campesinas). Cochabamba and Lima: AGRUCO-PRATEC.

Stern, S. J. 1987a. New approaches to the study of peasant rebellion and consciousness: Implications of the Andean experience. In *Resistance, rebellion and consciousness in the Andean peasant world, 18th to 20th centuries*, ed. S. J. Stern. Madison: Univ. of Wisconsin Press.

———. 1987b. The age of Andean insurrection, 1742–1782: A reappraisal. In *Resistance, rebellion and consciousness in the Andean peasant world, 18th to 20th centuries*, ed. S. J. Stern. Madison: Univ. of Wisconsin Press.

Sweet, D. 1995. The Ibero-American frontier mission in Native American history. In *The new Latin American mission history*, ed. E. Langer and R. H. Jackson. Lincoln and London: Univ. of Nebraska Press.

Temple, D. 2002. El quid pro quo guaraní. In *Ñande reko: La comprensión guaraní de la vida buena*, ed. J. Medina. La Paz: FAM Bolivia, PADEP/Componente Qamana.

———. 2003. *Teoría de la reciprocidad, Tomo III: El frente de civilización*. La Paz: Padep and GTZ.

Ticona, E. 1996. *CSUTCB: Trayectoria y desafiós*. La Paz: CEDOIN.

Villca, Juan de la Cruz. 2004. Personal interview. July 8.

Weber, M. 1997 [1978]. What is an ethnic group? In *The ethnicity reader: Nationalism, multiculturalism and migration*, ed. G. Montserrat and J. Rex. Cambridge: Polity Press.

Wolf, E. R. 1969. *Peasant wars of the twentieth century*. New York: Harper & Row.

Globalization and *Indígenas*: The Alto Balsas Nahuas

Frans J. Schryer

Mexico's native people, who can be identified by the Amerindian languages they speak, are referred to as *indígenas,* as opposed to *mestizos,* the Spanish-speaking majority. *Indígenas* comprise somewhere between six and thirteen per cent of Mexico's population, depending on which definition is used.[1] *Indígenas* are found in urban as well as in rural areas of Mexico and have also become part of the social makeup of the United States, where native migrants from Mexico and Central America are now recognized in the US census as "Hispanic American Indians" (Huizar Murillo and Cerda 2004). The increasing mobility of indigenous Mexicans, including those who come directly to large cities in the United States, is a manifestation of a broader process of globalization that is rapidly transforming the lives of all *indígenas*: those who leave their homes, those who remain behind, and those who move back and forth. This chapter looks at a predominantly Nahuatl-speaking region of Mexico, where about half of the population is currently working and living in various parts of North America.

Globalization and Mexico's Indígenas
Many researchers use the term globalization to refer to the integration of national economies into a worldwide system through foreign direct investment, trade, capital flows, and the spread of advanced form of technology and communication.[2] Globalization can have negative as well as positive effects; scholars put greater emphasis on one or the other, depending on their theoretical perspective and political orientation. Those who focus on negative impacts point out that globalization has resulted in increasing polarization between the rich and the poor in all parts of the world as well as new forms of social inequality. The literature on globalization's negative impacts on Mexico deals with three main topics: the establishment by international corporations of

industrial assembly operations (*maquiladores*), the influx of corn produced in the United States following the removal of tariffs, and the exponential growth of undocumented Mexican workers in all sectors of the American economy. Not all scholars dealing with these facets of globalization refer to Mexico's native people. Those who do, usually link globalization and *indígenas* when talking about rural poverty and marginalization. Their position is that the decline of local maize production, the erosion of social services, and increasing unemployment has had a disproportionate impact on native people.[3] Scholars writing about *maquiladores* may note that a large proportion of those who leave villages from marginal rural regions in southern and central Mexico to find work along the Mexican–American border are young indigenous women just as such women were more likely to work as domestic servants during the postwar boom period (Gutmann and Porter 1997). The most obvious and widely publicized connection between globalization and Mexico's *indígenas* is the Zapatista uprising in Chiapas following the signing of the North American Free Trade Agreement (NAFTA).[4] The website presence and political activity of the Zapatistas and their sympathizers in Mexico and abroad have become symbols for resistance against globalization and the struggle for indigenous rights.

Much of the researchers who examine the links between globalization and the fate of Mexico's native people portray *indígenas* as either helpless victims of global forces or political actors in opposition to those forces.[5] Both representations distort a more complex, diverse social reality. The image of impoverished indigenous Mexicans who become the vanguard of resistance against globalization glosses over creative forms of adaptation, resistance, or accommodation in areas of life other than the politics of dissent. Likewise, the portrayal of indigenous people as a universally exploited group (or alternatively the romantic vestige of a pre-capitalist world) ignores variations in the level of income and social conditions of this segment of Mexico's population. Instead, I attempt to provide a glimpse into the active agency and economic advancements that have been overlooked by scholars who, in some sense, *require* a downtrodden underclass to square with their notion of how the world works.[6] Even those writers who recognize the agency of indigenous people as protesters against the onslaught of globalization do not perceive the degree to which indigenous people might be willing and enthusiastic participants in globalization, including when they decide to work in the United States.

The process of globalization is closely intertwined with new patterns of international migration. In the case of Mexico, the majority of indigenous migrants are relocating to other parts of North America, mainly the United States.[7] In the 1990s, anthropologists studying the social and cultural dimensions of this international migration such as N. Glick-Schiller, L. Basch,

C. Blanc-Szanton (1992), M. Kearney (1995), and A. Portes (1996) coined new concepts, including transnationalism, to characterize the transborder lives of such migrants. The development of the concept of transnationalism represented a shift in theoretical orientation that emphasized inclusion of the society of origin of international migrants in research on migration, and a focus on the emergence of transnational communities. Empirical studies of transborder communities have provided new insights into the experiences and identities of international indigenous migrants. However, much of the research to date examines Mexican native peoples who work in agriculture, first as internal migrants to other parts of Mexico and then on the other side of the border, with some attention to the involvement of migrants in gardening, housecleaning, and child care.[8] Studies that include indigenous migrants in global urban centres, such as Los Angeles or New York, focus on the emergence of hometown associations and other civil organizations based on broader affiliations such as religion, region, or linguistic affinity.[9] This emphasis on civic engagement of migrants, some of whom have established organizations that operate in both Mexico and the United States, goes beyond a narrow focus on political activism and resistance to globalization. My case study builds upon, but also goes beyond, this pioneering work on transborder communities by including a greater range of social fields, including the world of crafts and arts, which also has a global dimension. The aim is to debunk a set of misconceptions and simplistic ideas about both globalization and what it means to be indigenous. The region I have selected to support my arguments is the Alto Balsas, located in the state of Guerrero, Mexico.

The Alto Balsas Nahuas

The name Alto Balsas Nahuas came into existence about two decades ago. It refers to a group (Nahuas) and the region they inhabit (named after the Upper Balsas, the section of a river). In many respects this group of native people epitomizes the indigenous and the local; most of them speak an Amerindian language (Nahuatl) and have their own way of life, characterized by unique customs and ceremonies generally associated with being *indígena*. They have occupied a specific territory for the past eight hundred years. At the same time, they use camcorders and are living and working in many other Mexican states. Moreover, they can be found in towns and cities in eighteen states of the USA (García 2002). Throughout their history, these Mexican *indígenas* have faced many obstacles and challenges. At the same time, they have found creative solutions to not only offset the negative impacts of external forces but also use them to their advantage. In order to better understand this indigenous group, in all of its diversity and complexity, it is useful to first situate the region with which they associated in a broader historical and ethnographic perspective.

Historical Background and Internal Diversity

The Alto Balsas region is an extension of the Iguala valley, whose largest population centre is Iguala (Guerrero). Originally inhabited by people whose material culture had Olmec features, the Alto Balsas was later populated by the Coixca, the Nahuatl-speaking ancestors of the current inhabitants. Their administrative centre was Oapan, which continued to be a site of political control after Aztecs conquered this part of Mexico, a hundred years prior to the Spanish conquest. Oapan was also the seat of a Catholic parish throughout the colonial period and beyond, until the parish was moved to Xalitla, the only village located on the paved highway that was built in the 1940s. The eighteen villages (*pueblos*) of the Alto Balsas region are located on both sides of one section of the Balsas River, and they are about equidistant from Chilpancingo, the state capital and the city of Iguala, which is a commercial centre.

In many respects the villages of the Alto Balsas are typical of other places in Mesoamerica whose inhabitants are indigenous. They have a cargo system, also known as a civil–religious hierarchy, an institution that involves obligatory public service as part of the duties that confer rights of membership in a community and access to land. Most of the land is legally defined as communal,[10] although individuals may buy or sell land to members of the same village. The cultivation of maize, beans, and squash, the staple diet of this region, involves slash-and-burn agriculture on steep hillsides and plough cultivation on flat or gently sloping land. Some individuals in each village also spend part of their time producing lime, charcoal, candles, bread, or reed mats for local consumption. Some of these items, which were once exchanged through a system of barter, are still sold at village festivals. People also visit other villages for major religious celebrations as part of a system of ritual exchanges that go well beyond the region under discussion. Their villages have been interconnected through such ritual exchanges as well as trade dating back to pre-Hispanic times.

The villages in the Alto Balsas region have many common features and their inhabitants could be considered as having a single regional culture. Yet each Nahua *pueblo* also has a strong local identity and there have been violent confrontations over land boundaries. There is little intermarriage and people in each village speak their own version of Nahuatl. Moreover, language use, an important indicator of social identity, is not uniform in the region. In all but two villages in the region, Nahuatl is spoken at home and on the street and children do not learn Spanish until they attend school. Yet the level of bilingualism varies; in the village of Maxela, Nahuatl has all but disappeared in the past four decades and the inhabitants no longer consider themselves *indígenas* although they are still involved in ritual exchanges with Nahuatl-speaking villages and they recognize common ties of kinship with the inhabitants of Ameyaltepec. For this reason most anthropologists still classify Maxela as an

"Indian" village.[11] In Xalitla, where Spanish is spoken on a daily basis, only the older generation and newcomers from other villages can still speak Nahuatl, although a group of people in Xalitla are trying to revive their native language and traditions. One of two elementary schools in Xalitla is officially bilingual, which means that their teachers emphasize the indigenous heritage of the students who sing the national anthem in Nahuatl. It is possible, although not common in Mexico, for people who speak only a smattering of an indigenous language to consider themselves to be *indígenas*.

There is also variation in the level and nature of intra-village conflicts. Some villages have become divided along religious lines, with the introduction of various Protestant denominations and a rift within the Catholic Church between charismatics and traditionalists. In addition, three villages have separate Roman Catholic churches whose members do not recognize the Pope and where mass is conducted in Latin. Ahuelican and Tetelcingo have the greatest number of denominations. In the case of Ahuelican, one of its residents introduced Protestantism in the early nineties. This young man had gone to live in Mexico City, where he became a Baptist, and, upon returning to Ahuelican, he converted several relatives. Their congregation had fifty members when I first visited Ahuelican in 2005. Initially there were tensions between this new sect and the Catholics because the Baptists refused to contribute to the cost of celebrations with Catholic origins. However, they continue to pay for their share of consumption of water and electricity and take part in the village government. Other villages have at times seen bitter conflicts related to competing loyalties to rival political parties. Indigenous people can be as united or riddled with infighting as any other human group. Yet at times the inhabitants of this region have united in the face of common threats.

Unlike other parts of Mexico, Spanish-speaking people (whether *mestizos* or Europeans) did not settle in any of the villages in the region under study. This was, in part, due to the fact that the land, prone to periodic drought, was not as attractive to outsiders. Moreover, the Alto Balsas lacked mineral resources, unlike the nearby region of Taxco, known for its silver.[12] Yet despite their marginal geographical location, the inhabitants of the Alto Balsas have always had contact with the rest of Mexico. Because people could cultivate only one crop of maize per year, they had to find other ways to make a living. Throughout the colonial era, and during the nineteenth century, men worked as mule skinners. A trail that ran through the Alto Balsas was the only route to transport the goods originating in the Philippines, as well as the Andean countries, destined for Europe. Spanish galleons arrived in the port of Acapulco once a year, and the goods had to be unloaded and put on mules. The Nahuas of the Alto Balsas knew how to transport pack animals and travellers across the sometimes turbulent Balsas river in the first stage of a long overland journey to Mexico City and then to Veracruz, where the merchandise was again loaded onto ships that crossed the Atlantic. The lives of the Nahuas of the Alto Balsas have thus been shaped by worldwide social, political, and economic forces for at least several hundred years. Globalization is certainly not a recent phenomenon; connections and interactions between places in different parts of the world, and the emergence of a single world economic system predates the Spanish conquest of Mexico.

The Nahuas not only worked as paid mule skinners and loaders, they also engaged in trading of their own. The main source of income for Nahua itinerant merchants until 1930 was to obtain salt along the coast (the Costa Chica of Guerrero) to be sold in the highlands. Using a system of barter, they traded food items such as onions and *pinole* (made from dried corn) for the salt that small-scale producers on the coast extracted from sea water. Others took their donkeys to the neighbouring *montaña* region to buy pineapples, mangos, and *chico zapote* to sell at fairs held in Cuetzala or Tacupulco. These forms of economic exchange ended in the 1940s due to the construction of a highway connecting Mexico City to Acapulco.[13] Subsequently, the inhabitants of the Alto Balsas became increasingly dependent on seasonal migratory labour to neighbouring regions. These labourers walked between one and five hours to the village of Xalitla to board buses to reach the city of Iguala and beyond. As a result, several of the younger men and women began working part-time in the rapidly expanding metropolitan centre of Mexico City. Most men earned daily wages cutting sugar cane in neighbouring regions to earn the money needed to buy basic necessities such as hats, sugar, and cotton cloth used to make clothes. Other sources of labour in the Iguala valley were a small mine in the town of Huitzuco, a watermelon orchard in the village of Santa Teresa, and a sawmill. The only change in standards of living and technology at this time was the introduction of tin and corrugated tarpaper for use as roofing material.

During an economic boom in North America following World War II, increasing revenues allowed the Mexican state to build up its social and physical infrastructure, including the building of additional schools in rural areas. Although several villages in the Alto Balsas region had already been affected by the arrival of schoolteachers who taught in one-room tile-roof houses, primary education gradually spread to neighbouring villages. In this period many children received their first exposure to the Spanish language and a small minority of people learned how to read and write. Some affluent parents sent some of their children to boarding schools in other parts of the state, and a parish priest who believed in the value of education set up parochial schools and provided assistance for their best students to continue their studies. This is how a small number of men (particularly from Xalitla and Pepeyocatitla) who later became lawyers, teachers, and anthropologists, initiated their professional careers. These men (at that time no women) were to play an important role as political leaders, as we shall see later. However, the majority of the Nahuatl-speaking population continued to be monolingual and illiterate. Even children with a minimal exposure to schooling in their villages picked up only a bare minimum of either written or spoken Spanish; consequently, by the turn of the century, most men and women above the age of sixty could not read or write.[14] Older people were more likely to have picked up some Spanish while working and travelling in other parts of Mexico.

Even today the degree of bilingualism and level of education varies from village to village. Ameyaltepec, which is today considered to be the richest village, was the least receptive to the introduction of schools where children learned Spanish. They were the last to get a *telesecundaria* (lower high school), where classes shown on a television screen are explained by a teacher in the classroom. In contrast, for the people of San Agustin Oapan, which used to have a larger proportion of households whose members worked as day labourers, education was considered essential for social mobility. In that village, more young people continue their education to become schoolteachers. These variations in language, religion, level of income, and education, plus the extent to which people see themselves and are labelled as *indigenas* by other Mexicans, can, in part, explain differences in patterns of migration and the emergence of new forms of migration.

A discussion of the continuities and discontinuities in social identity, language use, or customs cannot ignore how people make a livelihood. While almost everyone in the Alto Balsas continued to practise subsistence agriculture until the end of the twentieth century, the ongoing industrialization of Mexico (combined with the expansion of other sectors of the economy, particularly tourism) provided opportunities and new markets for the inhabitants of the Alto Balsas. Starting in the 1950s, the region experienced a veritable boom and every year fewer people continued working as seasonal wage labourers.

The Development of a Craft Industry

The emergence of craft production and the maintenance of the control of indigenous artisans over the marketing of their products is a story in itself. Originally the main form of craft production was pottery: women made jars for holding water and pots for straining the lime water used to soak corn. In the early fifties, several men in the village of Ameyaltepec experimented with painting the designs once applied to clayware on various surfaces. The most successful medium was the same type of bark paper (*amate*) once used by the Aztecs.[15] For several years, only three families were involved in painting *amates* on commission, but gradually the craft spread throughout the community. While one member of each family was generally more adept at drawing the designs, the whole family was involved in filling in the colours with acrylic paints. The craft of *amate* painting was also adopted in Oapan and several other villages where new styles were developed. Other forms of craft production were invented. Some villages specialized in making masks, carving wooden figurines, or painting *amate*-type scenes on ashtrays and bowls. Artisans in Ahuehuepan made clay necklaces and later began painting designs on carved wooden fish that were strung together to create mobiles.

The craft industry in the Alto Balsas is unique because the majority of artisans market their own products. The people who produced crafts for sale made frequent trips to other parts of Mexico to sell directly to consumers while continuing to grow maize. The income they earned enabled families to erect larger houses of adobe and cement and to eat better. The construction of these new homes was typically completed in stages and could take up to twenty years. As early as 1980, visitors were surprised at the complete transformation of such villages as Ahuehuepan and Ameyaltepec. In order to continue building new houses and acquire more material goods, many families expanded the market for their crafts to Cancun, San Blas, San Miguel de Allende, and other tourist cities, returning home for only a few months a year.

The ability of many Alto Balsas Nahuas to raise their standard of living through a combination of craft production, subsistence farming, and itinerary trade is an example of how indigenous people are capable of taking advantage of the opportunities that came with new forms of globalization following World War II. Although today the production and sale of handicrafts is not as lucrative as it was, some artisan households continue to make a living—and even prosper—from their profession by spending most of the year in Mexican urban centres and resort towns. For example, in the city of Cuernavaca, Nahua families from Ameyaltepec and San Agustin Oapan have built houses in a former squatters' colony located in one of the ravines not far from the city centre.[16] Artisan-vendors from Ahuehuepan live year round in the town of La Peñita where they walk up and down the beach selling necklaces to people staying in all-inclusive hotels in Rincon de Guayabitos.[17] Most craft vendors have diversified the range of crafts they sell, including items they do not themselves produce, and a group of artisans from San Juan Tetelcingo sell handicrafts and give lessons to tourists in Playa del Carmen, on the Mayan Riviera (see Morales Aguilar 2007).

The development of crafts, especially *amate* painting, cannot be divorced from the emergence of a new form of group identity. The craft industry transformed how people saw themselves as well as how they were seen by outsiders; the Nahuas of the Alto Balsas became well known as *amateros* not only at home but abroad. Most of the *amate* paintings were bought by tourists and middle-class Mexicans. Others were exposed to this indigenous form of art in expositions sponsored by the Mexican state. Those *amate* painters whose work is deemed to be outstanding have been awarded prizes and *amate* art produced by better-known artists has been exhibited in art galleries and museums in New York and Paris. The participation of indigenous Mexicans from the Alto Balsas region in the international field of arts and crafts represents another facet of the process of globalization.

In presenting an overview of the development of crafts and arts, it is easy to overlook the fact that not all villages of the region became involved in the crafts industry. People in at least two villages continued to work as agricultural labourers in the sugar cane fields of the neighbouring state of Morelos (Saldaña Ramírez, n.d.). Consequently, not all villages are equally prosperous. While standards of living have risen in the region as a whole, some villages, such as San Marcos and Tula, which do not have any crafts or arts, have a higher proportion of thatched-roof houses with mud walls. There is also diversity in income and standards of living related to the extent to which people who do produce crafts are involved in the marketing of their own products. The artisans of San Francisco Zumatlán are known for their production of wooden masks, but few of the producers sell directly to consumers. Rather, they sell to middlemen, including Nahua artisan-vendors from other villages in the region. In Maxela, the only village where painting *amates* is a specialty of women, artisans also sell directly to middlemen.

The Creation of a New Region

Although the Alto Balsas, as a region and as the home of a unique cultural group, has become well known to anthropologists, journalists, and politicians, this was not always the case. Foreign tourists might have become familiar with the crafts sold by Nahua artisans as early as the 1950s, but they would not know where those artisans came from; nor was the label *amateros* associated with a particular region. The villages in the Alto Balsas did not come to both national and international attention until the early 1990s, when a group of local political leaders appropriated a term hitherto only used only by hydraulic engineers. These leaders founded the *Consejo de Pueblos Nahuas del Alto Balsas* (CPNAB), an organization established to fight for the cancellation of the dam project. In so doing they also created a new regional identity.

The establishment of a regional organization is particularly noteworthy since there has never been an overarching administrative structure for the region. Even today the eighteen villages of the Alto Balsas belong to four different *municipios* (the Mexican equivalent of counties). Competition over who controls any village administration takes place in different arenas, with village leaders establishing ties with power holders in *mestizo* administrative centres like Tepecuacuilco and Zumpango that are quite distant from each other as well as being distant from the Nahua villages under their respective jurisdictions. Nor do the representatives of Nahua villages normally act together to find solutions to such common problems as water shortages or the lack of electricity, roads, bridges, and health clinics. This was the situation until the 1990s, when they faced a common threat. In 1991 it became apparent that the federal government was planning to build a hydroelectric dam in San Juan Tetelcingo[18] that would flood most of the region. More than half of their villages would have to be relocated. The inhabitants of a region that was flooded because of a similar dam project on another part of the Balsas River had not received adequate compensation and suffered a deterioration of living conditions in their new settlements.

This chapter will not dwell on the story of the mobilization of the inhabitants of the Alto Balsas Nahua *pueblos* and their success in persuading the president of Mexico to stop the building of the dam that would have been funded by the World Bank. I will only mention the main leaders were indigenous (Nahua) professionals, including an economist and several anthropologists who grew up in the village of Xalitla. These leaders set up an organization that included the authorities of all the villages in the region, who in turn mobilized people to attend demonstrations, set up roadblocks, and take part in a march to Mexico City.[19] They succeeded in 1992, in part because the Mexican president needed to present a good image to the rest of the world after the Zapatista uprising in Chiapas brought the issue of indigenous rights to international attention. Their victory illustrates that the globalization of indigenous rights movements can be advantageous for people who oppose such large-scale projects. Several leaders of the movement, who also became involved in regional and national organizations, subsequently made visits to other countries, where they met indigenous leaders from other parts of the world. In so doing, they became part of a global network of identity politics based on new pan-Indian (Amerindian) identities and an even broader international use of the label "indigenous people."

The emergence of new global identities is one component of the politics of resistance and protest at the international level. The creation of organizations of indigenous leaders seeking greater recognition for native peoples involves alliances and links with other groups who do not benefit from the other consequences of current globalization. Such leaders are part of an international anti-globalization social movement. However, such leaders do not always have broad-based support among the indigenous people they represent. In the case of the Alto Balsas, CPNAB lost credibility at the local and regional level around the turn of the century after several internal splits resulting from infighting among its leaders. In the case of the region of Guerrero, most of its inhabitants do not even use the name Alto Balsas nor do those inhabitants identity themselves as members of a common region. The organization set up to represent them has for all practical purposes ceased to function at the local or regional level, even though it still has a presence on the World Wide Web. Yet its principal leader still represents the Nahuas of the Alto Balsas in international forums.[20] The label Alto Balsas has also become well established at the national and international level.

The plan to build a hydroelectric dam in San Juan Tetelcingo originally brought together political leaders from different villages who had hitherto not acted in concert. The leaders who created this regional, as well as ethnic, identity were successful in having politicians and journalists adopt the name Alto Balsas Nahuas. This group label also became a form of social identity for indigenous intellectuals involved in Mexican and international politics. Anthropologists from outside the region who do research in this part of Guerrero have also adopted the label. It is not productive to make the argument that this group name is less real, or that there really are no Alto Balsas Nahuas because the majority of the inhabitants of the region do not see themselves this way. It makes more sense to say that the name has more salience in the world of politics. The label Alto Balsas Nahuas might well be used by more people in the region in the future if and when there is renewed mobilization against the building of a dam, should that project be resurrected.[21]

Today the vast majority of the inhabitants of the Alto Balsas region are not interested in, or even know about, the movement of anti-globalization in which the people who represent them are involved. Nor are they necessarily opposed to becoming involved in the process of globalization, as we have seen in the case of their entry into the craft industry. One must be careful in generalizing about all aspects of globalization and what globalization means for any group of indigenous people. Globalization has both positive and negative elements and the impact of broader forces present both challenges and opportunities for the indigenous inhabitants of rural Mexico. Moreover, globalization has many dimensions and is not restricted solely to the economy or international politics, which constitute social fields whose logic and dynamics are not the same as those of other social fields such as arts and crafts or religion.[22] These various social fields overlap to a greater or lesser extent and they each operate at the local, national, and international levels. Indigenous people in Guerrero are active participants in all of these fields, at each level, but not all to the same extent. Moreover, indigenous people do not have the same reputation or encounter the same level of prejudice in each field. How the people from the Alto Balsas are perceived and how they identify or change any of their multiple identities (as *indigenas,* Mexicans, *amateros,* or *campesinos*) varies according to each field of action. The ongoing transformation of social identities and the way they seek new ways of making a living as well as new forms of social recognition can be further illustrated by examining how the people from the Alto Balsas region have entered the international labour market, specifically in the United States.

New Challenges and Opportunities: The Global Labour Market

By the mid-nineties, the inhabitants of the Alto Balsas were preoccupied with matters other than the possibility of a hydroelectric dam. While the threat of the dam project no longer hung over their heads, the impact of broader changes resulting from NAFTA and other neo-liberal policies presented new challenges. The removal of subsidies led to a decline in subsistence agriculture at a time when *amate* paper was scarce and, as a result, the cost of making handicrafts increased. Simultaneously, the market for local crafts, which had already become increasingly competitive, reached a point of saturation. Many artisan-vendors can no longer making a good living and have opted to become migratory workers in the United States. In doing so, they are able to maintain higher standards of living. Even today, with increasing restrictions on international travel, their ability to cross the border, their success in finding work in a variety of urban occupations, and the way remittances are used demonstrate a high degree of agency and ingenuity as these Mexican indigenous people find ways to confront both the challenges and opportunities associated with globalization. Transnational migration and the development of transborder lives go hand in hand with the emergence of new group identities.

Historical Precedents

The inhabitants of the Alto Balsas region have known about the possibility of migratory work in the United States since the late 1940s, with the advent of the *bracero* program for agricultural workers from Mexico. At that time few people from the Alto Balsas region took advantage of this opportunity; while fifteen men from Ahuelican were recruited to work in Texas, California, or Arizona, fewer people from other villages were interested in this option. In the case of Ahuehuepan only two men went to work in the United States for several months in the early 1950s. Most people preferred to work at home or in other parts of Mexico. During the boom in craft production, in the late 1950s and 1960s, even fewer men (no women) ventured north. The outflow of transnational workers from the Alto Balsas did not begin until two decades later. Beginning in 1978, transnational labour—this time as undocumented workers—brought an increasing number of persons from several villages, particularly from Maxela, Xalitla, and San Miguel, to the United States.

With the end of the *bracero* program, which had provided work permits to Mexican workers until its termination in 1964, people interested in finding jobs in the United States had to first travel to a border city to find someone who could smuggle them across. The men who provide this risky but remunerative service are referred to in Mexico as *coyotes*. Most of those who thus go to work in the United States earn minimal wages, although a minority eventually obtain higher-paid jobs as work supervisors. Despite low wages (by American standards, not Mexican) these workers manage to earn enough money within their first year to pay off the men who brought them across the border. Although some seek out a coyote in Tijuana, the majority of illegal migrants depend on the services of well-known coyotes with local links. This can be illustrated by how people in the Alto Balsas region first started migrating without the required documents, which would have been almost impossible to obtain.

In the seventies, a man from the Spanish-speaking town of Tonalapa Del Rio (close to the city of Iguala), who had been in the United States, married a woman from Maxela. His home town is located in a region neighbouring on the Alto Balsas region, and most people in Maxela at that time still spoke Nahuatl. This man persuaded several of his new neighbours to take the risk of crossing the border, saying that they could earn eight dollars a day there, instead of the five pesos (less than a dollar) at home. He charged them three hundred dollars for taking them across, and they could pay him back in installments. On his first trip, he took six men with him, and soon more people wanted to go. This local coyote next found customers in Cuacoyula and Pipilula, Spanish-speaking villages located on the edge of the Alto Balsas region, but his steadiest customers were people from the Nahuatl-speaking village of Ahuelican. In 1978, he recruited a group of men and several women, from both Maxela and Ahuelican, and more and more people from Ahuelican asked him to take them across the border. Two years later, he took fifteen men from Maxela and more from Ahuelican. This trend accelerated during the economic downturn in Mexico in the 1980s.

Throughout the eighties and nineties, most people did not have too much difficulty crossing the border without documents, althought the trip was not without risks. Those caught by the US border patrol were sent back to Mexico, and sometimes it took several trips to finally reach their destination in the United States. In almost all cases an employer was already waiting for them, since people find jobs through the recommendations of friends and relatives already working in the United States. Initially most migrants worked in agriculture, but they quickly moved into a wide range of other occupations: both men and women from the Alto Balsas region currently work in garden centres, factories, big-box stores, and the garment industry. Their remittances have enabled families to continue building large two- and three-storey brick and cement houses in their home villages. Many households also now own one or two vehicles, as shown by the volume of traffic of cars and pickup trucks with American licence plates in the Alto Balsas region.

Starting in the early nineties, an increasing number of people, including many artisans, entered the international migratory flow. The mass exodus of people from Ahuelican and San Juan Tetelcingo started around 1992, while emigration to the United States from Ahuehuepan, Oapan, and Ameyaltepc began several years later. From the mid-nineties onward, it became typical for both male and female teenagers from the region to leave to seek their fortunes in *el Norte* as soon as they finished school. By the year 2000 as much as one-third of the households in some villages had family members living for anywhere from two to three years at a time in other parts of Mexico or in Los Angeles, Houston, and Atlanta.[23] Today only children and the elderly remain; individuals between the ages of sixteen and thirty-five are scarce. Nevertheless, the majority of migrants return for major festive celebrations, to marry, and whenever it is their turn to provide public service.

People who worked and lived in the United States prior to 9/11 generally returned to their hometowns once a year or at least once every two years. Today it is more common for people to stay for five years or longer, since it is becoming increasingly difficult to cross the border on the way back to the United States with new homeland security measures. Consequently, many people are separated from other family members for an even longer period of time. In conducting interviews, I repeatedly came across the expression "*Xok waahlaw*" (they do not come back any more). While it is still easy to return to Mexico, it is increasingly difficult to come back to the United States. Because the majority of the men and women from the Alto Balsas who live and work in the United States do not have work permits, authorities could, in theory, deport them at any time. Prior to 2007, this was unlikely to happen unless the migrant did something to break the law. Today local police, who used to turn a blind eye to illegal immigrants, need to report anyone without proper documentation to the migration authorities. In order to avoid deportation, some Nahuas borrow work permits from other migrants who have proper documentation and, in return, give a percentage of their earnings to the person who lent the papers. With the start of the recession in 2008, life for undocumented Mexicans has become more difficult. It is no longer easy to find work and those who have part-time jobs find they can work only two or three days a week, which is not enough to cover their living expenses. Hence, more and more people are returning to their home villages, where at least they do not have to pay rent. Nevertheless, the majority remain.

Today one can find Nahuas from the Alto Balsas all over the United States, although every Nahua *pueblo* has it preferred destination. The majority of those who emigrate from San Juan Tetelcingo live and work in Ontario, California, while people from Ahuehuepan are more likely to emigrate to Lincoln, Los Angeles, or Sacramento, California. One is more likely to find people from

San Miguel, Oapan, and Ahuelican in Houston. Some Nahuas from these and other villages are found in Chicago or in Atlanta, Georgia. While they all plan to eventually return to Mexico, those who have spent almost as much time in the United States as in their country of birth, and those whose children are growing up there, are forging a new way of life for themselves.

Life and Work in the United States

Initially only young men left to work in the United States. They would typically work for several years to save the money required to build a house and get married. Once married, a man would leave his wife in the village to raise his children until they were old enough to emigrate. Men made trips back to supervise the construction of their houses or to take their turn serving their hometown as unpaid office holders. Women started migrating to the United States a few years later. Young Nahua men and women who meet in the United States return to their village to get married. In some cases, they first cohabit and have children in the United States and only later return to Mexico to marry and have their children baptized. A more recent trend is for young people who are already engaged to migrate together, because they do not want to remain separated for a long time. They generally they live in common-law relationships for several years until they can save enough money to have a large wedding in their home village. Both men and women, of all ages, continue to migrate to the United States in order to improve their economic condition, following the example of those who return with money and cars. They know that in the United States one earns per hour what one earns per day in Mexico.

International migration has its own linguistic dynamics. The first migrants spoke little Spanish and improved their Spanish in the United States through contact with non-indigenous Mexican workers and managers. In most public spaces and at work they are immersed in an almost completely Spanish-speaking environment and most migrants learn little English. In contrast, Nahua children born in the United States or those who attend elementary school there after their parents migrated quickly learn English. Yet their parents and older siblings continue to speak Nahuatl when they return after work or school to the apartments and town houses they rent. They continue to speak Nahuatl while talking on the telephone with family members in Guerrero. While people in the Alto Balsas are becoming increasingly bilingual (in Spanish and Nahuatl), those who spend a long time in the United States are becoming trilingual. I have met children in the Alto Balsas who speak three languages fluently, although other boys and girls speak Spanish and English but no longer speak Nahuatl. Unlike their parents, these children, some of whom have never visited their parents' birthplace, no longer identify with, nor would they be considered, *indígenas*.

Nahua migrants replicate social and cultural patterns from their home region, including a tendency to identify and associate with people from their village of origin. This is true even for recreational activities. Men generally play sports with men from the same village, as long as they have a critical mass. In Houston I have observed young men from Ahuelican playing basketball in several parks. These basketball players organize annual tournaments in their home region where each team consists of players from the same village. Nevertheless people are aware that there are migrants who come from other villages of the Alto Balsas. They may already know each other, especially if they travelled together in larger groups when coming from Mexico or if they work for the same employer. People originating from different villages may give rides to such *paisanos* or attend national holiday celebrations attended by everyone from the same region.

Kinship patterns are likewise reproduced in the American context. As in the Alto Balsas, young people generally marry someone from their home village, although in some cases they may marry someone from another Nahua village, as they do at home. When this happens, it becomes even more important that a boy uses the services of an intermediary who will formally ask the girl's parents' permission for them to marry. If they have already eloped, the intermediary consoles the girl's parents, just as at home. Relations between children of different ages, even if they are born in the United States, also follow traditional patterns. When children of Nahua parents speak English among themselves, they use the Nahuatl words "wewe" and "pipi" to address an older brother or an older sister. At the same time, customs and values are modified in an American environment. There is more freedom in the United States to speak to and date members of the opposite sex without a chaperone. The role of women has also changed. Women work to earn their own money and drive. In places like Lincoln, California, women need a car to get to work or to look for a new job, but they also drive for other reasons. One woman from Ahuehuepan drives her family's pickup truck in Lincoln whenever they attend a party because her husband was picked for drunk driving, put in jail, and deported. He did not succeed in crossing the border again for at least another year, but his wife refused to return to Mexico.

Ongoing contacts between migrants and people at home in turn result in the partial transformation of patterns of social interaction and cultural values at home. Gender roles and traditional masculine values have changed in the Alto Balsas, where most men no longer work in agriculture (see García and Zárate-Hoyos 2005). In those villages where people are still engaged in subsistence agriculture, more women work in the fields. A few women who have never been in the United States now drive their family's pickup truck. Patterns of regional interdependency are also changing. Young women, as well as older people of both sexes who are in charge of corn production and house construction, supervise young male labourers who come from the poor neighbouring *montaña* region. They pay their hired hands with money sent by relatives working in the United States. The money earned by working in the United States has triggered conspicuous consumption. I have witnessed baptisms of babies that involved not only elaborate house parties but also an outdoor dance with a live band. Weddings are becoming increasingly elaborate. All of these events are taped with camcorders.

Not everyone who has gone to the United States succeeds. Two years ago, Ahuehuepan received news of the first death of a young man who died from dehydration while walking through the desert of Arizona. An emphasis on general patterns overlooks the variations, including both cases of failure or personal tragedies and exceptional success stories. Some migrants have not only built larger homes in their villages of origin but now live in suburban homes in large American cities. Moreover, with the recently increased homeland security program, life for illegal migrants is becoming more difficult. Until several years ago, illegal immigrants could report to a local police station and present their Mexican birth certificate to obtain an identity card that would allow them to obtain an American driver's licence. This is no longer possible; the only alternative is to buy fake identification at a Hispanic *pulga* (flea market). Increasing border security has not stopped the flow of illegal migrants into the United States, but it has made the process more dangerous and expensive for those crossing the border. Coyotes now charge double what they charged in 2002, but experienced indigenous migrants from the Alto Balsas without the necessary documentation are still finding ways to cross the border on their own. For most people, it is still worth taking the risk.

In order to provide a more complete picture of the impact of international migration and globalization, in all of their complexity, we need to look more closely at the destination of those who leave the Alto Balsas. In order to gain better insights into the experiences and career trajectories of these migrants, I will focus on Houston, a city that has migrants from several *pueblos* in the Alto Balsas.

Houston, Texas

Initially Alto Balsas Nahua migrants to Houston lived in the same apartment building, where many young men shared the same apartment unit. An apartment complex on Wirt Street by the name of "Cancun" still has a large number of occupants from the Alto Balsas. After staying in Houston for several years, young couples as well as extended families began to move into their own units or buildings in other parts of the city, while others rented townhouses. Families who have been in Houston the longest now live in several suburbs and in nearby towns such as Katy and Rosenberg (near Richmond). While most still rent, I know of several families, including one whose main breadwinner does not have legal documentation, who have managed to buy a single-family dwelling. Today people originating from different villages in the Alto Balsas may still live in the same building complex or on the same street. However, in general, the same pattern of spatial dispersal as well as clustering found in the United States overall is found in Houston; almost all of the people from San Miguel live on or near Beechnut and Brissonnet streets in the Bellaire area, while those from San Juan Tetelcingo live in the Katy area.

The migrants from the Alto Balsas region initially worked on the outskirts of Houston picking lettuce and peppers but later began working in Houston in construction and for landscaping businesses. One man from Ahuelican, who worked on a farm near Houston for three months in 1979, worked construction for six months in 1982 and returned for another stint of construction work in Houston in 1985. Upon returning to Mexico, this man gained employment as a paid secretary in the village townhouse, where he was also put in charge of the civil registry. He obtained this position because he was better educated than most people from Ahuelican. His family was relatively wealthy and his parents had sent him to study at a seminary in Mexico. This man, who is somewhat exceptional, never returned to the United States. The more common scenario is a much longer period of living and working in the United States, combined with frequent trips back and forth. A man from Maxela, whose father had worked on a chicken farm in California in the early sixties, was first recruited in 1980 to work in Houston as a carpenter's assistant. Like so many others who worked construction, his employment never lasted more than a few weeks at a time. In 1982, he obtained his first full-time job in a small ceramics factory, specializing in garden ornaments and interlocking patio stones. His boss noticed that he was drawing pictures of birds and flowers on a scrap of paper during a break. He had been learning how to paint *amates* since he was eight years old. His employer recognized his talents and for the next few years he drew all of the paper designs for the moulds used in a new line of patio stones. He then helped his boss by recruiting men from another village in the Alto Balsas to work as manual labourers until the government fined the owner for employing illegal immigrants.[24] This man from Maxela subsequently worked washing the cars that came from the assembly line of a new Ford auto plant until he found work in a supermarket. His case is also unusual because the majority of migrant workers from Nahua villages have worked for only one employer.

In the 1980s, migrants from the Alto Balsas who came to Houston were mostly young men employed in construction. Starting in 1983, migrants from both Maxela and Ahuelican began working for large department stores and supermarkets (especially the Fiesta and Kroger chains). Many stores in Houston continue to recruit workers from Ahuelican today, although others, such as Wal-Mart, no longer hire immigrants without work permits. A minority of Nahua migrants in Houston, including those from the village of Ostotipan, work in landscaping, and a few men and women work in restaurants as both dish washers and waiters. However, the majority work in the retail sector. The fact that most of these indigenous migrants in Houston work as white-collar workers goes against the stereotype of indigenous Mexicans working on farms or scrubbing floors. The case of Alto Balsas migrants in Houston also contradicts the image of the evil, exploitative *mestizo* coyote that profits from smuggling people across the border. Coyotes may themselves be *indígenas*.

Almost all of the Nahua migrants living in Houston were brought there by a coyote who was one of their own, since he came from the village of Ahuelican. This indigenous Nahuatl-speaking coyote, Julio,[25] had worked in the United States as an illegal immigrant in the eighties. Like several other emigrants from Ahuelican working in Houston at that time, he benefited from an amnesty for illegal Mexican immigrants granted during the presidency of Ronald Reagan. The papers he received allowed him to legally work in the United States and cross the border. Like his predecessor from Tonalapa, Julio personally escorted people from their village of origin to Houston and allowed them to pay him in installments. Soon his brother also became a coyote, although he worked independently. They both took up residence in border city of Reynosa but kept in close contact with their father in Ahuelican. Julio and his brother represent the type of independently run small-scale business ventures in smuggling that ended with the emergence of international criminal cartels who added smuggling people to drug trafficking to their dominion.

Julio and his brother were no longer able to smuggle across the border when a competitor from Reynosa made a deal with a large smuggling cartel. He informed the cartel that the two brothers were operating without paying for protection and, consequently, members of the cartel robbed, beat, and ran the brothers out of town. This new coyote, based in Reynosa, did not pick up migrants in Guerrero, nor did he escort them to Houston. The smuggling of illegal migratory workers has taken a new form, involving a larger number of people in both Mexico and the United States who each take care of a different leg of the trip. For example, the cartel pays men in several villages who own vans to bring groups of men to a small airport in Cuernavaca, where they board a plane to a city on the border. There someone else provides them with a place to stay until they are ready to be smuggled across the border. This system called *cadena* (chain) represents the globalization of organized crime, whose tentacles reach the smallest hamlets in Mexico. However, this new system of smuggling people across the border, and increased border control after 9/11, did not stop the flow of people, including indigenous Mexicans, across the border.

The people from the Alto Balsas region that continued to migrate to Houston at the turn of the century and beyond continue to work for the same large commercial retailing chains. The latest newcomers from Ahuelican are often the children of former migrants who have since returned to Mexico. For example, three brothers from Ahuelican who went north followed in the footsteps of their father. Their father was the first man from their village to work for nine months in the United States, as a *bracero*, in 1961. He returned several times to work in 1972, 1984, and 1989, until he retired to live full time in Ahuelican. He raised three sons, all of whom attended secondary school in the city of Iguala. The oldest son got a job in a shampoo factory in Mexico City but went to work in Houston when he needed money to pay for the education of his eldest daughter. He worked for a Fiesta store for a while, and the experience he gained helped him to get a similar job for a similar supermarket (Comercial Mexicana) in Mexico City. The second son was the first to go to Houston, as an illegal immigrant, in 1981, where he later obtained a work permit. He returned to Ahuelican for a large wedding and took his new bride back to Houston, where his children were born.

People from Ahuelican and other parts of the Alto Balsas living year-round in Houston are now more dispersed. While people from the same village still help each other, the differences in income, standard of living and lifestyles, even among those without documentation, are becoming more apparent. Some men have not only bought a pickup truck but are working as independent operators in landscaping. Unlike indigenous migrants from other regions of Mexico, the Alto Balsas Nahuas in Houston and other cities in the United States have not yet developed regional or hometown associations, although people from the same village do cooperate to send money home for community projects. In the case of Houston, I detected the creation of new forms of social identity.

Globalization and New Forms of Identity

International migration and globalization have resulted in new forms of identity, multiple group labels, and new stereotypes. Nahuas from the Alto Balsas refer to White Americans as *bolillos* (white buns). The one person from Houston who now has American citizenship does not consider himself as a "real" American, unlike the children of migrants born and raised in Houston. Such children, who grow up speaking both English and Spanish fluently, see themselves as both Mexicans and Americans rather than as *indígenas* even if they have learned the Nahuatl language. Variations and changes in group identity and corresponding lifestyle are also apparent in the field of religion. The majority of Nahua migrants in Houston are Catholics, and many homes have the same small altars and pictures of saints as in Mexico. They attend masses given in Spanish at several parishes, some of which have Mexican priests. Those who belonged to Protestant denominations in the village of Ahuelican had no trouble finding a North American equivalent. However, already existing Spanish-speaking religious institutions in the United States have also had a direct influence on Ahuelican. A man from Ahuelican first became a Pentecostal in Houston, where he joined a large Spanish-speaking congregation. When he went back to Ahuelican several years later, he started proselytizing and set up a Pentecostal congregation. There are close connections, partly based on kinship, between indigenous Pentecostals in Ahuelican and Houston.[26] The identities associated with this and other denominations, as well as other new hybrid ethnic-religious labels are part of an ongoing trend towards a set of ever more diverse multiple-group identities. Someone can be both *indígena* and Protestant. In Houston I also encountered new ethnic-racial labels.

In the United States there are Chicanos (Americans of Mexican descent) who see themselves as Aztecs (who spoke Nahuatl), even though they might not have any Nahua ancestry. One group of these Chicanos have organized a professional dance group specializing in Aztec dances. When they discovered there were recent migrants in Houston who spoke Nahuatl, they asked a man from Ahuelican to give them language lessons. This man, one of a few migrants who have American citizenship, had also taken on an Aztec identity as a result of his contact with an American writer not of Mexican descent. The American writer was initially surprised that migrants from Ahuelican in Houston did not know the history of ancient Mexico. When she realized they spoke Nahuatl, she told them they were descendents of Aztecs. To what extent other migrants from the Alto Balsas identify with their native ancestry, and want to maintain their indigenous language, varies from person to person. I am not aware of any contact between people from the Alto Balsas and Native Americans in the United States, but this is bound to happen since other native peoples from Latin America have joined with those from Canada and the United States as part of a pan-Indian movement.

Discussion and Summary
My case study calls into question simplistic ideas concerning both indigenous people and globalization. The process of globalization started a long time ago; indigenous people from the Alto Balsas region have been active participants, not passive victims, in this process for a long time, as shown by their involvement in trade and commerce throughout and beyond the colonial era. In the twentieth century, Nahuatl-speaking people from the Alto Balsas carved out a niche for themselves in the world of arts and crafts at a time when the influx

of tourists created a demand for souvenirs and *amate* paintings. Participation in the production and marketing of arts and crafts also provided the inhabitants of this region with a new sense of identity as *amateros*. *Amate* paintings achieved international attention when better-known artists were invited to attend international exhibitions. One of the better-known Nahua *amate* painters, Nicolás de Jesús, achieved notoriety while he was living years in Chicago as a young man. He made engravings and became part of a cultural movement by Chicanos. But he maintained his identity as *indigena* and decided to leave the United States to return to Mexico for the remainder of his life. In Guerrero, he assumed a public post in his native village of Ameyaltepec and introduced the technique of engraving to other full-time artists in the region. He is currently living in the Guerrero state capital of Chilpancingo but pays regular visits to his hometown where he owns a house.[27]

The story of Nicolás de Jesús is typical of a minority of Nahua artists, including Marcial Camilo from the village of Oapan,[28] who currently resides year round in Cuernavaca. They have an international clientele for whom they paint on commission, but they maintain contact with each other and with their relatives and neighbours in their home villages. Being *indígena* and producing what is seen as indigenous art allows them to succeed. However, being indigenous does not have the same symbolic importance in places where Nahua migrants work for wages, either in Mexico or in the United States, where they no longer use their artistic talents. These former craftsmen and artists no longer see themselves as *amateros,* although they might adopt new social identities, as we have seen.

In the United States transnational migrants from the Alto Balsas are more likely to be labelled, as well as to present themselves, as Mexicans rather than as Mexican native people, except under specific circumstances, such as in the world of education. However, these migratory workers, who continue to speak Nahuatl at home, identify with their villages of origin, where most of them continue to seek spouses and where they build large houses. New forms of globalization, combined with direct and more prolonged exposure to life in the United States, will probably result in cultural assimilation and the loss of an identity as *indígenas* for those members of the next generation of people from the Alto Balsas who will no longer return to their region of origin. However, more efficient forms of telecommunication and recording devices will facilitate the survival of multi-generational cross-border indigenous communities as long as people on both sides of the border continue to interact socially and influence each other. The existence of such cross-border communities may have more salience, and shape people's lives more, than the nation-states to which people legally belong.

In the Nahua villages of the Alto Balsas, people who have never been outside of Mexico are today *more* familiar with the apartment buildings, shopping malls, and gardening centres in American urban centres than they are with downtown Mexico City or their own state capital. Children growing up in the Alto Balsas watch not only television but also videos sent by uncles, fathers, or older siblings who live and work in the United States. These same children ride on the backs of donkeys at home and continue to speak Nahuatl. These Nahua *pueblos* have truly become globalized villages, as have so many other villages in Mexico and other parts of Latin America. To what extent people from these communities who continue to be *indígenas* may well depend on whether or not the Nahuatl language, as well as a separate group identity other than that of *mestizo* or Mexican, will survive in their home region. However, what it means to be *indígena* or Nahua may change over time.

A separate indigenous identity—or any other form of group distinction—is more complicated than language retention, the strength of group boundaries, or the relative importance of alternative group identities. The meaning of any group identity—whether that be Nahua, Mexican, American, or some combination of all three—also varies within different social fields. We have seen how the identity of *indígena* has more weight in the field of crafts and arts than in the labour market. Even within Mexico the knowledge and use of an indigenous language is a more important criterion for membership in an indigenous group in the field of education, than in the world of arts and crafts. It is easier for artisans from Xalitla who speak little if no Nahuatl to identify themselves, or be labelled, as *indígena* than for non-Nahuatl speakers from Xalitla who want to be recognized as indigenous teachers. The notion of being a native person likewise varies by country, since the group dynamics of what it means to be "Indian" or "Aztec" is different in Houston, Mexico City, or Paris. What it means to be indigenous is as prone to competing interpretations as is the definition of globalization.

The case of the Alto Balsas has broader implications for current debates about the nature of globalization. International migration and recent trends in globalization, such as the telecommunication revolution, have brought people in all of North America (and much of the rest of the world) closer together in terms of awareness of others. A new term, "global culture," implies that a worldwide culture is emerging, but some anthropologists argue that cultural values and social patterns today are characterized by greater complexity and more diversity. Along similar lines, political scientists and sociologists are debating the relative importance of national states in today's world, some arguing that the state is becoming less relevant and powerful compared to international corporations, while others point out that the nation-state, and national identity, are still crucial components of the new world order.[29] The story of the Alto Balsas region, whose villages have become cross-border communities, can illustrate the relative merit of both sides of these arguments. The increasing difficulties faced by its migrants entering the United States from the Alto Balsas illustrates the power of nation-states, particularly that of the American government as it tries to decrease the number of workers from the Alto Balsas and other part of Mexico who are currently working in the United States. In the case of Mexico, globalization has not eroded the ongoing expansion of the Mexican state, as it continues to build more schools in indigenous regions in order to create a single national culture.[30] However, there are strong countervailing trends. Some Nahua children, particularly those currently growing up in the United States, speak fluent Spanish but no longer see themselves as Mexican citizens.

In the case of the United States, the number of immigrants deemed as illegal is growing exponentially. In some towns the number of people speaking only Spanish will soon be greater than those speaking only English. There are Spanish television networks, whose viewers are more interested in soccer than American football. Recent trends in globalization include the creation of new group identities, such as the resurrection of the label "Aztecs." In Mexico, recent trends in globalization, including the implementation of a free trade zone (NAFTA), are eroding national unity and a greater degree of cultural homogeneity at the national level. This was not always the case. In the fifties, the impact of globalization triggered the growth of a crafts industry and the expansion of the national system of education in the Alto Balsas. More people started travelling to other part of Mexico. Together these developments made Nahuas more aware of the rest of Mexico, and they learned how to speak Spanish as they became more integrated into national life. Yet the recent globalization of Nahua villages as a result of transnational labour has made some of their inhabitants more familiar with the United States than with their own country.

Finally it is important to remember that the use of any group label, including that of *indígena,* glosses over intra-group diversity which may be as great as inter-group variations. In the case of the Alto Balsas, recent forms of globalization may result in such intra-group variation becoming even greater. The success of some Alto Balsas Nahuas, including visual artists with an international reputation, handicraft merchants who now own houses in several cities, powerful political leaders, or international migrants who have established thriving businesses, makes is easy to overlook the low incomes and exploitation of other people who belong to the same ethnic group. Yet the average income and standard of living for most of the still largely Nahuatl-speaking villages in the Alto Balsas are higher than those of other parts of the state of Guerrero, including regions inhabited by people who are not *indígenas*. Native people in the Alto Balsas now employ *mestizos* as bricklayers rather than the other way around. Overall, the indigenous people who were born and raised in this part of Mexico have so far been able to make globalization work to their advantage.

Notes

1 According to the website of the Commission for the Development of Indigenous People (CDI) (2008), thirteen per cent of the population of Mexico are of indigenous descent but only six per cent speak indigenous languages; the website http://www.cdi.gob.mx cites as its source one of its own publications (Navarette Linares 2008), which is itself available online.
2 For a comprehensive overview of the concept of globalization, see Sassen (2006).
3 For an example of a statement equating indigenous communities in Mexico with the agricultural sector, see Chodkiewicz (2004, 196).
4 Chiapas is the home to Tzeltal- and Tzoltil-speaking peasants. For an examination of the Zapatistia movement, NAFTA (TLCAN in Spanish), and indigenous issues, see Otero (2004, Chapter 8).
5 See Niezen (2004, 77). For an example of the depiction of indigenous people from Mexico as mainly poor peasant farmers who are then relegated to the lowest levels of ethnically segmented labour markets, see Fox and Rivera-Salgado (2004, 4).
6 I obtained this insight from an anonymous reviewer of an application for a fellowship for which I applied.
7 To date few Mexican indigenous people have come to Canada; however, there were some men from Oaxaca among the seasonal agricultural workers in the Canadian–Mexican guest workers program.
8 An example of a recent study is Lynn Stephen's (2007) *Transborder lives*, which deals with the transborder lives of indigenous migrants from Oaxaca.
9 See the introductory chapter, "Building Civil Society among Indigenous Migrants," in Jonathan Fox and Gaspar Rivera-Salgado's *Indigenous Mexican migrants in the United States* (2004, 1–61). A dozen such studies are included in Fox and Rivera-Salgado's *Indigenous Mexican migrants in the United States* (2004).
10 Legally, most of the land surrounding these villages, with land titles dating back to the colonial era, is classified as *tennenos comunales*. Three villages also obtained access to formerly privately owned land in the form of *ejidos* with the distribution of several estates in the valley of Iguala that bordered on the Alto Balsas region. Information regarding land tenure was obtained in the archives of the Registro Agrario Nacional (formerly Secretaria de la Reforma Agraria) in the state capital of Chilpancingo.
11 The anthropological literature on the Alto Balsas represents different, often diametrically opposed theoretical perspectives, including how to define ethnic groups. Catherine Good Eshelman (1988) argues that the adoption of craft production for sale has reinforced an economy of reciprocity at the local level. Her position is that there has been no capital accumulation resulting in class differentiation in Nahua villages. In contrast, Aline Hémond (2003) refers to one of these villages, Amayeltepec, as having an indigenous bourgeoisie. Another point of

contention is how to classify the two villages where Spanish has almost completely replaced the Nahuatl language. Good Eshelman (1988), who posits the reciprocity model, considers these two villages, Xalitla and Maxela, as internally class-stratified and no longer indigenous. In contrast, Hémond (2003) argues that these villages are part of a single social and cultural system, noting ongoing ties of kinship and ritual bonds between Nahuatl-speaking people and their now Spanish-speaking counterparts.

12 In contrast, the indigenous people in the rest of the Iguala valley lost most of their land shortly after the arrival of the Spaniards. For a comprehensive treatment of the colonial history of this part of Guerrero, see Amith (2005).

13 A paved highway connecting Mexico City to Acapulco (first built in 1927) was improved in 1955, cutting travel time to six hours.

14 I conducted a survey of the village of Ahuehuepan and have observed that almost all older people in other villages of the Alto Balsas region are also illiterate.

15 In 1950 *amate* paper, used by local shamans to create cut-outs used for ritual purposes, was only produced in the Otomí village of San Pablito Pahuatlán, located in the state of Puebla. With the introduction of *amate* paintings, producers from San Pablito began travelling to the Alto Balsas region to sell sheets of paper to Nahua artisans. See Good Eshelman (1988, 29–30).

16 This colony, whose inhabitants received title to the land they had occupied, is called Ampliación de Chula Vista.

17 I visited and spoke to vendors in these towns, located just south of Puerto Vallarta, which also has artisan-vendors from the Alto Balsas region. In total I have conducted over twelve months of fieldwork (spread out over various trips) in Mexico, spending most of my time in the village of Ahuehuepan.

18 Tetelcingo is the name of a village located about one kilometre from the place where the old highway from Mexico to Acapulco crosses the Balsas River.

19 Hindley (1996), who witnessed these events, wrote a dissertation on this movement and its leaders.

20 This discrepancy beween the reputation of a united region called the Alto Balsas (at the international and national levels) and how most of its inhabitants see themselves may change in the future, if plans to create a single administrative unit (a single indigenous *municipio*) come to fruition. People from the region might yet again unite within or across villages to oppose what they perceive as threats.

21 Although the current president of Mexico has confirmed that there are no immediate plans to resurrect this dam project, that possibility is included in the Plan Panama project, a development plan for both southern Mexico and Central America.

22 I am using the term "social field" in the same way as Pierre Bourdieu's notion of *champs d'action*. The historical development and dynamics of each field or subfield, each of which has its own logic of social practice, must be empirically discovered. See Bourdieu and Wacquant (1992, 97–98).

23 I conducted interviews with migrants during several trips to Houston.

24 This is the only case I am aware of where an *amate* painter who went to work in the United States was able to apply his artistic talents there. However, several *amate* painters who reside year-round in Mexico have made visits to American museums or art galleries as invited guests.

25 Julio is a pseudonym.

26 However, not everyone in the same family changes their religion. Neither the husband of the formerly non-Roman Catholic woman in Houston nor her son converted. In addition, her daughter, also in Houston, became a Jehovah's Witness.
27 He is mentioned on various websites and his life history appears in a book about contemporary Mexican artists. See Lara Elizondo (2004).
28 His life is described in Cowen (2005).
29 An overview of these debates and a source of the literature on globalization, including both cultural and economic trends is *The Globalization Website*, http://www.sociology.emory.edu/globalization/about/html.
30 In theory Mexico has a policy of pluriculturalism, which involves the recognition and preservation of the culture and languages of all its indigenous groups. In practice, Mexico's program of indigenous education (through what are called bilingual schools) do not teach native children to write or read in their own mother tongue, and its curriculum is almost identical to that used for the rest of Mexico.

References

Amith, J. 2005. *The Möbius strip (A spatial history of colonial society in Guerrero, Mexico)*. Stanford: Stanford Univ. Press.
Bourdieu, P., and L. Wacquant. 1992. *An invitation to reflexive sociology*. Chicago: Univ. of Chicago Press.
Chodkiewicz, J. 2004. Mexico: Global or Mexicano. In *Globalization and community*, ed. J. L. Chodkiewicz and R. E. Wiest, 191–210. Univ. of Manitoba Anthropology Papers 34. Winnipeg: Univ. of Manitoba Press.
Cowen, T. 2005. *Markets and Cultural Voices*. Ann Arbor: Univ. of Michigan Press.
Fox, J., and G. Rivera-Salgado. Building Civil Society among Indigenous Migrants. In *Indigenous Mexican migrants in the United States*, ed. J. Fox and G. Rivera-Salgado, 1–65. Center for US–Mexican Studies (UCSD)/Center for Comparative Immigration Studies (UCSD).
García, M. 2002. Nomadas viajeros y migrantes. La comunidad sin límites del Alto Balsas. Master's thesis for the Escuela Nacional de Antropología e Historia.
García, M., and G. Zárate-Hoyos. 2005. Las mujeres Nahua en el Alto Balsas de México: Administradores y generadores de remesas para el desarrollo humano. Paper presented at Centro para La Justicia Global, "Mujeres y Globalización." http://www.globaljusticecenter.org/ponencias.htm.
Glick-Schiller, N., L. Basch, and C. Blanc-Szanton. 1992. Towards a transnational perspective on migration, race, class, ethnicity and nationalism reconsidered. *Género y Sociedad* 3(1): 67–94.
Globalization Website. http://www.sociology.emory.edu/globalization/about/html.
Good Eshelman, C. 1988. *Haciendo la lucha (arte y comercio nahuas de Guerrero)*. Mexico, Fondo de Cultural Económica.
Gutmann, M. C., and S. S. Porter. 1997. Gender: 1910–96. In *Encyclopedia of Mexico*, Vol. 1, ed. M. S. Werner, 578. Chicago: Fitzroy Dearborn Publishers.
Hémond, A. 2003. *Peindre la révolte: Esthétique et résistance culturelle au Mexique*. Paris: CNRS.

Hindley, J. 1996. Indigenous Mobilization, Political Reform and Development in Mexico: The Struggle of the Nahua People of the Upper Balsas, Guerrero. Doctoral diss., Department of Government, University of Essex.

Huizar Murillo, J., and I. Cerda. 2004. Indigenous Mexican migrants in the 2000 US census: "Hispanic American Indians." In *Indigenous Mexican migrants in the United States*, ed. J. Fox and G. Rivera-Salgado, 279–302. Center for US–Mexican Studies (UCSD)/Center for Comparative Immigration Studies (UCSD).

Kearney, M. 1995. The local and the global: The anthropology of globalization and transnationalism. *Annual Review of Anthropology* 24(1): 547–65.

Lara Elizondo, L. 2004. Nicolás de Jesús: Amor a la tierra y su comunidad. In *Vision de México y sus amates (paralelismo en la practica de los siglos XIX y XXI)*, ed. L. Lara Elizondo, 219–25. Mexico City: Promoción de Arte Mexicano.

Morales Aguilar, B. 2007. Classes paint your own... *Regiones* 30 (July): 5–8.

Navarette Linares, F. 2008. Los Pueblos Indígenas de México. Mexico: CDI.

Niezen, R. 2004. Indigenous people in a global era. In *Globalization and community*, ed. J. L. Chodkiewicz and R. E. Wiest, 77–87. Univ. of Manitoba Anthropology Papers 34. Winnipeg: Univ. of Manitoba Press.

Otero, G. 2004. ¿Adios al campesinado? Burnaby, BC: Simon Fraser Univ./Porrúa: Univ. de Zacatecas.

Portes, P. 1996. Transnational communities: Their emergence and significance in the contemporary world system. In *Latin America and the world-economy*, ed. R. P. Korzeniewicz, 151–56. Santa Barbara, CA: Greenwood Press.

Saldaña Ramírez, A. n.d. La construcción de nuestra casa en Morelos: El caso de los Jornaleros Agrícolas de Tula del Rio, Guerrero. A paper presented for a workshop of the centre INAH-Morelos.

Sassen, S. 2006. Territory, authority, rights: From medieval to global assemblages. Princeton, NJ: Princeton Univ. Press.

Stephen, L. 2007. *Transborder lives*. Durham, NC: Duke Univ. Press.

Language Shift, Maintenance, and Revitalization: Quichua in an Era of Globalization

Rosario Gómez

Introduction

The early 1990s were marked by worldwide concern over the potential of globalization to increase cultural and linguistic homogenization (Crystal 2004). For many, this fear was confirmed as the world's dominant languages gained new speakers at alarming rates, threatening the already precarious existence of minority languages. This chapter examines the impact that globalization has had on the Ecuadorian variety of Quechua, known as Quichua, and explores some of the aspects of globalization that can be redirected to promote the maintenance and revitalization of minority languages. This will be accomplished through an examination of the global and local factors that, from the 1980s onward, have contributed to language shift, maintenance, and revitalization in Ecuador.

For centuries, Quichua and Spanish have coexisted in a variety of contexts of power, conflict, and diglossia.[1] While the language of the European invaders became the dominant language employed in the public, religious, academic, legislative, and judicial spheres, Quichua was relegated to marginalized indigenous communities.

Despite its inferior status vis-à-vis Spanish, Quichua has a relatively large number of speakers in comparison to other endangered languages around the world. Its sister varieties of Quechua are spoken over a large geographic expanse including Peru, Bolivia, Argentina, Colombia, and Chile. Estimates for the total number of Quechua speakers in South America range from 8 to 10 million.[2] In Ecuador alone, between 340,000 (INEC n.d.) and 3 million

(CONAIE n.d.) individuals are believed to speak Quichua—the low figure being attributed to a boycott of Ecuador's 1990 national census by indigenous peoples.

Despite these numbers, from the 1980s onward, intergenerational transmission as well as the domains in which Quichua is spoken has rapidly decreased, clearly indicating that this language is in danger of extinction (Hornberger and Coronel-Molina 2004, 9). Most linguists agree that across South America, other varieties of Quechua are also losing ground. The shift from Quichua to Spanish in Ecuador has been accelerated by a variety of factors, several of which will be examined below.

Language Shift
The tendency of monolingual Quichua speakers to adopt Spanish is neither a recent phenomenon nor can it be attributed to any one particular factor. In Ecuador, the linguistic diversity of the region, the widespread demographic and socio-cultural displacements of indigenous groups, and language ideologies have all contributed to the shift toward Spanish. These contributing factors have, to some degree, been intensified or mediated by the globalized cultural, economic and linguistic trends of recent decades.

Linguistic Diversity
Ecuador's internal linguistic diversity has been the most enduring of the factors contributing to language shift. In addition to the relative isolation of Quichua speakers in the Andes, the diversity of indigenous languages was furthered by both geographic and sociolinguistic factors. Ecuadorian Quichua can be divided into two principal dialectal variations: Highland and Lowland Quichua, which are further subdivided into sub-dialects, still in use today. Highland Quichua consists of three sub-varieties: (1) Northern (in the provinces of Imbabura and Pichincha); (2) Central (Cotopaxi, Tungurahua, Bolívar, and Chimborazo); and (3) Southern (Cañar, Azuay, and Loja). Lowland Quichua is subdivided into three distinct varieties: (1) Bobonaza (province of Pastaza); (2) Tena (Napo); and (3) Limoncocha (Orellana).

Such internal linguistic variation has caused disagreements among the speakers as they negotiate which variety of Quichua will be used as a unifying standard and which constitutes "authentic" Quichua (Hornberger and King 1998). In 1981, members of Indigenous Education at the Catholic University of Quito and speakers of the different varieties (von Gleich 1994) developed a standardized variety of Quichua to be used in the education system; the result was Quichua Unificado. Their aim was to rid Quichua of any Spanish lexical items and to replace them with Quichua equivalents or neologisms as well as to devise a standard orthographic system for all varieties of Quichua. Although this was intended to facilitate language acquisition and to promote the revitalization of Quichua, it in fact had the opposite effect: the tension that developed among speakers around the perceived authenticity of the language actually deterred the use of Quichua (Hornberger and King 1998).

Unified Quichua, a learned academic variety used by the young educated indigenous individuals, clashed with authentic Quichua spoken by older rural speakers. Because the distribution of the two varieties was imbalanced, communicative gaps emerged between younger and older speakers, especially in the more rural communities where older members are Quichua dominant. Authentic Quichua, which paradoxically contains numerous Spanish borrowings and has lost some of its morphological structure, was rejected by the younger educated members, who considered Unified Quichua as the purer standard form. Authentic Quichua and, by extension, its speakers, were rejected as inferior. Speakers of authentic Quichua, on the other hand, found Unified Quichua to be foreign and incomprehensible at times (Hornberger and King 1998). Thus, conflicts have arisen on two levels: first, between generations and, second, as a result of the social and educational distribution of Unified and authentic Quichua. This conflict further divides a linguistic community already threatened by Spanish, thereby reducing contact between speakers and diminishing opportunities for language use and spread. Ironically, these conflicts largely resemble those between Spanish and Quichua, which are based on language ideologies of superiority and social class structure. In addition to the linguistic diversity that has been a driving force in language shift, Quichua and its speakers have also experienced demographic and socio-cultural displacements[3] that have exacerbated the language shifts.

Demographic Shifts
During the 1970s, Ecuador experienced significant rural to urban migrations. At present, the urban population is estimated at 68.8 per cent of the nation's population (Centro de Estudios de Población y Desarollo Social 2007) and projections show that between one and three per cent of the rural population will relocate to metropolitan centres every decade (King and Haboud 2002). The majority of rural indigenous groups that have migrated to the cities have done so in search of salaried employment. Globalization and modern communication technology have raised awareness of the apparent prosperity that exists outside of rural communities. This increased awareness has created new incentives for indigenous people to relocate to the cities to seek out what is perceived to be a successful way of life.

The demographic shift has resulted in small clusters of urbanized indigenous communities with varying degrees of language loss due to the intensity and duration of contact with Spanish speakers. As indigenous groups scatter across diverse regions, social networks are disrupted and individuals lose the linguistic support systems in which Quichua was the language of interaction. In recent decades, indigenous individuals have tended to move farther from their originating linguistic communities; they have been bound not only toward metropolitan centres within Ecuador but also toward the United States, Canada, and Europe, particularly Spain.

Geographic factors, including natural disasters, have also contributed to the demographic shift. For instance, when the Tungurahua Volcano erupted in August 2006, more than 300,000 people were affected. The disaster wiped out several villages and forced the evacuation of residents to Ambato, the nearest city (Emergency Disasters Data Base 2007). Cataclysmic phenomena such as these force the migration of Quichua-speaking populations and cause the disappearance, albeit sometimes temporary, of Quichua from rural areas. Once in an urban context, Quichua speakers often acquire Spanish. This is especially the case with younger community members.

Socio-cultural Displacements

The increased contact with Spanish that results from the relocation of indigenous peoples to urban centres cannot alone account for the high incidence of language shift. When indigenous people migrate to the cities, their physical displacement is often accompanied by socio-cultural displacements. These displacements have arisen mainly from the pervasive low prestige accorded to this ethno-linguistic group and the social and economic limitations they endure. For centuries, Ecuadorian elites—white Europeans and *mestizos*— have associated indigenous peoples with rurality, poverty, and backwardness. Therefore, indigenous peoples in the pursuit of social mobility often shed their cultural symbols, including language, in favour of the dominant *mestizo* characteristics. The repressive social conditions that prompt socio-cultural displacements, though not as violent as wars or natural disasters, are just as damaging to the self-esteem of group members. Linguistic shame and discrimination are the leading factors that prevent speakers from using Quichua in the public sphere in urban contexts and cause individuals to deny or conceal their knowledge of Quichua (Gómez 2003).

Moreover, monolingual Quichua speakers often face discrimination in the employment sector; thus, migration to the cities implies a need to be proficient in Spanish. However, as the world's economies become increasingly interconnected, knowledge of English enhances an individual's global competitiveness, threatening both Spanish and Quichua in Ecuador. Advertisements for imported products such as toiletries, wines, and electronics completely bypass Quichua speakers and often contain English slogans. Spanish monolingual students, however, have the opportunity to attend bilingual schools in which English, French, or German is taught. In some private schools, these languages may even be the medium of instruction. However, such programs are accessible only to upper-middle and upper-class students and are provided to advance their educational and social opportunities, making them more competitive globally.

Although modernization and globalization are major factors leading to socio-cultural displacements, Dorian (2001, 6) asserts that they have also enabled isolated groups, particularly those involved in human rights and environmental issues, and to some extent commercial organizations, to build new global networks. The Otavalo community from Imbabura, for example, has maintained its culture, identity, and language as a result of its national and international reputation as traditional weavers and artisans. Through their organization, Manducarios Solidario, their products have reached markets in Japan, Germany, France, and Spain (Manducarios United 2008).

Language Ideologies
The physical and socio-cultural displacements reviewed above are profoundly embedded in language ideologies that determine linguistic behaviours. Quichua and Spanish speakers share beliefs about Quichua that are detrimental to the very core of indigenous identity and which manifest themselves blatantly in language shift. In Ecuador, Quichua has been undervalued by all members of society — who have accorded Spanish official, dominant, and literary status. This underpinning ideology continues to shape the beliefs and attitudes of Spanish and Quichua speakers. For instance, many indigenous people, especially those among the rural poor, prefer to have their children educated in Spanish because it provides increased opportunities to participate in mainstream society (Carpenter 1983).

Mestizo language attitudes are no different; although most *mestizos* identify Quichua as an ancestral language, they view it as a grammarless language and a symbol of the past that lacks relevance in contemporary society (Haboud 1993; 1998). According to Cotacachi (1997), many Spanish-speaking teachers continue to consider Quichua a useless or backward language with a deficient grammar and lexicon. An example of such beliefs is particularly evident in the linguistic behaviour of the younger generation of Spanish speakers who consciously avoid assibilated realizations of (r) and (ll), in words such as *carro* and *calle*, respectively, because they are associated with uneducated working class indigenous speakers who are influenced by Quichua (Gómez 2005).

Hornberger and Coronel-Molina (2004) observe that despite the pervasiveness of these beliefs, there is increasing acceptance of a symbolic use of Quichua as it plays a public and calculated role in political domains. In 1979, President Jaime Roldós delivered part of his inaugural speech in Quichua, a bold and unprecedented step at the time. More recently, President Rafael Correa concluded his speech marking the one-year anniversary of his government in Quichua: "Kunanmi runa hataripa kamayka shuk wata tukun kunankaman shinami tantarishpa, shuklla shina katina kanchik shina kakpika, pipash mana atinkachu, pipash mana ishankachu ñuka ecuadormanta panikuna wawkikuna, yuyarichik llaktaka ñami tukuykunapa kan kayaminchakaman" (2008).[4]

Correa has been praised for his ability to communicate with the indigenous population in their own language, having learned Quichua while volunteering in a remote highland town (*Financial Times* 2006). He has been lauded as an economist in a peripheral country that understands the economic damages of globalization first hand. As a citizen working with Quichua intellectuals, he is cognizant of the colonial damage inflicted upon the racialized sector of the population.

Nationwide indigenous movements, which use the language as a central symbol of indigenous resistance and identity, have also raised awareness of Quichua's significance. In many rural communities Quichua remains an important marker of ethnic identity; being indigenous means participating in a community and, by extension, speaking the language of the group.[5] Quichua continues to serve as a symbol of common goals and aspirations for self-empowerment.

Thus, in summary, the plurality of indigenous languages and dialects, the demographic and socio-cultural displacements of Amerindians, and the language ideologies prevalent in Ecuador have contributed in recent decades to the shift towards Spanish language dominance. In some cases, global trends, such as increased rural to urban migration and the large-scale diffusion of English and Spanish, have accelerated this shift. However, technology and increased communication have empowered some indigenous organizations to maintain their traditional values and languages while being incorporated into the global economy.

Language Maintenance and Revitalization

It is important to note, however, that an increased awareness about the detrimental effects of globalization on Quichua has triggered a large-scale reaction. Various measures to protect and revitalize indigenous languages have been undertaken by stakeholders, such as Ecuador's Ministry of Education and Cultures, in part as a response to pressures from indigenous groups and international entities. The following section will examine the recent shift in language and education policy in Ecuador and the local and global actors that brought about these changes. Although new rights and laws have been developed to protect minority languages and cultures, much remains to be done in terms of implementation and acceptance by the dominant Spanish-speaking community.

Educational Reform in Ecuador

Historically, policy shifts in Ecuador have revolved around the 1962/1974 agrarian reform, the oil boom of the 1970s — which improved education, communication, and utilities in rural sectors — and the political crises of the 1990s. In 1964, the Ecuadorian Education Plan (Plan Ecuatoriano de Educación) stressed the need to integrate the indigenous population into the mainstream education system (Yánez 1989, 76). The influx of international tourists interested in Ecuador's indigenous cultures initiated a cultural-identity-based shift among middle-class Ecuadorians in the 1970s, which paved the way for the significant language policy changes of the 1980s that aimed to reform the Spanish-dominant national education system by adopting bilingual education. In 1981, intercultural-bilingual education was officially sanctioned by the Ministry of Education and Culture in predominantly indigenous areas (Art. 000529). Instruction was to take place in Quichua (or another indigenous language) and Spanish. In 1983, a second provision (Art. 27 of the Constitution) required that Quichua (or the community's language) be the primary language of instruction in areas with predominantly indigenous speakers. Spanish was to be employed only for intercultural communication (DINEIB 1994, 5).

In 1986 the Confederation of Indigenous Nationalities of Ecuador (Confederación de Nacionalidades Indígenas del Ecuador, CONAIE) was established and was subsequently recognized by the government. Since its beginnings, CONAIE has attempted to guarantee indigenous peoples a political voice, advocating a national reform of the education system and the implementation of autonomous indigenous language literacy programs. As a result of CONAIE's initiatives, indigenous groups developed programs that employed Quichua and other indigenous languages as a means to embed the educational experience within an indigenous context. For example, the Indigenous Schooling Foundation (Fundación Runacunapac Yachana Huasi), implemented in the province of Bolívar, utilized Quichua as the language of instruction, taught Spanish as a second language, and aimed to enhance students' identification with their own communities (King and Haboud 2002; Caiza 1989).

The National Directorate of Intercultural-Bilingual Education (Dirección Nacional de Educación Intercultural Bilingüe, DINEIB), created in 1989, served to implement and monitor the education reforms. However, although bilingual education was thus legislated in the 1980s, it was not fully implemented due to a lack of programs and planning. The directorate was established due to the pressure applied by indigenous organizations and a series of talks between President Borja (1988–92) and the leaders of CONAIE (Selverston 1992). The DINEIB's mandate was to oversee schools in regions whose population was more than fifty per cent indigenous and to ensure the consistency, adequacy, and effectiveness of indigenous education (adhering to the agreed-upon usage of Unified Quichua in Quichua-speaking communities) throughout Ecuador (DINEIIB 1991). Among its responsibilities were the development of teaching materials, teacher training, the promotion of a standard orthography for indigenous languages,[6] the coordination of regional directorates in the twenty-two provinces, and the implementation and evaluation of health, environmental and education programs (DINEIIB 1991; Krainer 1996).

An unprecedented and important development in indigenous language education was the establishment of the first indigenous university in Ecuador, La Universidad Intercultural de Nacionalidades y Pueblos Indígenas Amawtay Wasi, which was officially opened in 2004, offering undergraduate degrees in agroecology, teacher training, and architecture and territorial planning. Plans to open a graduate-degree program cannot be implemented until 2010, as the National Council of Higher Education (Consejo Nacional de Educación Superior) requires that the university be operational for five years before offering graduate programs and degrees. In their words, the university "was established to be a space of both reflection and action, and grew out of a project of the nationalities and peoples of Ecuador and of all Abya Yala (the Americas). Our university works towards the decolonization of knowledge and is committed to reconstructing the concept and meaning of intercultural knowledge. The UIAW is an intercultural project whose purpose is to serve as a foundation stone in construction of a plurinational state and an intercultural society" (Universidad Intercultural n.d.).

Current language planning strategies continue to focus on the role of ideology; the maintenance of threatened languages; and human, linguistic, and cultural rights. The Board of Education, in line with the 1994 reforms of the Law of Education, approved the inclusion of indigenous peoples' topics in the national curriculum, including subjects such as cultural diversity in Ecuador, family and community customs, myths and legends, and ancestral teachings related to health and ethics (Soto 1997). These shifts in language policy are the result of negotiations and concessions within the larger framework of dialogues dealing with identity, ethnicity, and notions of the nation–state. In Ecuador in particular, these shifts have been largely influenced by forces such as: (a) the increased number of indigenous representatives in the Ecuadorian government; (b) steps taken by other Andean nations to recognize the multilingual, multicultural, and multiethnic make up of their populations; and (c) globalized efforts to protect and revitalize indigenous languages.

The Indigenous Presence in Politics
The inclusion of indigenous groups and individuals in the government in the last decade has marked a positive change for indigenous communities across

the country. Organizations such as CONAIE have been instrumental in applying pressure to the government to ensure that the multicultural reality of the country is reflected in policy. In 2002, CONAIE representatives were allotted key government positions, an unprecedented development that has granted previously marginalized segments of the population access to policy-making. There is also increasing indigenous representation at the municipal, provincial, and national levels. Of note was the 2001 appointment of Nina Pakari to the National Congress. Pakari (2001) proposed a constitutional amendment regarding the use of indigenous languages nationally, the provisions which included the inalienable right to use indigenous languages (Art. 2), the use of indigenous languages in public procedures involving indigenous citizens (Art. 3), and bilingual (Spanish and the corresponding indigenous language) written versions of state laws and judicial norms (Art. 5). In addition, the amendment called for the use of ancestral languages in public institutions and services, legislatures, courts, and the mass media and for the state to grant adequate facilities and resources to translators (Art. 6; Haboud 2000, 33). Additionally, the political party Pachakutik Plurinational Unity Movement–New Nation (Movimiento de Unidad Plurinacional Pachakutik–Nuevo País), founded in 1995, currently holds six seats (out of eighty-two members) in the National Assembly and provides Amerindians with a great deal of expectation for more equitable participation.

The Impact of Other Andean Nations
The shift toward intercultural-bilingual education was stimulated by national and international pressures on the Ecuadorian government to adopt a more inclusive policy; after all, similar shifts were occurring in neighbouring Andean countries and elsewhere (Godenzzi 2008). At the regional level, education policy reforms in Ecuador are inextricably linked to the fundamental changes in policies in Peru and Bolivia, which advocate the recognition and appreciation of indigenous cultures and languages while striving for intercultural-bilingual education.

In Peru, during General Velasco's administration (1968–75), Quechua was included in the Peruvian constitution as an official language and as such, was to be used at all levels of education (Art. 2) and in all legal procedures involving monolingual Quechua speakers (Art. 3). As a result, the ministry of education was charged with developing teaching materials and backing organizations committed to language spread (Art. 4; von Gleich 1994; see also Godenzzi 2008; Hornberger 1987; Pozzi-Escot 1988). Similarly, the Bolivian government implemented the education reform of 1996 which called for intercultural-bilingual education for all individuals at all social levels (Godenzzi 2008; King and Haboud 2002).

Cooperation among the Andean nations in recent years has been a significant factor in shaping language policies. One such Pan-Andean collaboration is the Training Program in Intercultural-Bilingual Education for Andean Countries (Programa de Formación en Educación Intercultural Bilingüe para los Países Andinos, PROEIB), which aims to develop human resources trained in intercultural-bilingual education. With headquarters in Bolivia, PROEIB boasts a membership of five Andean nations — Peru, Colombia, Ecuador Chile, and Bolivia;[7] its Ecuadorian centre is located at the Universidad Politécnica Salesiana in Quito.

Globalized Indigenous Movements

Although globalization has been generally considered a threat leading to the attrition of culture and language, affecting particularly languages that lack official status or that have very few speakers (Hamelink 2000; Phillipson 2000; Skutnabb-Kangas 2000), globalization has also been acknowledged as a constructive process that may unify and create networks of solidarity (Fishman 1991, 6). A good example of a positive effect of globalization in the domain of language and education policy is the worldwide movement toward the legitimization of minority language rights. At the international level, the recognition of linguistic diversity has been articulated formally. Perhaps the most influential language-planning medium has been the United Nations, as stipulated in Article 27 of the International Covenant on Civil and Political Rights (1966), which came into effect in 1976 (Office of the United Nations High Commissioner for Human Rights 2007). Subsequent declarations of the UN highlight the state's responsibility to "create favourable conditions" for minority groups (Skutnabb-Kangas 2000, 533), as is evident in the General Assembly resolution 47/135 of 1992 (Office of the United Nations Commission for Human Rights 2007). However, it was not until 1996 that the Universal Declaration of Linguistic Rights, the most progressive and influential of declarations dealing exclusively with language rights, was accepted in Barcelona and subsequently submitted to UNESCO (World Conference on Linguistic Rights 1996). The Linguapax Institute, born out of a UNESCO initiative, is an international NGO based in Barcelona that is charged with seeking solutions in the areas of peace research, democracy, and human rights, and has as its aim to promote peace through the respect of linguistic diversity and the promotion of multilingual education.

In addition to institutional global trends working to legitimize minority language rights, increasing co-operation among indigenous groups internationally is raising awareness of parallel developments around the world. Changes across the Andes have been prompted by direct pressures from indigenous organizations and international lending institutions concerned with creating more inclusive and egalitarian education systems (Luykx 2000). More than a dozen international organizations and associations are conducting research on endangered languages and supporting indigenous rights. These include the Endangered Languages Fund (n.d.), the Foundation for Endangered Languages (2007), the Hanns Seidel Foundation, Terralingua, and the International Clearing House for Endangered Languages. These come in addition to grant programs from organizations such as Documentation of Endangered Languages (DoBeS 2006) and GBS: Society for Endangered Languages (2006).

These organizations have the potential to become powerful instruments that promote transnational awareness and contact between indigenous groups. Recent global developments such as these, which foster not only the recognition of minority languages but also unprecedented collaboration among indigenous groups and advocates of indigenous rights, will no doubt continue to set the tone for language revitalization in Ecuador. Globalization does not have to signify the death of minority languages and the birth of one global culture. Indeed, what is occurring is not worldwide cultural homogenization but rather the increased sharing of particular values by certain social groups; and that is exactly what language awareness has become, or could become. Echoing David Crystal's recommendations in regard to all endangered languages, advocates of Quichua revitalization need to take advantage of these globalized processes and utilize technology in a fashion similar to other international movements. Thus, a language revitalization movement must reach the media and increase its presence on the internet. There are already encouraging signs for the future of Quichua: a proliferation of Quichua language websites now exist, including the presence of Quichua cultural material on YouTube. In addition, the private global enterprise Google has produced a Quechua version of its search engine and Microsoft, in collaboration with Peru's Ministry of Education, has produced Quechua versions of its Windows and Office software applications (Godenzzi 2008).

Challenges of Indigenous-language Education
In spite of the profuse national legislation passed throughout the Andes to promote cultural diversity and international assistance in the form of consultancy and experimentation, adequate and consistent implementation of such legislation has not been achieved.[8] The implementation of these reforms was ineffective due to the lack of trained and qualified teaching personnel and resources, bureaucratic obstacles, diverging opinions regarding the usefulness of indigenous languages within educational contexts, and conflicting interpretations of terms such as "intercultural" and "bilingual." Several aspects of the education reform remained ambiguous about what bilingual education meant at the practical level; the DINEIB had not specified in what language

instruction was to be conducted but rather had stressed the revival and maintenance of indigenous languages. As a result, bilingual education could be interpreted as the use and development of Amerindian languages as well as Spanish.

Critics have argued that in spite of the use of indigenous languages, there has been an overarching emphasis on the acquisition of Spanish, which eventually produces an incomplete form of bilingualism or, in fact, language shift. Admittedly, this scenario is still an improvement to educational systems in existence before the 1960s, in which Amerindian languages and cultural topics were completely excluded from the curriculum.

The definition of intercultural education is just as ambiguous. Whereas one definition may stress the affirmation of one's own culture and worldview as well as the appropriation of selective cultural aspects of other ethnic groups, King and Haboud (2002) state that interculturality entails not only interaction between two different cultures but also a political commitment to building a society based on equality. The discrepancy rests on the question of who the principal agents of intercultural education are. The rhetoric suggests that the stakeholders are all Ecuadorians. Thus, all segments of society should have equal and mutual involvement. In practice, however, the task has been handed off to indigenous groups and limited to the classroom. Outside of Amerindian communities, Quichua as a second language is not taught to Spanish-speaking students in public schools, nor is it used as a medium of instruction. In addition, outside of the public school system, Quichua instruction for Spanish speakers is almost nonexistent. Haboud (2004, 78) observed that in 2002 only two out of twelve universities in Quito (Universidad Católica and Universidad San Francisco de Quito) offered Quichua classes to students at large. Although some universities, such as La Universidad Indígena Intercultural, which is linked to PROEIB, specialize in Intercultural-Bilingual Education, it is evident that the Ecuadorian education system has placed the task of implementing interculturality in the hands of the indigenous population, which generally lacks resources, whether in the form of materials, funding, or trained human resources.

Moreover, government bureaucracy has caused further setbacks to the implementation of intercultural-bilingual education. In 1990, the agreed figure of $3.8 million of funding in support of DINEIB bilingual education services was never granted (Selverston 1992). In 1998, DINEIB put forth a proposal to write intercultural education into the constitution, on the basis of Ecuador's population being forty per cent indigenous and that therefore thirty per cent of the total education budget should have been invested in intercultural-bilingual education. However, national economic crises[9] resulting in cuts in education and health care (PROEIB Andes 1998, 2) have had a negative impact on indigenous language education.

Future Challenges

Crawford (2000, 66–73) has proposed a series of hypotheses stressing the pivotal role that the speech community itself plays in the process of revitalization, maintenance, or death of its own language. From Crawford's perspective, language shift and language revival are the result of internal changes within the community and a re-evaluation of the community's values. In Ecuador it is clear that responsibility for interculturality has been left to Amerindian communities and that the concept as of yet has not been embraced by the wider population. In addition, language planning must address more than just the linguistic needs of a community; it must be framed within a larger context that touches upon globalized changes that affect the community. Hornberger and Coronel-Molina explain that although this strategy might be viewed as "blaming the victim," it directs to an affirming strategy, one that places responsibility and some degree of control of the future of Amerindian languages in the hands of the speakers. "This is, we suggest, where it ought to be" (Hornberger and Coronel-Molina 2004, 52).

The vitality of Quichua depends on the cumulative day-to-day communicative decisions of its speakers and the value they attribute to interacting in this language. Thus, any language-revitalization enterprise must seek to raise the self-esteem of the speakers and to sensitize those who undervalue the language. As Mufwene (n.d., 42) suggests, language rights activists including NGOs, international NGOs, linguists, and academics need to articulate alternative ecologies in which threatened languages can be revitalized; they must make it clear in what ways speaking Quichua would make this group competitive with those shifting to monolingualism in Spanish.

Spanish and Quechua have co-existed in the Andes for centuries in situations of power, subordination, inequality, and mutual linguistic, cultural, and social influence, and Quechua has always been on the losing side. However, the fact that Quechua continues to be spoken by several million individuals across five nations is a feat in itself. Although it is difficult to predict with certainty the future of Quichua in Ecuador, the outlook appears optimistic; Quichua has received valuable support from the government, the indigenous community, and international organizations, and has benefited from some positive effects of globalization. Intercultural bilingual education has played a key role in language maintenance and the Ecuadorian model has been among the best in Latin America and the Caribbean, having articulated and planned a systematic set of goals, programs, and policies (Hornberger and Coronel-Molina 2004), although the lack of resources, trained teachers, and funding for these programs has hindered implementation. In spite of these difficulties, intercultural bilingual education continues to press forward not only in primary and secondary education but also in tertiary education with the foundation of the Amawta Wasi University. Nevertheless, in spite of these seemingly positive steps, linguists have cautioned that the total number of Quichua speakers is continually decreasing, giving way to Spanish and, to some degree, English as the world's economies become interconnected.

Notes

1. For more on diglossia see Ferguson (1959), Gumperz (1971), and Fishman (1967).
2. While Cerrón-Palomino (1987) estimates that there were 8 million Quechua speakers in South America, Hornberger and Coronel-Molina (2004) place the estimate at 8 to 10 million.
3. Referred to as "dislocations" in Fishman (1991, 55–65).
4. "Today the Government of the People's Revolution celebrates its first year, we must continue together, as one, as we have been to this day. This way, no one will conquer us, no one will overcome us sisters and brothers of my Ecuador, remember the nation now belongs to all of us! Until always." (My translation; original text of speech found at http://www.presidencia.gov.ec/noticias.asp?noid=12333&hl=true.)
5. In addition to language, ethnicity and territoriality also serve as identity markers (Haboud 2003, 191).
6. See Hornberger and King (1998) for a discussion on the problems of implementing a standardized Quechua in Peru.
7. Recently Argentina requested membership in the program.
8. See King and Benson (2004) for further discussion.
9. In the 1990s, Ecuador suffered its worst economic crisis and natural disasters, and a sharp drop in world oil prices caused the economy to plummet in 1999. Poverty drastically worsened, the banking system collapsed, and the national currency depreciated by approximately 70 per cent. The Mahuad government announced the dollarization of the national currency, the sucre (CIA 2007). In 2001, the inflation rate reached 22.4 per cent.

References

Caiza, J. 1989. Hacia un modelo de educación bilingüe autogestionaria. In *Pueblos indios, estados, y educación,* ed. E. López and R. Moya, 309–26. Lima: Programa de Educación Bilingüe de Puno, El Proyecto de Educación Bilingüe Intercultural del Ecuador, y el Programa de Educación Rural Andina.

Carpenter, L. K. 1983. Social stratification and implications for bilingual education: An Ecuadorian example. In *Bilingualism: Social issues and policy implications,* ed. A. Miracle, 96–106. Athens: Univ. of Georgia Press.

Centro de Estudios de Población y Desarrollo Social. 2007. *Estimaciones y proyecciones de la población total y tasas de crecimiento: 1950–2015.* http://www.cepar.org.ec/estadisticas/pobind1/pobind1.html.

Cerrón-Palomino, R. 1987. *Lingüística Quechua.* Cuzco: Centro de Estudios Rurales Andinos "Bartolomé de las Casas."

CIA (Central Intelligence Agency). 2007. Ecuador. *The world factbook.* https://www.cia.gov/library/publications/the-world-factbook/geos/ec.html.

CONAIE (Confederación de Nacionalidades Indígenas del Ecuador). n.d. http://conaie.nativeweb.org/index.html.
Consejo Nacional de Educación Superior. 2007. *Listado general de institutos.* http://www.conesup.net/lista_institutos.php.
Correa, Rafael, 2008. Informe a la nación. Gobierno Nacional de la República del Ecuador. http://www.presidencia.gov.ec/noticias.asp?noid=12333&hl=true.
Cotacachi, M. 1997. Attitudes of teachers, children and parents towards bilingual intercultural education. In *Indigenous literacies in the Americas: Language planning from the bottom up,* ed. N. Hornberger, 285–98. Berlin: Mouton de Gruyter.
Crawford, James. 2000. *At war with diversity.* Clevedon: Multilingual Matters.
Crystal, D. 2004. *Creating a world of languages.* Forum Barcelona 2004. http://www.davidcrystal.com/DC_articles/Langdeath5.pdf.
DINEIB (Dirección Nacional de Educación Intercultural Bilingüe). 1994. Modelo de educación intercultural bilingüe. *Pueblos Indígenas y Educación* 29–30: 5–142.
DINEIIB (Dirección Nacional de Educación Intercultural Indígena Bilingüe). 1991. La educación intercultural bilingüe en el Ecuador. *Pueblos Indígenas y Educación* 17: 31–67.
Dorian, N. 2001. Small peoples in globalization's grip: Can short-term disaster become longer-term opportunity? Paper presented at the American Association of Anthropology meetings. Washington, DC, November.
Emergency Disasters Data Base. 2007. http://www.em-dat.net.
Ferguson, C. 1959. Diglossia. *Word* 15: 325–40.
Financial Times. 2006. Rafael Correa: Chavista with a whip hand, 9 October.
Fishman, J. 1967. Bilingualism with and without diglossia; diglossia with and without bilingualism. *Journal of Social Issues* 23: 29–38.
———. 1991. *Reversing language shift.* Clevedon: Multicultural Matters.
Godenzzi, J. C. 2008. Language policy and education in the Andes. In *Encyclopedia of language and education,* ed. S. May and N. H. Hornberger, 2nd ed., vol. 1, *Language policy and political issues in education,* 315–29. New York: Springer Science & Business Media.
Gómez, R. 2003. Sociolinguistic correlations in the Spanish spoken in the Andean region of Ecuador in the speech of the younger generation. Ph.D. diss., University of Toronto.
———. 2005. Attitudes towards the assibilation of rhotics and palatals. Paper presented at the Joint Session on Hispanic Linguistics, organized by the Canadian Association of Hispanists and the Canadian Linguistic Association, London, ON.
Gumperz, J. 1971. *Language in Social Groups,* ed. A. S. Dil. Stanford: Stanford Univ. Press.
Haboud, M. 1993. Actitud de la población mestiza urbana de Quito hacia el Quichua. *Pueblos Indígenas y Educación* 27–28: 133–67.
———. 1998. *Quichua y castellano en los Andes ecuatorianos: Los efectos de un contacto prolongado.* Quito: Abya-Yala.
———. 2000. *Interculturalidad y sordera visual.* Mimeo: Universidad Politécnica Salesiana.
———. 2003. *Quichua and Spanish in the Ecuadorian highlands: The effects of long-term contact.* Quito: PUCE.
———. 2004. Quichua language vitality: An Ecuadorian perspective. In *Quechua linguistics,* ed. K. King and N. Hornberger, special issue, *International Journal of the Sociology of Language* 167: 69–81.

Hamelink, C. 2000. Human rights: The next fifty years. In *Rights to language: Equity, power and education,* ed. R. Phillipson, 62–66. Mahwah, NJ: Lawrence Erlbaum Associates.

Hornberger, N. 1987. Schooltime, classtime, and academic learning time in rural highland Puno, Peru. *Anthropology and Education Quarterly* 18: 207–21.

Hornberger, N., and S. Coronel-Molina. 2004. Quechua language shift, maintenance, and revitalization in the Andes: The case for language planning. In *Quechua linguistics,* ed. K. King and N. Hornberger, special issue, *International Journal of the Sociology of Language* 167: 9–67.

Hornberger, N., and K. A. King. 1998. Authenticity and unification in Quechua language planning. *Language, Culture and Curriculum* 11(3): 390–410.

INEC (Instituto Nacional de Estadísticas y Censos). n.d. *Resumen Ejecutivo del Censo de 1990.* Quito: INEC.

King, K. A., and C. Benson. 2004. Indigenous language education in Bolivia and Ecuador: Contexts, changes, and challenges. In *Medium of instruction policies: Whose agenda? Which agenda?* ed. J. Tollefson and A. Tsui, 241–61. Mahwah, NJ: Lawrence Erlbaum.

King, K. A., and M. Haboud. 2002. Language planning and policy in Ecuador. *Current Issues in Language Planning* 3(4): 359–424.

Krainer, A. 1996. *Educacion intercultural bilingüe en el Ecuador.* Quito: Abya-Yala.

Luykx, A. 2000. Diversity in the new world order: State language policies and the internationalization of Quechua. Paper presented at the 2nd Spencer Early Career Institute in Anthropology and Education, Chicago.

Manducarios United. 2008. http://openentry.com/granvalle/EN/.

Movimiento de Unidad Plurinacional Pachakutik–Nuevo País. 2007. http://www.pachakutik.org.ec.

Mufwene, S. S. n.d. *Globalization and the myth of killer languages: What's really going on?* http://humanities.uchicago.edu/faculty/mufwene/publications/globalization-killerLanguages.pdf.

Office of the United Nations High Commissioner for Human Rights. 2007. *Declaration on the rights of persons belonging to national or ethnic, religious and linguistic minorities.* http://www.un-documents.net/a47r135.htm.

Phillipson, R., ed. 2000. *Rights to language: Equity, power and education.* Mahwah, NJ: Lawrence Erlbaum.

Pozzi-Escot, I. 1988. La educación bilingüe en el Perú: Una mirada retrospectiva y prospectiva. In *Pesquisas en lingüística Andina,* ed. L. E. López, 37–79. Lima-Puno: Consejo Nacional de Ciencia y Tecnología, Universidad Nacional del Altiplano-Puno, y GTZ.

PROEIB Andes. 1998. http://www.proeibandes.org.

Selverston, M. 1992. The 1990 indigenous movement in Ecuador: Politicized ethnicity as social movement. Papers on Latin America No. 32, Institute of Latin American and Iberian Studies, Columbia Univ.

Skutnabb-Kangas, T. 2000. *Linguistic genocide in education—Or worldwide diversity and human rights?* Mahwah, NJ: Lawrence Erlbaum.

Soto, I. 1997. Educación de adultos y bilingüismo: El caso ecuatoriano. *Pueblos Indígenas y Educación* 37–38: 69–80.

Universidad Intercultural de Nacionalidades y Pueblos Indígenas Amawtay Wasi. n.d. http://www.amawtaywasi.edu.ec.

von Gleich, U. 1994. Language spread policy: The case of Quechua in the Andean Republics of Bolivia, Ecuador, and Peru. *International Journal of the Sociology of Language* 107: 77–103.

World Conference on Linguistic Rights. 1996. *Universal declaration on linguistic rights.* http://www.unesco.org/cpp/uk/declarations/linguistic.pdf.

Yánez, C. 1989. *La educación indígena en el área Andina.* Quito: Abya-Yala.

Afro-Brazilian Women's Identities and Activism: National and Transnational Discourses

Jessica Franklin

Recognizing the inability of the state to effectively challenge long-standing barriers and the hesitancy of Brazilian society to fully integrate and accept black[1] women as equal and contributing members, Afro-Brazilian women have drawn on transnational discourses and networks to redefine their identities and to counter their marginalization. Black feminist perspectives, mainly emerging from the United States, have influenced Afro-Brazilian feminists and scholars and have contributed to the development of a distinct Afro-Brazilian feminist identity. Increased dialogue between Afro-Brazilian women activists and activists situated throughout the African diaspora has also been critical in the Brazilian context. These individuals have worked to strengthen the rights and voices of African descendents through the continuous exchange of ideas and mobilization strategies across national borders. The heightened participation of Afro-Brazilian women in international policy arenas and forums—including the United Nations Fourth World Conference on Women held in Beijing, China, in 1995 and the United Nations Conference on Racism held in Durban, South Africa, in 2001—has also been significant in the fight against racism in Brazil and the incorporation of human rights norms and models into local initiatives and federal legislation.

International, national, and local discussions and activism related to racial and gender inequalities have undoubtedly transformed social and political relations and become powerful vehicles for change in the twenty-first century. The constructs of race, gender, and class take on particular significance for Afro-Brazilian women (Lovell 2006, 64). They have intersected to effectively shape their experiences in Brazilian society and their demands for social transformation. At the national level, a crucial step in the process of consciousness building has been the recognition that for marginalized populations, such as Afro-Brazilian women, historical patterns of discrimination are fundamental to the expression of individual identities. The shared experiences and historical struggles for survival by these women have become a source of common strength and provide a crucial foundation for resistance against the dominant discourses of racial and gender inequality in Brazil.

The Brazilian state and society have served as the sites of political and social exclusion in this case, asserting and reproducing racial and gender stigmas that have left many Afro-Brazilian women unemployed or underemployed and below the poverty line. Afro-Brazilian men also face extreme forms of racial and gender discrimination. However, they still have higher rates of income and life expectancy. In a Human Development Index (HDI) study accounting for gender and ethnicity, Afro-Brazilian men rank 104th while Afro-Brazilian women rank 114th out of a total of 174 countries (Sant'-Anna 2001). Blacks also remain largely invisible in the country's top political, media, and economic circles (Htun 2004, 63). Although the Brazilian government has attempted to increase their political representation at the federal and municipal levels, Afro-Brazilian women have yet to achieve adequate recognition or representation in formal politics. The policy changes which have occurred, including the 1996 adoption by the Brazilian Congress of a quota system of twenty per cent for female candidates in municipal elections and the extension of this mechanism in 1998 to twenty-five per cent for general elections, have proved largely ineffective (Htun 2002, 741).

Despite their low numbers in political office, Afro-Brazilian women activists have managed to increase public awareness of racial and gender inequalities and challenge negative stereotypes of black women. They have played an active role within their communities, participating in neighbourhood coalitions and religious, cultural, and social movements. Black women's organizations, such as the Black Women's House of Culture (*Casa de Cultura da Mulher Negra*) and Geledes Black Women's Institute (*Geledes Instituto da Mulher Negra*) have received international and national recognition for their work to combat domestic violence and systemic forms of discrimination, and to secure legislative and constitutional reforms expanding the rights of historically disadvantaged groups (Reichmann 1999; Lebon 2007). Afro-Brazilian women have openly challenged attempts to generalize their identities and experiences and have celebrated the existence of diversity in a state that has, until recently, defined itself as racially homogenous. Yet it is important to note that the novel understandings of "race," identity, and the nation expressed throughout Afro-Brazilian women's activism have not developed in isolation.

In this case, distinct forms of racial and gender consciousness have emerged through an ongoing interplay between domestic politics, society and cultures, and transnational ideas, exchanges, and dialogues.

In this article, I argue that several key national and transnational factors have intersected to influence the construction of Afro-Brazilian women's identities and their social mobilization. I consider the impact of racial distinctions created in the colonial era and state policy on the identities of Afro-Brazilian women, emphasizing the myth of racial democracy and its manifestations. I also discuss the extensive social and economic inequalities faced by black women in Brazilian society and consider how these disparities have influenced the emergence, agendas, and actions of the black women's movement since the 1970s. Lastly, I examine how black feminist approaches, networks amongst activists situated in the African diaspora, and international forums on human rights and racism have served as important tools in the identity formation process and enhanced the agency of Afro-Brazilian women.

Identity and the State

Early constructions of racial and gender identities in Brazil can be traced back to the colonization of the country by Portuguese settlers in 1500 and later to the transatlantic slave trade. Beginning in 1600, roughly 4.5 million African slaves from Angola and different areas in West Africa came to Brazil (Curto and Lovejoy 2004). As Brazilian historian George Reid Andrews asserts, "Europeans may have viewed Africans as sharing a common racial identity, but most Africans did not learn about the identity until they arrived in the New World and were informed that they were all 'blacks'" (2004, 21). In addition to becoming conscious of their identity through skin colour, blacks quickly learned that white colonizers determined their rights and livelihood. Extremely cruel forms of abuse were inflicted upon the non-white population in Brazil. African, indigenous, and mixed-race women were frequently raped, tortured, and forced into prostitution (Silva Jr. 2001). Martha Abreu describes how Brazilian women were commonly separated and caricatured based on their skin tone: white women were characterized as suitable for marriage, mixed race or mulata women were presented as a coveted object of desire and sensuality, while black women were viewed as labourers and child bearers (2005, 271).

In the mid-1930s, influential social historian Gilberto Freyre introduced the ideology of racial democracy in an attempt to present a different picture of racial and gender relations in Brazilian society. According to Freyre, an amicable relationship between Portuguese colonizers and African slaves, and widespread miscegenation among the Brazilian population, allowed for the development of a racially democratic society (1946). A crucial component of this ideology is the depiction of mulata women as responsible for the creation of a racially harmonious nation and also as a constant threat to white men's social positioning because of their sexual allure and cunning (Goldstein 2003; Caldwell 2007). Kia Lilly Caldwell argues that Freyre's work naturalizes the association of Afro-Brazilian womanhood with manual labour and sexuality, and in turn legitimizes and sanctions historical patterns of sexual exploitation and economic domination (2007, 57). Afro-Brazilian women continue to confront these colonial depictions, which remain very much alive in Brazil's historical accounts and social imagery.

Brazilian intellectuals have argued that the construction of the ideology of racial democracy was a purposeful act spearheaded by elites to minimize the fact that during and following the influx of European immigrants in the 1920s and 1930s, Afro-Brazilians consistently remained in disadvantageous economic and social positions (Fernandes 1969; Hasenbalg 1979). This blatant disparity was not attributed to race but was characterized as a long-term effect of the emancipation of slaves, a result of class discrimination or a sheer coincidence (Nascimento 2007, 18). The state's refusal to recognize racially distinctive groups and the existence of racism stifled the identity formation and collective mobilization of Afro-Brazilians for decades (Htun 2004, 64).[2] The majority of the population, including blacks, accepted that racism did not exist in Brazil and reproduced these false assumptions in daily life (Twine 1998).

Only recently have efforts to counter the myth of racial democracy and to reveal the continued marginalization of the black population come to the forefront. A significant shift occurred in the 1980s with the withdrawal of the military regime in 1985 and the centennial of the abolition of slavery in 1988. Black militants and intellectuals emerged to openly challenge the myth of racial democracy and to reveal the presence of pervasive forms of racial discrimination (Lovell 2006, 65). Several black organizations, particularly the Movimento Negro Unificado (MNU), were central to the politicization of race that defined this period. Various forms of social activism emerged during the early stages of Brazil's transition to democracy. Women, Catholics, landless peasants, and the urban poor worked alongside black movement organizations to demand improved economic and social policy from the state.

Despite the increased political mobilization of disparate groups over the past two decades, Brazil has faced marked challenges in the process of redemocratization. The opening of the country's economic borders to global capital has been met with economic decline. The liberalization of markets in the early 1990s opened Brazilian industry to higher degrees of foreign competition and pushed those already situated in vulnerable socio-economic positions into deeper disparity. In addition, the Brazilian government has faced pressure from the American administration to implement a well-established rule of law, forcing political leaders to be accountable to all branches of government and their constituents. Responding to this heavy criticism and seeking to show its vested interest in the re-democratization process, the country has recently embarked on the challenging process of replacing the notion of racial democracy with an American-influenced system of affirmative action. In 1995 the federal government, under the direction of President Fernando Henrique Cardoso, acknowledged the need to incorporate "revolutionary equality policies" (Reichmann 1999, 22) into Brazilian legislation. The National Human Rights Program has since presented specific policies aimed at improving the positioning of black individuals in Brazilian society, including the controversial adoption of educational quotas by individual states to increase the enrolment of black students in public universities (Htun 2004, 67).

The Mobilization of Afro-Brazilian Women

Despite some advances in legislation, the disproportionate and continued discrimination faced by Afro-Brazilian women is striking. According to the 2000 Census, Afro-Brazilians represent 48.5 per cent of the population. However, Elisa Larkin Nascimento, Director of IPEAFRO Afro-Brazilian Studies and Research Institute in Rio de Janeiro, contends that estimates increase to 70 or 80 per cent when discrepancies in self-identification are considered (2007, 44).[3] Researchers have estimated that the roughly 38 million black women in Brazil make up 23 per cent of the total population (Barsted and Hermann 2001). Their levels of employment, reproductive health, and income are substantially inferior to those of white women, black men, and the rest of the Brazilian population. Black women occupy the lowest ranks in the Brazilian labour market and are more prone to informal and uncertain forms of work. Nearly 80 per cent of black women in the Brazilian workforce are manual labourers, with most working as domestic servants for menial wages or job protection (Nascimento 2007, 47). Statistical analysts and researchers have pointed to systemic forms of racism and sexism to explain this trend, which has persisted in spite of Afro-Brazilian women's increasing education levels (see Lovell 2000; Safa 2007). Extreme racial disparities are also visible in the areas of health care and reproduction. Recent studies indicate sharp differences in terms of reproductive risks and access to health care between the white and black population. Although the infant mortality rate has dropped significantly in Brazil during the twentieth century, Lucila Bandeira Beato of Geledes asserts that the "differential between African descendant and white children is still very high" (Beato 2004, 771). Her findings show that between 1977 and 1993, the decline in infant mortality rates among the children of white mothers was forty-three per cent in contrast to twenty-five per cent for children of Afro-Brazilian women (ibid.). In addition to this, the incidence of maternal death is highest among Afro-Brazilian women.

In order to improve these conditions and to challenge the pervasiveness of racism in Brazilian society, black women became involved in the organization of the black movement and the communication of the anti-racist message in the early 1980s. However, many felt that this male-led and -dominated movement did not sufficiently address their needs and struggles (Lovell 2006, 66). Effectively marginalized by sexism in the black movement, several activists became more politically engaged in their communities and looked to the growing national feminist movement to voice their concerns. Yet, the marked differences in the social experiences of black and white women led to significant divisions. While a number of black women had turned to feminism to avoid the blatant sexism they encountered in black organizations, they quickly found that racial differences prevented the achievement of commonality in the Brazilian feminist movement (Caldwell 2007, 153). These exclusions provided the impetus for the creation of autonomous black women's organizations throughout the 1980s and early 1990s (Lovell 2006, 66).

Black women's organizations have sought not only to distinguish their focus and experiences from the feminist and black movements but to utilize the skills and lessons they had gleaned from these struggles. Heading up research on black women's experiences and organizing local forums and national conferences, Afro-Brazilian women's organizations have shed light on their historical socio-economic subordination in the Brazilian context. Activists achieved particular success with the inclusion of important anti-racist and anti-sexist laws in the 1988 Constitution. This was the first Brazilian Constitution to reject all forms of discrimination and to establish human rights as one of the core principles of the Federal Republic of Brazil. Black women's organizations were critical in the development of several amendments, including Item 42 of Article 5, which explicitly stipulates that the practice of racism is a serious crime punishable under law, and Article 215, which protects expressions of indigenous and Afro-Brazilian culture and those of other ethnically distinctive groups in Brazilian society (Barsted and Hermann 2001, 58–59).

In the new millennium the panorama of social mobilization in Brazil has changed, not only for black women's organizations but for all black-focused groups. According to Afro-Brazilian female activist and scholar Luiza Bairros, diverging political agendas and mobilization platforms have resulted in a critical fragmentation. In an interview in 2007 she explained that black organizations had previously adopted more nationally oriented strategies and had been largely influenced and represented by the predominantly male organizations. However, these organizations can no longer be identified as guided by one particular force or striving toward a specific goal. Each deals with different manifestations of racism and comes together as a collective to provide support on key projects. Examples are found in groups focused on *quilombos* (settlement communities created by runaway slaves before the abolition of slavery in 1888), domestic violence, and AIDS awareness. The most significant change is in the consciousness of these organizations of the similar struggles of other marginalized populations and the transnational linkages that have been forged along the lines of feminism, human rights, and social justice.

Building the Black Feminist Discourse
Despite that feminism in Brazil has in recent years received the distinction of being "Latin America's largest, most vibrant, and most diverse feminist movement" (Htun 2002, 73), it was not until the mid-1970s that feminism emerged in that country as a formidable political force and ideology (Pitanguy 2002). For years it was equated with mainstream feminism in the US, which was viewed as focused on middle-class white women and their struggle for equality in the workplace and in male-dominated literary and academic circles (Sadlier 1994, 164). As a result, little English feminist writing and teaching was translated into Portuguese. When variants of North American and European feminism began to receive increased attention in Brazil, they were met with support by some middle-class white women, who were already attending universities in higher numbers than men and making notable strides in formal politics (Still 1999). Marxist feminists saw this approach as insufficient because of its minimal consideration of class-based inequalities. They viewed Brazilian gender relations in the context of the broader class structure and appealed to the sisterhood of all women subordinated by the capitalist structure (Saffioti 1976). As a result, Brazilian feminist scholars and activists tended to reduce the importance of race and privilege the concerns of white women, not recognizing that their heightened social positioning was directly linked to the exploitation of black women in the domestic realm.

Since the late 1970s, feminists of colour in the United States, Britain, and various developing countries have questioned the presumption put forth by unitary feminist approaches that the complex identities and experiences of women could be generalized. Particularly in the United States, many black feminists have felt estranged from mainstream feminism and sought to create distinctive conceptualizations of feminism, gender, and identity based on their historical narratives and experiences.[4] They have criticized mainstream feminism for paying insufficient attention to the various ways that gender and womanhood are defined for women of other races, classes, religions, and cultures (ibid., 219). A central aspect of these perspectives is the assertion and recognition of difference, a position that rejects the prevailing notion that sameness produces harmony (hooks 1992, 1996).

The critiques of feminist theory emerging from US women of colour have particularly resonated with black Brazilian feminists, who were publishing their own critiques of mainstream feminism and producing studies on the marginalized position of black women in Brazilian society by the early 1980s (Gonzalez 1982; Carneiro and Santos 1985). These works identified significant limitations with Brazilian feminisms which often evaded racial differences and reinforced the myth of racial democracy. Former MNU leader and black feminist Leila Gonzalez argued that these works lost much of their impact by making abstract a fact of great importance — the pluricultural and multiracial character of Brazilian society (Gonzalez 1988). Afro-Brazilian feminist Sueli Carneiro later noted that "classic feminist discourse on women's oppression fails to account for the qualitative differences in oppression suffered by black women, and the effects of those multiple oppressions on black women's identity" (1999, 218). These women not only challenged the narrow conceptualizations of gender but also affirmed the importance of a distinct historical trajectory recognizing the multiple forms of discrimination faced by Afro-Brazilian women. Their works have strengthened the black female's perception of her position in Brazilian society and her determination to be represented in all significant spheres of national life (Duke 2003).

Emphasizing the Local

Several Afro-Brazilian feminists have adapted concepts and ideas emerging from black feminist scholars and authors in the United States to discuss their own lives and the specific cultural and social context of their environment. An example is found in my discussion with Lucia Xavier, general coordinator of Municipal and National Projects for the black women's organization Criola in Rio de Janeiro. Questioning her about the influence of non-Brazilian feminists on her perspectives, she responded that Afro-American feminists and scholars such as Angela Davis and bell hooks have had a substantial impact both on her individual perspectives and on the wider debates between feminists in Brazil (Xavier 2007). She explained that these writings provide a critical theoretical component in broader discussions of the historical stratification and social realities of black women in Brazil and offer significant insight into the construction of racial and gender identities.

Yet some Brazilian feminist scholars have suggested that the ideas emerging from the US context have been uncritically imported and are deserving of increased scrutiny. Maria Elisa Cevasco argues that Brazilian feminists need to discriminate among the ideas they import by putting them up against the stark realities of Brazilian history and society (1999, 174). Many of the activists I interviewed did make reference to the groundbreaking works of bell hooks, Alice Walker, Patricia Hill Collins, and others, but they also expressed the need for increased consideration of the local context in feminist analyses of black women's experiences and identities. Local activism, in the forms of neighbourhood associations, organizations for domestic workers, and women's collectives, have been extremely influential in the building of a collective social and political consciousness in Brazil. These engagements have empowered women in their homes, jobs, and communities and helped to address localized manifestations of racial and gender discrimination. The extensive involvement of Afro-Brazilian women in these local spaces demands increased examination not only in feminist scholarship but in social movements and Brazilian society.

The Importance of Intersectionality

A key adaptation from US black feminist discourses has been the theory of intersectionality. The intersectional paradigm focuses on how the understandings, interactions, experiences, and representations of an individual's identity are the product of intersecting constructions of race, gender, sexuality, class, and other identity forms. It examines the socially constructed nature of these categories and the role they collectively play in determining the individual's identity and social location. The extensive works of Afro-American female scholars such as Kimberle Crenshaw and Patricia Hill Collins have been crucial to the reconsideration of race, gender, and other identities as mutually influential constructs (Crenshaw 1991; Collins 2000). The influence of this paradigm is visible in recent black feminist writings in the Brazilian context. One of the most compelling works is that of Sueli Carneiro, who describes the importance of a feminist perspective that confronts the multiple types of oppression faced by black women. She identifies the emergence of a new feminist and anti-racist introspection that brings the struggles of the black movement and women's movement together and creates a new political identity deriving from the condition of being a black woman (2001). The challenge for Afro-Brazilian feminists will be to engage with Brazilian government and academia on these new and innovative ways to consider the identities and experiences of black women in Brazil.

Engagements with the African Diaspora

Situated within the broad transnational context, women of African descent share a distinct and complex history (Collins 2000, 231). Their similar experiences of historical exclusion from full citizenship and political equality have provided the necessary grounding for novel forms of transnational knowledge production, dialogues, and social organization between black women across the globe (Perry 2009). Yet some scholars suggest it requires more than shared experiences of discrimination to effectively construct and mobilize collective racial identities. Livio Sansone argues that Afro-Brazilian musical techniques, tastes in hair, and ideas of beauty run counter to essentialized representations of blackness and demonstrate more complex and contradictory uses of black culture and identity (2003, 174–76). He suggests that black cultures today are dictated less by slavery and colonialism and more by globalization and the diasporic character of ethnic identities.

While this perspective identifies the powerful role played by globalization in the process of identity formation, this argument is often contested by scholars and activists who suggest that the pervasive racial designations for black women developed in the period of slavery and colonialism still persist. Although the process of racialization may differ depending on the individual country, the detrimental impacts on black women's identities and self-image remain the same. Caldwell states that "the continuation of colonial social and economic relationships is perhaps most evident in Afro-Brazilian women's contemporary role as the mae preta or mammy" (Caldwell 2007, 73). By emphasizing the fluidity of Afro-Brazilian women's identities, the influence of historical oppressions and past narratives on individual and collective identities and social activism in the contemporary period is too easily dismissed. Current black women's organizations in Brazil have sought to challenge derogatory characterizations by celebrating the presence and contributions of black women in African culture and history. Chair of the Brazilian Network of Black Women's Organizations Jurema Werneck asserts that these groups have drawn on organizational and behavioural models developed by black women leaders that predate European colonialism. She explains that the honouring of African queens in cultural celebrations, the planning of religious gatherings and activities, and the clandestine or open meetings of women's societies are some of the historical activities that demonstrate black women's leadership, their responsibilities in the public and private realm, and their political impact (Werneck 2007, 103).

The Afro-Caribbean and Afro-Latin American Women's Network

Recognizing the congruency of their historical experiences and current social location with other women throughout the diaspora, Afro-Brazilian women activists have committed to the building of transformative transnational alliances. One of the most meaningful and influential transnational advocacy networks has been the Afro-Latin American and Afro-Caribbean women's network. Founded in 1992, it has provided black women with an autonomous forum to combat sexist and racist practices in their countries and across the region (Barr and Careaga 2002). For Afro-Brazilian female activists, the network has placed Brazilian racial dynamics in dialogue with those in other African diaspora communities. Women from thirty-three countries are represented, including Colombia, Costa Rica, Nicaragua, Peru, and the United States. Since its inception, regular forums have been held to discuss the impact of present neo-liberal economic policies on the cultural, spiritual, and political contexts of each country and how New Leftist politics and economic mandates affect the livelihood of black women.

The recent Managua Declaration, which emerged from the preparatory meeting for the Regional Conference of the Americas against Racism in 2006, reaffirms the network's commitment to collective leadership and the incorporation of perspectives of gender, ethnicity, and race in domestic policies and international measures. It also recognizes the importance of creating and expanding new alliances to positively transform the societies in which women of the diaspora reside. Despite its significant accomplishments, the network has faced notable challenges. Werneck argues this is because it has failed to develop "prompt strategies for common political actions and agenda setting" (2007, 111). Furthermore, she notes that the network has been unable to deal with internal differences and conflicts, and as a result has yet to establish a more concrete position in the face of economic globalization (ibid., 111). Yet, as Werneck correctly asserts, the obstacles faced by the Afro-Latin American and Caribbean Network represent many of the impasses faced by black women's organizations seeking to strengthen connections across the region and the world.

Encountering Obstacles

Despite the growing connectedness of citizens, organizations, and information, extensive contact between groups remains limited. Lucia Xavier stresses that funding is the most significant impediment to the transnational organization of black women. In discussing Criola's ongoing work with women's organizations across the Latin American region, she explained that "They are poor organizations... connections are still limited and slow... there is a problem of access. There are limited resources and salaries and this makes it difficult to get to know each other" (Xavier 2007). Funding for black women's organizations frequently comes from European-based non-governmental organizations and international agencies focused on social and economic development and human rights. These agencies provide a set amount for a particular time period or program, but often funding is removed or finished prior to completion of the specified goals. Activists also express hesitancy to take funds from certain institutions, especially those based in the United States, for fear their initiatives will be tainted by the underlying political agenda of the grant organization. Some Afro-Latin and Afro-Brazilian feminists hesitate to link themselves with their Afro-American counterparts, believing their situation to be completely different from that of black women situated in a developed country. Language barriers and educational backgrounds widen this divide. The task for Afro-Brazilian women lies in continuing to create sustainable cross-border coalitions with black women of the diaspora, recognizing that historical oppressions have resulted in common challenges and barriers to mobilization (Collins 2000, 235).

Entering the International Human Rights Arena

Since the early 1990s, a concerted women's movement has focused on the international human rights arena in their efforts to make countries more responsive to the realities of gender inequality (Romany 2000, 54). According to Barbara Schulman, human rights frameworks have proven effective because they are "transnational not only in concept but in formal structure" (2004, 104). The strategic turn towards human rights has generated exchanges and forums on identity, equality, and rights across territorial, political, and ethnic boundaries. Afro-Brazilian women have become actively involved in this movement, and in turn have contributed to a renewed interest in the relationship between race, gender, and human rights. Engaging in dialogue with women's organizations throughout the world, they have given visibility to the problem of racism in Brazil and the historical and cultural specificity of their identities and experiences.

Why Human Rights?

Recognizing that many of the challenges faced by their communities are linked to the same economic, social, and political forces marginalizing others around the world, Afro-Brazilian women activists have emphasized the importance of dialogue and action. While the campaigns of the international women's movement—focused on reproductive rights, eliminating employment barriers, and decreasing poverty and illiteracy rates—have been supported by Afro-Brazilian feminists, there has been a growing realization that the issues confronting black women in Brazil and across the region go far beyond gender discrimination. More specifically, what lacked was adequate consideration of the racial dimension of gender oppression. Realizing this disconnect, and identifying the powerful linkage between women's rights and human rights and the potential for widespread change, black women have seen a clear opening for their agenda. In this respect, Afro-Brazilian women have been able to access the spectrum of human rights through their support of women's rights, and, once in this sphere, emphasize the importance of race. Rosana Heringer, a long-time women's and minority rights advocate in Brazil, points out that the human rights approach serves as an umbrella that multiple perspectives and organizations can fall under (2007). In an interview in

2007 she told me that this arena holds a particular appeal for Afro-Brazilian women and other marginalized groups because it can be used to address the multiple forms of discrimination faced by this segment and to stimulate conversations with a government that has been resistant to internal criticism (Heringer 2007).

Applying Human Rights Models

The legal texts adopted by the United Nations and ratified by Brazil have proven to be strategic tools in the struggles to guarantee human rights at the national level. Afro-Brazilian women have called on the government to implement legislation based on the Convention for the Elimination of All Forms of Racial Discrimination (CERD) and the Convention on the Elimination of All Forms of Discrimination Against Women (CEDAW), which were ratified in 1968 and 1984, respectively. The most notable inclusion of anti-racial discrimination in Brazilian legislation was Law 7716 in 1989. This law deals with crimes resulting from racial prejudice. In 1997 the government expanded its focus to include acts arising not only from discrimination based on race or colour but also discrimination based on ethnicity, religion, or nationality. Other legal reforms introduced since the ratification of the CEDAW include legislation on the right to family planning, the criminalization of sexual harassment, and provisions for restraining orders in domestic abuse cases (Barsted and Hermann 2001).

Specific conventions have also been translated into movement activities. Some black women's organizations, such as *Fala Preta!*, have incorporated the Universal Declaration of Human Rights and the CEDAW in their statutes. *Geledes* has a legal studies centre that produces studies about racial inequality and the justice system in Brazil and seeks to improve existing national legislation. Their SOS racism program encourages individuals to speak up if they have been a victim of a racial crime and provides free legal assistance to those wanting to prosecute offenders. In this case, international human rights legislation has assisted black women in combatting inequalities and promoting new and multifaceted visions of citizenship and equal rights.

Beijing and Durban: Defining Moments for a Movement

The use of the United Nations as a forum to address and expose racial and gender divisions at the national level by Afro-Brazilian women can be traced back to the mid-1970s. *Manifestos das Mulhers Negras* (The Manifestos of Black Women) presented at the United Nations Decade for Women in the 1975 was one of the first documents that brought attention to black women's social exclusion and revealed the gendered aspects of racial discrimination in Brazil (Caldwell 2001, 223). At the World Conference on Human Rights in

Vienna in 1993, black women's groups were critical in the recognition of women's rights as human rights and lobbied for the organization of a World Conference focused on racism and intolerance, which culminated in Durban, South Africa in 2001. Afro-Brazilian female delegates at the 1994 World Conference on Population and Development in Cairo, Egypt, demanded freedom for discriminated groups to challenge racist and control-seeking policies.

In preparation for the Fourth World Conference on Women in 1995, over eight hundred women's organizations participated in the National Articulation of Brazilian Women for Beijing (Alvarez et al. 1998, 309). The Articulation facilitated the development of local women's forums and increased networking and cooperation amongst Brazilian women activists (Alvarez 2000). Historically uninvolved Brazilian states, such as the predominately black-populated northeast, played an instrumental role. This conference made significant strides in the recognition of race and ethnicity as causes of discrimination and factors of inequality. It also acknowledged the importance of domestic and informal labour in the global economy and demanded increased consideration of women's skills that are not sufficiently compensated in formal sectors of the economy (Correa 1995).

Afro-Brazilian activist and Professor Joselina da Silva suggests that it is the preparation for such conferences that has the most powerful influence on the strategies and cohesion of the black women's movement in Brazil. During an interview in 2007, she told me that the preparation process is the most significant course of action for the movement, more than participation in the event (da Silva 2007). The United Nations conferences provide a reason for women's groups throughout the region to meet and discuss what is taking place in the lives of black women. Activists are forced to define the mobilization goals and become organized by choosing delegates and engaging in discussion of the major issues at the municipal, national, and regional level. From this dialogue a distinct kind of motivation and excitement develops that propels the movement forward. She believes that the movement is strengthened through these extensive conversations because activists become more aware of the actual needs of the women they represent and more prepared to articulate their concerns on the international scale.

The Durban conference is often characterized as a watershed event for the black women's movement because it forced Brazil to expose and reject its widely held myth of racial democracy and showed the capacity of Afro-Brazilian female activists to advance race- and gender-specific claims. As the conference approached, race became a fiercely contested topic in Brazilian media and politics. The pronounced invisibility of Afro-Brazilians in political office, universities, and television programming became the focus of news stories, intellectual debates, and activist platforms (Htun 2004, 82). With the largest delegation outside of South Africa at Durban, Afro-Brazilian activists were able to incorporate many of their concerns into the conference proceedings and official documents. Drawing upon their previous experiences at international forums, black feminists worked closely with the Brazilian government delegation to clearly articulate their demands and to encourage open communication and collaboration. According to Edna Roland, the appointed rapporteur for Brazil at the meeting, the Platform for Action produced at the meeting went further on issues of antiracism and sexism than any of the previous documents emerging from United Nations conferences. In a recent interview with me, she discussed how the Platform specifically incorporates race and gender and recognizes the different ways in which racism materializes itself for men and women—an implicit reference to the complex situation in Brazil (Roland 2007). It also recommends policies of affirmative action and other reparations for victims of racism. In this respect, Durban was an extremely powerful experience for the country of Brazil and for Afro-Brazilian women, causing a drastic shift in the mindset of the population and strengthening the calls of historically marginalized groups to end racial discrimination (Htun 2004, 82).

Conclusion

Afro-Brazilian women have made notable strides in confronting racial and gender inequalities and countering negative associations of blackness and womanhood with poverty and weakness. However, their struggle to translate international commitments and conventions into national public policy continues. Proposed policies and projects to foster black women's health and educational and economic development have repeatedly fallen short because of restricted budgets or the diversion of funds. The Brazilian government has reiterated its commitment to support the Durban Platform for Action and to comply with the recommendations of the United Nations Human Rights Committee, but for the most part these statements have not been translated into action.

Several historical, civil, and political forces, including local and international feminisms, the redemocratization process in Brazil, and the international human rights movement, have influenced the redefinition of Afro-Brazilian women's identities. When examining the complexities in black women's identity formation and social mobilization, the impact of the national ideology of racial democracy and the deeply ingrained patterns of racial and sexual discrimination cannot be understated. However, racial, gender, class, and national differences, not ideas of sameness, have defined the latest phase in the search and struggle for Afro-Brazilian women's identity. They have built upon black women's history of survival and agency, enhancing their local activism and feminist practices and participating in transnational exchanges with women throughout the African diaspora. The universality of women's international human rights has been embraced by the movement, which continues to use international forums and existing human rights law as tools in changing their situation. Although rapid change has yet to occur in the national arena, Afro-Brazilian women are gradually gaining the leverage necessary to expose and challenge the manifestations of racism and sexism within the borders of Brazil and beyond.

Notes

This work was carried out with the aid of a grant from the International Development Research Centre, Ottawa, Canada.

1. This article uses the terms "Afro-Brazilian," "Afro-descendent," and "black" interchangeably to refer to Brazilians of African ancestry. Each term has been utilized to identify this segment of the Brazilian population in the scholarly literature and popular discourse on race relations in Brazil.
2. It should be noted that members of the Afro-Brazilian have historically utilized grievances of informal segregation and racial oppression to organize along racial and cultural lines, although not to the degree that has occurred in recent decades. The oldest Afro-Brazilian political party is the Frente Negra Brasileira (FNB), which emerged in 1930s. Its general message encouraged the moral uplift and material advancement of Afro-Brazilians and motivated blacks to participate in the political arena (Andrews 1991, 149).
3. The major challenge when attempting to grasp the economic and social plight of Afro-Brazilian women is the lack of systematic research articulating race, gender, and ethnic data in Brazil. An exception is found in Lebon's comprehensive analysis (2007). The critical barrier in the assessment of this data has been the arbitrary racial categorizations used in the Brazilian Census. Two categories are used to identify African descendants, *preta* and *parda*, which translate into "dark-skinned black" and "brown." To calculate the sum of the Afro-Brazilian population the two categories are combined. However, there has been a notable tendency among African descendants to classify themselves as white due to widespread whitening ideologies (Nascimento 2007, 44). These ingrained misconceptions have resulted in distorted figures.
4. Refer to the works of Amos and Parmar (1984), hooks (1984), Hull, Bell Scott, and Smith (1982), and Mohanty, Russo, and Torres (1991).

References

Abreu, M. 2005. Mulatas, criolos and morenas: Racial hierarchy, gender relations, and the national identity in Postabolition popular song. In *Gender and slave emancipation in Atlantic world*, ed. P. Scully and D. Paton, 267–88. Durham, NC: Duke Univ. Press.

Alvarez, S. E. 1998. Latin American feminism "go global": Trends of the 1990s and challenges for the new mellenium. In *Cultures of politics, politics of culture: Re-visioning Latin American social movements*, ed. S. E. Alvarez, E. Dagnino, and A. Escoban, 293–324. Boulder, CO: Westview.

———. 2000. Translating the global: Effects of transnational organizing on local feminist discourses and practices in Latin America. *Meridians: A Journal of Feminisms, Race and Transnationalism* 1(1) (Autumn): 29–67.
Amos, V., and P. Parmar. 1984. Challenging imperialism: Feminism. *Feminist Review* 17 (Autumn): 3–19.
Andrews, G. R. 1991. *Blacks & whites in São Paulo, Brazil, 1888–1988*. Madison: Univ. of Wisconsin Press.
———. 2004. *Afro-Latin America: 1800–2000*. Oxford/New York: Oxford Univ. Press.
Bairros, L. 2007. Interview by author. Salvador, Brazil. 26 October.
Barr, E. C., and G. Careaga, eds. 2002. *Poderes cuestionados: Sexismo y racismo en America Latina*. San Jose: Diseno Editorial.
Barsted, L. L., and J. Hermann. 2001. Black and Indigenous women: Law vs. reality. In *Brazil: Women and legislation against racism*, ed. L. L. Barsted, J. Hermann, and M. E. Vieira de Mello, 39–84. Rio de Janeiro: Cepia.
Beato, L. B. 2004. Inequality and human rights of African descendants in Brazil. *Journal of Black Studies* 34(6) (May): 776–86.
Caldwell, K. L. 2001. Racialized boundaries: Women's studies and the "question of difference" in Brazil. *Journal of Negro Education* 70(3) (Summer): 219–30.
———. 2007. *Negras in Brazil: Re-envisioning black women, citizenship, and the politics of identity*. New Brunswick, NJ: Rutgers Univ. Press.
Carneiro, S. 1999. Black women's identity in Brazil. In *Race in contemporary Brazil: From indifference to inequality*, ed. R. Reichmann, 217–28. Pennsylvania: Pennsylvania State Univ. Press.
———. 2001. Rendering Feminism blacker: The situation of black women in Latin America from a gender perspective, translated by Manuel de Freitas. *Lola Press* 16 (November). http://www.lolapress.org/index/authors.htm.
Carneiro, S., and T. Santos. 1985. *Mulher negra*. São Paulo: Nobel/Conselho Estadual da Condicao Feminina.
Cevasco, M. E. 1999. Importing feminist criticism. In *Brazilian Feminisms*, ed. S. Ribeiro de Oliveira and J. Still, 173–88. Nottingham: Univ. of Nottingham Press.
Collins, P. Hill. 2000. *Black Feminist thought: Knowledge, consciousness, politics of empowerment*. 2nd ed. Abingdon: Routledge.
Correa, S. 1995. Thank God it's over: Histories and geographies of Beijing, translated by V. Swarbrick. *Lola Press* 4 (November–March). http://www.lolapress.org/index/authors.htm.
Crenshaw, K. 1991. Mapping the margins: Intersectionality, identity politics, and violence against women of color. *Stanford Law Review* 43(6) (July): 1241–99.
Curto, J. C., and P. E. Lovejoy. 2004. Introduction. In *Enslaving connections: Changing cultures of Africa and Brazil during the era of slavery*, eds. J. C. Curto and P. E. Lovejoy, 11–18. New York: Humanity Books.
da Silva, J. 2007. Interview by author. Juaziero do Norte, Brazil, 31 October.
Duke, D. 2003. Alzira Rufino's *a casa de cultura de mulher negra* as a form of female empowerment: A look at the dynamics of a Black women's organization in Brazil today. *Women Studies International Forum* 26(4) (July–August): 357–68.
Fernandes, F. 1969. *The negro in Brazilian society*. New York: Columbia Univ. Press.
Freyre, G. 1946. *The masters and the slaves: A study in the development of Brazilian civilization*. New York: Alfred Knopf.

Goldstein, D. M. 2003. *Laughter out of place: Race, class, violence, and sexuality in a Rio shantytown*. Berkeley: Univ. of California Press.
Gonzalez, L. 1982. A mulher negra na sociedade brasileira. In *O lugar mulher*, ed. M. T. Luz, 87–106. Rio de Janiero: Edicoes Graal.
———. 1988. *Women organizing for change: Confronting crisis in Latin America*. Rome: Isis International in Coordination with DAWN.
Hasenbalg, C. 1979. *Discriminacao e desigualdades raciais no Brazil*. Rio de Janeiro: Graal.
Heringer, R. 2007. Interview by author. Rio de Janeiro, Brazil, 27 September.
hooks, b. 1984. *Feminist theory: From margin to the center*. Boston: South End Press.
———. 1992. *Black looks: Race and representation*. Toronto: Between the Lines.
———. 1995. *Killing rage: Ending racism*. New York: H. Holt and Company.
Htun, M. 2002. Puzzles of women's rights in Brazil. *Social Research* 69(3) (Fall): 733–51.
———. 2004. From racial democracy to affirmative action: Changing state policy on race in Brazil. *Latin American Research Review* 39(1) (February): 60–89.
Hull, G., P. Bell Scott, and B. Smith, eds. 1982. *All the women are white, all the blacks are men, but some of us are brave*. Old Westbury, NY: Feminist Press.
Lebon, N. 2007. Beyond confronting the myth of racial democracy: The role of Afro-Brazilian women scholars and activists. *Latin American Perspectives* 34(6) (November): 52–76.
Lovell, P. A. 2000. Gender, race and the struggle for social justice in Brazil. *Latin American Perspectives* 27(6) (November): 85–103.
———. 2006. Race, gender, and work in São Paulo, Brazil, 1960–2000. *Latin American Research Review* 41(3) (October): 63–87.
Mohanty, C. T., A. Russo, and L. Torres, eds. 1991. *Third world women and the politics of Feminism*. Bloomington: Indiana Univ. Press.
Nascimento, E. L. 2007. *The sorcery of color: Identity, race and gender in Brazil*. Philadelphia: Temple Univ. Press.
Perry, K. Y. 2009. The groundings with my sisters: Toward a black diasporic feminist agenda in the americas. *The Scholar and the Feminist Online* 7(2) (Spring). http://www.barnard.edu/sfuonline/africana/print_perry.htm.
Pitanguy, J. 2002. Bridging the local and the global: Feminism in Brazil and the international human rights agenda. *Social Research* 69(3) (Fall): 805–20.
Reichmann, R., ed. 1999. *Race in contemporary Brazil: Indifference to inequality*. Pennsylvania: Pennsylvania State Univ. Press.
Roland, E. 2007. Interview by author. São Paulo, Brazil. 11 October.
Romany, C. 2000. Themes for a conversation on race and gender in international human rights law. In *Global critical race feminism: An international reader*, ed. A. K. Wing, 53–66. New York: New York Univ. Press.
Sadlier, D. J. 1999. Theory and pedagogy in the Brazilian northeast. In *Brazilian Feminisms*, ed. S. Ribeiro de Oliveira and J. Still, 163–72. Nottingham: Univ. of Nottingham Press.
Safa, H. I. 2007. Racial and gender inequality in Latin America: Afro-decendent women respond. *Feminist Africa: Diaspora Voices* 7: 49–66.
Saffioti, H. I. B. 1976. Relationship of sex and social class in Brazil. In *Sex and class in Latin America*, ed. J. Nash and H. I. Safa, 147–59. New York: Praeger Publishers.
Sansone, L. 2003. *Blackness without ethnicity: Constructing race in Brazil*. New York: Palgrave Macmillan.

Sant'Anna, W. 2001. Ethnic/Racial and gender inequalities in Brazil: The possible revelations of the human development indexes and the development index adjusted for gender. *Proposta* 88/89: 16–33.

Schulman, B. 2004. Effective organizing in terrible times: The strategic value of human rights for transnational anti-racist feminisms. *Meridans: Feminism, Race, Transnationalism* 4(2) (Spring): 102–8.

Silva Jr., H. 2001. Black women and the need for specific judicial demands. In *Brazil: Women and legislation against racism*, ed. L. L. Barsted, J. Hermann, and M. E. Vieira de Mello, 39–84. Rio de Janeiro: Cepia.

Still, J. 1991. Introduction. In *Brazilian Feminisms*, ed. S. Ribeiro de Oliveira and J. Still, 1–14. Nottingham: Univ. of Nottingham Press.

Twine, F. W. 1998. *Racism in a racial democracy: The maintenance of white supremacy in Brazil.* New Brunswick, NJ: Rutgers Univ. Press.

Werneck, J. 2007. Of Ialodes and Feminists: Reflections on black women's political action in Latin America and the Caribbean. *Cultural Dynamics* 19(1) (March): 99–113.

Xavier, L. 2007. Interview by the author. Rio de Janeiro, Brazil, 4 October.

Legal Creolization, "Permanent Exceptionalism," and Caribbean Sojourners' Truths

Adrian Smith

Introduction

Over twenty thousand "unfree" labourers sojourn in Canada by way of the Seasonal Agricultural Workers Program (SAWP).[1] Since the inception of the SAWP in 1966, mostly male sojourners arrive from the Commonwealth Caribbean—as well as from Mexico and most recently Guatemala[2]—to pick tobacco and other horticulture, fruits, and vegetables.[3] The lives of migrant farm workers are entangled in complex social processes that, on certain accounts, are best captured by the idea of transnationalism (see Satzewich and Wong 2003; Basok 2004). In oscillating between Canada and the West Indies, these workers are ensnared within a provisional existence—the implications of which are not yet fully explored. Characterized in post-colonial theoretical terms as a condition of "inbetweenity," transnational migratory practices are said to encourage the formation of hybrid identities or hybridity. On this account, the post-colonial basis of workers' transnational existence rests on the mounting popularity of the post-national reimagining of the migration of people.

Satzewich and Wong (2003, 364, 376–78) accept the explanatory utility of the concept, reasoning "that the continuities and discontinuities accompanying transnationalism amount to a transformation of the political economy of immigration, race, and ethnicity" in Canada. They make clear, however, that it suffers certain limitations. Others are far less swayed by transnationalism's utility (see for example Kivisto 2001). In light of the discord, there is a need to make explicit the basis for any reliance upon transnationalism. While I employ the concept often as an intensifier, a short form stressing the social practices, encounters, and overall experience of migrant farm workers, I acknowledge that it is open to debate. Posing questions about how we understand the intricate rhythms of migrant farm workers' lives, I strive to interrogate the socio-legal[4] bases of their collective migratory experience, viewing that experience through the lens of law's role in shaping their collective consciousness and behaviour or, in a phrase, legal consciousness (see Smith 2005).

Where do Caribbean migrant farm workers, as participants in home as well as host labour markets, albeit in limited and discontinuous forms, develop their legal consciousness? How does the transnational working experience modify workers' conceptions of host marginalization and exploitation? How mobile is resistance—that is, do forms of resistance follow workers as they migrate? For Caribbean migrant farm workers who live and work in two worlds, where and how does their legal consciousness develop? Although these queries cannot be fully resolved here, at least not in a theoretical respect, they chart the contours of my ongoing project on workers' legal consciousness and resistance. That wider project marks an attempt to rethink, in the context of taking seriously law's essential relationship with capitalism, the role of law, legal institutions and legal education in the service of worker collective organizing and struggles. In view of an explicit commitment to praxis—understood here in a creative, emancipatory, and transformative sense—the idea of transnationalism must undergo a transformative recasting. To the extent that transnationalism signifies a re-envisioning of identity that encourages or even forges "a decrease in attachment to a particular state and to bounded notions of citizenship" (Satzewich and Wong 2003, 376), as is sometimes meant by the post-colonial notions of hybridity and inbetweenity, I contest the utility of the concept. Notwithstanding the underlying commitment to situate migrant workers at the forefront of post-national politics and openings, which is quite laudable, and in spite of the particular insights forged through post-national reimagination, academics have refrained from confronting the fundamental socio-legal realities that constitute this post-colonial "civility" (Purdy 1999). To be more explicit: "Dressing law in the borrowed garb of postcolonialism has made us blind to the ways in which law continues to function as it always has in the colonial context" (ibid., 218). Nowhere is this more evident than in the widespread disregard for the role of the nation-state in labour migration.

The role of the nation-state in constructing the policies and parameters of temporary labour migration and immigration more broadly remains indispensable. Indeed, in the context of the regulation of immigration flows to Canada, "state power has not disappeared from the twenty-first century landscape" (Satzewich and Wong 2003, 367). Fundamentally, "the nation-state still remains the site of power for the regulation and control of the flow of people" (ibid.; Sharma 2006; Aiken 2007).[5] It is on this basis that I turn to the idea of transnationalism. Eschewing the conventional wisdom in the fields of law and the social sciences that posits the decline, disempowerment, or transcendence of the nation-state, I opt for the pursuit of transnational lines of inquiry in a more nuanced way, acknowledging the continuing importance of the nation-state—both sending and receiving. The truths of these Caribbean sojourners are embedded at once in their transnational experiences as workers in home and host countries, and in a legal regulatory framework that facilitates their enduring marginalization and hyper-exploitation.[6] Borrowing and developing the concept of "permanent exceptionalism"[7] to illustrate the functioning of the regulatory framework, in particular the form of Canadian state intervention in migrant labour recruitment and retention, but also the enforcement and disciplining responsibilities of sending states, I explore how that framework conditions workers' transnational experiences.

In line with this more nuanced questioning, I develop the idea of "legal creolization" as a way to capture and characterize the transnational development of migrant farm workers' legal consciousness.[8] Conventionally understood, creolization depicts the processes of the intermixing of cultural features and traits which spawn distinct features and traits. Fundamentally, I strive to maintain congruence with the orthodoxy of creolization in Caribbean studies, capturing these transnational socio-legal processes in the specific historical context of Caribbean SAWP workers and in the more general context of Caribbean systems of labour domination. As such, legal creolization signifies the legal–cultural interchange or intermixing occurring through the circulation of Caribbean workers in the SAWP. Legal creolization accounts for the role of law, Caribbean and Canadian, in the continuous making and remaking of Caribbean creole society. But because I seek to clarify the legal structural and institutional obstacles for collective worker organizing, action and resistance, and because the SAWP framework cannot be disembedded from the unequal relations of global capitalism, we must draw on legal creolization to confront the role of Canada as a (legal) imperialist force.

The 'Permanent Exceptionalism' of the SAWP

Migrant worker programs have been a feature of Canadian labour markets since Confederation (Trumper and Wong 2007, 152). Organized around conceptions of race (as well as gender), guest worker programs turned on the potential exploitability of foreign workers. As Trumper and Wong (ibid.) contend: "The ideal of creating a British settler community was Canada's original nation-building goal, but the reality was that the Canadian capitalist class preferred non-white or less-white guest workers for agricultural and industrial work, infrastructure and railway construction, and domestic work." In labour-intensive agricultural production, as the rural labour force in Canada increasingly urbanized following World War II, as post-war reconstruction efforts depleted white Western European immigration to Canada, and more recently as the Canadian birth rate steadily declined (Gordon 2006, 110), growers have encountered problems of labour recruitment and retention. The dirty, difficult, and dangerous character of the occupation intensified these problems, as did the just-in-time specificities of agricultural production: at key moments growers demand a captive and unfree workforce—the undivided attention of workers during peak planting and harvest—but growers have little utility for these workers at other times. Alternative sources of labour were sought in agriculture (André 1990, 253) and resulted in the state's decision to facilitate temporary labour migration from Caribbean countries.

The incorporation of agricultural workers from the Caribbean was, to follow Vic Satzewich's seminal account, "structured by the idea of 'race,' and an ideology of racial superiority and inferiority" (1991, 179). According to Satzewich, "Black [and Indian] workers from the Caribbean were considered unfree migrant labour, in part because of the belief that they were 'racially' suited to long hours of back-breaking labour under the hot sun, that they were 'racially' incapable of full participation in Canadian society, and that their permanent presence in Canada would cause various social and 'racial' problems to arise" (1999, 323).

Having previously excluded Caribbean peoples on the rationale that they were not biologically suited for harsh Canadian winters, Canadian immigration policy underwent a "seasonal" change in the 1960s to permit the entry of West Indians on the basis of their supposed biological suitability to the hot and humid summers of Ontario, among other provinces. Thus, Canada's immigration policies mirrored racial ideologies of the day.

Yet, as Nandita Sharma remarks, "state immigration policies do more than reflect ideologies that help to legitimate unequal treatment, however. They also create the objective conditions for this discrimination to continue through the legislated denial of freedom" (2006, 138). As "state power in Canada materialized through racist social relations" (Gordon 2006, 108), the legislated denial of freedom rests on racial ideologies as well as on racist social formation.

To the extent that agricultural labour market forces have not overwhelmingly favoured capital, the Canadian nation-state has been called upon to assist growers in the achievement of superior market power. With the institutionalization of the SAWP, the Canadian state assumed overarching responsibility for the incorporation of foreign labour.[9] The scope of the scheme, however, extends more broadly to assign roles for growers and for the sending states. I employ "permanent exceptionalism" to apprehend and characterize the role of both receiving and sending national states in the SAWP. Much like the aphorism "there is nothing more permanent than temporary workers" (Martin 2003, 3), permanent exceptionalism captures the interplay between the SAWP's permanent and temporary or exceptional features. Both the receiving national state and the sending states draw on permanent as well as exceptional features to fulfill employers' recruitment and retention needs.

With respect to the Canadian state's mode of intervention in the agricultural labour market, permanent exceptionalism encapsulates the complex operation of the regulatory framework governing migrant farm workers. This framework includes a Memorandum of Understanding (MOU) between Canada and the labour-supplying countries, a tripartite contractual agreement formalizing the employment relationship and the statutory provisions of the federal Immigration and Refugee Protection Act under the auspices of the Non-Immigrant Employment Authorization Program (NIEAP), as well as applicable labour statutes, namely provincial employment standards and collective labour relations legislation, and social security laws. Functioning alongside community-based federal human resource offices, Foreign Agricultural Resource Management Services (FARMS) forms the SAWP's administrative arm. While growers assume a direct administrative function in the program, FARMS excludes the involvement of workers and their advocates. Through the Ontario Horticultural Advisory Committee, the state's service of capital's needs appears most denuded as growers work in partnership with federal representatives to set policy for the SAWP.

The MOU is constructed not as a binding treaty of international law (Verma 2003, 14) but as an "intergovernmental administrative arrangement" outlining the duties and responsibilities of state and non-state actors. The intent behind this particular form of legal institutionalization is the withdrawal of the program from the international legal sphere, including the forms of scrutiny (such as international human rights) that international law invokes. In so doing, it is designed to build exceptionalism into the SAWP's permanent structure—permanent insofar as the program exists, yet exceptional in reference to the ease with which the participating governments could eliminate the program. Treaties are not subject to cancellation or disruption in the same way that non-treaty arrangements are.[10] Thus, the MOU enshrines temporariness as a core feature of the SAWP.[11]

The SAWP fits within the Non-Immigrant Employment Authorization Program (NIEAP). It marks the fundamental basis of the legislated denial of freedom which is grounded in immigration or citizenship status. The responsibility of Citizenship and Immigration Canada (CIC), the NIEAP applies to individuals in possession of a valid Canadian work permit who travel to Canada for employment. SAWP workers may only work in Canada for eight months in a calendar year. The program formally distinguishes between citizens and permanent residents on one side, and non-citizens or "non-immigrants" on the other. Best characterized as a bonded forced-rotational system

(Wong 1984, 87), the NIEAP ties non-immigrants to specific employers imposing heavy restrictions on the labour market circulation of those characterized as such, restraining their geographic mobility within Canada and denying them the opportunity to remain in Canada after the expiration of their work permit. During their authorized work period, non-immigrants may not alter the conditions of their authorization, change occupations or take on additional work without the written approval of a federal immigration official. Thus, although it is typically presented as a labour mobility program, the SAWP relies paradoxically on the imposition of tight restrictions on the labour market and geographic mobility of its workers.

The NIEAP renders participating workers exceptional in that they represent a "foreign" exception to citizen rights and privileges. It is on this basis that the "deeply exclusionary impulses" of citizenship (Bosniak 2002) intervene to prevent migrant farm workers from receiving the full rights and privileges afforded to citizens. The "non-immigrants" distinction marks the formal juridical basis of the exceptional treatment. With "the only temporary feature of [the NIEAP being] the individual worker contracted to work in the country for a particular period of time" (Sharma 2006, 105), migrant workers are an exception by virtue of their temporary stay in Canada. Exceptionalism is therefore analogous to temporariness in the context of the NIEAP, serving to justify migrant farm workers' differential treatment vis-à-vis citizens or near citizens.

The legal categorization of migrant farm workers as "non-immigrants" brings into play the uneven and hierarchical dynamics of global capitalist relations. As non-immigrants, migrant farm workers are played off against citizen employers.[12] The non-citizen and citizen legal relation becomes a social relation in fact. In this respect, the weight of global capitalist relations is brought to bear on the capital–labour relationship. Historically, immigration policy in Canada has linked the accumulation of local capital to the logic of European and American capitalism. The NIEAP has some affinity with Canadian immigration policy at the turn of the twentieth century through which the state ensured its "participation in a wider transatlantic capitalist labour market" (Avery 1983, 9). Yet Eastern and Southern European immigrants "were at once candidates for Canadianization" receiving many of the basic rights afforded to citizens (ibid., 8). SAWP workers are deliberately denied those basic rights and privileges. As Sharma asserts (2006, 109): "The NIEAP allows employers to tap into the broader world market for labour and secure workers who come with conditions of unfreedom imposed upon them. Such terms give employers access to an internationally competitive labour force." The NIEAP fulfills a fundamental purpose within capitalism by linking the needs of growers to global capitalism. The Canadian state facilitates the "organiz[ation] of employers in Canada as internationally competitive" while "employers remain under no pressure to improve wages, working conditions, or pay rates" (Sharma 2006, 109). As a product of the NIEAP, the SAWP draws on unequal global capitalist relations, reproducing the hierarchy and unevenness that define those relations.

The SAWP tripartite employment agreement ensures growers enjoy considerable benefits through the denial of freedom in key areas of the employment relationship. The agreement grants growers the authority to repatriate workers prior to the end of their work term without justification. This sets the narrow parameters in which temporary labour migration to Canada occurs. In contrast to the "live-in" requirement imposed on migrant caregivers (see for example Stasiulis and Bakan 2005), the SAWP employment agreement requires agricultural workers to live on or near the farm. This imposes an additional restriction on workers' mobility and, in practical terms, a communicative restriction (pertinent to the exercise of freedom of association).[13]

The practical obstacles to worker transfers between farms also impose constraints. According to the employment agreement, transfers are possible with the permission of federal officials, liaison officers, and growers. However, liaison officers report several difficulties in effecting transfers (Verma 2003). A disgruntled grower is more likely to repatriate a worker than to approve a transfer. Potential recipient growers may not be willing to accept a worker perceived as a problem. Some growers loan or transfer workers to other employers without the prior authorization of the worker, Service Canada, and the respective liaison officer (see Service Canada 2006). This all but diminishes workers' only formal legal opportunity to countervail growers' repatriation authority. The fact that the employment agreement lacks explicit enforcement mechanisms further compounds the constraints encountered by workers.

In sum, the employment agreement renders workers an exception and creates an employment relationship in which the racialization of SAWP workers materializes. Insofar as it works to continue the racialized relations of the SAWP, the Canadian state ensures that the exceptional treatment of migrant farm workers becomes the rule and that exceptionalism remains permanent in the agricultural labour market. It is evident that efforts to market the SAWP as a model for temporary labour migration (see for example Greenhill 2000) endeavour for its continuation in Canada as much as for its proliferation abroad. Although individual workers are constructed in legal terms as temporary, the "availability of unfree workers [marks] a permanent feature of the labour market in Canada" (Sharma 2006, 105). Agricultural labour markets in Canada represent a paradigmatic case in this respect.

As a labour historian once stated, "agricultural workers have been historically, as they are today, casual labourers dependent upon irregular spates of ill-paid waged work" (Parr 1985, 96). Throughout the twentieth century, agricultural labour markets in Canada have represented a formative and enduring example of non-standard, precarious employment. The state's interventions in that labour market ensure that workers are excluded from virtually all meaningful protections under provincial labour laws, and that this exclusion persists. This has led to, in Eric Tucker's words, a vicious circle of exclusion and precariousness for agricultural workers.[14] Even when workers have secured modest victories in the form of protective labour legislation (See *Dunmore v. Ontario [Attorney General]*)—namely the recent expansion of occupational health and safety protection to agriculture in Ontario (see Ontario. Ministry of Agriculture, Food and Rural Areas 2005; Ontario. Ministry of Labour 2006)—these have been moderated by weak legislative reforms, implementation, and enforcement. Moreover, employers' power of repatriation prevents the normal operation of labour laws such that workers could not effectuate their rights under the province of Ontario's Occupational Health and Safety Act so long as the threat of repatriation governs the employment relationship. Thus, the employment agreement marks a largely successful attempt to harden the agricultural worker exclusion and render migrant worker exceptionalism permanent.[15]

The Incorporation of Foreign States

Just as the Canadian state functioned to bolster the labour needs of growers, it also sought to formally incorporate sending states and growers into the fray. As one federal official put it, the SAWP's "strength lies not only in the formal structure that has been put in place but also in the fact that all the key players are engaged" (Greenhill 2000, 5). This perspective overlooks the exclusion of workers from the SAWP's governance structure—a point to which I return below. Here, the task is to interrogate the incorporation of the Caribbean states. I contend that the SAWP represents concerted political means through which the Canadian state acts not only on its own terms and in concert with growers but, fundamentally, by encouraging the mobilization of sending state resources, to render workers cheap, marginalized, and exploited. Tasked with the selection and screening of workers, Caribbean states perform a crucial disciplining role. Increased awareness of the role of sending states does not detract from efforts to appreciate the historical significance of migration for advanced capitalist countries such as Canada. In fact, to preview an argument advanced below, it is in ascertaining the social and geographic dimensions of uneven global capitalist relations that we might begin to evaluate the basis on which Canada is said to constitute an imperialist force in global capitalism.

The idea of permanent exceptionalism also applies to the role of sending states in the SAWP framework. Pointing to employment generation and skills development, governing Caribbean elites find it "politically expedient" to promote temporary labour migration through the SAWP (André 1990, 246).

Calls for the use of Caribbean farm workers in Canada commenced in the late 1940s with governments in the region soliciting interest through the British high commissioner in Canada (Satzewich 1991). These countries continue to proclaim their desire to expand the size of the program. There are important questions about the specific economic benefits of the SAWP that cannot be answered here. Questions notwithstanding, Caribbean involvement represents a pressure toward rendering temporary labour migration to Canada permanent. That involvement, however, comes with stringent conditionalities. The Operational Guidelines (Annex I) contained within the MOU delineates the administrative structure of the SAWP. It provides participating countries with the opportunity to review the guidelines annually. Growers commence the labour recruitment process through a formal worker request, which requires a labour market opinion and approval from HRSDC. While employers are permitted to name specific individuals they wish to re-employ, sending countries are given control over recruitment, of appointing government agents who ensure the "smooth functioning of the program for the mutual benefit of both employers and the workers." It is quite "peculiar" that these states are incorporated into the SAWP to fulfill the interests of growers (Verma 2003, 23).

Sending states impose the conditions of unfreedom on workers even prior to migration. The disciplining of SAWP workers begins with the pre-screening process and extends to the prescribed responsibilities of liaison officers, the agents of the respective sending governments, who ensure workers do not stray from the dictates of the program. That these officers are meant to represent their governments and serve the interests of employers and workers alike is evidence of the contradictory nature of their disciplinary role. Agents themselves acknowledge the failure of the SAWP framework to furnish the tools to fulfil their specific duties. For instance, liaison officers admit that they are practically unable to facilitate the transfer of workers between farms (Verma 2003). Make no mistake, however: sending states impose heavy discipline to preserve their claim to SAWP participation. It is precisely in this authoritarian role that they clarify and demarcate the political limits of their economic developmental agenda.[16]

Sending states assume a disciplinary role, to be sure, but an equally profound aim lies at the root of the incorporation of Caribbean states. This relates to social reproduction. While growers draw from the pool of migrant workers for up to eight months each year, responsibility for the employment of these workers for the remainder of the year rests with the sending state. In effect, the Canadian state secures unfree labour by downloading onto sending states the costs of workforce training and social reproduction more generally (Sharma 2006, 134; Trumper and Wong 2007). The Canadian state also endeavours to minimize its indebtedness to migrant farm workers for the duration of their employment in Canada. This appears to be the case with social security protections, which are allocated to migrant workers on an uneven basis if at all. Even where they have been formally granted access, such as with workers' compensation if injured on the job, the fear of repatriation reduces the efficacy of these social protections in practice. The immediate point is that, as noted in a different context, "an expendable labour force takes its problems away with it when it is re-exported" (Böhning 1983, 35–37). The underlying point is to recognize how the SAWP legal regulatory framework functions to redistribute the reproduction needs of capitalism itself. In formally implicating Caribbean states, however, the SAWP reinforces the vested interests of sending states. This amounts to the introduction of a permanent feature and may undermine Canada's efforts to portray temporary labour migration as exceptional.

Conditioning SAWP Workers

The SAWP framework sets the parameters of the employment relationship and of community engagement more broadly (see Preibisch 2007). It is within these parameters that workers undertake resistance. In this sense, the SAWP framework conditions the vantage point from which workers and their allies elaborate their strategies of resistance. The framework utilizes permanent and exceptional features to construct the appearance of consent and to shape worker behaviour.

In facilitating the migration of workers from the Caribbean to Canada, the SAWP strives simultaneously for cross-border mobilization of labour power and the immobilization of workers. It promotes the movement of these so-called low-skilled workers across national borders while imposing constraints on their movement within Canada. In addition, SAWP workers face the burden of marginal and differential protections under provincial minimum labour standards legislation due to their non-immigrant distinction, which renders them exceptional and therefore not deserving of the rights, privileges, and protections afforded to citizens and near-citizen workers. They also must overcome the splintering of their ranks into tiny factions representative of the agricultural production process. With the effective denial of normal collective bargaining rights, the labour law regulatory regime ensures workers' collective power remains latent. Moreover, the rehiring mechanism, the naming process, seemingly forces an individual who desires to re-enter the SAWP to appease growers. If daily productive relations in the SAWP lie within a deeply exclusionary and racialized context, and if those relations function on a patchy and tenuous floor of workplace rights, it occurs under the forever gloomy cloud of employer reprisal and the threat of repatriation. These are the parameters, erected within the transnational web of responsibilities of the receiving state, growers, and sending states, in which worker behaviour is conditioned.

It is in the context of these specific and limiting legal regulatory parameters that I turn to the idea of legal creolization. I do so to divert attention away from analyses that overstate the ways workers are said to "consent" to exploitative working conditions, "reproduce" the system, or "avoid" collective challenge to the system,[17] as if the legal structural parameters explored throughout this piece have had little if any impact in constituting the SAWP's social formation, or as if workers cared only about economic gains or lacked the capacity to appreciate what they desire in productive relations. I turn to legal creolization also to keep alive questions of the role of the sending and receiving states in the processes of temporary labour migration to Canada. At its core, the framework rests on the relationship between law and the state within capitalist relations of production. Legal creolization is a way to acknowledge that the extent to which the specific and limiting parameters have a lasting effect on workers' consciousness and action is still, if only in a minor way, open to debate.

As far as I am aware, the phrase "legal creolization" has not been employed elsewhere. That said, there have been some initiatives aimed at characterizing the relationship between the development of law and colonialism. These efforts have linked the processes of creolization to the processes of law making in colonial Caribbean societies.[18] I employ legal creolization to confront the unique challenges posed by the SAWP's legal regulatory framework. It is designed to explore potential opportunities for collective worker organizing and legal education. Creolization, taken from discussions within Caribbean studies, is regarded as a continuous cultural process entangled in the making of colonial and post-colonial social formations in Caribbean countries. That is to say, the Caribbean constitutes creole societies that, while shaped by colonial and imperial relations with metropolitan centres, have taken on distinctive appearances of their own by virtue of the internal social dynamics and contestations.

Legal creolization offers a glimpse into the role of law in consciousness making. The concept aligns closely with legal or juridical consciousness, which represents an empirical concept and theoretical tool that may potentially aid worker organizing and legal education (see Smith 2005). Whereas the study of the legal consciousness forms an attempt to understand how law shapes worker consciousness and resistance, legal creolization is a way to foreground and characterize the transnational processes of legal consciousness formation. The claim then is that: how legal creolization develops—dialectically and contradictorily, I assume—has important empirical consequences and implications for worker organizing and education.

In casting legal creolization as an avenue through which workers might explore potential forms of resistance, we must appreciate the role of law in the construction of collective worker consciousness. To appreciate the significance of legal creolization we also must grapple with the role of the state and law in facilitating capitalist relations of production. I outline two ways in which we might utilize the concept of legal creolization. First, it is useful for the exploration of the historical continuities between the SAWP and earlier systems of labour regulation in the Caribbean. This feeds into the second way: to explore the historical and ongoing significance of the relationship between receiving and sending states. This is conducted as a socio-legal inquiry defined as an exploration of what law does as opposed to what law is.

Nigel Bolland's formidable comparative exploration of early-twentieth-century labour movement politics in the Caribbean provides a suitable basis from which to launch such an inquiry. Taking the colonial capitalistic control and exploitation of labour (and land) as a point of departure, Bolland observes "basic and long-term continuities in the contradictions of the relations of production, despite changes in the legal forms of these contradictions" (2001, 24). The legal breaks or ruptures that occurred in the course of post-contact Caribbean history, initially in the form of emancipation and later of independence are, for Bolland, "largely symbolic" (ibid., 22). On this account, the historical record reflects continuities from "slavery through Emancipation to independence to the present" in the dominant systems of labour, namely enslavement, indentured servitude, and free wage labour (ibid., 24). In a rigorously comparative and thoroughgoing way, Bolland sets about to appreciate the crucial interconnections, finding ultimately that in the face of formal legal structural shifts and alterations the core authoritarian roots of colonialism in the Caribbean remain in tact.

In a similar vein, Irving André asserts that the SAWP "approximat[es] much of the control (although not the brutality) inherent in slave labour but avoi[ds] the universal opprobrium attached to that system of labour" (1990, 245). In this way, André expresses sentiments held by countless migrant farm workers, activists, and critical commentators that the SAWP shares common features with slavery and indentured servitude (Smith 2005). Taken together and assessed in broad terms, both André's and Bolland's accounts appear to capture the broad historical contours of the dominant labour regimes governing workers in the Caribbean. Nevertheless, more rigorous and sustained socio-legal reflection and theorizing are required. This requires the development of appropriate socio-legal concepts.

Insofar as it rests on the notion of law as a predominantly symbolic form, Bolland's account relies too heavily on an overly broad approximation. Not only is a great deal lost in perceiving the formal legal breaks between labour regulation regimes as mere symbolism[19] but, in effect, we sidestep (perhaps even foreclose) more systematic consideration of what law does. Law functions as symbolism to be sure, but it is not merely symbolic; it serves a coercive function as well. If the task is to seriously consider law's myriad functions in capitalist relations, in particular the interplay between its symbolic and coercive functions, then we must overcome the analytical tendency toward overgeneralization. That is not to say "the symbolic" deserves any less consideration. The complexities of the historical development of a given regime of labour regulation call for different levels of abstraction and analysis to capture these relations in its entirety. In pursuing law's symbolic form we ought to emphasize "'the ethical–political aspect of politics or theory of hegemony and consent' but not at the expense of 'the aspect of force and economics'" (see Gramsci 2005, editors' introduction to "State and Civil Society," 207).[20] In short, this calls for an appreciation of the role of law and the state in capitalism.

Law and the State

In capitalist society, "the State is the entire complex of practical and theoretical activities with which the ruling class not only justifies and maintains its dominance, but manages to win the active consent of those over whom it rules" (Gramsci 2005, 244). Yet, while the state hinges on direct coercion it too must "organize consent by other means" (Wood 2002, 31). Indeed, the liberal state anchors its authority to govern in the idea of rational consent and employs ideological means to organize "spontaneous consent" or "social hegemony" of the subordinated masses (Gramsci 2005, 12). Hegemony and coercion operate in concert mutually reinforcing one another as "hegemony [is] protected by the armour of coercion" (ibid., 263). Through the interplay of consent and coercion, the state works to guarantee conditions necessary for the continuation of the capitalist mode of production, the essence of which is labour exploitation.

Law and the state are twisted together in the tangled mass of capitalism. The state is called forth to mediate productive relations (see Fudge and Tucker 2001). To do so the state turns to law: "Legality is a crucial, if not the primary, mode of regulating the contradictions that arise from capitalist production relations" (Fudge and Tucker 2001, 4). The law may straighten and bend, twist or flex under oppositional pressures or through shifts in social formation. Ideologically, law's distortions and contradictions work in the service of stat us quo social relations, serving as a distraction from law and the state's underlying connection to the furtherance of capitalism (see for example Smith 2005). In the face of law's myriad configurations, the state maintains its essential commitment to capitalism. That commitment "places limits and exerts pressures" (Fudge and Tucker 2001, 7) on the existing social formation.

As law serves to construct rational consent and to organize and configure the use of force, it is in this respect that we must accent the role of law in the politics of hegemony and consent without losing sight of law's formative role in the aspect of force and economics. As Merry, summarizing Hirsch and

Lazarus-Black (1994), asserts, "Law has a cultural capacity to construct categories, rules, and modes of understanding that shape the way people see the world and the ways they think they should behave within it, so that its power lies in the realm of culture and consciousness as well as in the imposition of force. But this form of power is never complete, and always subject to forms of contestation and revision" (Merry 2004).

The regulatory framework governing the SAWP operates in a very particular way. It ensures workers are unevenly captured under labour law protections and that this exclusion persists. The "non-immigrants" distinction is the basis from which virtually all other formal and legislated denials of freedom emanate. The distinction shapes the way workers engage with the world by altering the normal course of productive relations. Whereas the state typically mediates class relations, under the SAWP that function becomes far more one-sided and coercive.

That said, coercion does not flow from the Canadian state alone. Without detracting from my earlier attempt to note the historical continuities in Caribbean systems of labour domination, the SAWP presents a crucial difference that must now register. Whereas the exploitation of foreign labour has tended to refer to colonial relations within colonized societies, the SAWP occurs within Canada. The Canadian state assumes primary—but not sole—responsibility for labour recruitment and retention. In short, Canada recruits Caribbean states to fulfill capital's most pressing need for labour power. The Canadian state strives to complete its power, to maintain its dominance, effectively by tapping sending states' coercive capacities. The integration of sending states into the SAWP amounts to the disassociation of the Canadian nation-state's coercive capacity, if ultimately for the completion of its own authority and domination. This contradiction is perhaps as much a source of weakness as it is of strength and legitimacy.[21] In terms of weakness in particular, this opens the door for collective strategies of resistance that target both the sending and receiving states.

Yet coercion and consent function in concert. Much in the same way that an individual liberal capitalist state relies on rational consent, the incorporation of sending states into the SAWP means that the legal construction of consent occurs through both states. The receiving state and the sending state each look to the other to "organize consent by other means." The ensuing section strives to situate the receiving–sending state relationship within global capitalism.

Migrant Workers as 'Accidental Tourists'
In bringing in the Caribbean states, the SAWP invites questions about the character and significance of relations between the Canadian state and the sending states. An understanding of the relationship *between* states within the global nation-state system requires keen attentiveness to the historical devel-

opment of the existing social formation *within* states. This is particularly true in the context of Caribbean nation-states where colonialism and imperialist relations so heavily shaped the contours of the contemporary social formation, including labour relations (see Smith forthcoming).

In implicating sending states, the SAWP recasts and reconstructs the hierarchical relations of global capitalism as consensual relations between sovereign states with the equal and consensual engagement of the participating non-state social actors. In fact, the framework turns on and reproduces hierarchical relations within the nation-state system.

The Canadian state intervenes to transform migrant farm workers into marginal and exploitable factors of production for the benefit of Canadian capital. As we have observed, this occurs through a reliance on ideologies of race, through the creation of legal categories and distinctions beholden to those ideologies, through the institutionalization of growers as planners and administrators, and through the incorporation of sending states as enforcers. But to say that foreign labour power bolsters capitalism in Canada is not to address the impact on social relations in the periphery. It is not to speak to the constitutive role of colonialism in Caribbean societies (See Bolland 2001; James 1989), including the active participation of Caribbean ruling elites. All of this demands deeper exploration, but the critical task here is to note what we miss by neglecting the political economy of labour migration in the Caribbean.

Few scholarly accounts of the SAWP seriously consider the role of the Caribbean. We must appreciate temporary labour migration to Canada as having "its etiology in the historical experience of the Caribbean" (André 1990, 245). Labour migration constitutes "a process whereby labour is consciously exported as a rational means of promoting economic development within the sending countries" (ibid.). In actuality, according to Irving André, the exaction of labour power from the sending countries brings economic development to Canada at the expense of development in the Caribbean. Notwithstanding theoretical and empirical contestation over the dependency theory implications of André's thesis, particularly the idea that development and underdevelopment are different sides of the same coin (see for example Kiely 2007), there is a definite need to incorporate sending countries into the analysis of labour migration.

More specifically, there is an absence of reflection on the significance of the formalized relationship between Canadian and Caribbean states through the SAWP. That said, calls for more specific attempts to delve into the internal historical political economic factors and conditions that have driven workers to migrate need not detract from a wider attempt to implicate global capitalism. A commitment to interrogate the various roles assumed by the Canadian state in global capitalism must not ignore the state's role in encouraging the conditions for the exploitation of foreign labour. Labour migration is firmly situated within the conscious rational policies of so-called "core" capitalist states like Canada. This includes the specificities of the SAWP and Canada's immigration policies as well as the promotion of more general policy endeavours abroad.

By virtue of the SAWP and its immigration policies, Canada constitutes an imperialist force in global capitalist relations. Gordon states the case quite explicitly: "Migration must be understood historically as a product of unequal relations—imperialist relations—between countries of the Global North and those of the Global South. It is not by accident that large pools of migrant workers are drawn from the [...] Caribbean nations [among others ...], which have witnessed a long history of colonial subjugation at the hands of the West" (Gordon 2006, 112). But as we have seen, historical continuities notwithstanding, the SAWP differs from past colonial systems of labour exploitation in that the exploitation of foreign labour occurs not within the periphery but at the core. I have sought to illustrate how this important difference translates into socio-legal implications. The incorporation of sending states into the SAWP signifies that the juridical responsibilities of coercion are split between the receiving and sending states. The Canadian state "contracts out" aspects of coercion. Caribbean states assume that responsibility for the sake of political expediency. Yet it is not expediency alone. Global inequality produces real material disparities for a majority of the world's people. These disparities are reflected in the commitments of Caribbean states, albeit in a partial and fragmented way.

This understanding appears to disrupt articulations of imperialism as the imposition of external forces on colonial or former colonial societies—with "external" signifying "military" force in the case of old-style imperialism and "economic" force in the case of new. But it is not so much that the territorial dimension of core–periphery relations gives way, leaving only the social dimension (class and class-related) to explain hierarchy and unevenness in global capitalist relations. The geography may have inverted in some cases but the geographic dimension of foreign labour exploitation remains significant. The critical challenge is to "register instead their irreducible simultaneity" (Saul 2004, 24) in the context of a critique of imperialist relations of the SAWP. The reproduction and continuation of imperialist relations occurs through social as well as geographic means.

Given that successive Canadian governments have held the SAWP out as a model scheme for "managed migration" (Martin 2003, 22; Greenhill 2000), and that foreign governments, including the United States, have reciprocated, we must begin to interrogate the role of the Canadian state as a (legal-cultural) imperialist force in the Western Hemisphere. The fact that the SAWP regulatory framework shares commonalities with the H2-A worker program in the United States might encourage a skewed perspective. In light of the emergence of debates on the new imperialism, it might be tempting to view the SAWP as another example of the transference of American legal norms and understandings abroad — what has been recently referred to as Empire's law (Marks 2003; Bartholomew 2006). While I fully agree that "the United States has long played a pre-eminent role in the spread of legal forms across the world" (Bartholomew 2006, 1), we cannot discount the role of advanced capitalist countries, such as Canada, in adjusting those legal forms and putting them to the service of their own locally rooted capital. To do so would essentially let Canadian capital and the state off the hook. The Canadian state has long since facilitated the global drive of Canadian capital through national policies which facilitated absentee ownership in the Caribbean (see André 1990) and elsewhere, but also very recently through the support of the austere measures of international financial institutions. These policies remain the driving force behind the migration of workers in search of subsistence wages.

We might begin to confront the imperialist relations in which the SAWP is embedded by further exploring legal creolization. The task is to account for the implications of legal creolization on workers' struggles back home. Transnational workers are not "like an empty vessel that can be filled with any rubbish that capitalists like" (Satzewich 1999, 325). Nevertheless, workers do act as vectors.[22] And at key historical moments transnational workers have energized collective labour organizing and struggle through the transmission of emancipatory ideas and commitments.[23] What is clear is that migrant farm workers already transmit socio-legal understandings back and forth. What is open for exploration is how this transmission might be utilized to bolster collective worker organization at home and away. Those explorations must take migrant farm workers where they currently find themselves; engaged in transnational class struggle resisting the coercive forces of the Canadian and Caribbean nation-states.

Conclusion

Although one might be tempted to interpret the transnational lives of workers as the invention of an in-between world, a distinct socio-legal space, or alternative pocket of legality (phrase borrowed from Merry 2004, 571), such a reading would be misguided. The SAWP fits within the wider political economic developments of both Canada and the Caribbean and, indeed, is a point of convergence. It is this convergence that we might seek to exploit.

In light of the fact that throughout the second half of the twentieth century the Canadian state's role in labour recruitment and retention has been decisive, we must continue to take seriously its role in constituting hyper-exploitative relations of production in agriculture. Permanent exceptionalism characterizes the functioning of the legal regulatory framework of the SAWP, in particular the form of Canadian state intervention in migrant labour recruitment and retention but also the role of capital, strategic and administrative, and of sending states. Alongside the incorporation of Caribbean workers, the SAWP incorporates Caribbean states into local processes of labour recruitment and retention. Sending states assume a disciplinary role to be certain, but the crux of the incorporation of Caribbean states is to download the costs of social reproduction. In formalizing the vested interests of sending states, and in light of current political commitment of Caribbean governing elites and the temporary labour migration expansionist desires in sending and receiving states alike, this may mean more, not less, coercion from sending or receiving states, or from both.

The ongoing and decisive role of the nation-state demands that socio-legal exploration maintain an emphasis on the state and on capital. Legal creolization is an attempt to do so. The concept seeks to clarify the obstacles for collective worker organizing and resistance, and for legal education, conceived of as a creative, dialectical, and transformative force. In the context of the SAWP, the conventional hypothesis about how law is internalized and practised must be adapted to capture the transnational lives of workers.

The legal regulatory framework conditions and disciplines through the interplay of temporariness or exceptionalism and permanency. Workers are mobilized to work abroad and, at the same time, immobilized in political and geographic terms while in Canada. The denial of freedom occurs in various forms, but it is the growers' authority to repatriate workers and the mobility restrictions, encased within the non-immigrants distinction, that most constrain worker collective assertions of power. The truths of these Caribbean sojourners are indeed embedded within their transnational working lives and within the coercive legal regulatory framework of the SAWP. The task of formulating a more coherent praxis of collective resistance calls for attention to these transnational truths. In this respect, to say the state is important is not to valorize law and the state as the only or best means for workers to register collective gains. For the struggle to occur on different fronts and in different locales, migrant farm workers must be supported by the labour movement in Canada. If nothing else, legal creolization must remind the Canadian labour movement of its privileges and responsibilities as members of the international labour movement. It is as much a call for the labour movement in Canada to fight the systemic racism in its ranks, which serves as a key factor in the lower unionization rates of workers perceived as non-white and non-Canadian (Das Gupta 2006). Canada is as much a part of the struggle against imperialism as it is a site for the reproduction of neo-imperialist relations. Canada is still very much implicated in the reshaping of Caribbean identity.

Notes

1 There is an ongoing debate over the usefulness of the term "unfree" labour. Although that debate has largely taken place outside of the purview of socio-legal scholars, it turns on the role of law as a coercive force (see Hay and Craven 2004). As Hay and Craven (2004, 26) assert: "Law is always coercive, even when it is also simultaneously facilitative and enabling of social organization." I employ the term not to register "the simplistic antinomy" (Bolland 1997, 123) of "free" and "unfree" labour. This largely has been discredited through, for example, the presentation of evidence of the "proto-proletarian" nature of enslaved Africans in pre-Emancipation Caribbean societies (see Turner 1995). Rather, I consider it useful in characterizing certain types of workers who, to paraphrase Bob Marley, have no chains around their feet but are not free (see Smith 2005). While there is much unsettled in the free-unfree debate, I accept that, as Hay and Craven (2004, 27) do, "Coercion is a complex continuum of forms and practices." For more on this point I direct the reader to the works of labour historians Mary Turner and Nigel Bolland; and to a synopsis of the debate from a socio-legal historical perspective in Hay and Craven (2004).

2 In 2003, the federal government established the Temporary Foreign Worker Program (TFWP) — also known as the National Occupational Classification C and D Pilot Program or the Low Skill Workers Program — to move foreign workers into diverse sectors of the economy (Preibisch 2007).

3 It is not my intention to minimize the need for analytical exploration of the role that gender plays in the SAWP. Although Preibisch (2007b) is right to note that the SAWP is "not an all-male cast" there has been little research conducted into the experience of female workers in the SAWP. The program enforces a gendered division of labour. It allocates work along gender lines; and because workers travel without their families, it reinforces gendered divisions within familial (work) relations as well. We might also situate the family farm model of agricultural production and the constraints on social reproduction within feminist theorizing on the public–private distinction. The myth of the family farm, which is a cornerstone of the "agricultural worker exclusion" from labour law protection, relies upon the supporting ideology of the nuclear household or family. In the same way that the nuclear family is perceived as a "private" matter, sheltered from "the market" and state intervention, the family farm is similarly characterized.

4 I use the term "socio-legal" not to connote the study of the intersections of sociology and law per se but to capture the field of law and society in less awkward terminology. In contrast with legal positivist approaches which focus on the rule of law and on what law is, law and society stresses the role of law and what law does. In this respect, the field draws on interdisciplinary insights.

5 Mainstream globalization studies which advance arguments about national state decline, disempowerment, and transcendence, rely implicitly and explicitly on the idea that labour does not flow unchecked across borders. While I accept the premise that nation-states continue to heavily regulate flows of people, I do so with two qualifications. First, I reject the idea of the end of the nation-state. I have found Kiely's (2007) intervention useful in this respect. Second, I dispute the claim that labour migration does not enforce a division of labour. The fact that the Labour Side Agreement attached to the North American Free Trade Agreement permits the

relatively easy flow of professional classes across the national borders of member states while remaining all but silent on cross-border movements of low-skilled workers, seems to suggest otherwise. Following Kiely, I contend that "the neo-liberal view of the non-interventionist state is a myth...that sceptics take too seriously" (2007, 161). But to say the nation-state remains important "does not itself undermine the view that there has been a shift towards neo-liberalism, no matter how nationally specific, uneven and uncontested" (ibid., 162). At issue is the national state as a valid basis of politico-legal analysis. The state remains an issue of epistemological significance—albeit in a modified way. For an application of this understanding of the nation-state in the context of Caribbean international political economy see Smith (forthcoming).

6 This is a deliberate play on the name of feminist, former slave, and abolitionist in the United States, Sojourner Truth.

7 In short, "permanent exceptionalism" is employed by Panitch and Swartz (2003) to characterize the main thesis of their text. None of what follows is meant to detract from their seminal thesis about the institutionalization of "permanent exceptionalism" in Canadian postwar labour relations. While they do not explicitly address agricultural workers, I am indebted to their formulation.

8 Legal creolization refers to dialectical processes which are continually repeating themselves in the case of workers with lengthy service in the SAWP. In exploring the legal structural pressures on legal creolization, I am working from an elementary hypothesis: legal consciousness is initially formed in the country where each worker has spent her or his formative years—based on myriad factors including (formal) education, interaction with legal regimes and authorities, and the prominence of legal and constitutional values. Workers' legal consciousness is adjusted or modified abroad by experiences on the ground in Canada. These transnational socio-legal processes first became evident to me during qualitative interviews I conducted with Caribbean migrant farm workers in 2004 where different workers referenced specific labour law terminology not employed in Canada to question the efficacy of Canadian labour law.

9 The state works also to serve the interests of other factions of the capitalist class. For instance, immigration schemes can be "regarded as part of a regime of capital accumulation" (Satzewich and Wong 2003, 366). Whereas the Canadian business immigration program encouraged entrepreneurs to transfer significant sums of capital into Canada, the SAWP revolves around remittances. Remittances represent a source of capital accumulation in the exorbitant fees generated on wire transfer transactions for Canada's major financial institutions, who operate successfully in the Caribbean as well, for wire transfer companies such as Western Union, and for predatory lenders such as cheque-cashing and "payday" loan businesses.

10 As Verma (2007, 4n5) notes, the status of the current MOU between Canada and Jamaica, which is representative of the Canada-Caribbean SAWP relationship generally, adds to the SAWP's appearance of temporariness. Established in January 1995, it was to remain in force until terminated by either state with three months written notice. The MOU remains in effect as of September 2007.

11 This is not to make light of the relative tradeoffs between establishing a domestic regulated regime versus an international treaty regime that likely underwrote the decision to opt for the latter. Regulating labour migration through the Canadian

domestic legal sphere presents its own challenges. Insofar as the Canadian state is engaged, SAWP policy decisions are likely subject to the fundamental principles of administrative law, including the duty of fairness.

12 Similarly, albeit in intra-peripheral terms, an internal contestation also occurs within the context of growing competition between sending states in the SAWP. Labour exaction occurs through the splintering of the SAWP workers into factions working on farms, minimizing the potential for their collective assertion of power. The SAWP scheme draws on workers with different national, racial, linguistic, familial, and social backgrounds. The framework exploits the differences, transforming them into formal distinctions. This transformation occurs, for example, with the creation of distinct standard form agreements that apply to Caribbean and Mexican migrant workers, which overstate the differences between SAWP workers, and with citizen agricultural workers. In pitting non-citizen workers against citizen workers, and non-citizen Caribbean workers against non-citizen Mexican and Guatemalan SAWP workers, juridical distinctions elevate cultural difference to the height of real social (and biological) fact. This grossly overstates the real differences in the material and strategic interests of agricultural workers within and without the SAWP.

13 The "live on or near" requirement denies workers unrestricted accessing to their allies on other farms or in the community. This, in addition to the fact that workers seldom have telephone access in their living quarters, amounts to practical obstacles which inhibit collective organizing efforts mounted by groups such as Justicia for Migrant Workers.

14 Tucker (2006, 268) adds that "the legal exclusion of vulnerable agricultural workers from collective bargaining laws not only undermined their indigenous capacity to develop an organized voice but deterred organizations with resources from coming to their assistance."

15 The efforts of the Canadian state to support the re-regulation of labour markets through legislative rollbacks, declining state enforcement, and neo-liberal public policies of taxation has meant increasing precariousness in non-agricultural work organization in late-twentieth and early-twenty-first-century production relations.

16 In presenting the case in this way there is a tendency to occlude the social forces at play by proceeding as though the individual sending states are monolithic and ahistorical objects and not historicized venues in which social interaction and contestation occur. I attempt to address this challenge by calling for more rigorous exploration of the political economy of labour migration in the Caribbean.

17 Elsewhere I have argued that if, to paraphrase a prominent labour historian, social history evolves around conflict and resistance not acquiescence, then questions about why migrant farm workers consent to exploitative working conditions shift to the background (Smith 2005). The normative task is to foreground law's role in the modes of understanding that shape the way workers view the world and think they should behave within it. Because the subjective contestation in which Caribbean migrant farm workers find themselves turns on the role of law and the state in capitalism, efforts to highlight worker resistance, and worker resistance itself, necessarily must contemplate core juridical relations. For those sympathetic to the plight of these workers the task lies not in merely chronicling isolated tactics of worker resistance. Although necessary, chronicles of resistance prove insuffi-

cient in confronting the juridical bases of exploitation and marginalization. The critical task demands more than an educative purpose; it calls for an incessantly evaluative one.

18 Lazarus-Black (1994, 3) hints at a definition of legal creolization noting: "From the beginning, the process of creolization entailed a dialectical interplay of legalities and illegalities that challenged each other as they changed over time and forged New World legal sensibilities." Similarly, Patchett notes that: "The statutory and common law that arrived with the colonists from England provided only the base from which local courts and assemblies built a creole jurisprudence; the received law did not dictate the subsequent development of local law" (Patchett 1973, 67). More general theories of legal transplantation appear to lack the capacity to account for legal cultural intermixing.

19 This appears the case in discerning differences between the earliest guest worker schemes and indentured servitude where we find that despite the overlap between these regimes, a significant socio-legal difference exists. The uniqueness of the former lies not in its temporary nature but in the work permit issued to workers. That is, "indentured servants were generally encouraged to stay after the expiration of their contracts, while guestworkers [are], by definition, expected to leave" (Hahamovitch 2003, 72).

20 Gramsci has asserted that, "though hegemony is ethical–political, it must also be economic, must necessarily be based on the decisive function exercised by the leading group in the decisive nucleus of economic activity" (2005, 161). I agree with Jessop who, in a 1997 lecture in Japan, interprets this passage to signify "that the essential function of hegemony is to ensure the reciprocal relationship between the economic (and extra-economic) needs of the mode of growth."

21 I say "perhaps" because this is, in part, an empirical question. If it is to be pursued as such, we must be open to the complexity of, to use Ellen Wood's (2002) term, the "culture of legitimation" in capitalism.

22 My aim in employing the term "vector" is not to follow too closely to the definition that connotes an agent that carries and transmits a disease—unless we want to describe certain mainstream perspectives in global labour movements which promote legalistic strategies over collectivist ones as pathological. This idea of workers as vectors—phraseology suggested to me by Dayna Scott—may offer some insight into transnational worker organizing efforts insofar as first, transnationalism is seen to place these workers in a unique position that may have a vanguard potential, that is, a utility to drive collective organizing in Canada and the Caribbean alike; and, second, we regard the transmission of ideas on law, solidarity, and so forth as a credible process. Then, we might look to draw historical comparisons to dockworkers and other similarly situated workers to build an understanding of "transnational" tactics and strategies employed in the service of collective worker resistance.

23 There is of course a negative spin on the transmission of ideas insofar as legalistic strategies take precedence over collective action. The transference of legal norms and understandings and consciousness to the periphery amounts to legal-cultural imperialism. This transference has been an implicit, albeit underdeveloped, aspect of critical understanding with respect to ideas of legal transplantation.

References

Aiken, S. J. 2007. From slavery to expulsion: Racism, Canadian immigration law, and the unfulfilled promise of modern constitutionalism. In *Interrogating race and racism*, ed. V. Agnew, 55–111. Toronto: Univ. of Toronto Press.

André, I. 1990. The genesis and persistence of the Commonwealth Caribbean Seasonal Agricultural Workers Program in Canada. *Osgoode Hall Law Journal* 28(2): 243–302.

Avery, D. 1983. *Dangerous foreigners: European immigrant workers and labour radicalism in Canada, 1896–1932*. Toronto: McClelland & Stewart.

Bartholomew, A., ed. 2006. *Empire's law: The American imperial project and the "war to remake the world."* Toronto: Between the Lines.

Basok, T. 2004. Post-national citizenship, Social exclusion and migrants rights: Mexican Seasonal Workers in Canada. *Citizenship Studies* 8(1): 47–64.

Böhning, W. R. 1983 [1972]. The migration of workers in the United Kingdom and the European community. In *Dangerous foreigners: European immigrant workers and labour radicalism in Canada, 1896–1932*, ed. D. Avery, 35–37. Toronto: McClelland and Stewart.

Bolland, O. N. 1997. *Struggles for freedom: Essays on slavery, colonialism and culture in the Caribbean and Central America*. Belize City: Angelus Press.

———. 2001. *The politics of labour in the British Caribbean: The social origins of authoritarianism and democracy in the labour movement*. Princeton, NJ: Markus Wiener Publishers.

Bosniak, L. 2002. Critical reflections on "citizenship" as progressive aspiration. In *Labour law in an era of globalization: Transformative practices and possibilities*, ed. J. Conaghan, R. M. Fischl, and K. Klare, 339–52. New York: Oxford Univ. Press.

Das Gupta, T. 2006. Racism/Anti-racism, previous employment, and unions. In *Precarious employment: Understanding labour market insecurity in Canada*, ed. L. F. Vosko, 318–34. Montreal and Kingston: McGill-Queen's Univ. Press.

Dunmore v. Ontario (Attorney General) [2001] 3 S.C.R. 1016.

Fudge, J., and E. Tucker. 2001. *Labour before the law: The regulation of workers' collective action in Canada, 1900–1948*. Toronto: Oxford Univ. Press.

Gordon, T. 2006. *Cops, crime and capitalism: The law-and-order agenda in Canada*. Halifax: Fernwood Publishing.

Gramsci, A. 2005 [1971]. *Selections from the prison notebooks*. Ed. Q. Hoare and G. N. Smith. New York: International Publishers.

Greenhill, D. 2000. Managed migration best practices and public policy: The Canadian experience. Prepared for the International Organization for Migration Workshop "Best Practices Related to Migrant Workers." Santiago, Chile.

Hahamovitch, C. 2003. Creating perfect immigrants: Guestworkers of the world in historical perspective. *Labor History* 44(1): 69–94.

Hay, D., and P. Craven, eds. 2004. *Masters, servants, and magistrates in Britain and the empire, 1562–1955*. Chapel Hill and London: Univ. of North Carolina Press.

Hirsch, S. F., and M. Lazarus-Black, eds. 1994. *Contested States: Law, hegemony and resistance*. New York and London: Routledge.

James, C. L. R. 1989. *The Black Jacobins: Toussaint L'Ouverture and the San Domingo Revolution*. 2nd ed. New York: Vintage Books.

Jessop, B. 1997. L'Economia integrale, fordism, and post-fordism. Italian-Japanese Conference on Gramsci, Tokyo, 15–16 November. http://members.jcom.home.ne.jp/katori/Jessop_on_Gramsci.html.

Kiely, R. 2007. *The new political economy of development: Globalization, imperialism, hegemony.* New York: Palgrave Macmillan.

Kivisto, P. 2001. Theorizing transnational immigration: A critical review of current efforts. *Ethnic and Racial Studies* 24(4) (July): 549–77.

Lazarus-Black, M. 1994. *Legitimate acts and illegal encounters: Law and society in Antigua and Barbuda.* Washington, DC: Smithsonian Institution Press.

Marks, S. 2003. Empire's law. *Indiana Journal of Global Legal Studies* 10(1): 449–66.

Martin, P. L. 2003. *Managing labour migration: Temporary worker programs for the 21st century.* Geneva: International Labour Organization.

Merry, S. E. 2004. Colonial and Postcolonial law. In *The Blackwell companion to law and society,* ed. A. Sarat, 569–88. Malden, MA: Blackwell.

Ontario. Ministry of Agriculture, Food and Rural Areas. 2005. Farming operations to come under the occupational health and safety act. November. http://www.omafra.gov.on.ca/english/busdev/facts/ohsa.htm.

Ontario. Ministry of Labour. 2006. Improving occupational health and safety on farms. June. http://www.labour.gov.on.ca/english/news/2006/06-73b.html.

Panitch, L., and D. Swartz. 2003. *From consent to coercion: The assault on trade union freedoms.* 3rd ed. Toronto: Garamond.

Parr, J. 1985. Hired men: Ontario agricultural wage labour in historical perspective. *Labour/Le Travail* 15: 91–103.

Patchett, K. W. 1973. Reception of law in the West Indies. *Jamaican Law Journal* 17(35): 55–67.

Preibisch, K. 2007a. Foreign workers in Canadian agriculture: Not an all-male cast. *FocalPoint* (May–June): 8–9.

———. 2007b. Patterns of social exclusion and inclusion of migrant workers in rural Canada. Building Value in Temporary Migration Program, Sir Arthur Lewis Institute of Social and Economic Studies, University of West Indies (UWI), North–South Institute, University of the West Indies, Cave Hill, Barbados. 7–8 May. http://www.nsi-ins.ca.

Purdy, J. 1999. Postcolonialism: The emperor's new clothes? In *Laws of the Postcolonial,* ed. E. Darian-Smith and P. Fitzpatrick, 203–32. Ann Arbor: Univ. of Michigan Press.

Satzewich, V. 1991. *Racism and the incorporation of foreign labour: Farm labour migration to Canada since 1945.* New York: Routledge.

———. 1999. The political economy of race and ethnicity. In *Race and Ethnic Relations in Canada,* 2nd ed., ed. P. S. Li, 311–46. New York: Oxford Univ. Press.

Satzewich, V., and L. Wong. 2003. Immigration, ethnicity, and race: The transformation of transnationalism, localism, and identities. In *Changing Canada: Political economy as transformation,* ed. W. Clement and L. F. Vosko, 363–92. Montreal and Kingston: McGill-Queen's Univ. Press.

Saul, S. 2006. *Development after globalization: Theory and Practice for the embattled south in a new imperial age.* London: Zed Books.

Service Canada (Government of Canada). 2006. Caribbean and Mexican Seasonal Agricultural Workers Program: Termination policy. http://www1.servicecanada.gc.ca/en/on/epb/agri/termination.shtml.

Sharma, N. 2006. *Home economics: Nationalism and the making of "migrant workers" in Canada*. Toronto: Univ. of Toronto Press.

Smith, A. 2005. Legal consciousness and resistance in Caribbean seasonal agricultural workers. *Canadian Journal of Law and Society* 20(2): 95–122.

———. forthcoming. Transnational labour law, global governance and the Caribbean. In *Caribbean international relations in the twenty-first century*, ed. S. Wilson and O. Robertson.

Stasiulis, D. K., and A. B. Bakan. 2005. *Negotiating citizenship: Migrant women in Canada and the global system*. Toronto: Univ. of Toronto Press.

Trumper, R., and L. Wong. 2007. Canada's guest workers: Racialized, gendered, and flexible. In *Race and racism in twenty-first century Canada: Continuity, complexity, and change*, 151–74, ed. S. Hier and B. Singh Bolaria. Peterborough, ON: Broadview Press.

Tucker, E. 2006. Will the vicious circle of precariousness be unbroken? The exclusion of Ontario farm workers from the occupational health and safety act. In *Precarious employment: Understanding labour market insecurity in Canada*, ed. L. F. Vosko, 256–76. Montreal and Kingston: McGill-Queen's Univ. Press.

Turner, M. ed. 1995. *From chattel slaves to wage slaves: The dynamics of labour bargaining in the Americas*. Kingston, Jamaica: Ian Randle.

Verma, V. 2003. The Mexican and Caribbean Seasonal Agricultural Workers Program: Regulatory and policy framework, farm industry level employment practices and the future of the program under unionization. Report to the North–South Institute. Ottawa: North–South Institute.

———. 2007. The regulatory and policy framework of the Caribbean Seasonal Agricultural Workers Program. Building Value in Temporary Migration Program, Sir Arthur Lewis Institute of Social and Economic Studies, University of West Indies (UWI), North–South Institute, University of the West Indies, Cave Hill, Barbados. 7–8 May. http://www.nsi-ins.ca.

Wong, L. 1984. Canada's guestworkers: Some comparisons of temporary workers in Europe and North America. *International Migration Review* 18(1): 85–98.

Wood, E. M. 2002. Global capital, national States. In *Historical materialism and globalization*, ed. M. Rupert and H. Smith, 17–39. London and New York: Routledge.

PART TWO

Cuban Culture at the Eye of the Globalizing Hurricane: The Case of *Nueva Trova*

Norman Cheadle

> Mi país es pobre, mi piel mejunje,
> mi gobierno proscrito, mis huestes utópicas.
> Soy candidato del inventario de la omisión,
> por no ser globable.
> — Silvio Rodríguez

Introduction

Revolutionary Cuba occupies an exceptional place in the emerging global order due to its status as a virtual dropout from globalizing capitalism, which the economic embargo imposed by that order's American hegemon reinforces. Cuba's political and economic divergence is further sharpened by its geographical proximity to the United States. Even though the hemispheric regime of neo-liberalism underwritten by American military and economic might has been recently challenged elsewhere in Latin America—especially in Venezuela, Bolivia, and Ecuador—Cuba remains unique in that it has sustained a separate order for nearly fifty years now: for roughly half a century, Cuban culture has evolved under a radically different set of political, social, and economic parameters. However, no culture can be hermetically sealed off from other cultural influences, and least of all Cuban culture with its "supersyncretic archive," as Antonio Benítez-Rojo (1992, 155) once put it. Thus, its exceptionality notwithstanding, Cuba inevitably participates to some degree in the maelstrom of cultural flow swirling across the planet. Cuban culture, at once bracketed from and participant in a larger turbulent system, is at the eye of a hurricane.

By comparing globalization to a hurricane, I do not wish to strike the apocalyptic tone of such metaphors as Mario Benedetti's—globalization as "a volcano without name, its hurtful lava destroying fauna and flowers."[1] The hurricane metaphor suggests not the catastrophic, irrevocable displacement of earth and fire, but rather the mobilization of the airy element into a volatile and complex meteorological system, a storm that has always been proper to the Caribbean, indeed a routine occurrence there. After all, the word "hurricane" itself—bequeathed us, via Spanish, by an extinct Taino language—predates that first wave of Western globalization initiated precisely in the Caribbean by the Spanish Empire. What's more, the often violently heterogeneous cultural flows on and around the island of Cuba, which inspired Fernando Ortiz's neologism "transculturation," could perhaps be figured as a series of hurricanes, or even a single storm system mutating over time, to whose destructiveness the Caribbean has responded with creativity. However, just as both the scope and the violence of meteorological hurricanes are increasing due to the global warming brought about by capitalist consumerism, so the current phase of economic and cultural globalization becomes historically unprecedented in its far-reaching, violent effects. Todd Gitlin has even wondered if the "torrent of images and sounds" produced "under the sign of Mickey Mouse & Co." may not mean "an end to culture" (2001, 205–10). Thankfully, the (albeit brilliant and controlled) hysteria of a New York public intellectual grows out of a structure of feeling that is alien to Cuba.[2]

It may help to consider the hurricane model in terms of Arjun Appadurai's oft-cited model of global cultural flow, which proposes five non-coincident dimensions—ethnoscapes, technoscapes, finanscapes, mediascapes, and ideoscapes (1995, 296ff). The suffix *-scape*, according to Appadurai, indicates not only the "fluid, irregular shapes" of these dimensions but also that the relations among them are not "objectively given" but rather "deeply perspectival," "inflected very much by the historical, linguistic and political situatedness of different sorts of actors," from the nation-state down to the individual (ibid., 296–97). Let me forthwith make explicit the perspective of this article: the image of the hurricane is a totalized condensation produced by viewing those various flowing "scapes" and their disjunctures from the Cuban viewpoint, on the level of nation-state, as that viewpoint is adopted by the Canadian individual who, sympathizing with Cuba, writes these lines. Thus, though singular, the viewpoint being explicated here is not one-eyed but at the very least bifocal, both Cuban and Canadian. Even if this perspective is specifically situated, however, it is elaborated upon an objective premise. Throughout both the first and third worlds, the flow rate varies within the dimensions identified by Appadurai, as do the resulting disjunctures among them, but in general "the sheer speed, scale and volume of these flows" is of an order hitherto unknown in human history (ibid., 301). In the case of Cuba, by contrast, all five dimensions are so strongly overdetermined by geopolitics, and the flow of international capital is so reduced, as to set this island-nation apart within the general torrent: there is an objectively observable "flow differential" between Cuba and most of the rest of the world; as a result, the "turbulence index" is distinctly lower there.

A brief consideration of the first three of Appadurai's "scapes" will confirm the point. Cuba's *ethnoscape* registers a bare trickle of immigration and emigration, unlike the torrential planetary flows to the rich North from all across the Southern Hemisphere. Tourism, too, thanks to the American legal prohibition against its own citizens visiting Cuba, is only a fraction of what it might otherwise be. The *technoscape* also changes slowly in Cuba, whereas it rushes quickly in the developed world and erratically in the developing world. Cubans, for example, have ingeniously learned to make do with their fleet of ageing Ladas. While rapid, capital-intensive advances in medical technology can actually diminish access to health care—in small-town Canada, for example, where there is also a chronic shortage of doctors—by overburdening the budgets of local hospitals, low-tech Cuba not only provides universal health care efficaciously but produces a surplus of qualified doctors. The notoriety of the Helms-Burton law makes comment on the *finanscape* from a Cuban perspective almost superfluous. True, there is some capital investment from countries such as Canada and Spain, mainly in the tourist industry, but Cuba is sheltered from the vagaries of vast anarchic flows of speculative finance capital that can wreck national currencies overnight. Cuba's *peso convertible* (CUC) mediates between the international monetary system and the *moneda nacional* (MN), providing a cushion against shocks in the global economy, though by the same token the dual currency system generates a destabilizing differential within the domestic economy. Many consumer goods such as refrigerators are sold only in CUCs, and not everyone has access to those figleafed American dollars.

Ethnoscapes, technoscapes, and finanscapes, in Appadurai's concept, form a group; the "deeply disjunctive relationships" among them must be accounted for by any "elementary model of global political economy" (Appadurai 1995, 298). Mediascapes and ideoscapes, "[b]uilt upon the disjunctures" of the other three "scapes," are in turn closely related to one another. The *mediascape* refers both to images and information created by the media and to the electronic means of their distribution; the *ideoscape*, to ideologies and counter-ideologies in a restrictive sense of these terms, i.e., concatenations of ideas in discourses oriented to sustaining or capturing state power. The two groups of "scapes" seem to correspond to the traditional Marxian dichotomy of base (the economic means of production) and superstructure (ideology, culture).[3] But in recent decades the dialectic between base and superstructure has taken a new twist. As Veit Erlmann has observed, "Western hegemony in the late twentieth century is no longer a matter of 'materially' subjecting the periphery to the cycles and economic interests of the center, but of manufacturing sense, of producing amid the rampant discontinuities of the postcolonial world a sense of connectedness by injecting into the seamless, medial flow 'realities' and actualities that have been generated by purely electronic means" (1999, 181); and that "it is the monopoly on explanation that Western bourgeois thinking seeks to restore, not imperial rule as such" (ibid., 183). No doubt, but the "monopoly on explanation" that produces the "realities" of medial flow achieves economic domination just as surely as traditional imperialism once did. George Yúdice, in *The expediency of culture*, has pointed out that, in capital's new regime of accumulation through the neo-liberal globalization of the planet, culture is no longer merely an ancillary support but is in fact integral to the process (2003, 192). Culture, he continues, "increasingly becomes a part of business and economic development departments, as was recently the case of the City of Miami Beach with the creation of a liaison for the entertainment industry in the economic Development Division" (ibid., 195). Yúdice goes on to conduct a case study on Miami as a centre where culture, instrumentalized in the media and ideoscapes, plays a salient role in the new globalizing regime.

Cuba and Miami: Eye and Eyewall of the Hurricane

A recent headline from *El País* reads: "La caída del muro de Florida" [The Fall of the Florida Wall] (Caño 2007), a reference to the old Berlin Wall and to a purported fading-away of the old, rabidly anti-Castro generation of Miami Cubans. I propose to replace the metaphor of the wall of bricks and mortar with that of the "eyewall" that encircles the eye of the hurricane. The eyewall is a circular band within the hurricane where the storm system's winds are moving at the greatest speed; it is where the system's kinetic force is most intensely concentrated (US Department of Commerce 2007). If the island of Cuba is at the eye of the swirling vortex of cultural currents in a storm system powered by neo-liberal capital accumulation, the eyewall of the storm is a band that runs straight through Miami.

In 1898 the United States chose Miami as headquarters of their security state vis-à-vis Latin America (Yúdice 2003, 196); since the Cuban Revolution in 1959, "the U.S. government has pumped billions of dollars into the Cuban exile community to transform it into a showcase" in an attempt to dazzle both the Cubans who remained on the island and other minorities within the United States who may have been attracted to Marxist and anti-imperialist critical frameworks (ibid., 197). Thus, from a military/police centre of command and control, Miami evolved into an economic one: a case of "politics by other means," orchestrating a new Pax Americana, as Jorge Nef and Alejandra Roncallo describe it (see Chapter 1 in this volume). In the current regime of transnational capitalism, in which the mediascape is a crucial site of domination, the traditional dominance of the United States is shared among new transnational capitalist entities. True, the two dominant Spanish-language networks Univisión and Telemundo, both operating chiefly out of Miami, are still American-owned; together they reach over 100 million viewers throughout the United States and Latin America. But two global media conglomerates, Spain's Telefónica and Germany's Bertelmann, made a deal to merge Terra, Telefónica's internet provider, with Lycos to create Terra Lycos, one of the world's largest internet companies. The American project of hemispheric dominance is merging with a larger transnational project of dominance, one of whose centres is Miami. For multinationals and cultural celebrities alike, Miami is a convenient location, being easily accessible to Europe, the United States, and Latin America. And of course, as in other major capitals of both the United States and Latin America, the good life enjoyed by Miami's movers and shakers and beautiful people is surrounded by the dystopia of conflict and poverty, especially among the local American blacks and Haitians (Yúdice 2003, 200–10).

When Yúdice calls Miami "the cultural capital of Latin America," this (mock-)honorific designation should properly be understood as meaning the command-and-control centre from which the culture industries extract value from Latin American culture, then re-disseminate it globally. Miami is producing a new Latin-ness, no longer solely Cuban but generalized: a kind of virtual Latino-ness (Yúdice 2003, 206). Arlene Dávila, whose book *Latinos, Inc.* exposes the invention/exploitation by corporate America of the category "Latino," points out an emblematic example of this process in Antonio Banderas, who on Telemundo broadcasts the slogan "Latinos are hot" to seduce corporate advertisers (2001, 1). The Spanish movie actor, who has spectacularly trivialized on screen such Latin American figures as Che Guevara and David Siqueiros, has also become a key outrunner of the transnational corporate operation of cultural extraction and accumulation.

Paradoxically, however, even as Miami's powerful extraction machine sucks cultural values from Latin America, flattens them out and empties them in order to better rebroadcast them back to their original producers, the Floridian city is not especially good at *producing* cultural value. This is quite clear in the music industry. As musicologist and *nueva trova* expert Robin Moore observes, "in contrast to Cuba itself, Miami has produced few figures of national or international stature.... Miami has become a centre of commerce and of recording and distributing music but not of artistic effervescence," a state of affairs that leads to the common perception that Miami is in fact "culturally impoverished" (2006, 254). But this does not necessarily mean that Miami uninhibitedly exploits the wealth of the island's music, as it does to the rest of Latin America. The lingering ideological animus of Miami

Cubans against the Revolution ensures that most Cuban musicians, especially those associated with the *nueva trova*, never perform in Miami—or anywhere else in the United States, thanks to the Miami–Cuban lobby's exorbitant influence in Washington.[4] Poor Cuban Miami, so close to its parent island and so far from the cultural plenitude it forsook!

Nueva Trova vis-à-vis 'World Music'

The *nueva trova* is anathema to Miami ideologues because its music, more than any other, is closely associated with Revolutionary Cuba. The musical movement arose spontaneously in the 1960s in consonance with international musical currents, especially the political protest song in both North and South America. Only later, in 1972, was it officially recognized and baptized as the *nueva trova* by the Cuban state. A cultural form born in the new circumstances created by the Cuban Revolution of 1959, though not an invention of the new regime, *nueva trova* may thus be considered as a synecdoche of revolutionary Cuban cultural identity, and so it will be worthwhile to consider how *nueva trova* is situated in relation to the first-world culture industries, in particular the extremely successful commercial phenomenon known as "world music."

I begin by recalling a verbal exchange that took place at a conference in Havana in December 2006. The music and film critic Frank Padrón had just delivered a plenary address on the *canción cubana contemporánea* in which he traced the *nueva trova*'s development from the mid-sixties to the present, highlighting the heterogeneous artistic influences, national and international, that had inflected that development. In the ensuing discussion, he was asked if, in his opinion, the *nueva trova* would eventually be integrated into the globalizing tendency of pop music known in musical shorthand as "world music." Padrón (2006) emphatically rejected the suggestion. He maintained that, even though exotic new influences have always and continually made themselves felt in *nueva trova*, this song form, in spite of its evident eclecticism, has its own specific integrity that resists the fragmentation, carnivalization, and "pastiche-ization" typical of the postmodern cultural condition.

As a Cuban intellectual, Padrón was clearly staking out an ideological position. In the history of Cuban popular music, there have been debates throughout the twentieth century about what constitutes authentic "Cuban" music. Since the 1920s, there have been successive reactions against the *son, filin, nueva trova*, and rock.[5] Even though the cultural motive for rejection varied from case to case, ranging from racism to anti-North-Americanism, the common denominator was the fear that *cubanidad* was being contaminated. It seems obvious, given the content of his plenary address, that a similar xenophobia could not be the motive for Padrón's rather vehement rejection of "world-musicalization."

On the other hand, the most striking thing about Padrón's account of *nueva trova* was its apoliticism. This stands in sharp contrast to Clara Díaz's history of *La nueva trova* (1994; re-edited in 1997). Díaz makes it clear that aesthetic and political avant-gardism went hand in hand from *nueva trova*'s beginnings in the mid-1960s. She openly affirms the principle of political voluntarism: first, the ideologico-aesthetic principles, inspired by Fidel's "Palabras a los intelectuales" speech, were forged, by stages, in various official instances and articulated in publications such as *El Caimán Barbudo*; then an elite core of musicians — Silvio Rodríguez, Pablo Milanés, and Noel Nicola are the leading triumvirate — set out to create a new musical form that would body forth those principles. Over and over again she makes it clear that the ultimate determining instance is politico-ideological.[6] María Figueredo, scholar of the *nueva canción* — the pan-Latin American musical movement in which the Cuban *nueva trova* originally participated — concurs when she cites the one and the other as "one of the strongest [cultural] responses" to post–WW II American imperialism (2003, 182). It is quite remarkable, then, that Padrón should completely bracket this dimension of his subject. In fact, he is much closer to the North American authority Robin Moore, who, though he does not depoliticize *nueva trova*, does point out the uneasy fit of *nueva trova*'s new aesthetic project with its political instrumentalization. Moore states baldly that "what came eventually to be called the *nueva trova* movement gained popularity in the 1960s not because of government policy but in spite of it" (2006, 153). Tracing the ups and downs of the movement's relationship to the state, Moore shows that the *nueva trova* has flourished in a kind of dialectical tension with officialdom. For the sake of the Cuban socialist project, the *trovadores* have criticized where they have seen problems, and often paid the price for their contestatory lyrics. But in the first instance, Moore concludes, their music represents "an implicit critique of capitalist culture" (2006, 167). One may posit, then, that Padrón and Díaz, respectively, reflect the two poles of the tension between, on one side, musical/cultural independence and, on the other, the will of the state bureaucracy to politically instrumentalize musical/cultural expression. Indeed, this very tension may be an index of the robust health of Cuba's cultural scene.[7]

If Padrón's position reflects neither xenophobia nor a Cuban version of "political correctness," how should one read his stance against *nueva trova*'s integration into "world music"? The term "world beat" and its synonym "world music" began to circulate widely in the mid-1980s; in Goodwin's and Gore's succinct definition, it referred to "any music that originates in, or borrows substantially from, the musical traditions of regions other than North America and Western Europe," but also includes "minority" music of the West such as "zydeco, Celtic sounds and Bulgarian folk music" (1990, 65). By 1990, the same authors could write: "World Beat is now institutionalized within the music and media industries. The form of that institutionalization is deeply shaped by Anglo-American hegemony in the music media" (ibid., 66–67). As such, it provoked a debate among progressive circles in the West: one camp celebrated it as the demise of rigid Western cultural dominance and the inclusion of the formerly marginalized; the critics saw a new form of cultural imperialism (ibid., 64). However, it quickly became clear to all that it was not a case of old-fashioned cultural imperialism but that something more subtle was going on. Veit Erlmann reframed the question thus: "contrary to the commonly held view that world beat is the voice of difference, articulating an Other and its distance from the Western self, I propose to explore the notion of world beat as an 'empty' semantic field, as a form of cultural practice that rests on completely altered notions of truth, meaning, and Utopia and that replaces these with what I call an aesthetics of the sono-dramatic" (1999, 181), which can be summed in Erlmann's words as "an aesthetics of amnesia, an a-semantic synchronicity" (ibid., 7). We shall return presently to the sono-dramatic, but for the moment let us note the cautious neutrality of Erlmann's tone. For if, as Erlmann posits earlier, "music no longer signifies something outside of itself, a reality, the truth" but instead "becomes a medium that mediates, as it were, mediation" (ibid., 6), then it would seem more forthright to say that the ideas of truth, meaning, and Utopia are not just "altered" but in fact emptied out and neutralized. Veitman's caution when postulating the sono-dramatic seems to reflect a certain paralysing ambivalence with regard to world music that prevails among progressive circles throughout the West. For example, the *Guardian Weekly* carries a regular column under the rubric "World Music" that informs its readers of the latest products marketed in a category that the progressive newspaper's editors apparently feel no need to problematize. Indeed, the greatest consumers of world music are probably those who think of themselves as progressive, anti-imperialist, culturally open-minded, etc. We enjoy listening to Buenavista Social Club, even if we cringe before Wim Wenders's film as we watch Ry Cooder present the Cuban musicians as a musical *objet trouvé* and then bow before the audience in Carnegie Hall as smugly as a magician who has just pulled a rabbit out of his hat.

Goodwin and Gore (1990, 65) trace the origin of the term "world beat" to Dan Del Santo, a musician and DJ from Austin, Texas, who made an album by the same name in 1982. They also speculate on the term's possible provenance from Jack Kerouac's novel *On the road* (1957), where he "wrote about tuning into a cosmic 'world beat'" (ibid.), a connection that would reinforce the notion's countercultural pedigree. The German music critic Diedrich Diederichsen, for his part, proposes a rather different and anterior origin for the term "world music." Publicly, Diederichsen cuts through the ambiguity of postmodernist theorizing and openly expresses his contempt for world music, both on the aesthetic level for its musically trite multiculturalism and for its political nullity (2002). Writing in a scholarly venue, Diederichsen (2004, 122) suggests that it was Karlheinz Stockhausen who coined the term in his 1973 article titled "Weltmusik." But Stockhausen was developing *Weltmusik*'s ideological-aesthetic program before that; in the notes written for his recording of *Telemusik* (1966), he wrote: "I wanted to come closer to an old and ever-recurrent dream: to go a step further towards writing, not 'my' music, but a music of the whole world, of all lands and races. I am sure you will hear it all in *Telemusik*" which, he goes on to tell us, quotes music from Japan, Bali, the southern Sahara, Spain, Hungary, Amazonia, China, and Vietnam (qtd. in Wörner 1973, 58). Thus, for Diederichsen, the notion of world music comes not from American pop- or counterculture but rather from the international high-art avant-garde, specifically from 1950s and '60s Minimalism. In their radical experimentation with sound, and informed by academic ethnomusicology, the Minimalists drew from non-Western music, Eastern music above all, in a cultural move that challenged "Western music's claim to absoluteness." The political correlate of this international cultural shift is manifested in the liberation movements throughout the third world and within the United States itself; indeed, some radical experimenters in sound such as Terry Riley and Steve Reich gave their music "an explicitly [progressive] political component" (Diederichsen 2004, 122). What began in the rarefied sphere of serious avant-garde music soon impinged upon pop music and culture, and indeed tended to break down the barrier between serious or high-brow music and pop(ular) music.

According to Diederichsen (2004, 128), "Minimalism's program of the fundamental exploration of sound contains within itself the seeds of extremely disparate, even antagonistic, projects." On one hand, "it opposes the surface appearances of culture," an impulse connected to a Marxist "critique of the commodity and consumer culture"; on the other, "it implies the essential priority of primeval forms and phenomena," leading to "a religious mysticism" that sooner or later "culminate[s] in the appeal to reactionary and anti-Semitic figures like C.G. Jung and many New Age gurus." Picking up the argument where Diederichsen leaves it, one might suggest that in recent decades in the capitalist West this antagonism has been resolved in a perversely Hegelian fashion. If the thesis was the Marxist critique of superficial commodity culture and the antithesis a quasi-mystical valorization of non-Western music, then the perverse synthesis is what we may call "world-musicalization," which, putting the bleakest face on it, is an aspect of "the cultural economy" that Jeremy Rifkin has defined as "the selling and buying of human experiences" (cited in Yúdice 2003, 34), including the ersatz mystical.

The 'Global' and the (non)-'Globable'

As an example of perverse world-musicalization, let us consider the advertising copy that Jericho Beach Music uses to promote the Canadian-Inuk throat-singer Tanya Tagaq Gillis. The sensationalist tag "the Jimi Hendrix of throat singing" appears at the head of the webpage. We read on to learn that Tagaq "has brought an ancient Inuit vocal game to the heights of the experimental music scene." Diedrichson's thesis seems to be confirmed: the reference to the 1960s countercultural icon is glancing; the text really wants to situate the traditional ethnic form in the avant-garde context, exemplified here by the Kronos string quartet, whose David Harrington is credited with the Jimi Hendrix comparison. Then we learn that Tagaq has collaborated and toured "with some of *the world's leading global artists*" (my emphasis), such as Bjork. Now, this text — pitched to the up-market yuppie consumer — is written in good expository English, so let us assume that the mention of "world" and "global" in the same syntagm is not due to sloppy redundancy. It is not about the world's leading artists but rather its leading *global* artists. So what does the qualifier "global" mean here? The obvious answer would be that it is mere hyperbole ("the world's leading global artists" would be more succinctly phrased as "the world's *globallest* artists," *global* being an amplifier of the superlative "leading"), but the enigmatic qualifier may also suggest some ideological supplement, whose nature is suggested as the text develops:

> Like Bjork, Tagaq makes music that is both decidedly unusual and universally appealing on a most primal level. Her innovative, solo style of throat singing seeks to push the boundaries of emotion and to express the primitive instincts she believes still reside deep within our flesh. She describes her evolution over the past six years as a process of going deeper and deeper into her performance to the point where she virtually "leaves her body" and lets the expression take over. (Tagaq 2007)

In this passage, the rapid accumulation of ideologemes — "primal level"; "primitive instincts" that "reside deep within our flesh" — build to the climax of extra-corporeal experience, surely a sublime object of New Age ideology, to borrow Slavoj Žižek's phrase. The New Age discourse is confirmed as the text continues; we read about the "cosmic coincidences" that led to Tagaq's collaboration with with Bjork and the Kronos Quartet. Furthermore, though the text is circumspect enough to avoid saying so directly, we are clearly meant to infer that Tagaq has privileged access to the "primal" and the "primitive" because she is Inuk, i.e., from a "primitive," non-Western cultural tradition.

Žižek has argued that "obscurantist New Age ideology is *an immanent outgrowth of modern science itself* — from David Bohm to Fritjof Capra, examples abound of 'dancing Wu Li masters,' teaching us about the Tao of physics... and so on.... [T]hese obscurantist shoots are not simply imposed from the outside, but function as what Louis Althusser would have called a 'spontaneous ideology'... as a kind of spiritualist supplement" (2001, 216). It may be less spontaneous than Žižek suggests. Karlheinz Stockhausen surely played a discursive role in elaborating the New Age ideological supplement when he grandly announced in "Weltmusik" the imminent end of the "religion of science" and the advent of a time "in which the musical in humanity—the resonance of all rhythms in mankind and their harmonization through music— echoes through all culture" (Stockhausen 1989, 325). In Heideggerian fashion, Stockhausen blithely assumes the Westernization of the entire world; through a "rapid process of dissolution, the diverse cultures of today will devolve into the one, more unified *world culture*" (ibid., 319), which will be ineluctably hegemonized by the West: "The standard of European culture will persist and even grow in fascination for all other peoples. Our great responsibility consists in this, and therefore demands that we maintain as many crystallizations of other cultures in their present form as is at all possible. The cultural museum of the earth, in which the musical museum plays a really essential role, cannot be avoided" (ibid., 321).

Stockhausen's dream of museifying the whole world is a more grandiose version of the older, more modest museifying impulses of nineteenth-century imperialism. What is new in Stockhausen's project initially appears contradictory: on one hand, we are to have the "crystallizations" of non-European cultures in a planetary museum under the curatorship of the European masters; and yet, on the other hand, all cultural diversity is to "dissolve" into a single world culture. In sum, all Otherness is to be absorbed into the (Western) One but at the same time preserved as a collection of neutralized traces. Stockhausen is perhaps a founding ideologue of what Erlmann diagnoses as the "aesthetics of the sono-dramatic," in which musical sounds, de-linked from their historical-cultural matrices, are brought together in an atemporal amnesiac present. Here is how Stockhausen writes about his piece *Kurzwellen* (1968): it is "the opening up of a new consciousness" and "a higher unity" in which the "earlier antitheses between old and new, between far and near, between the known and unknown, are resolved. *Everything* is *simultaneously* the *whole*. The notion of time is swallowed into the mind's past" (qtd. in Wörner 1973, 69). To return to the example of Tagaq, the cultural form of throat singing is to be preserved in the sono-dramatic aspic of "global" music, but its historicity will be suspended there, its signifying power dissolved in the simultaneous whole.

It must be acknowledged that the analysis of this example of world-musicalization is based solely on the elaborate infomercial dedicated to her by Jericho Beach Music on the Web. The intrinsic aesthetic quality of Tagaq's music is not being considered here; it is rather a question of the *mediation* of her music through world-musicalizing discourse. The writer(s) of Tagaq's promotional text are not necessarily cynical propagandists who confect their pitch from some abstract, extra-cultural space, some *hors-culture*. They move within an ambient, hegemonic cultural matrix, one in which Tagaq and Bjork and David Harrington are themselves caught up. Though I admit that I am bracketing the question of Tagaq's aesthetic value, it is difficult to imagine how one can truly bypass the culture industry's mediation of her music, how one can undercut, as Erlmann (1999) puts it, the "mediation of mediation."

As a counter-example to the world-musicalization of Tagaq and the "sono-dramatization" of Inuit throat singing, let us consider how tradition is referenced in the song entitled "Juan Pandero" by the *nueva trovadora* Rita del Prado (1998). Del Prado is practically absent from the Western mediascape. Thus, in direct opposition to the example of Tagaq my brief analysis of del Prado's song is based entirely on its recording on CD.[8] Exquisitely melodic, the song's instrumentalization—the singer's voice accompanied by acoustic guitar—represents a reaffirmation of *criollo* roots.[9] The lyrics are, at first blush, quite simple. The song begins as a traditional ballad about a crime of passion, but the tale morphs into one about the origin of the Cuban *trova* and finally adds up to a densely coded statement about the cultural significance of the *nueva trova*, a statement that ultimately would carry political nuances as well. Over the course of the song, the name Juan Pandero (John Drum) becomes Juan el Panadero (John the Baker). "Para los trovadores, tú fuiste el aurora, Juan el Panadero" [For the *trovadores*, you were the dawn, Juan el Panadero] is the last line of the song. In a review of the recently published *La trova en Santiago de Cuba: Apuntes históricos*,[10] we learn that the quasi-legendary Juan el Panadero did indeed exist historically and is held to be Cuba's first *trovador* (Zamora Céspedes 2007). I have not yet been able to consult the book, so it is impossible for me to hazard an interpretation of the musical lore that del Prado is drawing upon and shaping into the signifying content of the central line of her song, which for the outsider is only a hollow rhetorical affirmation: "No hay Cuba sin trova" [There is no Cuba without trova]. It *can* be noted, however, that the eastern city of Santiago de Cuba is extremely rich in musical traditions, being the birthplace of a long line of important Cuban musicians in more recent history, from Compay Segundo back to Pepe Sánchez (1856–1918) and Sindo Garay (1867–1968). The latter two, in Clara Díaz's account (1997, 8), were national-liberationist paragons of Cuba's *trova tradicional*, the musical movement that she considers the originary antecedent of the *nueva trova*. Santiago is also the most "African" of Cuban cities; the Afro-Cuban forms *son* and *danzón* developed there and continue to be heard in some strains of the *nueva trova*. Thus, in singing about a semi-mythical *trovador santiaguero* (Juan el Panadero), Rita del Prado is alluding to a richly layered musicological history that is rife with both cultural and political significance for Cubans. How she is musically moulding and lyrically interpreting that cultural history and how she relates that tradition to the present are questions that, for now at least, remain beyond the competence of the outsider who writes these lines. This is *not*, however, because there is some arcane mystery at stake, one buried in the primal (or primitive) flesh of a fetishized Other, nor, conversely, because the signifying power of a complicated musical past has been swallowed into a Stockhausian simultaneity. Rita del Prado, classified by Robin Moore (2006, 161) as a member of the second-generation *novísima trova* that came of age in the 1990s, almost certainly is positioning herself and her art by laying claim to the tradition of the Cuban *trova* "*tout court*," but her aesthetic/rhetorical move is at antipodes from the sono-dramatic acid-bath of world-musicalization. As for her assertion that "no hay Cuba sin trova," regardless of whatever else it may mean, we can infer that the line says at least this: that Cuban culture's very survival depends on the continued vitality of its music, and so that music must not be reduced to the "global" nor to the ahistorical, amnesiac, simultaneous whole.[11]

Given Rita del Prado's almost complete absence from the mediascape, she can hardly be considered a global artist in the lexicon of the purveyors of world music. Is this because there is something inherently "non-globable" about her music? A glance at another pair of examples, both of them Cuban musicians, will suggest an answer. Compay Segundo, ever since the Cooder–Wenders intervention, must surely be included in the ranks of global artists; Pablo Milanés, by contrast, does not qualify as such. And yet, as Robin Moore points out, the recordings that Milanés made in the 1980s in the *Años* series "include essentially the same material that has made such a splash in conjunction with the Buena Vista Social Club" (2006, 290n12). Is this not because Compay Segundo and Pablo Milanés are situated at quite different junctures of the ideo- and mediascapes? In the narrative popularized by Cooder and Wenders, the musicians of the Buena Vista Social Club had been languishing in the darkness of socialist Cuba until the American pop star and the German filmmaker, white knights of liberal tolerance, came along to rescue them into the sunlight of globalness, at the same time unlocking their music from its captivity since the 1959 Revolution. Pablo Milanés, by contrast, is one of the two most important icons of the *nueva trova*, music that cannot be dissociated from the Revolution. The fact that, in reality, both Compay and Pablo were playing similar music in the same general cultural scene, one that has been very much alive these last four and a half decades, is not, of course, what counts. Milanés, child of the Revolution, is irredeemable; the octogenarians of Buena Vista Social Club could be portrayed as relics of the good old years of Papa Hemingway's Cuba.[12]

It is a scantily publicized fact that both Pablo Milanés and the other outstanding figure of *nueva trova*, Silvio Rodríguez, have been nominated for the Latin Grammy Awards, the former in 2006, the latter in 2007 (Vázquez 2007). But for well-known geopolitical reasons, the music sector of the "virtual Latino-ness" industry—one branch of world-musicalization—has not yet been able to gain a definitive purchase on either of these Cuban musicians. Milanés did not win the Grammy, nor was he allowed by American authorities even to attend the ceremony, and Silvio Rodríguez's nomination fizzled out the same way.[13] This, in spite of the efforts of David Byrne, whose former rock band Talking Heads was active in the world-music scene of the 1980s, to bring Rodríguez "into the light" of world music fame.[14] The illustrious figure of Silvio Rodríguez—musician, poet, *diputado* in the Cuban government—is indeed world famous, but in a non-global way. As he himself has remarked wryly, he is not quite "globable." Asked in an interview how he felt when he heard that he had been nominated for the Grammy, he answered with exquisite irony: "Recibí la noticia en República Dominicana, esperando un ciclón, y pudiera decir que me sentí como Compay Segundo cuando fue 'descubierto' por Ry Cooder" [I received the news in the Dominican Republic, waiting for a cyclone, and I could say I felt like Compay Segundo when he was 'discovered' by Ry Cooder] (Rodríguez 2007b). Joking aside, we may say that Silvio is still waiting for the cyclone—let's call it the hurricane—of world-musicalization to overtake him; figuratively situated at the eye of the storm, he never quite gets dragged through the eyewall of the hurricane.

Nueva Trova and 'Alter-Globalization'

If the situation of Silvio Rodríguez, perhaps *nueva trova*'s most representative figure, reflects the situation of this genre in the eye of the hurricane, it should be mentioned that this figure is rendered visible in large part thanks to another kind of eye that opens within the planetary mediascape. Much of the research for this article was facilitated by the *Portal de Trova*, a website dedicated not only to *nueva trova* but also to matters related to the international *nueva canción* and its sequel generation. *Portal de Trova* collects news items, reviews of music and books, opinion pieces, and even academic articles on *trova* from both Cuban sources and from online publications throughout Spanish America. Launched in 2000, the website aims to put the technology of "the web of webs" at the service of people "throughout the world so that they may be acquainted with the songs of Silvio [Rodríguez], Pablo [Milanés], Vicente Feliú, and Noel Nicola, and Cuban culture in general."[15] It seems to propose, in effect, an alternative globalizing project for the constitutively "non-globable" *nueva trova*. At the same time, it quite consciously functions as an institutionalizing organ for *nueva trova* by sponsoring, for example, literary and musical contests in honour of the recently deceased Noel Nicola. Both these tendencies—alter-globalizing and institutionalizing—may be read as indicators of *nueva trova*'s status at this point in its evolution.

The current tendency toward institutionalization is no doubt a consequence of the generational character of *nueva trova*. Robin Moore (to whom I am largely indebted for the information deployed in this and the following paragraph) remarks in his synthetic subchapter "Defining *Nueva Trova*" (2006, 136–42) that its musical heterogeneity has made it difficult to pin down musically, and so "it has been defined less in musical terms and more by the *generation* that created it and its meanings" (ibid., 141; my emphasis). The generation that created *nueva trova* is being succeeded by new generations; hence the natural tendency toward institutional memorialization. But consideration of *nueva trova*'s originary heterogeneity suggests that the *Portal del Trova*'s alter-globalizing discourse was already present performatively in *nueva trova*'s musical eclecticism, its blending of both international and local sources. *Nueva trova* grew out of the South American *nueva canción*, but with a significant difference: "*Nueva canción* represented an attempt to valorize folk traditions that were absent in the national media [in Chile, Argentina, Uruguay]. By contrast, early *nueva trova* represented something different, a conscious break with local influences and an effort to create a cosmopolitan blend of local and international genres" (ibid., 137). Other notable international influences are 1960s rock (Rolling Stones, Beatles, Bee Gees) and folk rock (Phil Ochs, Pete Seeger, Bob Dylan).

On the local side, two related older genres inform *nueva trova*. It renews the tradition of the *vieja trova*, in that both emphasize the song's lyrics and texts and its emotional messages. Another source is *filin*, which infuses the traditional Cuban *canción* (romantic song) with North American jazz idioms. Both these local genres meet in the work of Pablo Milanés, the "innovative traditionalist" (Moore 2006, 145) who is credited by historians for writing the first piece of *nueva trova*, a song titled "A mis 22 años." Silvio Rodríguez, on the other hand, is described by Moore as an "internationalist" (ibid., 145). Distinct and complementary figures, the two singer-songwriters coincide artistically in the importance they place on the lyrics of their songs, which—reflecting a tendency quite atypical for the Caribbean—are not primarily meant for dancing but rather for self-expression on themes poetical, political, ethical, philosophical. And they share with their generational cohort a common ethos, at once "patriotic and rebellious" (ibid., 143). In sum, *nueva trova*'s founding generation is both individualistic and politically committed, anchored in Cuban tradition and open to global influences.

It is this set of meanings and values that I am characterizing as the performative alter-globalizing impulse of *nueva trova*. The qualifier that surely sets it apart from world music is "patriotic," a quality that most "global artists" would shun as definitely uncool. Thus, in *nueva trova*, the value of social/political *engagement* has a more concrete valence than does the politically correct but abstract idealism of world music groups such as *Manu Chao*. Like world music, *nueva trova* blends styles, a predilection that led James Lawrence Robbins (1990, 435) to describe the *novotrovadores* as "culture brokers." The descriptor is no doubt equally apt for the global artists of world music, but the mode of culture-brokerage is not the same: it is the difference between, in the former case, solidarity with a concretely-based revolutionary project and, in the latter, a directionless and placeless "mediation of mediation." In a word, *nueva trova*'s utopian universalism is firmly grounded in *cubanidad*, a concrete cultural and musical tradition in evolution: unlike world music, *nueva trova*—pace Deleuze and Guattari—has steadfastly refused deterritorialization.

As is evident even its name, the *novísima trova* that came into its own in the 1990s represents a generational change—not a total break with *nueva trova*, but rather an intensification of the original movement's complementary tendencies of "innovative traditionalism" (in singer-songwriters such as Gerardo Alfonso, Heidy Igualada, Rita del Prado) and "internationalism" (in Carlos Varela or the duo Gema y Pável). In Rita del Prado's ballad "Juan Pandero" can be seen a refinement and vindication of the tradition of the Cuban *romance* (ballad), a genre with historical roots five centuries deep. The great Cuban musicologist Alejo Carpentier (1979, 28) has remarked that Cuba is one of the countries in Spanish America where the romance tradition has best been conserved; del Prado reinforces and extends this tradition with a creatively conservative aesthetic. Carlos Varela, by contrast, one of the most famous of the *novísimos*, has a sound "virtually indistinguishable" from the music of U2 or Sting, according to Robin Moore (2006, 162). But in this aesthetic move, is Varela really behaving so differently from the early founding figures of *nueva trova*, Noel Nicola and Vicente Feliú, who "began their musical careers in the mid-1960s playing Elvis and Beatles covers and emulating rock combos" (ibid., 139)? Like his musical forebears, Varela is especially known for his powerful and often bitingly critical lyrics; and like his erstwhile protector Silvio Rodríguez, his relations with the state bureaucracy have not always been smooth (ibid., 162).

What *is* new, however, is that for years, now, Varela has been recording in Spain and Venezuela (Moore 2006, 162); clearly, the *novísima trova* is becoming implicated in the international recording industry, and so Cuban music is to some extent leaking into the medial flow of the global culture industry. The move toward institutionalization, exemplified in the *Portal del Trova*, is perhaps a partial bulwark against that industry's howling winds.

Conclusion

There is a discomfiting paradox for progressive-minded advocates of multi- or inter- or transculturalism (and the related notions of hybridity and *mestizaje*). Žižek, following Frederic Jameson and Alain Badiou, has phrased it this way: "the thriving of differences [celebrated by today's multiculturalism] relies on an underlying One: on the radical obliteration of Difference, of the antagonistic gap" (2001, 238). Let the Faustian figure of Stockhausen and his program for *Weltmusik* serve as a stark reminder of this uncomfortable truth. Nevertheless, that gap remains open, like the eye of a hurricane, precisely along the precarious eyewall that separates music such as the *nueva trova* (in spite of its transcultural eclecticism) from world music, and that demarcates Cuban culture (its supersyncretic archive notwithstanding) from cultural globalization. Senel Paz said in an interview not long ago that "[s]ería una catástrofe desde el punto de vista internacional que lo que significa Cuba para el imaginario colectivo latinoamericano llegue a una frustración" [it would be a catastrophe from the international perspective if what Cuba means for the collective imaginary of Latin America were to end in frustration] (Paz 2007). That catastrophe is not yet upon us.

Notes

The epigraph translates: "My country is poor, my skin a gungy mix, / my government outlawed, my hosts utopian. / I am a candidate for the inventory of omission, / for not being globable" ("Fronteras," from the CD *Expedición* [2002]). An alternate version of the second sentence appears as a tag at the bottom of the *Portal de Trova* webpage: "Mi voz no cuenta en las campanas de información, por no ser globable" [My voice doesn't count in the clangor of information, because it isn't globable].

1 In an interview with Carlos Montero of Radio Nederland, Benedetti asserted that "La globalización es un volcán sin nombre. Y su lava hiriente y derramada acaba con las faunas y las flores." The text is reproduced by the *Portal de Trova* (Benedetti 2007).

2 Recall Benítez-Rojo's lovely personal anecdote about the Cuban missile crisis of October, 1962 (1992, 10–11). He had only to watch the way two old black women were walking down the street in Havana "in a certain kind of way," he writes, in order to know "at once that there would be no apocalypse." The crisis was not resolved by statesmen, he concludes, but by "the culture of the Caribbean" (ibid., 10). There is no evidence to suggest that those women are not still walking that walk.

3 The Marxian construct is only implicit. Appadurai's model aims at "a tentative formulation about the conditions under which current global flows occur: *they occur in and through the growing disjunctures between ethnoscapes, technoscapes, financapes, mediascapes and ideoscapes*" (1995, 301).

4 Incredibly, since 11 September 2001, Cuba not only remains on the United States' list of proscribed "terrorist" nations, but Cuban performers are even less likely to gain access to the United States than their counterparts from Iran, Algeria,

Morocco, and other Middle Eastern countries that the Bush administration associates with Islamic terrorism (Moore 2006, 252). At the same time, the American authorities have for decades tolerated terrorism on the part of conservative Cuban-American leaders, who "throughout the United States have used their economic clout to discourage entrepreneurs and even universities from contracting Cuban musicians. They have also used bomb threats, and in some cases, actual bombings, in order to scare club owners for the same purpose" (ibid., 255).

5   In the 1920s, Eurocentric racism in the Cuban bourgeoisie reacted against the *son*, claiming that this African form was undermining the true *cubanidad*. In the 1950s, the *filin* [feeling] movement was criticized for being influenced by North American jazz and blues (Manduley López 2007).

6   In her account of the "Gestación y nacimiento del movimiento de la Nueva Trova," for example, Díaz starts with the I Encuentro Internacional de la Canción Protesta (celebrated in the Casa de las Américas, 24 July–8 August 1967). "La Resolución Final de este Encuentro dejaba manifiestos los principios ético-artísticos de sus participantes, al decir [que] 'la canción es un arma al servicio del pueblo, no un producto de consumo utilizado por el capitalismo para enajenarlo'" (1997, 21–22).

7   This health is confirmed by the recent debate over the *quinquenio gris*, the years between 1971 and 1976 when the repressive Luis Pavón Tamayo presided over the Consejo Nacional de Cultura and put a chill on Cuban culture affecting *nuevos trovadores* like Silvio Rodríguez (Moore 2006, 148–49). When, in January 2007, Pavón Tamayo and two other high-ranking cultural bureaucrats of the same period (Jorge Serguera and Armando Quesada) appeared on Cuban television, a storm of protest broke out (Vicent 2007). As a counterexample suggesting the absence of such a tension in the United States, consider this recent public relations manoeuvre by the US State Department: they actually hired the Los Angeles–based rock band Ozomatli, whose lyrics are explicitly contestatory and strongly critical of the Iraq invasion, and sent the group on a tour of Islamic countries—in order to improve the United States' image there! (Celis 2007).

8   A search on Google turns up only two web-sites containing parsimonious biographical/promotional material (one is at *Cubamusic.com*, partnered by Sangy of Italy and Artex of Cuba; the other is the Spain-based *Portal Latino*). Nor have I found a written version of the lyrics of Rita del Prado's song. The recording is from the fourth and last volume of *Antología de Nueva Trova*, whose title connotes a will to cultural conservation.

9   The Uruguayan musicologist Lauro Ayestarán notes that "[e]l instrumento criollo por excelencia es la guitarra" (1967, 10).

10 Lino Betancourt Molina, *La trova en Santiago de Cuba: Apuntes históricos* (Santiago de Cuba: Andante, Editora Musical de Cuba, 2007).

11 As a non-Cuban example, consider the meaningful vindication of traditional indigenous music that groups like *Inti-Illimani* and *Illapu* (both Chilean) undertook in the 1960s and beyond, with the result that "a large public became familiar with musical forms such as 'Yaravíes,' 'Carnavalitos,' Morenadas,' 'Huayños,' 'Bailecitos,' all indigenous Andean music hitherto virtually unknown except to the peoples of the highlands of Peru, Bolivia, Ecuador, Argentina and, to a certain extent, northern Chile" (Figueredo 2003, 186–87). These forms were not thus dissolved into ahistorical simultaneity but, on the contrary, were resignified through

a re-elaboration of those peoples' cultural memory in a manner harmonious with their own cultural/political aspirations.

12 See also Ana María Dopico's trenchant analysis of the Wenders film: "Symbolically erasing the Cuban musical present as well as forty years of history, Wenders reveals an eternal Cuban age in faces whose truths are immanent, redemptive, and amnesiac all at once" (2002, 486).

13 The Dominican-born Juan Luis Guerra swept the 2007 Latin Grammys, celebrated in Las Vegas, winning six of them. The only other multi-award winner was Ricky Martin (Ilich 2007). Nor has the election of Barack Obama changed the situation. On the occasion of Pete Seeger's ninetieth birthday (3 May 2009), the legendary American folksinger invited Silvio to attend the celebration. The US State Department refused to issue the visa necessary for Silvio to attend (CubaDebate 2009). Unable to attend, Silvio wrote to his "admirado y querido Maestro Pete Seeger" a birthday letter, recalling moments in their decades-long friendship that remain significant—personally, musically, and politically (Rodríguez 2009).

14 "The Talking Heads' album *Remain in light* was, according to the band, inspired by Nigerian afrobeat" (Goodwin and Gore 1990, 70). David Byrne visited Silvio Rodríguez in Cuba several years ago (Rodríguez 2007a) and in 1991 brought out under his Luaka Pop label the CD *Canciones urgentes: The greatests hits of Silvio Rodríguez*, re-released in 2003. The website of CD Universe (cduniverse.com) lists the album under six categories, including World Music and Nuevo [*sic*] Trova. Technically, then, world music has in fact made a very tentative claim on Silvio, even though it still finds *nueva trova* too foreign to spell it properly. On the other hand, neither Silvio nor *nueva trova* figures in Timothy Taylor's encyclopedic work on *Global pop: World music, world markets* (1997).

15 *Portal de Trova*'s mission statement can be found at http://portal.trovacub.com/modules.php?name=Content&pa=showpage&pid=4.

References

Appadurai, A. 1995. Disjuncture and difference in the global cultural economy. In *Global culture: Nationalism, globalization and modernity*, ed. M. Featherstone, 295–310. London: Sage.

Ayestarán, L. 1967. *El folklore musical uruguayo*. 2nd ed. Montevideo: Arca.

Benedetti, M. 2007. Interview with Carlos Montero: La globalización es la agonía sin fin de la esperanza. Portal de Trova. http://www.portal.trovacub.com/ modules.php?name=News&file=article&sid=1094.

Benítez-Rojo, A. 1992. *The repeating island: The Caribbean and the Postmodern perspective*. Trans. J. Meraniss. Durham, NC: Duke Univ. Press.

Caño, A. 2007. La caída del muro de Florida. *El País Digital*, 18 February. http://www.elpais.com/articuloCompleto/internacional/caida/muro/Florida/elpepint/20070218 elpepiint_10/Tes.

Carpentier, A. 1979. *La música en Cuba*. Havana: Editorial Letras Cubanas.

Celis, B. 2007. EE UU intenta seducir con el rock. *El País Digital*, 12 August. http://www.elpais.com/articuloCompleto/internacional/EE/UU/intenta/seducir/rock/el pepiint/20070812elpepiint_13/Tes.

CubaDebate. 2009. Gobierno norteamericano impide a Silvio Rodríguez a asistir a homenaje a Pete Seeger. *CubaDebate*, 3 May. http://www.cubadebate.cu/index.php?tpl=design/especiales.tpl.html&newsid_obj_id=14946.

Dávila, A. 2001. *Latinos, Inc.: The marketing and making of a people*. Berkeley: Univ. of California Press.

Del Prado, R. 1998. Juan Pandero. *Antología de la nueva trova*. Vol. 4. Havana: EGREM.

Díaz, C. 1997. *La nueva trova*. Havana: Editorial Letras Cubanas.

Diederichsen, D. 2002. Interview with Mariana Enríquez: El francotirador. *Página 12*. 12 December. http://pagina12.com.ar/diario/suplementos/radar/9-517-2002-12-12.html.

———. 2004. The primary: Political and anti-political continuities between minimal music and minimal art. Trans. J. Gussen. In *A minimal future? Art as object 1958–1968*, ed. A. Goldstein, 111–31. Los Angeles: Museum of Contemporary Art; Cambridge, MA: MIT Press.

Dopico, A. M. 2002. Picturing Havana: History, vision, and the scramble for Cuba. *Nepantla: Views from the South* 3(3): 451–93.

Erlmann, V. 1999. *Music, modernity, and the global imagination*. New York and Oxford: Oxford Univ. Press.

Figueredo, M. 2003. The Latin American song as an alternative voice to the new world order. In *The new world order: Corporate agenda and parallel reality*, ed. Gordana Yovanovich, 178–200. Montreal: McGill-Queen's Univ. Press.

Gitlin, T. 2001. *Media unlimited: How the torrent of images and sounds overwhelms our lives*. New York: Henry Holt.

Goodwin, A., and J. Gore. 1990. World beat and the cultural imperialism debate. *Socialist Review* 20 (July–September): 63–80.

Ilich, T. 2007. 2007 Latin Grammy award highlights & winners. *About.com: Latin music*, 9 November. http://latinmusic.about.com/b/2007/11/09/2007-latin-grammy-awards-winners.htm.

Manduley López, H. 2007. ¿Se debiera morir quien por bueno no lo estime?" *Portal de Trova*. 8 September. http://www.portal.trovacub.com/modules.php?name=News&file=article&sid=1133.

Moore, R. 2006. *Music and revolution: Cultural change in socialist Cuba*. Berkeley: Univ. of California Press.

Padrón, F. 2006. La vanguardia musical y poética en la canción cubana contemporánea. Plenary address to the I Coloquio Internacional de Estudios de Diálagos Interartísticos: La literatura y su relación con las artes. Centro Hispano-Americano de Cultura, Havana, Cuba.

Paz, S. 2007. Interview with María Luisa Blanco: La Revolución no se ha alimentado de la crítica. *El País Digital*, February 19. http://www.elpais.com/articuloCompleto/cultura/revolucion/ha/alimentado/critica/elpepicul/2007.

Robbins, J. L. 1990. Making popular music in Cuba: A study of the Cuban institutions of musical production and the musical life of Santiago de Cuba. Ph.D. diss., University of Illinois, Urbana-Champaign.

Rodríguez, S. 2007a. Interview with Jorge Smith: Los laureles me dan sustos. *Cubasí*, 8 August. http://www.cubasi.cu/desktopdefault.aspx?spk=160&clk=166847&lk=1&ck=85985&spka=35.

———. 2007b. Interview: Seguí creyendo que la cultura podía más. *La Jiribilla*, 7 September. http://www.lajiribilla.cubaweb.cu/2007/n330_09.html.
———. 2009. Carta de Silvio Rodríguez a Pete Seeger. *CubaDebate*, 4 May. http://www.cubadebate.cu/index.php?tpl=design/opiniones.tpl.html&newsid_obj_id=14956.
Stockhausen, K. 1989. World music. Trans. B. Radloff. *Dalhousie Review* 69 (Fall): 318–26.
Tagaq. 2007. *Jericho beach music*. 24 March. http://www.festival.bc.ca/jerichobeach/?artist=tagaq.
Taylor, T. D. 1997. *Global pop: World music, world markets*. New York and London: Routledge.
US Department of Commerce. National oceanic and atmospheric administration. 2007. Hurricanes: Structure. 22 February. http://hurricanes.noaa.gove/prepare/structure.htm.
Vázquez, O. 2007. Silvio entre los cantautores. *Granma*. 30 August. http://www.granma.cu/espanol/2007/agosto/juev30/silvio.html.
Vicent, M. 2007. El recuerdo del "quinquenio gris" moviliza a intelectuales cubanos. *El País Digital*, 13 January.
Wörner, K. H. 1973. *Stockhausen: Life and work*. Trans. B. Hopkins. Berkeley and Los Angeles: Univ. of California Press.
Yúdice, G. 2003. *The expediency of culture: Uses of culture in the global era*. Durham, NC: Duke Univ. Press.
Zamora Céspedes, B. 2007. De la trova caliente. *La Jiribilla: Revista de cultura cubana*. 23–29 June. http://www.lajiribilla.cu/sumario/aprende.html.
Žižek, S. 2001. *Did somebody say totalitarianism? Five interventions in the (mis)use of a notion*. London and New York: Verso.

From Pablo Neruda to Luciana Souza: *Latin America* as Poetic-Musical Space

Maria L. Figueredo

> "*Tierra mía, sin nombre, sin América*"
> "Land of mine, without a name, without América"
> Pablo Neruda, "Amor América (1400)," *Canto General* (1950)

> "*Así la poesía no habrá cantado en vano.*"
> "So that poetry would not have sung in vain."
> Nobel Prize in Literature acceptance speech (1971)

Of the Latin American poets being set to music today, Pablo Neruda (1904–73) takes the lead, given the capacity of his poetry to express a specific "situatedness" while fluidly moving across and into other cultural spaces. The most comprehensive online database of songs set to music by various musicians from across the globe, Musicalizando.com, lists 173 songs inspired by Neruda's poems.[1] This catalogue was created by Colombian poet Hugo Cuevas-Mohr in 2004, a year that becomes pivotal for witnessing a number of recordings and performances of Pablo Neruda's work, given that it marked the centenary of his birth. Other poets of stature in literary history and in their relationship to music are included in the catalogue, such as Alfonso X-El Sabio, Sor Juana Inés de la Cruz, Gustavo Adolfo Becquer, José Martí, Delmira Agustini, Rafael Alberti, Rosalía de Castro, César Vallejo, Jorge Luis Borges, Mario Benedetti, and younger writers Giaconda Belli and Bernardo Axtaga. Poets in Spanish-translation who appear include Walt Whitman, Fernando Pessoa, Arthur Rimbaud, and Bertold Brecht (http://www.musicalizando. com/catalogo/).[2] Yet none of these have provoked the same level of response by musicians as Neruda. Not even Uruguay's Mario Benedetti (1920–2009)—with 50 entries— comes close, although Benedetti is well recognized internationally for his

167

collaborations with musicians such as Daniel Viglietti (Uruguay), Joan Manuel Serrat (Spain), and Alberto Favero (Argentina). Neither do poets such as Federico García Lorca (Spain, 1898–1936) with 130 entries, nor Rafael Alberti (Spain, 1920–99) with 54, compare, although both had close ties with Neruda and influenced his work during the Spanish Civil War era. His experiences in Spain (commencing in 1934 with his appointment as consul in Barcelona), together with his other travels throughout his diplomatic career, had a profound effect on his view of the social role of poetry and his identity as a Latin American. It was following that period (1927–43) that Neruda came to write his *Canto General* (1950), a turning point in his work and in his international recognition (Franco 1975, 17). Over half a century has elapsed since that publication, yet Neruda's poetry continues to fuel musicalizations. In 2004, several compact discs appeared including Luciana Souza's *Neruda*, the compilation of various artists *Neruda en el Corazón*, and the Lieberson classical music interpretations in *Neruda Songs* by husband-and-wife team Lorraine (vocalist) and Peter (composer).

One of the most recent settings of Neruda's poetry, completed in 2004 by Brazilian composer and vocalist Luciana Souza, serves to focus on the resonances that Neruda's poetry has gathered since his lifetime. Her collection of settings bridges the Americas and Europe by using rhythmic inflections of the original poetry, her own Brazilian-jazz compositions, and classical music by the Catalan composer Federico Mompou, yet transposing the verbal text to a third language: English. Thus, she problematizes the notion of the linguistic and cultural tension. Souza's collection of settings of ten of Neruda's poems portrays the role of poetic–musical space in the constructions of the "Latin American" since the 1980s.[3] These lyrical and musical spaces carry within them the historicity of definitions of identity and encapsulate them in their very structures. At the same time they are able to cross cultural boundaries as the reception of Latin American styles of music becomes more embedded in other countries, through the presence of communities built by exile and migration. These musical spaces are easily transported but are as sheltering to cultural identity as physical spaces. They also have the capacity to mitigate our connection to nature, constituting both what is common to all, and what makes us unique as expressions of geographical specificities. The rhythms representing identity are a correlative of our time and space coordinates. As Paul Miller in *Sound Unbound* reminds us, "the Goethe and Schelling adage that 'architecture is nothing but frozen music,' becomes reverse engineered, remixed into a different scenario—and we thaw the process. Music becomes liquid architecture" (2008, 7). The questions I propose to address in this chapter are: (a) why do musicians continue to find inspiration in this Chilean-born poet of "América"?; and (b) if identity has a sound, what does Neruda's poetry express about it?

Neruda and Luciana Souza

Brazilian-born singer and composer Luciana Souza's musical renditions of Neruda are not included in the musicalizando.com catalogue for the obvious reason that they are set in the English language. Souza (2004b) chose to interpret the English translations by Alastair Reid, W. S. Merwin, Nathaniel Tarn, and Stephen Pascott (including those which Neruda had approved in 1961). She states that among the reasons for recording the poems in English rather than in their original Spanish were: (a) that she found the pronunciation too close to her original Portuguese mother tongue, making it harder to distinguish any subtleties in the contrasted inflections; (b) that many of Neruda's poems had already been interpreted musically in Spanish; and (c) that she could express her bicultural experience as an international student in the United States. She moved to New York in the 1960s at the age of eighteen to study jazz. In this way she felt she could combine her training in English to reflect her hybridity.

The definition of hybridity operating in this discussion is that rooted in the notions that popular music and poetry had already integrated by the middle of the twentieth century[4] in poets such as Nicolás Guillén[5] of Cuba. Pablo Neruda,[6] in his own poetry, had often sought the musical form as a correlative of the poem but did not achieve the same degree of integration, the levels of a rhythmic sense of identity that Guillén was able to express in his creation, the *poema-son*. In his poetry, both African and European lineages are fused beyond a binary relationship, forced to be reconciled in the voice of the same poet, who represents the voices of all hybrid subjects, regardless of their heritage. What Latin American poets such as Guillén had been able to do was find a literary model for this through music.

However, Souza's use of English for the Neruda musical settings is not without inherent tensions. In one way it encompasses a historical acknowledgement of a criticism of globalization equal to cultural colonization. This implies a criticism of the values and practices of the dominant cultures. In another way, her selection and Neruda settings portray a new view of immigrant and cultural outsider, as someone who settled in New York as a student of jazz and who, thus, also appropriated the English language in a creative way. Rather than negate this fact, her settings come into dialogue with the contexts in which Neruda wrote in Spanish, where the Brazilian and Latin American perspectives remain implicit in the historicity of his poetry and her voice. Although at first glance there appears to be no external tension in Souza's settings, there is a musical tension that underscores the majority of her compositions. This is communicated not only in the juxtaposition of bossa nova, jazz and Catalan musical genres, but also in her vocalizations, in changes in tempo and rhythm, and in the chord progressions. In the content of the poems, and the new associations formed in Souza's arrangement, the tension is more acutely an internalized one, where the singular first person subject that appears in each of the poems grapples with finding a reflection, a relationship in similarity and in difference to the larger community as a whole. At the turn of the twenty-first century, the viewpoint has changed from the Nerudian passage through the half-century of Cold War politics and military dictatorships in Latin America to a new globalized environment, with the United States as epicentre of cultural production. In the last decades of the twentieth century, Brazil became increasingly an important economic force and a country whose powerful cultural production became more an object of attention outside its borders (Perrone and Dunn 2001). Having opened its cultural perspective further into cross-cultural and translational interactions with Spanish America, it then became, in the 1990s, more of a draw in the English-speaking world. The experiences of those who, after exile and migration, established themselves in Canada and the United States found new expression by combining the music of their countries of origin with other musical genres, styles, and audiences. Able to share it within different linguistic communities, this forged new interpretations of identity and new ways of negotiating between cultural spaces. This in turn becomes a space of ambiguity and complexity, replacing former binaries and strict categorizations.

For this to occur it is necessary to redress previous notions of self-determination. This twenty-first-century grappling with issues of becoming oneself is what Julia Kristeva (2009) discusses in her recent work on feminist and existentialist Simone de Beauvoir. As in Beauvoir, the fundamental question of how to supersede binary social and political divisions was also evident in Neruda's work, particularly in the poems Souza selected for her settings. In all ten poems the perspective circumvents its regional markers, and is founded on problematizing the concept of identity as plural and as a process of "becoming," and not as a biological imperative. In these poems, even the original masculine voice is not gendered in a specific way but rather generalized, and as such becomes a representative human voice, moving beyond even a regional conception. Kristeva has recently applied literary reception "at the start of the new millennium to the question of 'the tension between the singular and the political'" (Keltner 2009, 225). As Kristeva suggests in "Beauvoir and the risks of freedom," the anthropological revolution of the feminists like Beauvoir could be extended to the considering our paradigms of social equality in general, to posit "transcendence as freedom" (2009, 226). The poems chosen for Souza's *Neruda* also communicate this common theme as Souza states in the sleeve of the disc: "Neruda and Mompou share a certain universality to their creation—their work is not masculine or just Latin American or Spanish—their art is honest, raw and personal, arising from their experiences" (2004a). For Rosemary Sullivan, "the core of Neruda's genius" is the articulation of the ambiguity of the self in relation to "Solitude and Multitude" as "one of the primary obligations of the poet in our time" (2007, viii). The solitudes Neruda experienced, in his travels as a Latin American in consular posts throughout the world, through exile, and as a man, led him to consider the linguistic barriers and bridges that form us. In her song cycle *Neruda*, Souza asserts this solitude–multitude structure by alternating poems with this theme, as we shall see.

The selection of Neruda's poetry in music reveals each political moment's wrestling with questions of identity. Foregrounding the individual who seeks his or her place in a larger community, first in the national sense, then in the regional and continental, and finally in the global sense (if such is as yet possible), the move of the poetic voices in Neruda's poems manifest an awareness of the individual–community arc that moves in an increasingly hybridized environment as the twentieth century progressed. Recent settings of poems to music and their recordings and performances, such as those realized by the Brazilian singer Souza, mirror that inherent dialogue between musical styles traditionally considered separately, yet that belie common ground if not common origin. Consider, for example, points of contact between the jazz creations of the United States and those of the Afro-Latin rhythms of the Caribbean and later in the Southern Americas. Souza's interpretation of "Tonight I Can Write" features a piano-based accompaniment which fuses jazz melodies with a minimalist Brazilian vocal style and English lyrics. An analysis of the ways Neruda's poems appear in the repertoire of current musicians, such as Souza, reveals a return to the importance of the performative, or ritual, and lyrical aspects of poetry, that is, a return to the oral roots of all poetry. As Juan Pablo Neyret writes:

> The origins of poetry were oral and its existence was oral until the invention of printing. The Greek rhapsodies, the Nordic *skalds*, the French troubadours and balladeers, the Spanish *juglares* conserve the musicality of the word and simultaneously accompanied them with music until Gutenberg gave birth to his new galaxy. From that point on, and even with the emphasis that had always been maintained on the phonic aspect, poems became the object of silent reading. However, poetry preserved its orality as a subterranean river that surfaced in the twentieth-century with the advent of mass media: radio, television, cinema and the record. (2002, 1)[7]

By 2004, when Souza recorded her compact disc of poems, *Neruda*, there was to be added to this the impact of Neruda's literary vision as a symbol of hybridity in the post-1980s Latin American consciousness.

Néstor García Canclini, author of "Notas recientes sobre la hibridación" (2004) explains this phenomenon of the hybrid that is the basis of Latin American identity. García Canclini's work attempts to provide a theoretical context on interculturality and hybridization to reformulate the question of "Latin-ness" or of the "Latino." He asserts that "latinidad" cannot be an isolated territory after the fall of the defensive rhetoric of the nation-state. Rather, it has always been a hybrid construction, "a confluence of contributions from the Mediterranean countries of Europe, the indigenous American and African migrations. These fusions that constitute what is Latin American are now expanded in their interaction with the Anglo due to the voluminous presence of Latin migrants and cultural products in the United States. Beyond this, what is 'latino' interacts and also remodels itself in a dialogue with cultures in Europe and even in Asia" (2004, 1).[8]

Souza does not mention her audience as a factor for explaining her decision to record the song cycle entirely in English. It is interesting to note that Souza had experienced success singing in her mother tongue, with such Grammy-nominated recordings as *Brazilian Duos I* and *II*, for Best Jazz Vocal Albums. Her 2003 recording in this category, *North and South* also received a nomination. In 2005, Luciana was awarded Female Singer of the Year by the Jazz Journalists Association. Her reasons for choosing English translations as the language for the record, interestingly, stem from what she considered the closeness of Portuguese and Spanish, and the difficulty this would cause in her vocal interpretation. To select the poems and set the arrangements for the album, Souza states in a radio interview that she recorded her own voice reciting the poems in Spanish and in English to set them to music. She allowed the meter and inflection of particular parts of the enunciated verses to lead the musical interpretation. Set primarily in 3/4 time, Souza admits it was liberating to work in this form rather than her prevailing previous work with Brazilian music, set predominantly in 2/4 binary time. Unlike her previous recordings, where a quartet or a quintet accompanied her performances of Brazilian music, the pieces of the *Neruda* CD were quieter. At her New York live performances in 2004, Souza cited from Neruda's memoirs and recited his poetry between the songs, wanting, as she stated, to "be him" for each performance.

Souza Sings Neruda

> "De tantos hombres que soy, que somos
> no puedo encontrar a ninguno:"
> "Of the many men whom I am, whom we are,
> I cannot settle on a single one."
> "Muchos somos," *Estravagario* (1958)

The selection of Neruda for the recording is explained by Souza in personal and political terms. By Souza's youth, Neruda's poetry was well known and canonized in Brazil, and in Latin America in general, as much for its political as its personal themes.

Having grown up in the 1960s, Souza witnessed a period of turmoil for musicians in Brazil. The military dictatorship was unkind to musicians, often jailing them or forcing them into exile. This occurred to several friends of Souza's parents (Da Silva 2005) and to well-known musicians such as Caetano Veloso, who became another symbol of the *transcultural* in Latin America (see Perrone and Dunn 2001). In "Caetano Veloso and the Meaning of Exile" Derek Beres draws a link between Neruda and Veloso in their experiences with "progressive, social poetics" (2007, 1) and the political effects of their engagement. While Caetano Veloso works mainly as a musician and composer, he has become widely regarded for his poetic lyrics. The result is "a natural fusion of sound and poetry" (ibid.).

Veloso, like Neruda, experienced the pain of exile. As Beres describes (2007, 2),

> Co-founding the Tropicália movement alongside Gilberto Gil and Gal Costa in 1967, Veloso's aim was to redefine Brazilian music, taking traditions started by his inspirations (among them, Bossa Nova legend João Gilberto) and propel the culture's artistic heritage ahead. Tropicália was a reaction against both the oppressive limitations imposed by the government, as well as lack of musical innovation. Drawing from the anthropophagic philosophy of modernist Oswald de Andrade, partial agendas included reprocessing foreign information to create original art, as well as establishing common ground between urban citizens and rural neighbours, closing the economic rift.

Similar to Neruda, Veloso and his peers in the Tropicália movement, such as Gilberto Gil, "were temporarily imprisoned and banned from making public appearances. After performing two farewell shows in July, 1969, the pair left for exile in England, not returning for almost two years" (Beres 2007, 2). What Beres finds in common between Veloso and Neruda, however, cannot be encapsulated in mere political terms; Beres sees in both a "revolutionary and romantic" nature (ibid.):

> The genres are inseparable; to be a poet of one is to work with in the other. Both politics and relationships speak to the potential freedom of humanity. The opportunity to build within another, create community based on respect and trust, and evolve is the foundation of both society and family. Two of Pablo Neruda's most loved collections span these topics: *Canto General* [1950], his political opus, and *The Captain's Verses* [1952], a starry-eyed, heartfelt classic. His pen was sword and sooth, a soft lover tempering the flames of hell within. Veloso carries the same weaponry.

The debate of "sword versus pen" is internalized in poetry that writes the political and the personal as two sides of the same coin, as Neruda and Veloso do. Nobel Prize recipient in 1971, Neruda was named Ambassador to France the same year. Over his lifetime he would go on to serve as a diplomat to various other countries. It was his first posting as consul in Spain (1934–38), however, that had initiated Neruda's political engagement. This view was expanded into a universal search for liberation after Neruda's experience of exile, which coincided with the increased international attention his work received. After years of being abroad in Spain, Mexico, France, and other countries during his exile, Neruda returned to Isla Negra, Chile, in 1972. Already sick with leukemia, he found his nation on the verge of civil war. Neruda died two weeks after the bloody military coup that overthrew Salvador Allende in September 1973. In the same year the world was immersed in conflicts: Palestine–Israeli wars and Cold War politics in Europe and Latin America.

Neruda's poetry manifested an evolution towards a transcultural strength following his experiences of both exile and migration. Thus, Neruda's work can be considered in light of Edward Said's well-known suggestion to "consider the entire world a foreign land" (2000, 185), because this,

> makes possible an originality of vision. The majority of people are conscious above all of one culture, one environment, one home; the exiled are conscious of at least two, and that plurality of vision gives rise to a consciousness that—to use an expression from music—is that of counterpoint.... For an exiled person, the routines, expressions and activities of life in the new environment occur inevitably in contrast with a memory of things from the other place. In this way, the new place and the previous one are vivid, real, and exist in counterpoint. (qtd. in García Canclini 2004, 8)

The ability of Neruda's poetry to frequently integrate the expression of this counterpoint to lift itself beyond strict categories of nationalisms or regionalisms has granted it relevance to diverse audiences. The ability to hone the dialogic nature of counterpoint brings implicit a clarity and resonance of each point in the complex relationship of voices.

Neruda of América, Global Neruda

By the time Souza arrived in the United States, Neruda's work was widely read and regarded as a major influence on world literature. What had led to this point is a well-known fact in literary history; yet what is to be questioned is how Neruda continues to play such an important role as a symbol that crosses the regional differences of Latin America, reaching also beyond the traditional linguistic divide between Brazil and the rest of the Spanish-speaking Americas.

For Gabriel García Márquez, Pablo Neruda was "the greatest poet of the twentieth century—in any language" (48). His words and their history remain significant today. This is caused by the clear impact his work continues to exert today on musicians of various backgrounds, due to its breadth and the voracious nature of his attempt to reflect life in poetry. As a reflection of this fact, Neruda's work has been extensively translated—into musical forms as well as literary—and is readily received around the world.[9]

His travels as consul and his experiences in Spain had sparked the origins of his epic work *Canto General* (*General Song*), which is a history of Latin

America in verse as well as a personal testimony as a Latin American (Franco 1975, 17). In *Canto General*, Neruda included a special section he titled "The Heights of Macchu Picchu," published separately in 1948 (the same year he was exiled from Chile). Neruda had visited the Incan ruins of Peru in 1943. Built in the mid-fifteenth century, and standing at eight thousand feet, the city of Machu Picchu gave Neruda the perspective to see his Americas from a temporally and geographically unifying viewpoint; in this way he distanced himself from the divisions that had resulted from the effects of Spanish and Portuguese colonial rule. The unique location of Machu Picchu had protected it from the sixteenth-century conquistadors; this seeming indestructibility had appealed to Neruda. The poet links the rock of the Andean mountain range to the mythical and emotional level of interpretation he chooses to see in the geographical space his vision encompasses. In "Alturas de Machu Picchu," as González Echeverría states, "Neruda's vision is refocused by the presence of these ruins...an allegiance to a collectivity with nature to create beauty and justice. [But it is an allegiance] also marred by violence, abuse and betrayal.... Neruda summons the voice of *América* as he tells the story of Columbus, the conquistadors, the resistance of Tupac Amaru, the Bolivarian revolution and the betrayal of its hopes to his present" (cited in Prashad 2007, 7). Machu Picchu became a symbol of an alternative "*América* without *América*", that is, without the defensiveness and inferiority complex of having inherited a colonial past. This vision contained the essence of more than one imagined *América*. Inherent in that vision was a desire for an experienced *América*, wiser because of the lessons of history, able to build upon a different system of values. In the stones of Machu Picchu Neruda saw the confluence of nature and human work, an Incan construction cradled in the rocks of the Apu mountains. As Franco writes, in this work: "Nature and history become the oracles which offer the key to human destiny" (1975, 18). For Franco, Neruda's position as "the witness, as the man who has seen and touched and now transmits the truth to others" is evidenced in this Section 11 of "The Heights of Machu Picchu":

I see the ancient being, the slave, the sleeping one, Blanket his fields—a body, a thousand bodies, a man, a thousand women swept by the sable whirlwind, charred with rain and night.	veo el antiguo ser, servidor, el dormido en los campos, veo el cuerpo, mil cuerpos, un hombre, mil mujeres, bajo la racha negra, negros de lluvia y noches, con la piedra pesada de la estatua

The individual witness now joins the multitude of others in the present that assumes many pasts. The perspective of witness allows for a multifocal and plural vision filtered through one voice.

Situated as the second section within *Canto General*, a monumental work of 340 poems divided into fifteen sections, "Alturas de Machu Picchu" became part of the process of examining the cycles of construction and destruction in an epic interpretation of the geographical, historical, and political reality of America. In "The Heights of Macchu Picchu" Neruda merges his desires as a man with his desire as a Latin American:

> Come up with me, American love.
> Kiss these secret stones with me.
> The torrential silver of the Urubamba
> makes the pollen fly to its golden cup.
> The hollow of the bindweed's maze, the
>   petrified plant, the inflexible garland,
>   soar above the silence of these
>   mountain coffers.
> (Kerrigan 1970, 184, 190)

> Sube conmigo, amor americano.
> Besa conmigo las piedras secretas.
> La plata torrencial del Urubamba
> hace volar el polen a su copa amarilla.
> Vuela el vacío de la enredadera,
> la planta pétrea, la guirnalda dura
> sobre el silencio del cajón serrano.

Although the central theme is the struggle for social justice, it is rooted in the individual's love and desire for self-realization as physical and transcendental at the same time. Beyond this, the Temucan-born Neftalí Ricardo Reyes Basoalto of Central Chile, who had worked as a leftist politician and had witnessed the atrocities of repression, the pain of exile, and the wounds of solitude, now reaches across these contextual markers to envision a sense of human justice that encompasses the human condition.

Canto General (1950) signaled a change in Latin American letters. By the 1980s his poetry would have an impact on the work of English-language poets in the United States. It was also at this midway point of the twentieth century, according to Angel Rama, that a new frame of reference arose for a new discourse in Latin America about Latin America. The term *transculturation* used by Rama, as defined in his 1982 publication, *Tranculturación Narrativa en América Latina*, serves our discussion of poetry in song. As Juan Poblete cites Rama's terms, the transcultural is "a dialectic between direct producers (the creator of a cultural text) and indirect producers (the public), where the work appears simultaneously as a creative individual exercise and a social and collective work; this constitutes its conditions of possibility and its sources" (2002, 6). Poblete notes that "the public" in Rama's conception largely coincides with the collective producer (the *pueblo* or the people) whose cultural work allows and solidifies the work of the transcultural writer. As such, the work must be postulated and constructed a priori by the transculturator with the indirect help of the *pueblo*. That is, the public exists as a potential *pueblo* (ibid.). According to Patricia D'Allemand, the value of Rama's book is that it posits "transculturation as a modernizing alternative model" (qtd. in Poblete

2002, 7). As Poblete postulates, "the secondary national discourse in Rama... is that he incorporates a culturalist and anthropological dimension to the analysis. The singular modernizing and urbanizing European project [as Rama saw it] now finds itself opposed to the concept of cultural pluralities founded on the processes of regional transculturation" (2002, 7–8). In other words, "what Rama calls transculturation is analogous to what Jesús Martín Barbero denotes as the cultural truth of Latin America: the concept of *mestizaje* or hybrid not only as a racial question but also as plot or a thickening agent of our modernity. This hybrid that mixes the indigenous with the rural, the rural with the urban, the folkloric with the popular and the popular with that of mass reception" (Poblete 2000, 8).[10]

This can be achieved in aesthetic narrative or poetic form. Rama proposed that popular Latin American culture as an active substratum of contemporary cultural life can be rescued in literature; it is seen as a way of superseding the antonyms of national culture and what could be determined as the intellectual elite. The massification of popular culture commencing in the 1960s and 1970s in new forms of production and reproduction explains this phenomenon to a large extent.

Partaking in this technological shift and beyond the literary translations of his works, Neruda participated with musicians of the *nueva canción* movement, and later his poems were also set to music by interpreters from all parts of the world, including Chilean singer Angel Parra of the *nueva canción,* the Chilean group Quilapayún, Greek singer Mikis Theodorakis, among many others into the 1980s, such as the Canadian band Red Rider.

The *nueva canción,* or *new song,* movement in Latin American music emerged in the mid-1960s, taking root in South America, especially Chile and other Andean countries. It was to have widespread effect during the times of heightened political turmoil in South America until the mid-1980s. The *nueva canción* combined traditional Latin American folkloric idioms and popular urban forms with progressive, often politicized, lyrics. It gained great popularity throughout Latin America and is sometimes called a precursor to *rock en español.* Angel Parra, son of Violeta Parra, the Chilean folklorist of the *nueva canción* movement, set Neruda's poetry to music with the involvement of the poet. *Arte de pájaros* was released as an LP in 1966 by Angel Parra, based on Neruda's book of poetry of the same name, and published in the same year. In subsequent years, Angel Parra would travel extensively, helping to maintain the *nueva canción* tradition in expatriot communities in Europe, North America, and Australia. This tradition affected the poetry set to popular music in Latin America during the second half of the twentieth century and the climate in which Neruda's poetry was adopted into the repertoire of other international artists.The inseparability of textual production and performance/reception reclaims the space of dialogue between author and reader/listener in a time marked by constant flux and cultural migration.

The legacy of the *nueva canción* movement brought a partnership of literature and music that was seen to carry the weight of social messages that could reach beyond borders and convey certain values. A well-known folkloric piece "Tonada de Manuel Rodríguez" is a text by Neruda with music by Vicente Bianchi. Though called a "*tonada*," or a traditional Chilean song brought by Spanish settlers, it was musically rendered as a "*cueca*" (or "*zamacueca*," the most popular musical song form of Chile dating from 1824) as had been set out by Neruda in the original text published as part of *Canto General*. Like other musical forms that extended through various regions, often cutting across national borders, given their existence prior to the nineteenth century (see Ayestarán 1967, 136–37), the poetry of Neruda's vision by *Canto General* reached out to communities of the imaginaries of the peoples rooted in a sense of belonging to various places. This "Tonada" is a lament for a fallen fighter. The community mourns and the poetic voice speaks on behalf of their shared plight:

Que se apaguen las guitarras,	Silence all guitars
que la patria está de duelo.	for our native land mourns.
Nuestra tierra se oscurece.	Our land turns dark.
Mataron al guerrillero.	They killed the guerilla fighter.[11]

The cry for justice is localized in Chile:

En Til-Til lo mataron	They killed him in Til-Til
los asesinos,	the murderers
su espalda está sangrando	his back is bleeding
sobre el camino	on the road

but is extended to encompass other similar situations in the generalized "nuestra tierra." Notable as well is the connection between the land and the sentiments of the plural poetic voice:

sobre el camino, sí.	on the path, yes,
Quién lo diría,	Who would have guessed
él, que era **nuestra** sangre,	he, who was **our** blood
nuestra alegría.	**our** joy.
La tierra está llorando	**The earth is crying**
vamos callando	**we leave in silence** (emphasis mine).[12]

In Souza's *Neruda* it is possible to draw on these allusions because by the 1980s Neruda's name had come to stand metonymically for a body of thought on social justice, a community based upon shared values that could cut across borders and divide each country internally. This association with Neruda occurred to such an extent that in 1983 his name was chosen by the Canadian band Red Rider (once fronted by singer Tom Cochrane) as the title for what would become their best-selling album. The songs are not strictly musical settings of the texts of his poems but rather allude to themes derived from a reading of his poems, such as the track "Light In the Tunnel / Human Race."

Moreover, the diversity of Neruda's themes, reflecting the connections between the individual and the collective perspectives, was captured musically in the two-compact-disc compilation *Neruda en el Corazón* (2004). "Tonada de Manuel Rodríguez" was included as the second track of the first disc. In this version it is interpreted by Ana Belén (b. 1951), a Spanish actress and singer who worked with Víctor Manuel in the 1970s on compositions known for their social and political content. The rest of Disc 1 contains eighteen settings of poems interpreted by artists from across the Spanish-speaking world, mostly from Spain (Vicente Amigo, Miguel Bosé, Sole Giménez, Pedro Guerra, Víctor Manuel, Enrique Morente, Carmen París, Miguel Poveda, Miguel Ríos, Joaquín Sabina, Joan Manuel Serrat, Antonio Vega), with others from Latin America: Jorge Drexler (Argentina), Adriana Varela (Argentina), Pablo Milanés (Cuba), as well as Mexican-American Julieta Venegas, and Lucio Dalla of Italy. Disc 2 contains thirty-five recitations of Neruda's poems. Twenty-three tracks are of Neruda's voice (Disc 2, tracks 5–27). One recitation is by Matilde Urrutia (Disc 2, track 3) of "Soneto 94"; the others are various voices in Spanish (Disc 2, tracks 1–2) and in English (Disc 2, tracks 28–35).

Neruda and Mikis Theodorakis

Outside of the Americas, in Europe, Neruda's poetry also had an impact. When Greek singer and composer Mikis Theodorakis set the poetry of Neruda to music in the 1970s, he selected six poems from *Canto General*, including "Algunas bestias," "Voy a vivir," "Los libertadores," "A mi partido," "Lautaro" and "Vienen los pájaros." By this time, *Canto General* had become the "bible" of Latin America (Theodorakis 2007). Theodorakis' (2007) official website states that *Canto General* became a "cry of revolt against all forms and all forces of oppression." Theodorakis discovered *Canto General* in 1971 when, exiled from Greece, he was on a concert tour of Chile at the invitation of president Salvador Allende. His musical setting of thirteen parts of the poem is a major choral work. He was to premiere the first seven parts in Chile in September 1973, in the stadium of Santiago. On 11 September, however, the military junta under Pinochet overthrew and assassinated Allende, initiating a period of severe repression of dissidents; Neruda died soon afterward.

Theodorakis gave his first performance of the work in his native Greece, after the end of the military regime his own country had suffered. Upon hearing of Neruda's death, Theodorakis played some part of the *Canto General* in each of his concerts until the restoration of democracy in Chile in 1993 (Wagner 2004).

Souza's *Neruda*: The CD, 2004

Interestingly, none of the poems of *Canto General* are found in Souza's settings of Neruda's work, yet they are implied in the organization of the pieces. América appears as much as the personal beloved of the individual self, as an imaginary about what it means to be a member of Spanish América.

Luciana Souza's recording, titled simply *Neruda* (2004), is an hour-long song cycle that takes Neruda's poems into the twenty-first century and celebrates, as many were doing that year, the hundredth anniversary of his birth. As a song cycle, it is important to consider that the ten poems set to music now constitute a new, whole, unified musicality. The *Neruda* song cycle is scored for piano (played by Venezuelan Edward Simon), voice, and percussion (by Souza). The group of songs is linked together with the theme of solitude–multitude that runs throughout the pieces. Contained in each text is an emphasis on the self's search for identity as representative "of the many…who I am" (Neruda, "We Are Many"). The ten songs composed by Souza are interwoven among the piano compositions of Catalan composer Federico Mompou (1893–1987). Souza made selections from his work "Música callada" or "Silent Music." Mompou, a twentieth-century composer, is best known for his piano solos in "Songs and Dances." Working mainly in tonal music, his style is spare with a sound architecture of few instruments. The Mompou pieces serve as starting points and bridges between the songs Souza composed and arranged for the ten poems. The theme of silence is carried throughout the pieces, as it also appears as a strong ingredient in the Neruda poems that Souza arranged in the following order:

1. "House" (originally titled "Casa")
2. "We Are Many" ("Muchos Somos")
3. "Sonnet 99" ("Soneto 99")
4. "I Will Come Back" ("Yo Volveré")
5. "Memory" ("La Memoria")
6. "Loneliness" ("La Soledad")
7. "Sonnet 49" ("Soneto 49")
8. "Poetry" ("La Poesía")
9. "Leaning into the Afternoons…" ("Inclinado en Las Tardes…")
10. "Tonight I Can Write…" ("Puedo Escribir los Versos…")
    (Souza, 2009, inner sleeve, 1).

The specific project came about after Souza grew somewhat obsessed with Neruda after reading his work and discovering that they shared a common birthday. As she admits in one of her reflections on Neruda, her reasons for choosing his work was based on the ease and accessibility she felt upon reading it, so much so that it felt like her own words: "In the beginning, all Luciana knew was that Pablo Neruda's poetry spoke directly to her and even for her. 'For years I've sent Neruda's poems to friends for anniversaries, births, and other special occasions,' she says. 'It felt like I could have written those words myself. He of course says everything much better than I could, but still, some of his poems felt like mine'" (Sunnyside 2004, 1). For Souza, poetry was daily bread: "Souza's everyday use of poetry goes back to her childhood in São Paulo, Brazil. Luciana's mother, the prominent songwriter Teresa Souza, literally raised Luciana and her four siblings on poems. 'At every event my mother would quote poetry. She has an incredible memory, so for example, every time there was a little fight among us kids, my mother would seize the opportunity to make peace by quoting something by poets like Drummond and Dante'" (ibid.).

These personal connotations perhaps led Souza to place the poem "House" as the first in her *Neruda* song cycle.

The quotidian aspect of "House" at first sight highlights the difference in translation between "home" and "house," both of which can be termed as "*casa*" in everyday spoken Spanish. Although "*hogar*" is the typically more direct translation of "home," it can also be used interchangeably with "*casa*." Not so in English, in which "house" makes a distinction. Nevertheless, "House" soon departs from the daily particular sense of place to allude to a universal meaning. In Souza's interpretation, this piece is driven by percussion, setting a rapid pace for the opening of the song cycle:

Perhaps this is the house in which I lived	Tal vez ésta es la casa en que viví
when neither I, nor earth, existed	cuando yo no existí ni había tierra,
when everything was moon, or stone,	cuando todo era luna o piedra
or shadow	o sombra
with the still light unborn.	Cuando la luz inmóvil no nacía.

The connection in the first two verses between the poetic voice's personal house and the planet as human dwelling is a shift that occurs swiftly at the beginning of the poem. The doubt of the poetic voice is caused by questions about the nature of belonging and the uncertainty of memory. This is expressed in Souza's voice through a raise in melody line at the end of each verse. The doubt continues in the next six verses of the poem:

This stone could then have been	Tal vez entonces esta piedra era
my house, my windows, or my eyes.	Mi casa, mis ventanas o mis ojos.
This granite rose recalls	Me recuerda esta rosa de granito

something that lived in me, or I in it,   algo que me habitaba o que habité.
a cave, a universe of dreams inside the skull: cueva o cabeza cósmica de sueños,
cup or castle, boat or birth.   copa o castillo o nave o nacimiento.

Her vocalization of the verbal text pushes forward rapidly, only stretching more languidly on certain words. For instance, when reaching the next section of the poem, she holds the words "depths" and "soul" in the fifteenth verse [emphasis mine]:

I touch the rock's tenacious thrust,	Toco el tenaz esfuerzo de la roca,
its bulwark pounded in the brine	su baluarte golpeado en salmuera,
and I know that flaws of mine subsisted here,	y sé que aquí quedaron grietas mías,
wrinkled substances that surfaced	arrugadas sustancias que subieron
from the **depths** into my **soul**,	desde profundidades hasta mi alma,
and stone I was, stone shall I be, and for this	y piedra fui, piedra seré, por eso
caress this stone which has not died for me:	toco esta piedra y para mí no ha muerto:
it's what I was, and shall be-the tranquility	es lo que fui, lo que seré, reposo
of struggle stretched beyond the brink	De un combate tan largo como el
of time.	tiempo.

The reverse arpeggios of these verses musically imitate the falling rock evoked in these verses, while the fast tempo set by the piano and percussion reiterate the passage of time. The song culminates in a piano solo starting midway through the track (at 2:07). Lasting for the remaining 2:08 minutes, the piano solo onomatopoeically conveys the contradiction and tension between the binary theme of struggle (with time and place) and tranquility (of the acceptance of it). The voice returns to repeat the above-cited section of the poem; the rapid articulation ends at "soul" and lingers over the "stone" verses (vv. 16–17), to end with a scat vocalization that serves as a counterpoint to the piano and percussion.

"We Are Many," the second song on the disc, is slower in tempo, emphasizing the contemplative state of the poetic voice. Juxtaposed with the previous poem, what surfaces is a heightened preoccupation with the relationship of self to society. The self becomes ambiguous and fragmented as it decides how to respond to its spatially determined experiences:

Of the many men whom I am, whom we are,	De tantos hombres que soy, que somos
I cannot settle on a single one.	no puedo encontrar a ninguno:
They are lost to me under the cover of clothing.	Se me pierden bajo la ropa,
They have departed for another city.	Se fueron a otra ciudad.

No percussive element is evidenced here, as if to remove the burden of time. Not until the last three stanzas does this cadence become steadily contemplative. This musical section coincides in the text with a self-critical tone in the poetic voice, as it regards the vain, lazy, and escapist tendencies that have caused a lack of awareness in relation to society and being:

But when I call upon my dashing self	Pero cuando pido al intrépido
Out comes the same old lazy self,	me sale el viejo perezoso,
And so I never know just who I am,	y así yo no sé quién soy,
nor how many I am, nor who we will be being.	no sé cuántos soy o seremos.

From this point in the song cycle, the question of "who I am" and "who we will be" is followed by a change in musical style, from experimental jazz to another earlier Latin American musical genre influenced by jazz: the bossa nova. This internationally renowned form of Brazilian music is a derivation of *samba*[13] and jazz.

The Music of Silence, or the Language of All

"Sonnet 99" is the third piece of the collection. Within the cycle of songs, "Sonnet 99" stands out not only because it is the only bossa nova piece (this sub-genre originating in the 1960s is experiencing a renaissance in Brazil among a new generation of musicians such as Bebel Gilberto, Kay Lyra, and Phillipe Baden Powell), but also for its musical and lyrical strength. Furthermore, it is emblematic of the thematic content. To compose this piece, Souza sat at the piano and found herself at the key of G major and it naturally became a bossa nova. Arpeggios abound on the entire album, but particularly in this rendition, in the fourth verse, "violins will have the fragrance of the moon," highlighting its relevance for the way in which the poetic voice is the centre of perception of a larger unnamed reality. One of the main components of the poems highlighted in Souza's selection is the repetition of poems that allude to a Nerudian pantheism. As Vilches suggests, this implies a type of *cosmovisión* in which the human being — microcosmos — is found inserted in the *gran universo* (2004, 51–56). The vision is manifested in certain predominant leitmotifs. In the vocalization and selection of emphasis of various aspects of the interpretation we find an association with themes and literary devices in Neruda. The pre-Columbian aspects that are so prevalent in *Canto General*, for example, are not directly cited in Souza's song-cycle selections, although the original imagery does appear connotatively in the primary emphasis on the four natural elements, the metaphors of stone and silence, and the interplay of solitude and multitude.

Neruda's "Sonnet 99" is displaced on the written page in traditional sonnet form. It is not until it is recited, or sung, that its cadences display variances from the traditional rhythmic structures. The sonnet, originally a poetic form of Italy, has been present in Hispanic letters since the Renaissance. The form was resuscitated in the literary period of *modernismo hispano* (from the end of the nineteenth century to the beginning of the twentieth century) in the work of Rubén Darío. As Sullivan points out in her introduction to the translation of these texts by Gustavo Escobedo, "In writing *100 Love Sonnets* Neruda's intention was to create a new sonnet form, retaining the fourteen-line structure, but abandoning the traditional rhythms and rhymes that filtered out or over-refined the poet's raw human voice" (2007, viii–ix). In his dedicatory note of October 1959 to Matilde Urrutia (whom he married in 1955), Neruda explains this conscious effort:

> When I set myself this task I well knew that along the side of each sonnet, through their elective inclination and elegance, the poets of all times laid out rhythms sounding like silver, crystal or cannon fire. With much modesty, I made these sonnets out of wood; I gave them the sound of this pure and opaque substance, and they must reach our ears thus. As you and I walked through the forests and beaches, lost lakes, ashen latitudes, we picked up fragments of wood, of timber exposed to water and the weather. From such soft relics then, with an axe, a blade, a pocketknife, I built these woodworks of love and I raised small houses of 14 boards each; so that your eyes which I adore and sing to, may live in them. With my reasons for love established, I give you this century: sonnets of wood that were only able to arise because you gave them life. (Sullivan 2007, ix)

Neruda's totems stand as expressions of a poet singing to life through an instrument that is both a work of nature (wood) and of human expression (word).

Neruda popularized the sonnet form so that it sounded as natural as a *romance*. As Souza sings it we become aware that the traditional rhythm of the sonnet is displaced into a natural division of enunciation and a varied rhythmic structure. Rather than hearing it as a strict hendecasyllabic form, the following pattern emerges, following Souza's vocalization: 8, 15, 10, 11, 8, 11. Traditionally, the sonnet consisted of two quartets and two tercets of eleven syllables, with a consonantal rhyme structure. Instead Neruda used free rhyme. Furthermore, while in the Renaissance the sonnet contained a change in theme or turn of tone between the second quartet and the first tercet, in Neruda's "Sonnet 99" there is no major change, except in the sole mention of time: "Aunque no sea como está dispuesto." After this verse the poem returns from the present to the use of the future tense. The subjunctive verb mentioned at this turn toward the present invokes a moment of doubt. In the music, as in the English version of the sonnet, this change is more notable. The introduction of the subject pronoun in the second person, rather than the impersonal form as it appears in the original, implies a more emphatic turn towards presence. This is articulated musically by Souza in a rising of the notes in her voice, to subsequently allow the melody to fall back into a lower range. The English translation by Stephen Tapscott that Souza uses does not follow the syllabification of the sonnet, also preferring free verse. However, in Souza's musicalization we note that she permits the music to complete the necessary beats for the metric of the traditional sonnet.

The central theme of "Sonnet 99" is silence, one that stands as an eternal presence behind the dialogue of two lovers. This is communicated through a first-person voice, who sees itself in the physical world as a fusion of all the senses, and as giving voice to that experience in creative expression. The underlying silence that is present everywhere oversees the entire cycle of the poem, moving from the <u>universal</u> to the **singular** in interweaving movements, and in two main sections (stanzas <u>1</u>–2; stanzas <u>3</u>–4):

Other days will come, <u>the silence of plants and of planets</u> will be understood, and so many <u>pure things</u> will happen! Violins will have the fragrance of the moon!	Otros días vendrán, será entendido el silencio de plantas y planetas y cuántas cosas puras pasarán! Tendrán olor a luna los violines!
Maybe the bread will be **like you:** it will have **your voice,** your wheat, and other things—<u>the lost horses of autumn</u>—**will speak with your voice.**	El pan será tal vez como tú eres: tendrá tu voz, tu condición de trigo, y hablarán otras cosas con tu voz: los caballos perdidos del Otoño.
And even if it's not what **you'd prefer,** <u>love will fill huge barrels</u> like the ancient honey of the shepherds, and there **in the dust of my heart** (where so many plentiful things will be stored), **you will come and go** among the melons.	exactly, Aunque no sea como está dispuesto El amor llenará grandes barricas como la antigua miel de los pas tores, y tú en el polvo de mi corazón (en donde habrán inmensos almacenes) irás y volverás entre sandías.

Although Sullivan argues that the poems of *100 Love Sonnets* "are the poems of his [Neruda's] solitude" (2007, viii), both sonnets included in Souza's song cycle display a merging of the poetic beloved with a universal concept of communion, harmonious with the natural world.

As previously considered, the first two poems of Souza's CD, "House" and "We Are Many," represent the particularity of home and the daily existence of the subject "I" within the larger collective and social project; this creates a multiplicity of the self. "Sonnet 99" is the culmination of the transcendental project that seeks to respond in a new way to the bifurcations of the self previously evident. As we see in "We Are Many," the search for the self is mirrored in others, and the need for dialogue is a desire for communion with others and with the land:

While I'm writing I'm far away;	Mientras escribo estoy ausente
and when I come back, I've already gone	y cuando vuelvo ya he partido:
I would like to know if others	voy a ver si a las otras gentes
go through the same things I do,	les pasa lo que a mí me pasa,
have as many selves as I have;	si son tantos como soy yo,
and see themselves similarly;	si se parecen a sí mismos
and when I've exhausted this problem	y cuando lo haya averiguado
I'm going to study so hard	voy a aprender tan bien las cosas
that when I explain myself	que para explicar mis problemas
I'll be talking geography.	les hablaré de geografía.

The melancholic tone of the musical setting at the beginning of the recording suggests that the search is yet unfulfilled. However, the musical tone shifts halfway through the song into a dissonant and increasingly accelerated tempo, echoing the poetic voice's frustration:

But when I call upon my dashing being	Pero cuando pido al intrépido
out comes the same old lazy self	me sale el viejo perezoso
and so I never know just who I am	y así yo no sé quién soy
nor how many I am, nor who we will be being.	no sé cuántos soy o seremos.
	(verses 28–31)

This question is not resolved until "Sonnet 99," with the fulfillment and union expressed in the text, and also in the fourth track, "I Will Come Back," where there is acceptance of the ambiguous and tenuous nature of identity: "here I shall be perhaps both lost and found – / here I shall be perhaps both stone and silence."

The images in "I Will Come Back" organize themselves along two main axes: "stone" and "silence." The first-person voice sees itself inserted into a collective history and then it dissolves into nothing: "Some time, man or woman, traveler, / afterwards, when I am not alive, look here, look for me here / between the stone and the ocean." The biological and cultural travel ends in a no man's land that represented by a space called "silence":

for here is where I shall come, saying nothing	porque aquí volveré sin decir nada, sin voz, sin boca, puro,
no voice, no mouth, pure,	aquí volveré a ser el movimiento
here I shall be again the movement of the water, of	del agua, de

its wild heart	su corazón salvaje,
here I shall be both lost and found –	aquí estaré perdido y encontrado:
here I shall be perhaps both stone and silence.	aquí seré tal vez piedra y silencio.
	(verses 8–14)

Souza presents this piece with voice and percussion only. Her vocal tone is placed in a higher range, and the melody line forms one continuous drive to the end, culminating on and drawing out the final word: "silence." In the text, the connection between presence and silence, the insistence on the spatial quality of this connection seen in the repetition of "here," and the natural elements (stone, ocean, light, storming, water) blend with the mention of the "wild heart" or physical life (emphasized in the percussive force of the music). To return, therefore, is to memory, and to a physical awareness, "dust to dust."

The subsequent piece, "Memory," is introduced by a Mompou composition, whose pathos and stillness resonate with the previous text. Taking as her compositional departure the final chord of the Mompou piano solo, Souza begins her setting of "Memory." Souza's vocalization is melancholic in tone. A change occurs at verse 12,

I have to make the air again,	Tengo que hacer de nuevo el aire,
steam, the earth, leaves,	el vapor, la tierra, las hojas,
hair, and bricks as well,	el pelo y también los ladrillos,
the thorns which pierced me,	las espinas que me clavaron,
the speed of the escape.	la velocidad de la fuga.
	(verses 11–15)

At this point the solo piano picks up the tempo and, by the eighteenth verse, begins to play in rhythmic counterpoint. The repetition of this verse, "Take pity on the poet," creates a type of chorus; to this Souza adds "take pity on me" in the final repetitions. Throughout the poem, the first-person voice considers the collective experience in an attempt to see how it can participate in both the natural and social worlds. This task is based upon a remembering that is also a creating:

I have to remember everything,	Tengo que acordarme de todo,
keep track of the blades of grass, the threads	recoger las brisnas, los hilos
of the untidy event, and	del acontecer harapiento
the houses, inch by inch,	y metro a metro las moradas,
the long lines of the railway	los largos caminos del tren,
the textured face of pain.	la superficie del dolor.
…	…
I cannot measure the road	ni puedo medir el camino
which may have had no country,	que tal vez no tiene país

or that truth which changed,	o aquella verdad que cambió
which the day perhaps subdued	y que tal vez se apagó de día
to become a wandering light	y fue luego luz errante
like a firefly in the dark.	como en la noche una luciérnaga

The references to exile ("the road is / which may have had no country") and to migration ("or that truth which changed"), as they are tentatively communicated in the shifting conclusions in the passage of times ("may have"), are transcended by a natural metaphor: "the road" becomes "a wandering light"; this suggests the road is a method for knowing and for creating a new world for the self.

In the sixth track of the cycle, "Loneliness," the emphasis is placed upon the effects of history, the ebbs and flows of time and space, and social alienation. Loss and negation dominate the poem:

The not-happening was so sudden	Lo que no pasó fue tan súnito
that I stayed there for ever,	que allí me quedé para siempre,
without knowing, without their knowing me,	sin saber, sin que me supieran,
as if I were under a chair,	como debajo de un sillón,
as if I were lost in the night-	así fue aquello que no fue,
so was that which was not, as so I stayed there for ever."	y así me quedé para siempre.
	(verses 1–7)

The silence here is that of observation, as the poetic voice stands apart from the "dancing and living" of the other characters in the poem. This creates a sense that silence has spatial determinants, and that "not speaking" is a physical separation:

It is what has not happened to me	Es lo que no le pasó a uno
that determines the silence,	lo que determina el silencio,
and I don't want to go on speaking	y no quiero seguir hablando
because I stayed there waiting;	porque allí me quedé esperando:
in that place and on that day	en esa región y aquel día
I have no idea what happened	no sé lo que me pasó
but know I am not the same.	pero yo ya no soy el mismo.
	(verses 14–20)

Souza reiterates the last verse, "but I know I am not the same" until it becomes imbued with another meaning, that of the painful experience that an outsider feels when they are not in their usual cultural context. The misunderstanding then becomes the experience of loneliness. It is another aspect of solitude, of singularity. The Mompou piece placed after this poem expands the mood of emptiness.

Following it, "Sonnet 49" gives way to a preoccupation with time and eternity. Its tempo is a sharp contrast to those of the previous songs. Here it is base on a cascading percussive wood instrumental arrangement. The text inscribes the subject immediately into the present: "It's today: all of yesterday dropped away." Recalling "Sonnet 99" with hopeful longing, nature and beloved are fused once more: "no on can stop the river of your hands // No one can stop the river of your hands." Juxtaposed with the previous song, the beloved appears as a solution to loneliness: "You are the trembling of time, which passes / between the vertical light and the darkening sky." This hope and the presence of love explain the reason for the poetic voice's creative expression: "That is why I sing to the day and to the moon, / to the sea, to time, to all the planets, / to your daily voice, to your nocturnal skin." The Mompou piece placed at this point in the song cycle echoes the lighter tone, but not without some residual, underlying melancholy.

Subsequently, "Poetry" describes the subject's project within the social panorama; the poetic voice examines how the worlds that came before it fuse together. From this dance between the micro and the macro bursts forth the fervour of what happened when the poet went out into the world and "Poetry" found him; indeed, it seems to have thrust itself upon him like a natural phenomenon:

And it was at that age... Poetry arrived in search of me. I don't know, I don't know where it came from, from winter or river. I don't know how or when, no they were not voices, they were not words, nor silence, but from a street I was summoned, and from the branches of night... there I was without a face and it touched me.	Y fue a esa edad... Llegó la poesía a buscarme. No sé, no sé de dónde salió, de invierno o río. No sé cómo ni cuándo, no, no eran voces, no eran palabras, ni silencio, pero desde una calle me llamaba, desde las ramas de la noche, de pronto entre los otros, entre fuegos violentos o regresando solo, allí estaba sin rostro y me tocaba. (verses 1–13)

Souza's vocal and piano setting moves at a steady pace, the piano creating a binary structure between the bass and chord notes. Holding the notes over certain words near the end of the text, phrases such as "the universe" and "my heart broke loose on the wind," stand out after the rush of articulated verses that preceded. The turning point, "and suddenly I saw / the heavens / unfastened / and open, / planets," move from the particular poet's recollections ("pure / nonsense, / pure wisdom / of someone who knows nothing") to the ever-widening frame of universal reference:

palpitation plantations	Plantaciones palpitantes
shadow perforated,	la sombra perforada,
riddled	acribillada
with arrows, fire and flowers	por flechas, fuego y flores,
the winding night, the universe.	la noche arrolladora, el universo.
	(verses 33–37)

The staccato rhythm appears to imitate the shorter verses of the original text. The verses vary in length, ranging from hendecasyllables in the early stanzas, to those of only one syllable: "void." This structure implies cycles of disintegration and production of language that seek to reflect the path of the poet.

After this follows "Leaning into the afternoons" in which the dialogue between the feminine and the masculine reappears. It is as if the self needs to steady itself against the perturbing questions of identity in relation to time and space, and does so by establishing a renewed connection with the beloved. Souza underscores the theme of love with a melancholic tone, recreating the lengthening of the text, now in alexandrine verse. To end with "Tonight I Can Write the Saddest Lines" seems at first to be a break with the previous momentum of the song cycle. Yet placing "Leaning into the Afternoons" after "Poetry" and before "Tonight I Can Write" prepares the interpretation for forging a link between the literary act as an ontological examination, one that finds its resolution in the loving act.

This poem, otherwise known as "Poema 20," is from Neruda's second collection, *Twenty poems of love*, written when the poet was twenty years old. Souza explains that her first impression of the mood of the poem translated musically into minor chords. She later decided to set it in D major, a key with several sharps, in order to resist the obvious tones of sadness. In this way, she achieves greater movement and range that reflects the shifts we witness in the poetic voice's experience of love. What stands out is the presence of silence in this piece and the parallel structure between the piano and vocal melodies that imitate the original pairs of verses. To end at the beginning, as it were, the song cycle suggests a return to an origin that is a poet expressing love: "Puedo escribir los versos más tristes esta noche" // Oír la noche inmensa, más inmensa sin ella. / Y el verso cae al alma como al pasto el rocío ("Tonight I can write the saddest lines. // To hear the immense night, still more immense without her / And the verse falls to the soul like dew to the pasture").[14] The elements of writing, listening to silence, and the metaphors of the natural environment, all give way to a song in verses 17–18: "Eso es todo. A los lejos alguien canta. A lo lejos. / Mi alma no se contenta con haberla perdido" ("That is all. In the distance someone is singing. In the distance. / My soul is not satisfied that it has lost her.").[15] Thus, the spatial aspects of music are reinforced. The place where the lover is, beyond the reach of the poetic voice, is traversed by song.

The singularity of the poetic voice that is at the core of the entire collection (of poems and of songs) has as its desire a need for connection. For her *Neruda* song cycle, Luciana Souza has selected poems of both solitude and multitude, finding in these poems, as many other musicians have done, her own expressions of geography and language. Though Neruda's experience of home began in Temuco, Chile, he did not see this as an impediment to connecting beyond the local. Through his life and times he was able to construct an *América* without *América*, reinterpreting inherited mythologies, reintegrating visions from across the three Americas and into other parts of the world, to give voice to both the singular and the plural aspects within each human voice. That dialogue between the plural voices represents the Latin American experience today. Luciana Souza understands this experience musically, as do many of us. As she explains on her recent CD *Tide*: "geography and language have played a big part of my life. Feeling uprooted and disoriented, but also aspiring to be centered and calm—a real dichotomy of feelings, but somehow thriving in the memories and in the unknown. Poetry and music have carried me around, as has love" (2009). When asked in an interview in May 2009, "to describe her sound," Souza answered: "I guess what I do is Brazilian jazz. The rhythm of Brazil is so present in my interpretation yet it's also infused in the freedom of jazz. I draw from these two sources.... Where is home? Music is home for me" (Sert 2009, 20). By setting Neruda's poems to music and arranging them in her particular song cycle, Souza simultaneously finds recognition of her Brazilian-ness, and of her Latin-ness, while inspiring renewed vigour into the Neruda's words to present a twenty-first-century interpretation of their meaning.

Notes

Translations in the epigraphs are my own.

1 Of these, seventeen are recited poems, rather than sung renditions. Please refer to the following website for details: http://www.musicalizando.com/catalogo/ index.
2 The principal objective of musicalizando.com is to promote the poetry of the main Spanish-language poets of all epochs and to serve as a virtual musical catalogue "where one can hear the poems in song, read the original text, consult the biography of the poet, the musician and the interpreter, as well as see the album in which the piece appears" (Cuevas-Mohr 2004, 1). In effect, the site creates a multi-sensory reading of each text. The interactive readings are also transcultural in that one can experience the same poem in different musical settings by various interpreters from across the Spanish-speaking world.
3 For more considerations of the relationship of poetry and popular music in Latin America, see Figueredo (2003; 2005) and Bethell (1998).
4 Poets of the Latin American Modernist movement, led by Rubén Darío, gave rise in subsequent generations of poets writing under the literary influence of

"Americanismo" (Ellis 1985), to a renewed focus on the *synaesthesic* possibilities of language for creating new forms and for sustaining a universal literary expression that was also reflective of the social and cultural context in which it was born on Latin American soil; the emphasis on the musical is key.

5   For more on this topic, see Ellis (1985), Bajini (2003), Benítez-Rojo (1998; 2001).
6   For more on this topic in relation to Pablo Neruda, see Aparicio (1987).
7   My translation.
8   My translation.
9   In addition to those listed in the works cited for this chapter, other translations include the following: Robert Bly (1970); James Wright (1970); Merwin, Anthology (1962) and *Veinte Poemas de Amor*, Cape Editions (1970). The translations used in this chapter, from the 1970 and 1975 translations of *Selected Works*, were initiated in conversation by Nathaniel Tarn with Pablo Neruda in 1962 when they both attended the P.E.N. Conference in Bled, Yugoslavia (as cited in the Editor's Foreword, 1970 edition). In a recent article, Vijay Prashad (2007) reveals that many extracts from Neruda's *Canto General* are available in several Indian languages, such as a recent translation into Hindi of selected verse in Chandrabali Singh's *Pablo Neruda: Kavita Sanchayan* (Sahitya Akademi, 2004) and an earlier volume translated by Prabhati Nautiyal, *Ruko-o-Prithvi* (Sahitya Akademi, 1997).
10 My translation.
11 My translation.
12 My translation.
13 The history of *samba* contains within it the seeds to understanding the heart of an experience that can be termed "Latin American." Within it are contained the Nerudian preoccupation with becoming the self and the spaces of solitude and multitude that form an identity in context. The Brazilian context contained in the *samba* could be extrapolated to other regions in Latin America. If there is one aspect to be highlighted it is this: the blending of cultures has its most poignant manifestation in the way the popular music has evolved in each region. Brazilian musician and composer Marcos Aristides (2000) writes,

> Brazil at the end of the nineteenth century, with the end of bondage, the population of African origin, abandons the fields in search of work in urban centers. For cultural and economic reasons, the city of Rio de Janeiro attracts many of the former slaves, as well as European immigrants, the majority of them Portuguese, who come to Brazil in pursuit of economic prosperity, fleeing from poverty in their birthplace."
>
> A place known as *Cidade Nova* ("New City") located on the outskirts of Rio de Janeiro (which was eventually to become the neighbourhood of Estácio), once abandoned, became the main point of convergence for these migratory waves. This also meant that it was a point of convergence of several cultures that mixed together in a kind of melting-pot. The people gathered around musical groups to dance, sing and celebrate life, each group bringing its cultural element for this *festa*. Those of African origin came with their rhythms, percussion and the custom of playing music in community; the Portuguese brought in their suitcases poetic songs and melodies rich in melancholy beauty.

The typical instruments of each of these cultures are fundamental ingredients of this composite. The African drums united with the guitars, the *cavaquinho* and eventually the flute, becoming the main components of the band that, almost always in an improvised way, livened up the get-togethers. The people present took turns singing. Each person in the audience could (or had to?) ask the group to accompany him/her in a song of his/her choice. The meetings of this type became known as *Roda-da-Samba* ("Wheel of Samba"). The more modest levels of society in Rio de Janeiro carry on with *rodas-da-samba* until today. There are *rodas-de-samba* held every weekend in the suburbs of Rio de Janeiro. Even Rio's most famous event, the Carnival, with its parades of samba schools, has its origins in these events.

14 Translation by W.S. Merwin (Franco 1975, 31).
15 Translation by W.S. Merwin (Franco 1975, 31).

References

Aparicio, F. 1987. Música y poesía en La Barcarola de Pablo Neruda. *Revista Iberamericana* 53(141): 767–86.
Aristides, M. 2000. Terra Coda. Publicity materials for the Latin American musical group. *Terra Coda*, Geneva, 4 April.
Ayestarán, L. 1967. *El folklore musical uruguayo*. Montevideo: Arca.
Bajini, I. 2003. Nicolás Guillén en la música y la música en Nicolás Guillén. *Annali di Ca' Foscari. Revista della Facoltà di Lingue en Letterature Straniere dell'Università di Venecia* 42(1): 5–22.
Benítez-Rojo, A.1998. The role of music in the emergence of Afro-Cuban culture. *Research in African Literatures* 29(1): 1–6.
———. 2001. Cuba in three keys: Rhythm, music and literature. *Review: Latin American Literature and Arts* 63: 17–22.
Beres, D. 2007. Caetano Veloso and the meaning of exile. *Rattapallax*, February 4. http://www.rattapallax.com/fusebox_02veloso.htm.
Bethell, L. 1998. *A cultural history of Latin America: Literature, music and the visual arts in the 19th and 20th centuries*. Cambridge, New York: Cambridge Univ. Press.
Cuevas-Mohr, H. 2004. Musicalizando. Fundación "Verso a Verso" para la difusión de la Poesía. http://musicalizando.com.
Da Silva, L. T. 2005. Luciana e a sua paixão de cada dia. *Voz Lusitana* 2(16): 6.
Ellis K. 1985. *Cuba's Nicolás Guillén: Poetry and ideology*. Toronto: Univ. of Toronto Press.
Figueredo, M. L. 2003. Latin American song as an alternative voice in the new world order. In *The new world order: Corporate agenda and parallel reality*, ed. G. Yovanovich. Montreal: McGill-Queen's Univ. Press.
———. 2005. *Poesía y canto popular: Su convergencia en el siglo XX. Uruguay, 1960–1985*. Montevideo: Linardi y Risso.
Franco, J. 1975. Introduction. In *Pablo Neruda, Selected Poems: A bilingual edition*, ed. N. Tarn, trans. A. Kerrigan, W.S. Merwin, and N. Tarn, 13–23. Toronto: Penguin.
García Márquez, Gabriel. With Plinio Apuleyo Mendoza. *The Fragrance of Guava: Conversations with Garcia Marquez*. New York: Verso, 1983.

García Canclini, N.. 2004. Noticias recientes sobre hibridación. 3 December. http://acd.ufrj.br/pacc/artelatina/nestor.html.
Keltner, S.K. 2009. Introduction to "Beauvoir and the risks of freedom." *PMLA* 124(1): 224–26.
Kristeva. J. 2009. Beauvoir and the risks of freedom. Trans. C. Porter. *PMLA* 124(1): 226–33.
Miller, P. D. 2008. In through the out door. In *Sound unbound: Sampling digital music and culture*, ed. P. D. Miller, 5–19. Cambridge, MA: MIT Press.
Neruda, P. 1970. *Selected poems*. Ed. N. Tarn, trans. A. Kerrigan, W.S. Merwin, A. Reid, and N. Tarn. London: Jonathan Cape.
———. 1970/1975. *Selected poems: A bilingual edition*. Trans. J. Cape [1970], and A. Kerrigan, W.S. Merwin, A. Reid, and N. Tarn [1975]. Toronto: Penguin Twentieth-Century Classics.
———. 1991. *Residencia en la tierra*, ed. H. Loyola. Madrid: Cátedra.
———. 2004. *La barcarola*, ed. H. Loyola. Buenos Aires: Debolsillo.
———. 2007a. *100 love sonnets: English and Spanish bilingual edition*, trans. G. Escobedo, introduction R. Sullivan. Holstein, ON: Exile Editions.
———. 2007b. *Reflexiones de Islā Negra*. August 26. http://www.neruda.uchile.cl/coleccionlibros.htm.
Neyret, J. P. 2002. Catorce versos dicen que es Sabina: Canción y poesía en "Ciento volando." *Espéculo* 20. *Revista de estudios literarios.* Univ. Complutense de Madrid. http://www.ucm.es/info/especulo/numero20/sabina.html.
Odell, J. 2005. A Brazilian in New York: Luciana Souza explores her roots. *Down Beat* 72(7): 32–35.
Perrone, C., and C. Dunn, eds. 2001. *Globalizing Caetano Veloso: Globalization as seen through a Brazilian pop prism*. Gainesville: Univ. of Florida Press.
Poblete, J. 2002. Trayectoria crítica de Angel Rama: La dialéctica de la producción cultural entre autores y públicos. In *Estudios y otras prácticas intelectuales latinoamericanas en cultura y poder*, comp. D. Mato. Caracas: CLACSO, Consejo Latinoamericano de Ciencias Sociales.
Prashad, V. 2007. I was among them: Pablo Neruda turns one hundred. 7 February. http://www.cpim.org/marxist/200402_Neruda.doc.
Red Rider. 1983. *Neruda*. Compact disc. EMI Music Canada.
Said, E. 2000. *Reflections on exile and other essays*. Cambridge, MA: Harvard Univ. Press.
Sert, A. 2009. Brazilian Singer Luciana Souza mixes poetry and jazz to make her own brand of music. *Venice Magazine* (May): 20. http://www.lucianasouza.com/pdfs/venice09.pdf.
Souza, L. 2004a. *Neruda*. Compact disc. New York: Sunnyside Records.
———. 2004b. Interview with John Schaefer: Beyond Bossa Nova. WNYC.org.93.9 FM. 8 April. http://www.wnyc.org/shows/soundcheck/episodes/2004/04/08.
———. 2009. *Tide*. Compact disc. New York: Verve Music Group.
Sullivan, R. 2007. Introduction. In *100 Love Sonnets, Pablo Neruda*, trans. G. Escobedo, vii–x. Holstein, ON: Exile Editions.
Sunnyside Interview. 2004. "When Luciana Souza began..." http://www.sunnysidezone.com.
Theodorakis, M. 1975. A mi partido. *Canto General*. LP. Minos.

———. 2007. Gospel of our time: *Canto General. Mikis Theodorakis*. 4 February. http://www.mikis-theodorakis.net/canto-e.html.

Vilches, P. 2004. Cuerpo de mujer, grandes colinas: La subjetividad femenina como geografía ecológica en la poesía de Pablo Neruda. In *Neruda, 100 años*, ed. Sophia Austral. 51–56.

Wagner, Guy. 2004. Pablo Neruda. *Theodorakis: The home page*, 8 March. http://en.mikis-theodorakis.net/index.php/article/articleview/208/1/56.

The Transculturation of *Capoeira*: Brazilian, Canadian, and Caribbean Interpretations of an Afro-Brazilian Martial Art

Janelle Joseph

On sunny Sunday afternoons in the summer of 2005, I observed passersby being hailed into Trinity Bellwoods Park, a large green space in downtown Toronto. Pedestrians were attracted by the sounds of the syncopated rhythms played on an *atabaque* and *pandeiro* (Afro-Brazilian percussive instruments) and the sorrowful, melodic cry of a *berimbau* (a bow-shaped instrument integral to capoeira). Near the source of the music, a dozen people formed a circle, clapped their hands and sang songs in Portuguese. In the centre of the circle, two muscular black men wearing only white pants with coloured cords hanging around their waists spun and weaved around each other, kicking and escaping with acrobatic grace and dancers' flair. That summer these *capoeiristas* (capoeira practitioners) gathered in the park often to practise and perform a fighting sport mixed with dance.

Be it the transformation of the First Nation's game of baggattaway into what is now known as Canada's national sport, lacrosse, or the embrace of cricket by immigrants from former British colonies, the presence of sport in Canada has always been predicated on border crossings. Thus, it is no surprise to find the Afro-Brazilian martial art capoeira performed on streets, in parks, and at capoeira schools called *academias* in Toronto, Canada. How do we theorize the political, emotional, and recreational significance of capoeira for its practitioners in Canada? What are the local exigencies of the teachers, students, and setting that result in the transculturation of this sport? What path will it travel as it evolves? In the following pages I draw on participation, observation, informal conversations, and off-site interviews carried out with one group I refer to as Ginga Capoeira (GC). I have been a member of this group for eight years but acted as an ethnographer at classes, performances, parties, and meetings for six months in 2005.

I follow Fernando Ortiz (1995) who explains transculturation as the complex process of cultural transmission and diffusion. Uprooting and transplanting a cultural form is followed by compromise, sharing, and ultimately a transformation into a new cultural whole based on the conglomeration of various cultural traditions within one territorial space. Ortiz's (1995) comparative study of crop production in Cuba emphasizes individual agency in selecting *parts* of a dominant discourse and reveals the embedded nature of any business in historical particularities and interpersonal social relations. Meanings associated with a business product are always adapted to suit a local setting, and styles and subtleties are modified as a result of collaborations, parody, and mis/incomprehension. This theory can be applied to other cultural phenomena, such as capoeira, to explore how economic opportunities, contradictory identities, and social capital are generated in a myriad of multicultural spaces.

Capoeira students outside Brazil are often curious about how capoeira in their country compares to the "real thing" in Brazil, assuming there is a major gap in quality (Delamont and Stevens 2008; Essien 2008; Joseph 2008a). Rather than lament a loss of authenticity as a result of capoeira's globalization, or essentialize capoeira in all of Canada or Brazil, I show that this martial art is constantly subject to growth, development, and modifications dependent on particular historical and social contexts. Many historians and cultural theorists have described capoeira as the result of diasporic movements, colonialism, and resistance practices in Brazil (Assunção 2005; Lewis 1992). The examination of this multifaceted physical activity in Canada provides evidence of the transculturation that results from more recent migration patterns, the exoticization of Brazilian culture in North America, and the class, age, gender, national, and racial identities of teachers and students.

I begin by situating this study within the literature on sport and cross-cultural exchange. I show that sports and athletes are altered when they enter what Pratt (1992) refers to as "contact zones." I describe the (con)text of capoeira and its transplantation to Canada and the GC group in particular. My objective is to demonstrate how an Afro-Brazilian cultural form and its community of devotees can transform due to the influence of (a) class, age, and gender on the intensity of violence accepted by students, (b) teacher's commodification of their talent, and (c) Caribbean-Canadian diasporic identities. The body and physical activity are undertheorized elements of globalization studies. Therefore, in this chapter I use sport as a lens to examine global cultural flows and transformations.

The Sporting 'Contact Zone'

In Canada, sports that originated elsewhere are taken up not only by recent immigrants striving to maintain a connection to their homeland, but also by "host land" nationals and other immigrants, thus creating "diaspora spaces" (Brah 1996) or "contact zones" (Pratt 1992). In these spaces, Pratt explains, "peoples [once] geographically and historically separated come into contact with each other and establish ongoing relations, usually involving conditions of coercion, radical inequality, and intractable conflict" (1992, 6). Pratt draws on Ortiz's (1995) term, transculturation, to describe how "subordinated or marginal groups select and invent from materials transmitted to them by a dominant or metropolitan culture" (Pratt 1992, 6), but we can no longer think of Southern countries as merely receivers. Within "diaspora spaces" relations of inequality and conflict between majority and minority groups are ongoing, but Brah also points out boundaries "of belonging and otherness, of 'us' and 'them,' are contested ... [and] African-Caribbean, Irish, Asian, Jewish and other diasporas intersect among themselves" (1996, 209). Thus, I investigate not only majority/minority relationships but also how lateral interactions (between Caribbean and Brazilian immigrants, for example) take shape. Attention to local nuances of identification, performativity, and conflicts of transculturation are key to understanding the complexities of transnational flows.

In the past two decades increasing attention has been paid to transnational migrants—those who regularly cross borders between their "home" and "host" nation. Recently, sociologists have demonstrated the significance of sport as a transnational practice (Klein 2007; Giuliannotti and Robertson 2007). For example, Major League Baseball celebrities such as Ichiro Suzuki have a significant impact on international tourism, east–west politics, and US and Japanese cultural identities and nationalisms (Nakamura 2006; Collins 2007). In addition to important dyadic relationships, scholars have shown that transnational networks develop though sport to include multimodal travel, kinship, economic, political, and environmental links (Giuliannotti 1999; Gupta 2004; Joseph 2008b; Taylor 2006).

When sports are introduced into entirely new cultural settings, the implications for the players are great and the sports themselves are sometimes drastically transformed. Donnelly (1988; 1993) noted that sport is less a totally incorporated aspect of popular culture and more an area in which values, ideologies, and meanings may be contested. For instance, in the United States, players altered rugby into gridiron football, a game less based on tradition and equivocal rules and more upon division of labour, individual success, and strict man-to-man contact, in line with mores of the United States (Reisman and Denney 1951, 289). Kalarippayattu, a martial art unique to the Southern Indian state of Kerala, provides another cogent example. This martial art has recently succumbed to pressures to gratify tourists by eliminating the spiritual ambience of traditional forms and emphasizing its dance elements; the reconceptualization of kalarippayattu as a performance art is based on karate and street-fighting styles mediated by iconographies and ideologies of Hollywood, Bollywood, and Hong Kong film industries (MacDonald 2003; 2007). Many studies have shown that globalized sports' meanings shift based on the intentions of the athletes and the cultural context of play.

My study contributes to an analysis of the transculturation of sports and globalization more broadly. As suggested by Jorge Nef and Alejandra Roncallo in this volume, "the Americas" should be considered as an integrated whole. I show in this chapter that based on the class, culture, and nationalities of athletes, capoeira is now a sport of "the Americas." This chapter demonstrates the transculturation of the sport into a Brazilian, Caribbean, *and* Canadian phenomenon.

Capoeira (Con)Text: Brazil and Canada

To understand how Ginga Capoeira (GC) teachers and students have transformed the martial art, it is necessary to first describe its text—that is, answer the question: What is capoeira? I then outline its context—that is, its history, transformations in the Brazilian setting, and transplantation to Canada.

Capoeiristas use a variety of terms to describe what they do; whether it is termed as a *luta* (fight), *jogo* (game), *dança* (dance), or *esporte* (sport), capoeira remains an alternative physical activity and a resistance practice. Capoeira once expressed enslaved Africans' music and movement cultures, their desire for freedom and their need for a black space in a white-controlled society. *Capoeiristas* subverted the discourses of the dominant social institutions explicitly, through defiance of laws that prohibited Afro-Brazilian public gatherings, and symbolically through the structure of the game.

To play capoeira, two people intertwine their bodies in an acrobatic, dance-like, and even comedic physical conversation, led by the music of the *bateria* (band)[1] and encircled by their peers who sing and clap. The music is used to create rhythms to impel the shoulders and hips of all within earshot, to bring energy called *axé* and spectators to the circle formation called a *roda*. The music directs the tone of the movements to be aggressive or playful: there is always a martial component, but depending on the rhythm of the *berimbau* (lead instrument), the attacks are either slow and feigned, allowing time for an escape, or fast and deadly.[2]

Players attempt to dominate their opponents by demonstrating superior balance, acrobatics, flexibility, and style in their dance; anticipating the next move and blocking it, offering an immediate counter-attack; using *malícia* (trickery) to confuse the opponent and a mastery of aesthetics to impress the audience; or through deployment of a hard kick or take-down manoeuvre. In fact, a *capoeirista* can show advanced skill by stopping a kick inches from an opponent's face, or sweeping a fellow *capoeirista* off his or her feet but gently placing him or her on the ground. Even in an aggressive game, this mock-violence or friendly-fight element of capoeira contrasts with most martial arts, such as Korean taekwondo or Thai boxing, where the objective is always to execute strikes and dominate the opponent. In capoeira, the constant play of attack and counterattack, or call and response (foundational to most African based movement and music practices) makes ascertaining the "winner" always subjective.

Throughout the fifteenth to twentieth centuries, slaves and low-income rural and urban blacks practised capoeira secretively for entertainment and, importantly, to fight against plantation owners, police, and rival groups, and gangs (Assunção 2005; Lewis 1992). Scott observed that subordinate groups draw on Western mechanisms and ideas juxtaposed with indigenous beliefs and vocabularies to fashion out of their ordeals "a 'hidden transcript' that represents a critique of power spoken behind the back of the dominant" (1994, xii). This certainly applies to the case of Brazil's lower classes, who engaged in a hidden transcript that is as rich in complexity as the domination was severe. Where creative resistance was required, transculturation occurred, resulting in syncretism, hybridity, miscegenation, and creole cultures of post-colonial societies across the Americas.

The practice has always been dominated by men and is traditionally associated with the lower classes, black male sexual virility, and folk life in northeast Brazil (Lewis 1992). Illegal until the 1930s, the first transplantation of the martial art occurred with the permission of then-president Getúlio Vargas, who aimed to modernize Brazil and promote his conception of "racial democracy" (equality among races). One of capoeira's most renowned luminaries, *Mestre* Bimba, is said to have copied the techniques and fashions of local Japanese karate schools when he formally institutionalized the activity by creating the first legal capoeira training *academia* (school). M. Bimba removed capoeira from its origins in the *quilombos* (escaped slave villages), *favelas* (slums) and *ruas* (streets), symbolically marking the end of prohibition and allowing an Afro-Brazilian cultural form to gain respectability among Euro-Brazilians (Assunção 2005; Lewis 1992).

Capoeira was further mainstreamed through transplantation from predominantly black Bahia to the rest of Brazil. It was incorporated into the nation-states' elaborate plans for military police training, and eventually evolved into "a technique for demonstrating Brazilian courage in confrontations with other nations' champions who employed their own emblematic fighting forms" (Downey 2002, 3). Capoeira became a key component of folklore shows in attempts to bolster the nation-state's claims to racial democracy, which were key to Brazil's outer-national relations. Western Europe and the United States, each grappling with racial politics, eagerly accepted the martial art as a transportable symbol of multicultural unity in the early 1970s. Two decades later, capoeira made its way to Canada, infused in the bodies of migrants with little formal education, but the necessary corporeal and business acumen to augment their income through performing and teaching the exotic, "authentic" Brazilian martial art. Capoeira has emerged to become a public transcript: it is performed in streets, parks, and public spaces in metropoles across Brazil and around the world. Its pleasurable aspects certainly continue to be highlighted; however, capoeira's messages of resistance have shifted in accordance with the social position of *capoeiristas*. Today, the oppressors are said to be individual: "insecurities, and a lack of coordination or confidence" (Essien 2008, xiv) can be overcome through allegiance to the game. In sum, "pure" Brazilian capoeira has consistently undergone changes and continues to transform as it develops and spreads around the world, adapting to new settings and participant needs.

Establishing Authenticity within Ginga Capoeira (GC)
Capoeira can now be found in most major Canadian cities. The first GC teachers in Toronto had little capoeira experience but copious enthusiasm and business savvy. They started their own classes in parks and community centres, wherever free or inexpensive space was available and they had a devoted, albeit naive, group of students, such as Vão and Gigante: "My first teacher was one of the only people in Toronto that was teaching capoeira ... that's the only thing I knew in terms of it being exposed to me, so whatever capoeira I seen was like amazing ... [but] the capoeira I was doing with [him], it was *traditional* but it wasn't focusing on the sport as capoeira is today.... It wasn't like the *real* deal" (Vão 2005).[3]

In hindsight, Gigante has little respect for the first capoeira teachers he met: "If you can do one or two movements that nobody has ever seen before, you can pass yourself off as somebody that is more qualified than you actually are ... because people see them as being Brazilian, they speak Portuguese and can hold a *berimbau* [instrument] without it tipping over, 'Oh, they must know what they're doing'" (Gigante 2005a).

The first capoeira students in Toronto realized novices had duped them when a handful of experienced *capoeiristas* migrated from Brazil to Canada in the late 1990s. Vetted by a guru in Brazil, these real *capoeiristas* had decades of training behind them, could perform magically in the *roda*, had a mastery of other Afro-Brazilian music and dance forms, and were well respected in the international capoeira community. Vão, Gigante, and most of their peers switched teachers immediately.

With twenty-two years of capoeira experience, Sol, an Afro-Brazilian who co-founded Ginga Capoeira (GC) sees himself as a savior of capoeira in Toronto: "To make capoeira keep growing here there must be true *capoeiristas* who have the experience, who devote all that they have, who take their lifetime to learn and share, not just wake up one day and call [themselves] *mestre* (master)" (2005).

With the passion and devotion of a *"true capoeirista,"* Sol teaches regularly and now has a devoted following of close to sixty students.

In 2004, with Sol's permission and supervision,[4] three Jamaican-Canadians, Vão, Gato Preto, and Risão, who had been training eight to ten years, started teaching capoeira. Many of Sol's students have travelled to Brazil but none of these student-teachers has made it there due to economic and familial constraints. Nevertheless, Vão, Gato Preto, and Risão distinguish themselves from the so-called *mestres* who originally duped them when they were introduced to the art. They purport to teach "real" Brazilian capoeira. Below I show that despite claims to purity, many factors mediate the local experience of capoeira in Toronto. The influence of class, age, and gender on the tolerated level of violence, and the influence of commodification on the teaching style of capoeira classes is unique to the specific cohort of GC students and teachers in 2005. Furthermore, Vão, Gato Preto, and Risão's Jamaican-Canadian nationality and their personal connections to their African roots, Caribbean ethnicity, and this Afro-Brazilian martial art offer an exceptional insight into the transculturation process.

The Influence of Class, Age, and Gender

Many Brazilian teachers leave their homeland in part because they are unable to make a living from capoeira there. Sol's search for more wealthy students led him to teach a cohort in Canada that is in a higher class bracket, older, and less experienced with capoeira than his students in Brazil. These factors, along with student responsibilities (e.g., a mortgage, children, or career) and the localized expressions of gender, have implications for the levels of contact, aggression, and violence in the game.

GC *capoeiristas* are typically employed young adults between twenty and thirty-four years old. Due to their other responsibilities, such as school, family, and work, GC students are less willing to take risks with their bodies and the bodies of their peers in the *roda*. This results in less aggression and contact in their games compared to Sol's students in Brazil. Pulinho (2005a), a middle-class Canadian with four years of experience, perceives playing rough as "kid's stuff." Feliz (2005), a middle-class Canadian with 1.5 years under her belt, believes that adults should "play with control," otherwise someone could get hurt. Serpente, a middle-class Brazilian who spent three years training in Brazil before moving to Canada, vehemently disagrees:

> I always hear [my teacher] say, "Oh, you don't wanna get hurt, tomorrow everybody has to go to work." I think that yeah, that's nice... but how you gonna learn and see if you can kick someone if you don't [kick hard]? And then you go to a roda somewhere you gonna play some Brazilian people... so you gonna get kicked and then you never could kick someone. Sometimes I think this is wrong, the way we go, because you don't wanna hurt nobody, but to test your reflex, to test your power you gonna have to do that. (Serpente)

The fine line between "playing with control" and "testing your power" is a contentious issue amongst group members who work as bankers, lawyers, graphic designers, pilots, teachers, and Ph.D. students and do not want to risk injury.

Jonathan, a middle-class Canadian who has trained capoeira for four years acknowledges the benefits of testing his power, but has no intention of encountering a "real" Brazilian *roda*, because health and safety, career, family, and other recreational pursuits are his priorities over learning to kick and be kicked. Once an avid rugby and football player, he is no longer interested in participating in a violent sport model and echoes the sentiments of others in the group. He says (2005):

> I took capoeira because it's a sport that's physical and I can do a lot of things that I've always wanted to try to do [such as acrobatics and music], but the contact part isn't something that I'm interested in getting involved in.... I've got work and I've got family and I've got bills and all that kind of other stuff and so there's a lot of things I can't contribute extra time and effort to if I'm hurt.

Similarly, Gigante (2005b) explains that it is his age that precludes him from engaging in dangerous activity. "After 30 [years old] you don't heal as fast!" he reminded me. This attitude is common amongst many of the middle-class Canadian players, including myself, who remained after class one day to try to practise a takedown technique, a *tesoura* (scissors). After a few unsuccessful attempts, and being reminded that a GC member had once dislocated his elbow when it had been performed on him, we decided that we were "too old" to practice *tesouras* and turned our efforts to a less dangerous manoeuvre.

Sol sometimes compares GC students to his students in Brazil who kick faster and harder. They are a younger and predominantly male group that is embedded within a culture where capoeira is understood as a potentially violent martial art and means of self-protection. Essien (2008, 69) describes his experiences in Brazil, where violent encounters in the *roda* were not taken personally. The age and comfortable employment conditions of Canadian *capoeiristas*, combined with a "polite Canadian culture," compel GC students to keep their other responsibilities in mind, take fewer risks with their own and their opponents' safety, and take violent encounters more personally than *capoeiristas* in Brazil are reported to do.

Because capoeira is relatively new to Canada, there are proportionally fewer experienced players. One consequence of inexperience is inferior skill and a smaller amount of intentional contact. Beginners are often introduced to capoeira through a performance or demonstration on the street or in a park, where *capoeiristas* emphasize the beauty, not the martial aspect of the movements. This leads to the misconception that capoeira is more of a dance than a martial art. When beginners get into the *roda*, they mimic what they have seen in demonstrations and often play far apart from one another; therefore, contact is nearly impossible. *Capoeiristas* with more experience play closer together, which gives them more opportunities to take an opponent off his or her feet or to apply a strong kick to the body.

One advanced Canadian player who spent three months playing capoeira in Brazil explains why the *rodas* there featured more fights. In our group "you hold yourself back because you don't have confidence in your opponent" (Gigante 2005a). The majority of students in his class are beginners, so he avoids making contact with them. Essien explains that due to the larger pool of capoeiristas, greater access to talented *mestres* and high standards for technical precision, Brazilian players participate with great intensity and aggression, and these types of games are considered normal (2008, 69).

Serpente grew up in a Brazilian environment where violence in the *roda* was normalized. She is quite proud of her ability to use her kicks effectively. She explains that in Brazil the advanced *capoeiristas* are numerous and competitive, what she calls "hungry," setting the tone for a rough game that sometimes incites violence even among the beginners. "I saw some people being thrown out, you know, almost breaking out the wall and it is scary—your heart starts to beat and you [think] 'I have to go in there? Oh my god!'" (2005). Despite her fear and lack of experience, she did "go in there" and performed as aggressively as her advanced peers: "I wasn't that flexible yet, but I kicked [my opponent] in her face. I gave her a *martelo* [hammer kick] in her mouth.... I left there so happy" (ibid.). Serpente is an exception in the Canadian setting; most women express difficulty in learning to make physical contact with other players because they have limited experience with contact sports and do not want to hurt their friends or themselves.

Capoeira is embedded in a history of hyper-masculinity in Brazil. Like hockey or rugby in North America, women are marginalized and though some break barriers and play with men, they are often considered masculine women. In response, a hyper-feminine comportment (i.e., makeup, long hair, revealing uniforms) is the norm for female *capoeiristas*. In capoeira groups outside Brazil, "traditions such as women not being respected as capoeiristas have been challenged" (Essien 2008, xviii). Because of the dance and gymnastic elements (feminized sports in Canada), women are more likely to be regarded as ideal capoeira participants and GC students are more than fifty per cent female; the majority of these women do not like to fight and display low levels of aggression in the *roda*.

Even some men express uninterest in violence: "If I wanted to beat someone up, I'd take jiujitsu or judo or something, you know? I love the beauty of the movements so I'm gonna use my strong *gancho* (hook kick) to look good—I'm not about to kick someone's face in" (Curioso 2005). GC is seen as a space for the expression of sporting femininities and alternative masculinities. Curioso, a middle-class Canadian with three years experience, is quite clear that "meatheads" or "jocks" (athletes who value violence) are not welcomed.

As Sol's students in Canada gain more experience, witness more games between advanced students, subordinate their other responsibilities, improve their technique and the proximity with which they play, and shift their gender constructs, the GC game will more closely resemble that found amongst Sol's Brazilian students. Until then, the game will appear to be transformed into a style of play with less aggressive technique.

The Influence of Commodification

Martial arts are well known as sites to develop discipline, courage, self-assurance, and a lethal body; typically the *mestre* teaches students proficiency in a very strict manner. Due to the demographics and desires of the Canadian GC students, however, they are less likely to over-conform to a teacher's unpleasant requirements. If a teacher wants to maintain his students and income he makes fewer and less strict demands of them. Additionally, teachers who recognize that some students are interested only in the physical exercise aspects of capoeira may sell the art as an exotic fitness practice.

Participants describe capoeira *mestres* in Brazil and those who are newly immigrated to Canada as more strict, and as having higher standards of discipline than Canadian teachers. When *mestres* come directly from Brazil for the annual *batizado* (graduation) event, many GC students are shocked by the demands placed on them. During one workshop I attended, each student was made to do pushups every time anyone made a mistake and 200 abdominal crunches was the punishment for drinking water without permission. This workshop was followed by a twenty-minute tirade about showing respect for *mestres*. In the change room afterwards many *capoeiristas* expressed disbelief that we had "paid him to come and torture us." I have since wondered whether this *mestre's* "torture" was merely a staged performance designed to market the *batizado* and support the myth of superior Brazilian capoeira.

Serpente (2005) claims her Brazilian teacher had a difficult time adjusting to Canadian students when he first arrived:

There was a guy that trained with us. He was Brazilian and he was maybe here [in Canada] thirty years and he start to talk to [my teacher], "You know you gonna have to change your ways. People here they are different. They don't like... when the teacher screams [at] them, they think it's disrespectful and if you kick them like maybe they won't come back." That was really hard to change, to try to do things different than he was trained in Brazil and how he used to train his [Brazilian] students.

Ultimately, Serpente's teacher made some concessions because he acknowledged that his passion was a commodity that only has value if there is a consumer demand. Delamont has observed that in Britain "the capoeira teacher has to build loyalty and assert authority in a precarious financial situation" (2006, 164). In some settings, authority may be secured through intimidation and physical punishment of students. Within GC that "don't fly" (will not work) (Vão 2005). As I have explained elsewhere (Joseph 2008a), a teacher must adjust his teaching to suit his students' needs if he wants to pay rent, bolster his reputation, and maintain or augment his income.

The commodification of alternative sports is not a new phenomenon; Rinehart (2003) notes the process of commodification is not only one-way or top-down, the corollary of greedy corporations taking advantage of innocent individuals. Athletes themselves are often the instigators of the "sell-out," working to develop respectable incomes and icon status and subsequently risking destroying their authenticity and credibility.

Recognizing that many Canadians are interested in capoeira for its value as a fitness pursuit rather than a martial art, some unscrupulous GC students "auto-graduate themselves as *mestres*" (Assunção 2005, 182) and generate income from what I have termed capo-workout, capo-robics and other capoeira-fitness hybrids. Many *capoeiristas* and scholars choose to discount, ignore, or marginalize capoeira that is presented as the latest exotic workout (Essien 2008; Assunção 2005), yet this formation provides important evidence of transculturation. It is essential to analyze how physical activities, including judo, tai chi, zumba, and yoga, are initially valued for their ability to provide an outlet for creativity, an alternative view of the body and kinetic expression, yet are subsequently simplified, divorced from their cultural contexts and philosophical or spiritual practices, and infused with Western imperatives of rationality.

Despite, or perhaps due to, the representation of capoeira as counterculture, elements of this martial art have made their way to the vanguard of fitness cultures in Canada in just over one decade. *Mestre* Acordeon, the foremost contemporary capoeira *mestre* in North America explains that "Afro-Brazilian is a redundant term. African folklore is at the heart of Brazilian culture" (2005). The absence of African folklore from the heart of Canadianness, in contrast, makes Afro-Brazilian culture seem exotic; capoeira's unusual corporeality can add a taste of Brazilian spice to a fitness class.

My suspicions that capo-workouts are booming in popularity in Toronto were confirmed one afternoon when I ran into an acquaintance of mine. She invited me to a capoeira class she had just joined at a community centre close to my house. I had not heard of a new group in the area and asked for the name of the group and her *mestre*, basic questions for every *capoeirista*. She did not seem to understand what I was asking. "It's just capoeira" was her reply. When I asked if there would be a *roda* at the end of the class, she asked, "What? A hoedown?" The reason for her misunderstandings became clear when I arrived and saw a former GC student, Avaro, leading the class. He had trained with GC for a few years and had apparently stopped to spend his evenings working at a community centre where he taught simplified capoeira drills to music played on a stereo. He did not teach his students the Portuguese language, capoeira songs, history, or instruments. Neither did he demonstrate how to use capoeira techniques against an opponent in a *roda*. I managed to stay until the end of the one-hour class but left feeling furious with Avaro for teaching capoeira without permission from our *mestre* and for leading his aerobics students to believe they were "doing capoeira."

A few months later, Gato Preto, an established GC teacher, invited me to join him at one of his classes. When I arrived I discovered that in addition to his GC duties, he was teaching a capo-workout class at Bally's, a popular international fitness studio, where he meets clients' needs with his own version of the martial art. In his classes Gato Preto "artfully fuses together dance movements and techniques with the Brazilian martial art Capoeira into an energizing and invigorating total-body workout. The class focuses on cardiovascular work, toning and strengthening, all to the beat of exciting Brazilian music... [and] is the latest in [Bally's] continuous effort to provide our members with exciting and innovative ways to stay active and healthy" (Bally Total Fitness 2005).

Although Gato Preto's capo-workout featured a *roda* and was more similar to a traditional capoeira class than Avaro's, I remained frustrated that their students are not exposed to the multiple facets of capoeira and suggested that capo-workout classes devalue the "true" art. He assured me that students who take these types of classes may become interested in joining more traditional capoeira groups, so his proselytizing only helps GC. While this may be true, what I believe is also likely is that a fitness student might become interested in personal training capoeira sessions with Gato Preto or Avaro; therefore, capo-workouts may provide entrée into a lucrative fitness career and disguise the depth of capoeira.

My resentment of these student-teachers abated as I reflected on their student populations and motivations. Every teacher, whether in Brazil or Canada, selects particular elements of capoeira and excludes others to target a particular audience. Gato Preto and Avaro responded to a need they saw among women looking for a unique fitness class to maintain their interest and offered a one-hour, high-intensity exercise regime. My own teacher, Sol, saw how his students were sometimes vulnerable in the *roda* and began to teach jiu-jitsu manoeuvres we could use to respond to certain capoeira techniques that land us on our backs. Capo-jitsu could be placed alongside the capo-workout as an example of what Cheadle (in this volume) calls a "perverse synthesis," the fetishization and transformation of exotic culture in order to profit from it. While these types of transformations may not be unique to the setting outside Brazil, I draw on particular GC examples to demonstrate what form the transformations may take in environments where the general population knows little — in some cases nothing at all — about a cultural phenomenon. GC "teachers not only *in*struct capoeira, but they also *con*struct this activity in Canada" (Joseph, 2008a, 508).

There is an inherent contradiction in the rising commodification of capoeira in all its forms: capoeira originated amongst the first anti-capitalism protestors, enslaved Africans who used their embodied practice to resist oppression; today it can be sold for profit. Both in Brazil and in Canada, participants may take a capoeira class at a community centre, gym, or *academia* because they are searching for something different, special, authentic, or alternative. What they end up practising may be a class where they are "tortured" with exercises before a *roda* or where they learn to kick but not to sing. Both versions of the capoeira class are a result of the desire to marry a passion for capoeira with a need for income in the absence of major endorsements, magazines, or competitions, and demonstrate the transculturation that occurs when a cultural practice is commodified.

The Influence of Caribbean-Canadians

Students' racial and ethnic backgrounds sometimes influence their attraction to capoeira. Essien describes his book *Capoeira beyond Brazil* as an opportunity to share his "unique viewpoint as a non-Brazilian capoeira instructor, who is also black" (Essien 2008, xiv); however, he does not offer an analysis of how race generally, or his identity as a black man specifically, has influenced his participation in this martial art. My study has found that one unique aspect of the transculturation of capoeira is revealed through an analysis of the instruction of three black, Jamaican-Canadian student-teachers, Vão, Gato Preto, and Risão, who each run *academias* in the Greater Toronto Area. In 2005 nearly sixty per cent of the GC members were their students. Though none of them have been to Brazil they are adepts who have gained the respect of their students and teacher, Sol.

In her exposition on teacher clout in capoeira, Delamont asserts that "race and nationality, the former literally embodied and the latter culturally embodied, are crucial parts of the capoeira teacher's authority and authenticity" (2006, 166). The three Jamaican-Canadian student-teachers draw on their blackness to adduce their authority and authenticity in this martial art. Vão, Gato Preto, and Risão consistently affirm the African ancestry of the martial art and, furthermore, position Jamaica as kindred to Bahia, Brazil, the birthplace of capoeira. Their similar climates, ethnic composition, styles of cooking, carnivals, and philosophies—encapsulated by the expressions "Out of many, one people" in Jamaica and "racial democracy" in Brazil—make them have "basically the same atmosphere" Vão (2005) argues. Vão and his peers emphasize not only the current similarity between the regions but also the ancestral, diasporic links. Vão can draw a clear (albeit imagined) ancestral line back to the enslaved Africans who originated capoeira. "I have a link to it and most let's say Islanders or African descendant people might have a link to capoeira in a certain sense" (ibid.). He instructs his students to find out about the role of capitalism in slave history and to learn about maroons,[5] not only in Jamaica and Brazil but all over the Black Atlantic.

Gato Preto says his students and friends share with him how important capoeira is to their black identities: "I feel it is really good to bring them back to their roots.... The singing, the music, even though it's a different language they still have an African, I'd say flavour to it.... [I am] bringing a black art to the community" (2005a). Gato Preto elides the Brazilian roots of the art form when he discusses his students' motivations for playing. Describing it as a "black art" gives him authority as a black teacher.

Capoeira games and classes are occasionally wrapped up with *samba de roda*, samba dancing inside a circle. *Capoeiristas* relax, celebrate, and flirt with quick dance steps. Men and women enter the circle together and perform improvised choreography, which is often sexually suggestive and requires prodigious control of the hips, shoulders, and especially feet. When Risão, one of the Jamaican-Canadian student-teachers, takes his chance to shine in the *roda*, his samba steps usually (d)evolve into hip gyrations of another sort. In observing this, Gato Preto giggled, "We always a tro' a dutty wine in," meaning that they (his Jamaican-Canadian peers), are always wining (a sensual Caribbean dance), even when they should be dancing samba (2005b). The perception that the *capoeirista* is a dark-skinned man with a beautiful, muscular body and a reputation as a consummate seducer and stimulator of women is a stereotype once promoted derogatorily by upper-class white Brazilians but now endorsed by many *capoeiristas*, Afro-Brazilians and Jamaican-Canadians alike. Dancing, musical, and sporting proficiency are the epitome of heteronormative, hypermasculine virility in both Brazil and Jamaica (Willson 1997; Davis 2006).

Vão, Gato Preto, and Risão encourage their students to enter the *samba de roda* and express themselves but rarely offer dance or music instruction.

Pulinho complained about non-Brazilian teachers one day after a *samba de roda* at Risão's academy: "They can offer the [capoeira] movements, but they can't offer the culture and they can't offer the music, you know they just don't walk like a Brazilian, you know?" (2005b). Due to their inexperience with broader aspects of Brazilian culture, and their confidence in a Jamaican style of dancing and speaking, GC student-teachers deny their junior students access to a "real Brazilian" experience. Instead their students might learn to "*jookin de roda*" (Gato Preto 2005b), a Patois pun that equates *samba* and *jookin* (a Jamaican dance with sensual hip thrusting), and must turn elsewhere to learn Portuguese.

In addition to samba, the language and music of the capoeira *academia* is also different when taught by Vão, Gato Preto, and Risão. The *roda* remains a predominantly Portuguese playing space with music typically dominated by a syncopated rhythm on the *atabaque* (drum); however, Jamaican patois has crept into the training spaces and dancehall drumbeats are occasionally mixed in. When these three are in charge, the dance, language, and music of capoeira help to create not only a Brazilian capoeira *academia* but also a "black space" (Carrington 1998; Sansone 2003).

Another black Caribbean-Canadian student, Sombra, has often discussed with me local multiculturalism politics and the desire to exhibit this art form during Black History Month, for instance, while he recognizes that black Caribbean and Brazilian peoples and cultures are marginalized all other months of the year. I started capoeira, in part, because of my desire to associate with the only sport I know of that has black origins and to connect with my African roots. Sombra also feels a sense of racial pride because capoeira puts black culture into the spotlight in a positive way: "Capoeira is not just like hip hop or whatever where you wear the clothes and walk like this [with a limp] ... there is so much more. You know, there's the history, the philosophy, this is *real* black culture" (2005). Where mainstream hip hop is often associated with obnoxious American culture and black deviance, Sombra and I explored other avenues for a sense of black community.

Davis (2006) and Walcott (2003) discuss the importance of positive black role models, opportunities to negotiate freedom, the discovery of a sense of home, and safety among peers in the creation of black Canadian identities. Black "immigrants estranged in large metropolitan centers like Toronto, continue to look back to the Caribbean [and Brazil] in search of alternative signifiers, and in search of a cultural and national identity that can shield them from marginalization and racism" (Davis 2006, 24). Discrimination is the inevitable reality of life in Canada, where blacks are offered citizenship and multicultural incorporation but excluded from a sense of belonging based on cultural and racial differences from the dominant Anglo group (Davis 2006;

Walcott 2003). Like wearing dreadlocks or speaking patois, learning capoeira in the GC group provides access to conspicuous markers of blackness—both Brazilian and Jamaican.

Within GC, diasporic reformulations of roots and racial categories shape the discursive descriptors of capoeira and belonging. Since the martial art's inception the cultures of many groups have conjoined to transform its practice, which speaks to Brah's (1996) theorization of the lateral links between various ethnic groups. Today, in Canada, it continues to develop organically as "a prime example of a 'counterculture of modernity,' a 'transcultural, international formation' of the Black Atlantic rather than only African or Brazilian" (Assunção 2005, 30). Capoeira student-teachers fuse Canadian, Jamaican, and Brazilian cultures and create a new cultural environment.

Conclusion

Capoeira defies categorization. It is exclusively neither dance nor martial art, neither acrobatics nor sport, neither philosophical nor physical practice, yet all these at once. Keeping capoeira's penchant for syncretism in mind, it is easy to reconcile the thoughts of Vão the *capoeirista* and Sansone the ethnicity scholar, or to appraise the dance steps of Risão, who teaches the martial art, alongside the findings of Delamont, who researches capoeira embodiment. This martial art takes on a new face based on the participants' experiences, goals and cultural constraints, which, as I have shown here, are mediated by class, culture, and nationality.

The phenomenon of global circulation of cultural products and people is not new. Capoeira developed in a contact zone. Assunção (2005, 42) provides an example of early capoeira's transformation: the African languages of the original *capoeiristas* were replaced by Portuguese "since one of the main attractions consisted precisely in the questions or comments thrown to the public by the solo singer, that change was necessary in order to adapt to a wider multiethnic audience." The martial art continues to be transformed in spaces where, as Pratt (1992, 4) describes, new people and cultures meet, clash, and grapple with each other, borrowing and lending in both directions, creating creolized intercultural texts. Today the multi-ethnic audience consists not only of European and African descendents in Brazil but also of many other ethnic groups in various countries around the world, including Canada.

I return to Ortiz (1995), who coined the neologism "transculturation." He claimed that multiple cultures conjoin in the transculturation process to build onto preceding elements and form a new cultural whole. Capoeira continues to incorporate elements of the cultures of its devotees. I have shown how capoeira has transformed to accommodate middle-class students' aversion to danger and desire for fitness, altered to take advantage of teachers' need for money, and renewed itself to provide a diasporic resource for Caribbean-Canadians. Capoeira is a constantly evolving cultural practice that takes on new meanings as it crosses borders, based on the local needs, attitudes, and understandings of students and teachers.

Notes

1. The *bateria* consists of usually one *atabaque* (drum), one or two *pandeiros* (tambourines), and one to three *berimbaus*, which are bow-shaped lead instruments that emit sound when the wire is hit with a stick. The *berimbau* pitch is varied by manipulating a *dobrão* (stone) against the wire and amplified with a *cabeça* (gourd) held against or away from the musician's belly. The *berimbau* player usually holds a *caxixi* (shaker) to add a percussive element to the melody. The music is one of the most important elements of the *roda*.
2. These two styles are generally described as *Capoeira Angola* (slow attacks using playful and expressive techniques and contorted postures) and *Capoeira Regional* (fast kicks with aggressive manoeuvers and acrobatics).
3. Within capoeira, devotees are given nicknames that reflect their personalities or physicality. I have given pseudonym nicknames to all participants to protect their anonymity.
4. Another student-teacher, Gigante, a Canadian of English descent with nearly ten years experience, teaches at Sol's *academia* (school) in Sol's absence. His cultural background inevitably has an influence on the way he teaches, the analysis of which is beyond the scope of this chapter.
5. Maroons were enslaved Africans who escaped bondage and ran away into the mountains and jungles all across the Black Atlantic. Experts in guerrilla warfare, they won battles against individual slavers and colonial governments. Maroons were agents of active protest against slavery and in Jamaica in 1739 became the first group in the New World to be granted their freedom by a colonizing European power.

References

Assunção, M. R. 2005. *Capoeira: The history of Afro-Brazilian martial art*. London: Routledge.
Bally Total Fitness spices-up group exercise roster with Brazilian import, Boneco Capoeira. 2005. *Business Wire*, 3 May. http://findarticles.com/p/articles/ mi_m0EIN/is_2005_May_3/ai_n13667062.
Brah, A. 1996. *Cartographies of diaspora: Contesting identities*. New York: Routledge.
Carrington, B. 1998. Sport, masculinity, and black cultural resistance. *Journal of Sport & Social Issues* 22(3): 275–98.
Collins, S. 2007. "Samurai" politics: Japanese cultural identity in global sport—the Olympic games as a representational strategy. *International Journal of the History of Sport* 24(3): 357–74.
Curioso. 2005. Personal communication. 7 March.
Davis, A. 2006. Translating narratives of masculinity across borders: A Jamaican case study. *Caribbean Quarterly* 52(2–3): 22–38.

Delamont, S. 2006. The smell of sweat and rum: Teacher authority in capoeira classes. *Ethnography and Education* 1(2): 161–75.
Delamont, S., and Stevens, N. 2008. Up on the roof: The embodied habitus of diasporic capoeira. *Cultural Sociology* 2(1): 57–74.
Donnelly, P. 1988. Sport as a site for "popular" resistance. In *Popular cultures and political practices*, ed. R. Gruneau, 69–82. Toronto: Garamond.
———. 1993. Subcultures in sport: Resilience and transformation. In *Sport in social development: Traditions, transitions and transformations*, ed. A. Ingham and J. Loy, 119–45. Champaign, IL: Human Kinetics.
Downey, G. 2002. Domesticating an urban menace: Reforming capoeira as a Brazilian national sport. *The International Journal of the History of Sport* 19(4): 1–32.
Essien, A. 2008. *Capoeira beyond Brazil*. Berkeley, CA: Blue Snake Books.
Feliz. 2005. Personal communication. 7 June.
Gato Preto. 2005a. Interviewed by author. 31 May.
———. 2005b. Personal communication. 15 June.
Gigante. 2005a. Interviewed by author. 25 May.
———. 2005b. Personal communication. 15 June.
Giuliannotti, R. 1999. *Football: A sociology of the global game.* Cambridge: Polity Press.
Giuliannotti, R., and R. Robertson. 2007. Sport and globalization: Transnational dimensions. *Global Networks* 7(2): 107–12.
Gupta, A. 2004. The globalization of cricket: The rise of the non-West. *International Journal of the History of Sport* 21(2): 257–76.
Jonathan. 2005. Interviewed by author. 30 May.
Joseph, J. 2008a. Logical paradox of the cultural commodity: Selling an authentic martial art in Canada. *Sociology of Sport Journal* 25(4): 498–515.
———. 2008b. Going to Brazil: Transnational and corporeal movements of a Canadian-Brazilian martial arts community. *Global Networks* 8(2): 194–213.
Klein, A. 2007. Towards a transnational sports studies. *Sport in Society* 10(6): 885–95.
Lewis, J. L. 1992. *Ring of liberation: Deceptive discourses in Brazilian capoeira*. Chicago: Univ. of Chicago Press.
MacDonald, I. 2003. Hindu nationalism, cultural spaces and bodily practices in India. *American Behavioural Sciences* 46(11): 1563–76.
———. 2007. Bodily practice, performance art, competitive sport: A critique of kalarippayattu, the martial art of Kerala. *Contributions to Indian Sociology* 41(2): 143–68.
Mestre Acordeon. 2005. Personal communication. 15 July.
Nakamura, Y. 2006. The samurai sword cuts both ways: A transnational analysis of Japanese and US media representations of Ichiro. *International Review for the Sociology of Sport* 41(1): 79–88.
Ortiz, F. 1995. *Cuban counterpoint: Tobacco and sugar*. Trans. Harriet de Onís. Durham, NC: Duke Univ. Press.
Pratt, M. L. 1992. *Imperial eyes: Studies in travel writing and transculturation*. New York: Routledge.
Pulinho. 2005a. Interviewed by author. 29 March.
———. 2005b. Personal communication. 16 June.
Reisman, D., and R. Denney. 1951. Football in America: A study in culture diffusion. *Am. Quarterly* 3: 309–25.

Rinehart, R. E. 2003. Dropping into sight: Commodification and co-optation of in-line skating. In *To the extreme: Alternative sports, inside and out*, ed. R. E. Rinehart and S. Sydnor. Albany, NY: SUNY Press.

Sansone, L. 2003. *Blackness without ethnicity: Constructing race in Brazil.* New York: Palgrave Macmillan.

Scott, J. C. 1994. *Domination and the arts of resistance: Hidden transcripts.* New Haven/London: Yale Univ. Press.

Serpente. 2005. Interviewed by author. 26 May.

Sol. 2005. Interviewed by author. 13 February.

Sombra. 2005. Personal communication. 20 July.

Taylor, M. 2006. Global players? Football, migration and globalization, c. 1930–2000. *Historical Social Research* 31(1): 7–30.

Vão. 2005. Interviewed by author. 19 May.

Walcott, R. 2003. *Black like who?: Writing black Canada.* 2nd ed. Toronto: Insomniac Press.

Willson, M. 1997. Playing the dance, dancing the game: Race, sex and stereotype in anthropological fieldwork. *Ethnos* 62(3–4): 24–48.

Kcho's *La regata*: Political or Poetic Installation?

Lee L'Clerc

In 1994, an installation entitled *La regata* (1993–94) appeared in the landscape of Cuban art. Because of its concealed or perceived symbolism and because of the ethical and ideological questions it continues to elicit, it soon found itself within the realm of political controversy. First exhibited at the Fifth Havana Biennial and now in the Ludwig Museum in Cologne, this installation by the Cuban artist Alexis Leiva Machado, better known as Kcho, consists mainly of an arrangement positioned on the ground consisting of old shoes, perishable objects, and miniature boats and rafts made from wood, paper, and Styrofoam; together these items form the shape of a boat.

That this installation was to be immediately identified in relation to the Cuban rafter crisis that occurred during the same year as the Biennial was to be expected. Was it a coincidence that just around the corner, along the shore of Havana's seawall, El Malecón, many were leaving Cuba for the United States on inner tubes and homemade rafts? The work, it seems, could not have been read any other way, for Kcho's display does not appear to merely simulate the event; these small and fragile objects have been described as "tragi-comical reminders of the improbable raft constructions many Cubans have used in their attempts to flee to the USA" (Poupeye 1998, 190).[1] And if this installation is not an attempt to represent reality, what are we to make of the suggested geographical direction given to it? In what appears to be an incriminating visual sign of political and cultural involvement that further establishes how the real finds its way into Kcho's visual narrative, *La regata* is heading north, pointing to Miami, or to *"la yuma,"* as Cubans refer to the United States. Given the work's apparent context dependency, can there be any other possible interpretative assessment of *La regata*? All the elements of the installation, within the Havana space, seem to encourage the viewer to see the work not for what it is in itself, or in relation to some sporting event, as the title suggests, but as a culturally determined experience dependent on identification. In short, there exists in this installation much evidence that directs us to see not unconscious symbolism (to use Hegel's expression) but a cultural simulation, in which the art work appears to be mirroring and acting upon a real situation that was happening just then.

In this article I want to sketch a possible interpretative approach to *La regata* and thus attempt to rescue it from imported narratives grounded in politics and ideology.[2] I will argue that this installation is not in itself political art, but art that becomes political because it has been perceived as a simulation within a symbolic order and therefore has been identified and contextualized within a particular event said to be its background of reference. Although it is difficult to disconnect Kcho's installation from the socio-historical realities from which it emerges, I want primarily to address the work itself so to demonstrate how it interferes with the political narratives attributed to it, whether they are counter- or pro-revolutionary. Further, by examining a postcolonial approach to Kcho's work, though mainly through remarks regarding aesthetics and that of the artist's position when identified according to national or local narratives, I aim to show how this theoretical position excludes aesthetic experience and the work itself in favour of finding political and ideological discourses of "other voices" on the surface of the artwork. By the same token, in entertaining Gayatri C. Spivak's suggestion that "when a narrative is constructed, something is left out" (1990, 18), and in considering *La regata* as a material referent and as a site of transformations through which it asserts itself, I wish to explore how other relations can be established.[3] Therefore, without suggesting that this installation is, in Kantian terms, without purposiveness, or that it remains outside social concerns because it is a thing in itself, I draw attention to the aesthetics of *Arte Povera*, to the theatricality of display and metaphoric constructs of art installation, and to a poem, contexts that will upset the fixing of meaning and against which Kcho's work can be best understood.

It may be argued that to explain *La regata* according to the political boundaries or the socio-historical context of the day is to suggest that the installation was coloured by the rafter crisis and, therefore, that the artist mainly set out to record or to reconfigure this event. Clearly, it is by virtue of a constructed interrelation between the artwork and event that a political response is stimulated. Or, as Jacques Rancière shows in *The politics of aesthetics*, it can be said that it is not the work itself but "the state of politics that decides that artworks appear to harbour a political critique" (2006, 62). In this sense, the work's visual impact is instantly reduced to a political narrative mainly centred on the collective consciousness of *los balseros,* a politically disaffected people who had no other option than to seek a better life some ninety miles away. The social and political themes that the art work is said to introduce become substitutes for the aesthetic experience. Thus manipulated to be linked to a sociohistorical and political frame of reference, *La regata* is embraced for promoting a critical view of the Cuban revolutionary process. Kurt Hollander, for example, has linked Kcho's work to the specific political situation of the day. He writes: "Outside the island, *balseros* have until recently been welcomed as evidence of Cuba's political oppression, economic decadence and popular discontent" (1994, 45).

Moreover, to empathize within the realms of politics, if not to emphasize the wrongs of the Castro government, is to conceive *La regata* as a temporary monument to those who lost their lives while crossing the sea in such desperate conditions. At the level of the symbol, the work allows for this kind of interpretation. A humanitarian element can be ascribed to the installation, for it seems to evoke as much a sense of human presence through the shoes, children's toys, and egg trays as it suggest loss through bodily absence. The political narrative is even the more justified by the fragility of Kcho's little artifacts as seen in relation to the actual rafts. Yasmin Ramirez, for instance, sees the iconography of Kcho's *balsas* as an "effort to exploit the potential of this politically loaded symbol" (1996, 97). Whereas Héctor Antón Castillo, who questions the ethical position of the artist for exploiting the human tragedy of *los balseros* in the name of art, sees the work as a "simulacro de arte político" (2006, 49).

To be sure, this seemingly politically sensitive work invokes the sea as a space to be crossed and won, suggests displacement or unrealized journeys, and certainly raises ethical and ideological questions. It also expresses and offers, as we come to believe when looking at these crudely made sculptures and weathered found objects, a symbolic warning: In order to arrive at that place beyond the horizon where life is said to be better, one must not forget about the "Damned Circumstances of Water Everywhere,"[4] and one must be prepared to be burnt by the sun and taken hostage by the sea and its sharks. However, there are questions that need to be asked: Does the work refer to the process of leaving, traversing, and arrival? Or is it metaphorically haunted by journeys to be completed or by those peregrinations that had already crossed the sea? Who are those who have been transported or are going to be transported? Can absent bodies condition the significance of how this installation comes into play? And if the experience of a journey is mediated through the body, who is to be remembered in this sea of unrepresented bodies?

There are no clear signs assigned to *La regata* that facilitate identification with the rafter crisis or that indicate that this was the event intended for symbolization. This installation does not represent an inventory of an outside reality. There is no attempt in the work to elaborate on whether those who are alleged to have been transported were the victims of Fidel Castro's regime or illegal economic migrants disguised as political refugees. The work does not recognize the reason for any apparent political or economic displacement, nor does it recognize that this was a voluntary or a forcibly imposed exile. Individual memory may be understood through the worn shoes and tattered egg cartons, but there is no identification with personal narratives, nor, as Hollander observes, "any mention of life before or after" (1994, 45).[5] No one is remembered. This work is not a monument and does not claim to bear witness to the event. Interpreting the work for its symbolizing function may suggest a narrative about *los balseros,* yet the representational function of these carefully arranged objects suggest instead, as I will discuss later, an artistic gesture mainly grounded on aesthetic experience.

Further, it is paradoxical to see Kcho's installation in terms of a metaphoric journey, whether it stands for a Cuban experience or that of other rafters in other parts of the world. One may share Hollander's conviction that the work "[focuses] exclusively on the journey" (1994, 45). True, navigation and the idea of travelling are clearly conveyed within Kcho's fragile objects. Even the meaning of a metaphor, not just as a figure of speech in the Aristotelian sense, appears literally embedded within the work itself: "With its origins in Greek words meaning *carrying, transferring, transporting,* the metaphor is clearly a sympathetic linguistic figure for exile. The metaphor uncovers the qualities of one thing by shifting our attention to another. This displacement of meaning, this "defamiliarisation," suggests a consonance between metaphor and migration's actual estrangements (Osborne 2000, 127).

Still, the idea of Kcho's installation suggesting voyages across the sea is questionable if we consider, as Georges Van Den Abbeele writes, that "a voyage that stays in the same place is not a voyage. Indeed, the very notion of travel presupposes a movement away from some place, a displacement of whatever it is one understands by 'place'" (1992, xvi).[6] At any rate, navigation and travelling can be stressed as being central to interpretation, although the only symbolic journey that has taken place is that of the work itself, which left for Cologne rather than for Miami. In the end *La regata* does arrive, but at the only place many works of art wish to go, a museum, where, notwithstanding the ramifications of being commodified, it will be visualized for posterity and remembered within the context of art history, not politics.

Meanwhile, interpretation provides a framework that is grounded not on what the work is but on what the work is said to be — a simulation — and what it seems to be saying through metaphor. Narratives are brought from the outside in an attempt to assess the work or to assert that its meaning is revealed through the event that is assumed to be the origin of the work. The artwork is therefore removed from its own reality, and its coming into being is regarded as repetition, or simply reduced to the understanding that its existence owes to the transferring of an idea into an image so that we see similarities with other existing realities. Viewed against a 1990s Cuban backdrop, as defined by the tragic dimension and experience of Cuba's *balseros*, this installation is certainly rearticulated and contextualized by political discourses critical of the Cuban revolutionary process.

This is not to say that *La regata* does not allow for this kind of political interpretation. But it is necessary to question the limitations of imposed interpretations grounded on imported narratives in order to open up "Otros horizontes" (the title of another of Kcho's works) and thus the possibility of negotiating meaning and establishing other relations. As Gayatri C. Spivak has noted, "when an end is defined, other ends are rejected, and one might not know what those ends are.... What is left out? Can we know what is left out? We must know the limits of the narratives, rather than establish the narratives as solutions for the future" (1990, 18–19).

Let us briefly consider another social and political narrative that can be constructed around the rafter crisis, if we are to believe that this is the work's background of reference. Namely, a narrative that tells the story of an enterprise grounded on counter-revolution and egoism by people perceived as deserters (Hollander 1994, 45) and for whom the community had no value. True, *La regata* may allude to "the problems of the immigrant who embraces the sea route as a means of access to the great metropolis" (Montes de Oca Moreda 1999, 12), but it can also stand as a visual testimony to the "self-destructive 'crab barrel' mentality of placing individual over communal progress" (Poupeye 1998, 172). Within a pro-revolutionary context it would be said that the *balseros* are not political heroes, as claimed by Cubans from the Miami community, but—as Fidel Castro described the 124,700 Marielitos who left for the US in 1980—people "who don't have revolutionary genes, revolutionary blood, minds adapted to the efforts of heroism of a revolution" (qtd. in Fernández 2002, 26).[7] And within this orientation, it would also be said that the artist does not assume the role of witness, nor does he become a representative of the *balseros*. He is merely providing a cultural referent for us to reflect upon, which involves the choreographing of very fragile objects, and through which unfolds a history of the risk, danger, and possible tragedy of irresponsible people undertaking such journeys in such pathetic embarkations.

This is perhaps the moment to say something about post-colonial criticism, given that *La regata* is a work produced outside the so-called dominant Western cultural centres (is there a centre?); is interrogated within a defined geopolitical space; and, as with other works by this Cuban artist, fits within the context of "Art in the Age of Post-colonialism and Global Migration" (the title of a 1996 group show in Graz). In briefest outline, for I have no intention here of trying to deal with the extensive field of post-colonial criticism, I shall merely quote Homi Bhabha in relation to issues of aesthetics, despite the fact that his work is largely concerned with textuality and "with the process of 'intervening ideologically'" (1994, 22). Because it is relevant to our present discussion and because it shows Bhabha's commitment to post-colonial criticism, this passage is worth quoting at length:

> Culture as a strategy of survival is both transnational and translational. It is transnational because contemporary postcolonial discourses are rooted in specific histories of cultural displacements, whether they are in the "middle passage" of slavery and indenture, the "voyage out" of the civilizing mission, the fraught accommodation of Third World migration to the West after the Second World War, or the traffic of economic and political refugees within and outside the Third World. Culture is translational because such spatial histories of displacement... make the question of how culture signifies, or what is signified by culture, a rather complex issue. It becomes crucial to distinguish between the semblance and similitude of the symbols across diverse cultural experiences — literature, art, music ritual, life, death — and the social specificity of each productions of meaning as they circulate as signs within specific contextual locations and social systems of value. The transnational dimension of cultural transformation — migration, diaspora, displacement, relocation — makes the process of cultural translation a complex form of signification. (Bhabha 1994, 172)

And a paragraph earlier, Bhabha explains that postcolonial criticism "forces us to confront the concept of culture outside objets d'art or beyond the canonization of the 'idea' of aesthetics, to engage with culture as an uneven, incomplete production of meaning and value... produced in the act of social survival" (ibid.).

Certainly, a postcolonial perspective enables us to consider *La regata* as a cultural sign through which notions of identity and nationality can be formed. It can also be conceived, in Edward Said's words, as a "sort of theatre where various political and ideological causes engage one another" (1994, xiii). In this sense, this installation can be apprehended as a site that allows for a certain understanding not only of the world we live in, but also of a certain fragmentation in Cuba's history and its political present.[8] It follows that the artwork can be turned outward to speak to us about a certain condition or an historical event. And in this scheme, the location of gesture — social, political, or economic — within a value system that is said to exist in the work, and that is said to be directly linked to a particular disenfranchised local narrative, is of prime importance. In *La regata*'s case, again, it can be said that it is the collective experience of the rafters that becomes the work's gesture, the medium of truth, and what in turn exposes Cuba's socio-political reality, though more in terms of Cubans' frustrations than of Cuba's achievements. Clearly, if "people went into the gallery and cried" because "the installation evoked the tragic fate of so many Cubans who have taken to the seas over the years," as a Cuban exile said about another of Kcho's installations (Lowinger 2000, 1–2), the ethical and political implications of *La regata* can overshadow the aesthetic existence of the object itself and other possible relations. And I venture to say that, if *La regata* invites this kind of imposed interpretation, on the one hand it is because it provides a framework of certain conditions of existence with which some viewers can identify, while on the other it is because it is understood as a political compromise bound up with semblance. In any case, whether or not the imposed interpretation is one that reflects the needs of the audience, in the present context the work is reconstructed and integrated within a system of particular cultural and political values. Thus, critical reflection is authenticated through what appears to sustain the installation: the mirroring of ideology and of a social context.

Without categorizing or suggesting that the above passage by Bhabha defines the post-colonial attitude toward aesthetics, it might not be going too far to say that this approach is mainly concerned, not with the object itself or with aesthetic experience, but with the causes that led to the object's creation and how the art object is eventually apprehended for its functionality as a translatable sign. This is not to say that the object is abandoned or that its presence is concealed; rather, within the post-colonial context, the artwork becomes a mere accessory at the service of a semiotic venture that has invested in a narrative centred on political and ideological discourses. There is no narrative in *La regata* unless it is experienced for its literalism or colonized by language.

Similarly, in the attempt to discover in the artwork political motivations and signs of cultural dislocation, migration, or anti-master discourses, a post-colonial approach bypasses the possibility of considering not only aesthetic experience but also that which makes the work (e.g., composition, form, materiality, and colour). According to this approach, it can be argued that the artwork becomes subservient to its symbolic function as it is articulated from the outside, if not authenticated by fixed narratives or associations located outside the artwork. On this argument also rests the view that it is the outer reality of the artwork, where the political order of things is said to be inscribed, that guarantees the viewing public a grasp of the world. Thus, if a post-colonial approach strives to pass beyond aesthetics, it is because it does not recognize in the thing itself or in its becoming the source that provides the kind of information that confirms how culture signifies or how the world is politically and ideologically schematized. Must we overlook the sensuous elements that are also part of the artwork's own texture?

Yet, there is aesthetic inquiry within a post-colonial approach, despite Bhabha's claim that it goes beyond the canonization of the idea of aesthetics.[9]

The attention is placed upon the work's surface, where aesthetic perception is said to occur and meaning is said to be inscribed. But then, this is not the space of art, not merely the space on which the artist has left signs and traces of his or her hands or the gestures of the body. The surface is embraced as a textural space where we are to read or find imprints of unfairness, or, to borrow from Rancière, "where conflict and injustice take time to appear and express themselves" (2007, 267).[10] This is, again, the space within which certain features of the artwork are isolated so that the object can be articulated, modified, exchanged, and reduced for the purpose of establishing nonaesthetic relations with the world.

It must be said that although a post-colonial approach to this installation may not help us find our way through aesthetics or the poetics of the installation, it can help us understand the Otherness of the artist within a dominant Eurocentric universalism, as well as the reasons for political analogies that seem necessary to reinforce the significance of the work. Yet, despite the good intentions and whatever the reasoning may be when rearticulating an artist's work, there is a risk of "speaking for the Other," as Spivak remarked in her critique of "literary critics and other kinds of intellectuals" who "speak for the masses" (1990, 56). How can an artist—no matter who purports to represent him or her—avoid being identified, accounted for, or set apart as being from the other side? Caged as the Other, within the inequitable cultural relationship between Western culture and the so-called Third World, the artist thus enters the universal art stage as some exotic bird whose incomprehensible language or name seems better explained by critics, who in turn have a vested interest in the political convictions and concerns said to be embedded within the artist's artifact, the bearer of a message. As the Cuban art critic Gerardo Mosquera has written, "Postmodern interest in the Other has opened some space in the 'high art' circuits for vernacular and non-Western cultures. But it has introduced a new thirst for exoticism, the carrier of either a passive or a second-class Eurocentrism which, instead of universalising its paradigms, conditions certain cultural productions from the periphery according to paradigms that are expected of it for consumption by the centres" (2005, 220).[11]

It is unclear how much the rhetoric of cultural diversity frees the artist and his or her work from the margins, for both artist and work seem to remain enclosed within the exotic context from which they are intended to be freed. It is clear, however, that to view *La regata* as a social construct rooted in a specific history of cultural displacement, as Bhabha does, is an attempt to explain the work within a certain mode of discourse. Moreover, to classify artists according to national or local narratives can be counterproductive, considering how interrelated Western and non-Western cultures are in this age of so-called globalization.[12] Consider the answer by the Argentinean artist

Guillermo Kuitca when asked about his position within a Latin American cultural milieu: "I find Latin American countries have different answers to the same questions. I answer as an Argentinean, but I am questioned as a Latin American. I don't represent my culture in my paintings in that sense. I can't even say that the work is Argentinean. I like the traditional stance that infers that to acknowledge your own place is to be universal" (1993, 46).

Similarly, in her recent novel *Otras plegarias atendidas* (2003), Cuban novelist Maylene Fernández Pintado mirrors how the reception of post-1959 Cuban art is often validated or understood as being emblematic of political differences between the Cubans in the island and those in Miami. To be sure, cultural manifestations that are critical of the Castro government exist inside and outside, and much of the political dialogue held in kitchens, streets, farms, and *solares* is grounded in the "here" and "there," to use Fernández Pintado's terms (2003, 148). But to critically view post-Revolution Cuban art as grounded within geopolitical conditions is to limit Cuba's cultural process and its artists to the realm of a political struggle. As the main character in Fernández Pintado's novel says: "Y es como si el mundo sólo tuviera dos grandes continentes con una inmensa masa de agua insurcable en el medio: Miami y Cuba y todas las opciones, matices y dudas existenciales, se resolvieran sólo con decir aquí o allá" (ibid.).

The argument I have been using to try to rescue *La regata* from political intrusion carries a risk. In questioning the circumstances under which this installation is said to exist, I have set out to underscore the interpretative nature of political and ideological frameworks and to argue that not only is the artwork a thing that is already a commentary on itself, but also that the link between the world and the artwork is articulated by an object that is a thing in itself.[13] I also recognize that verbal supplements to artworks, or imported narratives brought to them, mainly confirm and justify the interpretative nature of who interprets or who sets out to explain within the limitations of his or her own contextual frames of reference. Yet, we do not want to bury the aesthetic evidence of the work under a socio-historical and political frame of reference, or to arrive at the claim that *La regata* finds its truth within the artist's homeland and, according to preconceived knowledge of information, within the reality of a local event.

Now, if aesthetic signification is to open up, and a recognizable source for the very texture of *La regata* is to be found, visualization then must be addressed. Let us consider, first of all, the art of *Arte Povera*, a primarily aesthetic movement—though it has been argued that it was not a movement but a trend—within which Kcho's work can be said to find its place.[14] As defined by the Swiss curator Jean-Christophe Ammann,

> "Arte Povera" designates a kind of art which, in contrast to the technologized world around it, seeks to achieve a poetic statement with the simplest of means. This return to simple materials, revealing laws and processes deriving from the power of the imagination, is an examination of the artist's own conduct in an industrial society.... A way of "dropping out" which is by no means a denial of society, but which instead asserts a moral claim: the subjectified sensibility in its objectified authenticity reflects a natural recollection of environmental phenomena, both universal and individual. (1999, 226)

While in the words of German Celant, who first coined the term, the *Arte Povera* artist

> mingles with the environment, he camouflages with it. He broadens his threshold of perception, and he sets up a new relationship with the world of things. He does all this, however, without reworking that world.... Consequently all his endeavours aim solely at extending the realm of the sensible. [The artworks] do not offer themselves as affirmations or indications of values, or even as models of behaviour. They appear instead as the proof of a contingent, precarious existence. (1999, 198)

In looking at Kcho's work, now confined to a European museum space and no longer supposedly on its way to the land of the free or coloured by the drama of the unfolding crisis that was happening outside during its Havana days, the work seems to have transcended the political and ideological symbolisms that were attached to it when first exhibited. Unless there is a label in the museum walls directing us to see this work in relation to *los balseros,* it is difficult to think of *La regata* as suggestive of a political narrative. What viewers (or at least this viewer) find themselves exploring upon encountering this work by Kcho is a floor arrangement that "addresses the viewer directly as a literal presence in the space," as Claire Bishop says about the art of installation (2005, 6). We are certainly invited to physically experience it, and to engage our senses with the texture, smell, composition, and the silence of these objects.[15] Unquestionably, *La regata* provides an interpretative space into which viewers bring their own personal or universal narratives, but as with the art of the *Arte Povera* movement, the essential reality of the work seems to me to lie in the physicality and materiality of the objects upon which we also reflect.

The very nature of these materials accounts for their texture and their odour after having been exposed to the elements or the lights of the museum and renders this work liable to acquire a different colour as it continues to age. Moreover, the transformation and blending of organic and human-made material ensures also a process of decomposition. The skin of the surfaces will deteriorate, the metal will oxidize, and other materials will disintegrate. It is precisely this process of decomposition, in addition to the work's mutism, that entails both the work's inner and outer expressions. On the other hand, the way in which these objects stand in relation to each other (representation), arranged harmoniously and suggesting a certain rhythm or movement toward the same direction, yet immobile and insecurely distorted, and showing evidence that they have undergone a certain transformation either by nature's own doing or by the gestures of the hand, entails the poetics of the work.[16] Thus, what makes these objects come into being stands as a reminder of what they will become, evidence of other physical modifications. We are very well aware of their fragility. And, like memento mori, what can be said to be inscribed on the surface of these objects is the passing of time.

Beyond imported narratives, the dematerialization of the physical, as evoked through the temporality and the tactile qualities of these objects, is as central to the understanding of this work as is their entire spatial arrangement. True, some will argue that the effect of these manufactured or found nonfunctional objects is purely visual, but Kcho succeeds nonetheless in bringing together sculpture, found objects, and the concept of art installation into an aesthetic unity. Through the art of installation, Kcho is able to construct the kind of theatricality that heightens the spatial experience of the viewer who is confronted with the display of sensibly choreographed sculptures and found objects serving as props. Through the found objects, a wink to a tradition that goes back to Duchamp and the Dadaist, the artist draws attention to material culture (toys, shoes, Styrofoam, etc.) and to their being material signifiers. Meanwhile, his sculptures—crudely recopied several times in different materials, scarred by natural marks or handmade scratches, and serving to bring the work into a coherent spatial patterning—maintain their own presence and suggest playfulness.

Indeed, the work is playful. It recalls the type of game Cuban children play (as I used to) when the streets fill with water after heavy rains and they send their homemade little embarkations down the street in a sort of regatta competition. The work even brings about memories of that familiar warning that can still be heard today by many a mother: "¡Niños, no se mojen!" The artist himself has stated the following: "The first work in which I used the element of a boat, ship, or raft, or however you call it, is related to one thing, my childhood. I completed *La regata* (Regatta) during 1993–94. The implication was of a child's game" (Kcho 1997, 66).[17] And yet, as someone who arrives at the moment the game is finished, we can only apprehend these objects in their present form. Their life can not longer be traced back to their origin. We know that their raw and worn appearance bears the imprint of a past and of their having been used, but their past is denied to us. From this point of view, any verbal supplement to the art object remains subject to the present reality of the object.

Having come this far, it must be acknowledged that, in analyzing art for its purpose or function, or explaining it in connection to some other reality or verifiable model so to determine its meaning, the actual practice of artmaking and witnessing the becoming of the artwork, which is solely the experience of the artist, are often overlooked. No less true is the fact that there are as many ways to respond to an artwork as there are valid theories on art. And, as Morris Weitz points out, "that there is no extant true theory is supported by the disagreements among the theories themselves. [For each] theory purports to enumerate the defining properties of art and to succeed in this endeavor as its competing theories do not" (1989, 153). Yet we are going to continue to talk about art either in terms of narrative, symbols, materiality, or colour. We may analyze it according to the artist's intention, or according to ascribed meanings based on perception or experience, or in relation to the world or to the work itself. We may even be tempted to agree with Donald Kuspit that ours is the era of the "anti-aesthetic" and of *The end of art*:

> In a post-aesthetic art world the work of art becomes a bully pulpit, and the artist tries to bully the spectator into believing what the artist believes. He becomes a self-righteous bully preaching to us (or rather at us) about what we already know—the ugliness and injustice of the world—without offering any aesthetic, contemplative alternative to it.... Social criticism is no doubt a noble cause, and changing the world for the better is no doubt a heroic enterprise, but it is far from clear that art is effective at both. The artist is not exactly the best person to educate us to the realities of the world nor the best person to help us endure and even overcome our suffering. (2004, 37)

Despite all, we persist, because where there is art there are experiences, and questions will be asked and links will be formed. Yet, with regards to Kcho's *La regata*, I am in agreement with Rancière when he proposes that "we should not simply ask how representations will translate into reality. Artistic forms are not purely subjective while political acts are objective realities" (2007, 264). Accordingly, we must be able not only to negotiate between political and artistic boundaries in the face of continuing changes in both politics and contemporary art but to consider also that the continual shifting of art and politics upsets any attempts at localization of meaning.

To embrace Kcho's *La regata* as political at the expense of the poetic, or vice versa, is to create unnecessary conflicts. Similarly, we must go beyond the idea that this work of art stands as a testimony to post-Revolutionary Cuban identity. The artist has stated: "Cuba is not Fidel lying on the Caribbean" (Kcho 1997, 73). In fact, from an interpretative context, far from addressing the rafter crisis of 1994 or referring to what may be seen as "postcolonial migration" (Bhabha 1994, 5), *La regata* bears witness to a Cuban history and an identity that have been shaped by a process of arrivals and departures, from 1492 to the present. As Fernando Ortiz wrote in 1949:

No creemos que haya habido factores humanos más trascendentales para la cubanidad que esas continuas, radicales y contrastantes transmigraciones geográficas, económicas y sociales de los pobladores; que esa perenne transitoriedad de los propósitos y que esa vida siempre en desarraigo de la tierra habitada, siempre en desajuste con la sociedad sustentadora. Hombres, economías, culturas y anhelos; todo aquí se sintió foráneo, provisional, cambiado, "aves de paso" sobre el país, a su costa, a su contra y a su malgrado.... Ya en esos elementos hay factores de cubanidad. (1993, 13–14)

The greatness of *La regata*, notwithstanding the agreements and disagreements, is that it can find its place both within the political, whether right or left, and the poetic. But equally important, this installation can be said to stand as a cultural referent to universal issues of migration and, to borrow from Alexandre Melo, as "an affirmation that all identities are constructed and reconstructed in a process of dislocation and adjustment in which we are simultaneously ourselves and all others, inhabiting a virtual frontier space between different spaces, times, memories, and imaginings" (1995, 211).

Finally, I would like to propose that we consider the following poem, because it enables us to establish a more convincing interrelationship between the seeable and the sayable, and because it allows us to underscore the supposed "strict ambiguity" that is said to contribute to the understanding of Kcho's installation as "un simulacro de arte politico" (Antón Castillo 2006, 49). Indirectly linked by subject matter to *La regata*, this poem by the Cuban poet Dulce María Loynaz, entitled *Cementerio de barcos* (1994, 229), tells the story of a destitute boat, presently anchored in an unfamiliar space, and impoverished by its own physicality. This is not a poem about the recording of a history but the first-person narrative of a boat that can no longer travel the sea and now appears to be meditating on the passing of time, on its condition, and of those visited spaces that can no longer be remembered with certitude but with nostalgia. Its speech, we recognize, is filled with pathos. Its present sorrows are recited from an uncertain shore, or what is now a cemetery where it exists among other useless boats. Further, the boat's story does not start at the beginning but at an imprecise and single moment when it was abandoned to its fate. We begin to listen to what seems to be the end of a life, or what could very well be the farewell of a disintegrated spirit. We are not told of any past experiences, which are inscribed on the boat's surface, and no information is given to us about the circumstances of those passengers of past voyages or those who may have been responsible for this boat's fate. Perhaps only the present is accessible to us because the boat has lost its memory, as it tells us. But we learn that it suffers from leprosy, that it is disconnected from its environment, its patria, and that it finds itself grounded on a territory that denies its nature and imprisons it to its own destiny. "I am here," the boat says, "immobile," "quiet," "empty," and "dead." The boat seems to want closure, but it cannot be achieved because it is kept alive by its imprisonment. Sadly, it is this imprisonment and therefore the boat's uselessness that provide for our contemplation. All in all, this poem is an account of what has become of this boat since being anchored in its present space. We may discern what it used to be, but we can only listen and take on what this boat, that says "I," says to us. It is the boat's story, or rather, selected fragments of a longer story upon which we will construct our own.

> Echaron — no sé quien y no sé cuando —
> ancla al mar en esta orilla incierta.
> Soy un barco inmóvil,
> y por tanto tiempo lo he sido
> que he perdido
> la memoria de las rutas y de puertos,
> la memoria de que una vez hendía el horizonte.
> Ahora estoy aquí, quieto,
> en un lugar desconocido,
> sin otra compañía que otros barcos
> inmóviles también o medio hundidos
> en el agua aceitosa.
> Padezco ya la lepra de los escaramujos,
> la nostalgia del mar que era mi patria,
> y hasta de lo que apenas conocí,
> la tierra.
> Se fueron ya los que por dentro
> de mí, movíanse conmigo.
> Estoy vacío, soy un barco muerto
> o solo vivo en esta dura,
> pesada ancla que me amarra
> al légamo del fondo todavía. (Loynaz 1994, 229)

Notes

1. A similar claim is made by Dannys Montes de Oca Moreda: "This work is shaped by the fragments left by a culture of immigrants and emigrants, for whom the sea is transformed into an essential source of meaning" (1999, 12).
2. For the purpose of this essay there is a need for me to clarify what I mean by politics and ideology in order not to fall into the ongoing debate on: What is politics? What is ideology? I am going to subscribe to more general terms, as outlined, though somehow disapprovingly, by Terry Eagleton in his valuable study, *Ideology*. Politics here "refers to the power process by which social orders are sustained or challenged, whereas ideology denotes the ways in which these powers processes get caught up in the realm of signification" (1991, 11).
3. Although Jean Baudrillard's *Simulation* represents a valuable study, in particular his analysis of "the successive phases of the image" (1983, 5–13), I'm guided here,

however, by Theodor W. Adorno's claim that, "What makes existing artworks more than existence is not simply another existing thing, but their language" (1997, 104).
4 I am using here the English translation of *La maldita circunstancia del agua por todas partes* (2001), the title of a 1993 etching on paper by the Cuban artist Sandra Ramos, and as an alternative view to that of Hector Antón Castillo, who is critical of Kcho for "banalizar comercialmente, mediante repiticiones injustificadas ... las secuelas humanas del fatalismo geográfico que implica la 'maldita circunstancia del agua por todas partes'" (2006, 46).
5 A similar observation is made by José Manuel Noceda Fernández, who writes, "Human presence was noticeable by its absence.... There was no room for anecdotes, and identities disappeared" (2002, 59). In addition, Hollander has noted that "Cuban art dealing with the *balsa* theme can be seen as warning, memorial or wish fulfillment, but also as merely trendy.... After all, the *balsa*, a social phenomenon that has existed for decades, has only recently become the vogue in art. This is no coincidence, coming as it does at time when Cuban art is of great international interest and when more Cuban artists are leaving the island than ever before (1994, 45).
6 Furthermore, Van Den Abbeele points out that, "travel can only be conceptualized in terms of the points of departure and destination and of the (spatial and temporal) distances between them" (1992, xviii). See also Nancy Spector's essay "Travel as Metaphor" for an insight into the work of another Cuban artist, Felix Gónzalez Torres, whose work makes reference to "announced journeys not yet made and borders not yet crossed" (2006, 249) — as it may said to be evoked in *La regata* as well.
7 However, it is important to note a difference between *los balseros* of 1994 and *los marielitos* of 1980. Those who left in 1994 were said to be victims of the so called "Special Period" — that period of economic crisis that Cuba experienced beginning in 1991 after the breakup of the Soviet Union. On the other hand, the Mariel Cubans were made up, according to Fernández, of four groups of immigrants: "ex-political prisoners and other dissidents that were pressured to leave by government officials ...; 'several thousand social undesirables comprised of petty criminals, mentally disturbed persons, homosexuals [sic] and juvenile delinquents'; 'antisocials' (a category which included religious evangelists such as Jehovah's Witnesses, alcoholics, prostitutes, vagrants charged under the 'Dangerousness Law' of 1979); and individuals with family members already living in the U.S.... (by far the largest segment)" (2002, 20). And as Hollander points out, *los balseros* were welcomed by the Miami Cubans as "heroes," while in Cuba, in the views of Roberto Robaina, former president of the Communist Youth, they were seen as "deserters" (1994, 45).
8 Consider also José Manuel Noceda Fernández's view, who writes that Kcho's *La regata* does not "belong to any specific symbolism" and can be "connected to questions regarding the reorganization of land following the transnationalisation of the environment and the experience of human life" (2002, 59).
9 I am not very clear what Bhabha means by the "'idea' of aesthetics," for he neither provides criteria for aesthetics nor locates the "idea" within any of the various disciplines within which art is object of study.
10 Rancière is here referring to the surface of cinematic projections in theatres or museums. He further explains that "Today the 'surface' has a bad reputation: The Marxist critical tradition that called for seizing the reality hitherto concealed from us morphed, by way of Debord and Baudrillard, into the idea that there is nothing

behind the surface, that it is the place where all things are equivalent, where everything is equivalent with its image, and every image with its own lie" (2007, 267). See also Bhabha, who sees "the surfaces of cinematic signification" as "the grounds of political intervention" (1994, 19–20).

11 On the other hand, see Nelly Richard's most valuable essay, "The Cultural Peripheries: Latin America and Postmodernist De-centering" (1995, 217–22), in which she explains why "the narratives of encounter and disencounter between Latin America and postmodernity are particularly difficult to analyze."

12 As Wolfgang Iser writes, "What in the classical imperial hegemony was an intertwining of power and legitimacy has now changed into a growing awareness of the intertwining cultures" (2006, 183–84).

13 For a very insightful study on the double character of art and a position that seeks to "underscore...a certain streak in Marxist thought...which insists on such a paradoxical autonomy of art" (2002, 220), see the essay by Krzysztof Ziarek (2002), "The Social Figure of Art: Heidegger and Adorno on the Paradoxical Autonomy of Artworks."

14 It should be noted that the artist himself has acknowledged his indebtedness to the practices and aesthetic of *Arte Povera*: "At one time I was very interested in Italian art—Futurism and Arte Povera" (1997, 73).

15 As Claire Bishop points out, installation art has been referred to as "the type of art into which the viewer physically enters, and which is often described as 'theatrical,' 'immersive' or 'experiential.'" And it differs from other traditional art forms, "in that it addresses the viewer directly as a literal presence in the space. Rather than imagining the viewer as a pair of disembodied eyes that survey the work from a distance, installation art presupposes an 'embodied' viewer whose senses of touch, smell and sound are heightened as their sense of vision" (2005, 6).

16 Rancière distinguishes among three different regimes of identification with regard to art in the Western tradition: the ethical, the poetic or representative, and the aesthetic. For him, "the poetic—or representative—regime of the arts breaks away from the ethical regime of images. It identifies the substance of art—or rather of the arts—in the couple *poiïsis/mimïsis*" (2006, 21). For Rancière, "the regime *poetic*" is understood "in the sense that it identifies the arts...within a classification of ways of doing and making, and it consequently defines proper ways of doing and making as well as means of assessing imitations." And it is called "representative insofar as it is the notion of representation or mimïsis that organizes these ways of doing, making, seeing, and judging" (Rancière 2006, 22).

17 Estrella de Diego, on the other hand, notes that, "El elemento reiterado son los barcos, barcos frágiles, de juguete, que se acumulan imposibles como *La regata*, barcos construidos con libros cuyo destino último es convertirse en papel mojado, barcos que se reflejan desde el techo, barcos en tierra que apuntan obstinados hacia un centro convenido, hasta chocarse" (2000, 46).

References

Adorno, T. W. 1997. *Aesthetic theory*. Trans. R. Hullot-Kentor. Minneapolis: Univ. of Minnesota Press.

Ammann, J-C. 1999. Visualized thought processes: The young Italian avant-garde (1970). In *Arte Povera*, ed. C. Christov-Bakargiev, 226–27. London: Phaidon.

Antón Castillo, H. 2006. De cómo el caimán se mordió la cola al salir de su isla. *Artecubano: Revista de Artes Visuales* 1(11): 45–49.
Baudrillard, J. 1983. *Simulations*. Trans. P. Foss, P. Patton, and P. Beitchman. New York: Semiotext(e).
Bhabha, H. K. 1994. *The location of culture*. London: Routledge.
Bishop, C. 2005. *Installation art: A critical history*. New York: Routledge.
Celant, G. 1999. Arte Povera (1969). In *Arte Povera*, ed. C. Christov-Bakargiev, 198–200. London: Phaidon.
Diego, Estrella de. 2000. Soy Ulises, hijo de Alertes. In *Kcho: La columna infinita*, 37–52. Madrid: Museo Nacional Centro de Arte Reina Sofía.
Eagleton, T. 1991. *Ideology: An introduction*. London: Verso.
Fernández, G. A. 2002. *The mariel exodus: Twenty years later*. Miami: Universal.
Fernández Pintado, M. 2003. *Otras plegarias atendidas*. Havana: Unión.
Hollander, K. 1994. Art, emigration and tourism. *Art in America* (October): 41–47.
Iser, W. 2006. *How to do theory*. Malden: Blackwell.
Kcho (Alexis Leyva Machado). 1997. Interview with Kellie Jones. In *No place (like home)*, comp. R. Flood, 66–77. Minneapolis: Walker Art Center.
———. 2006 [1993–1994]. La regata. Museum Ludwig, Köln. *Artecubano: Revista de Artes Visuales* 1(11): 47.
Kuitca, G. 1993. Interview with Josefina Ayerza: Guillermo Kuitca on the map. *Flash art* (November–December): 45–47.
Kuspit, D. 2004. *The end of art*. Cambridge: Cambridge Univ. Press.
Lowinger, R. 2000. Making waves. *Artnews* (June). http://www.artnewsonline.com.
Loynaz, D. M. 2002. Cementerio de barcos. *Dulce María Loynaz: Poesía*. Havana: Letras Cubanas.
Melo, Alexandre. 1995. Transoceanexpress. *Parkett* 44 (July): 207–11.
Montes de Oca Moreda, D. 1999. Island: Historical fictions and histories from fictions. In *While Cuba waits: Art from the nineties*, ed. K. Power, 9–21. Santa Monica, CA: Smart Art Press.
Mosquera, G. 2005. The Marco Polo syndrome: Some problems around art and Eurocentrism, trans. J. Flórez. In *Theory in contemporary art since 1985*, ed. Z. Kocur and S. Leung, 218–25. Malden: Blackwell.
Noceda Fernández, J. M. 2002. Kcho's jungle. In *Kcho: La jungla*, 57–63. Torino: Hopefulmonster.
Ortiz, Fernando. 1993. *Etnia y sociedad*. Havana: Editorial de Ciencias Sociales.
Osborne, P. D. 2000. *Travelling light: Photography, travel, and visual culture*. Manchester: Manchester Univ. Press.
Poupeye, V. 1998. *Caribbean art*. London: Thames and Hudson.
Ramirez, Y. 1996. Kcho at Barbara Gladstone. *Art in America* (June): 97.
Ramos, S. 2001. La maldita circunstancia del agua por todas partes. In *Art Cuba: The new generation*, comp. H. Block, ed. and trans. C. Franzen and M. Feitlowitz, 125. New York: Harry N. Abrams.
Rancière, J. 2006. *The politics of aesthetics*. Trans. G. Rockhill. London: Continuum.
———. 2007. Art of the possible: Fulvia Carnevale and John Kelsey in conversation with Jacques Rancière. *Artforum* (March): 256–69.
Richard, N. 1995. The cultural peripheries: Latin America and Postmodernist de-centering. In *The Postmodernism debate in Latin America*, ed. J. Beverley, M. Aronna, and J. Oviedo, 217–22. Durham, NC: Duke Univ. Press.

Said, E. W. 1994. *Culture and imperialism*. New York: Vintage Books.
Spector, N. 2006. Travel as metaphor. In *Felix Gonzalez-Torres*, ed. J. Ault, 249–67. Göttingen: Steidldangin.
Spivak, G. C. 1990. *The Post-colonial critic: Interviews, strategies, dialogues*. ed. S. Harasym. New York: Routledge.
Van Den Abbeele, G. 1992. *Travel as metaphor: From Montaigne to Rousseau*. Minneapolis: Univ. of Minnesota Press.
Weitz, M. 1989. Art as an open concept: From the opening mind. In *Aesthetics: A critical anthology*. 2nd ed., ed. G. Dickie, R. Sclafani, and R. Roblin, 152–59. New York: St. Martin's Press.
Ziarek, K. 2002. The social figure of art: Heidegger and Adorno on the paradoxical autonomy of artworks. In *Between ethics and aesthetics: Crossing the boundaries*, ed. D. Glowacka and S. Boos, 219–37. New York: State Univ. of New York Press.

Collective Memory of Cultural Trauma in Peru: Efforts to Move from Blame to Reconciliation

Jennifer Martino

Acts of commemoration may take various forms, such as visiting a memorial site, browsing through old photographs, and composing, performing, or dedicating a creative work. It is through this active engagement in the preservation of memory that we pay homage to individuals and groups. How do we decide, however, which people and events are to be honoured while others are condemned or simply forgotten? Collective memory of more than twenty years of conflict between the Partido Comunista de Peru—Sendero Luminoso (Communist Party of Peru—Shining Path) and the military in Peru provides an interesting context in which to consider this question. In 1980 Sendero Luminoso sought support from impoverished indigenous populations in a *guerra popular* against the Peruvian state (CVR 2003, 1). What began as a promise to bring a "new state of workers and peasants" that would ease the suffering of the Peruvian rural majority ended in a conflict that officially lasted until the year 2000 and is estimated to have claimed the lives more than 69,000 people (ibid.). Nearly ten years later, Peruvians continue to struggle with the memory of this cultural trauma. Multiple perspectives have emerged regarding who should be classified as victims and who should be hailed as heroes, as well as who should be recorded in history as the perpetrators. The issue of commemoration has surfaced as a secondary conflict, at odds with the government's mandate to promote reconciliation among the Peruvian people.

The question of how to move forward in the context of seemingly incompatible interpretations of the past is well served by a conceptual framework of collective memory. In this chapter I explore the role that the Peruvian *Comisión de la Verdad y Reconciliación* (Truth and Reconciliation Commission, hereafter referred to by the Spanish acronym CVR), as well as three specific cultural works have played in building a new collective memory of the violence that occurred during Peru's period of greatest internal conflict. As cultural works emerging after the initiation of the CVR investigation, Yuyanapaq: para recordar (both phrases mean "to remember," the first in Quechua and the second in Spanish), a memorial titled El ojo que llora (The Eye That Cries) and Santiago Roncagliolo's novel *Abril rojo* (Red April) address issues highlighted by the CVR final report, including the significance of diverse perspectives and whether or not responsibility for atrocities committed can be adequately assigned through a process of identifying some citizens as victims and others as transgressors.

Established in June 2001, the CVR has taken the important step of acknowledging the need to construct a new historical narrative of political violence in Peru through incorporation of diverse perspectives and hidden histories. Collective memory has hereby been employed as a tool for contending with cultural trauma, marked by the disruption of a group's world view after exposure to periods of socio-political crisis. The aforementioned cultural works have each contributed to this construction by effectively blurring the lines between victim and transgressor and encouraging spectators to actively question these categories. Through engagement with these works, spectators are provided with a significant opportunity to work through both collective and individual memories of this period of conflict in Peru while reflecting on the process and potential consequences of locating blame. A brief introduction to the concept of collective memory as defined by Diana Taylor, Susan Crane, and George Lipsitz will help us to understand the concept of cultural trauma in general and the Peruvian experience with its process of potential reconciliation in particular. Ultimately, these concepts will be applied to the aforementioned cultural works in order to discuss their potential impact on the Peruvian process of reconciliation.

The significance of collective memory to Latin American Studies was highlighted in September 2004 when the first regional forum, "Memory and Identity," was held in Montevideo, Uruguay. From the forum emerged a call for Latin America, "the magic multicoloured continent," to be "rediscovered from the inside" as it learns "to look upon itself" (Ganduglia and Rebetez Motta 1994, 12). In the published conference proceedings, forum organizers conclude that because socio-cultural factors invariably determine political and economic realities, public challenges cannot be adequately met without collective memory—which plays a key role in dealing with crisis—by taking advantage of the wisdom gained from the "collective experience of the people lived through their own senses" (ibid.).

Cultural critic Diana Taylor has defined collective memory as sensual experienced related to public policy, affirming that memory is "embodied and sensual, that is, conjured through the senses; it links the deeply private with the social, even official, practice" (2003, 82). Susan Crane, a historian, also supports the notion of embodied memory with political consequences. Crane maintains that "we can think about collective memory as being expressed by historically conscious individuals claiming their historical knowledge as part of personal, lived experience, expressed autobiographically in terms of what has been learned. The 'site' of collective memory is thus removed from an external representation of preservation and returned to the individual who remembers" (1997a, 1383).

Both scholars contribute to the greater body of work on collective memory addressed by the Uruguayan forum by articulating the need to recognize the contribution of individual bodies (and hearts/minds) to collective understanding of the private and public. They also acknowledge that the knowledge built by the collective may well hold the key to resolving both public and private challenges.

George Lipsitz, in turn, has enlisted the term "counter memory" to make a case for the recognition of the individual as a valid source of historical memory. Given that lack of appreciation for embodied memory has produced mistrust among those who "know all too well that historical narratives relating stories of 'human' progress all too often conceal the inhuman oppressions of race and class upon which the triumphs of 'civilization' rest" (2001, 212), Lipsitz argues that it is critical that narratives of marginalized collectives are no longer devalued while widely recognizable untruths are legitimized and preserved by the archive. Like Taylor and Crane, Lipsitz positions the individual body as a source of knowledge earned through lived experience, with much to offer in both the public and private spheres.

Although the applications of collective memory are easily identifiable within the work of each of the aforementioned scholars, it is more difficult to extract a specific definition of the term. Taylor maintains that "cultural memory is, among other things, a practice, and act of imagination and interconnection" (2003, 82). Crane also takes an embodied and participatory approach to collective memory, which she defines as "lived experience" as opposed to historical memory, which marks "the preservation of lived experience, its objectification" (1997a, 1373). According to Crane, rather than necessitating that an expert speaks for the Other, collective memory allows individuals who have lived an experience to speak for themselves and serve as a legitimate source simply because they *remember*. Lipsitz too places focus on the average individual's potential contribution to knowledge, identifying what he terms "counter memory" as "a way of remembering and forgetting that starts with the local, the immediate, and the personal...look[ing] to the past for the hidden histories excluded from dominant narratives" (2001, 213).

In Peru, the CVR has acknowledged the need to incorporate diverse narratives and hidden histories in a newly constructed version of the 'truth.' The final report was based on more than 17,000 testimonies gathered through both interviews and public hearings (Milton and Asesor 2007, 148). Coming from a place of embodied experience and often countering official versions of the more than twenty years of conflict, each of these testimonies have undeniably had an impact on the construction of a new, collectively produced, historical narrative. It is important to note, however, that although the CVR investigative process marks an impressive effort to incorporate diverse voices, it was not logistically possible for the CVR to reach many of those affected by cultural trauma. Furthermore, only one of the CVR commissioners spoke and understood Quechua, the native language of seventy-five per cent of the victims. As a result, although the historical narrative of Peru's internal conflict has been significantly amplified by interviews and public hearings, it is certain that many histories remain hidden from the dominant narrative.

The aforementioned challenges have caused some members of civil society to publicly question the validity of the CVR report, even going as far as to call the CVR a "lie commission" (Milton and Asesor 2007, 151). The concept of verifiable truth is particularly significant in the context of cultural trauma, wherein justice and retribution depend heavily on acknowledgement of human suffering on both an individual and collective basis. Sociologist Jeffery Alexander tells us that cultural trauma occurs when "members of a collectivity feel that they have been subjected to a horrendous event that leaves indelible marks upon their group consciousness, marking their memories forever and changing their future identity in fundamental and irrevocable ways" (Alexander et al. 2004, 1). He suggests that "it is by constructing cultural trauma that social groups, national societies, and sometimes even entire civilizations not only cognitively identify the existence and source of human suffering but 'take on board' some significant responsibility for it" (ibid.). It is often the case, however, that social groups refuse to recognize the suffering of others and victims are left to address trauma on their own. In this case, scholars like Alexander suggest that societies "cannot achieve a moral stance," resulting in diffusion of responsibility as well as projection of this responsibility on others (ibid.).

When individual memories of cultural trauma do not form part of the collective memory of greater society and various individuals are left to suffer alone, the process of reconciliation and social cohesion is made difficult if not impossible. The Peruvian case is particularly interesting in this regard, as even a cursory glance at the evidence raises the question of how such significant trauma could have persisted over a twenty-year period. The fact that traumatic episodes were continuously silenced throughout the course of the conflict provides a potential answer to this question. The CVR has acknowledged that "the lack of information [during the period of conflict] regarding grave human rights violations seriously put in question the principals of transparency and responsibility that a democratic regime should sustain" (CVR 2003, 20). When lack of information and transparency causes histories to remain hidden, the resulting historical narrative is fundamentally flawed and calls for increased representation of diverse perspectives.

Various artists, authors, national intuitions, and civil society groups have also contributed to the formation and explanation of collective memory of cultural trauma. Yuyanapaq: Para recordar, El ojo que llora and *Abril rojo* each contribute to collective memory of cultural trauma in Peru by providing spectators with an opportunity to have a physical and psychological encounter with the conflict, and work through their individual and collectives memories as they react to the material at hand.

Yuyanapaq: Para recordar, described as "a compelling look at political violence in Peru," is an exhibit of 40 of the 250 photographs brought together by the CVR with the goal of "shed[ing] light on the human dimension of a wartorn society" (UC Davis 2008). The inauguration of the exhibit marked the first step in releasing the final report of the CVR to the public. During the opening speech, the president of the CVR stated that, although the images capture only specific seconds in time, together they form a chain that allows us to "challenge the logic of time, which is passing, allowing us to achieve a sort of permanence" (CVR Presentación n.d.). He identifies the photos as playing an important role in "expanding time" and illustrating "a past that imposed on our present to call our attention and, why not, wake us up" (ibid.). The exhibit provides a venue for previously unexpressed memories to emerge from individual hearts and minds and join collective consciousness. As a result, memories are no longer relegated to the past but are actively lived in the present.

Spectators of Yuyanapaq are invited to walk through a timeline of cultural trauma, experiencing a collective experience of photographs, text, and audio recordings of victim testimonies and videos of news coverage from the period. Photo editors had two goals when selecting exhibit pieces, that of explaining the chronology of events and of communicating the suffering of the victims. Curator Mayu Mohanna explains the selection process in the following way: "When we went out to look for the photographs, we needed to reconstruct what happened. We made a list of the most important events during those 20 years. We had clear goals of finding photographs of those events, and another goal, that was much more subjective, which was to find photographs that spoke to us through the victims and their pain" (qtd. in Hoecker 2007, 35).

The editors ultimately chose to approach the subject of trauma through the abstract theme of suffering rather than by focusing on the physical evidence of violence. Mohanna identifies rejection of the exhibit on the part of spectators as one of the fundamental concerns of the editors, expressing a desire to incite a reaction of acceptance rather than recoil: "We consciously tried to create an exhibit that had the power of evidence, but we are photojournalists. We chose to communicate the message in a way that people wanted to look at the message, and wouldn't reject it" (qtd. in Hoecker 2007, 37).

My personal experience of the exhibit in December 2008 in Lima is one in which individual memories and experiences of trauma emerged as a fundamental theme. Although it is clear from the photographs that violence took place at the site where the picture was taken, the emphasis appears to be on trauma resulting from this violence rather than the act of violence itself. By pairing photographs of individuals with written descriptions of the conflict, memories of cultural trauma present throughout the display are provided with a semblance of the physical body that is so central to the concept of collective memory. Diana Taylor has suggested that the body functions as a "site of convergence binding the individual with the collective, the private with social, the diachronic and the synchronic, memory with knowledge" (2003, 80). She envisions cultural memory as something that is "mapped" directly on the body (particularly that of the *mestiza*), reflecting "racialized and gendered practices of individual and collective identity" (2003, 86).

When observing close-ups of individuals such as Celistino Ccente (see figure 1), who suffered wounds after being attacked with a machete in Ayachucho by Shining Path militants, the impression is given that memories of trauma are being passed to the spectator from the victim. It is as if the man has something to tell us, but because he has been silenced by history we will have to use the collective narrative to gain an understanding of what his message may be. Although Ccente was not able to record his testimony in written or oral form, photographic presence in the exhibit allows him to contribute to collective memory by indirectly "claiming [his] historical knowledge as part of a personal, lived experience" (Crane 1997a, 1383).

It is precisely by providing spectators with the opportunity to develop a connection to the victims and build on their own collective memory of cultural trauma in Peru that the curators hoped to contribute to the process of reconciliation, while at the same time ensuring that such events are not permitted to reoccur. Curator Mohanna is quoted as stating that:

> From the beginning we knew we had to choose images that were very symbolic, that would become icons and create a visual memory that would reject violence and now we think that we have achieved these icons. If you showed the average Peruvian the photograph of the hands [by Vera Lenz], or if you showed the photo of the man with the covered eye [the photo of Ccente by Oscar Medrano], these images are in their visual memory.... It is incredible, when people look at that photo they think terrorism, violence and the CVR. (qtd. in Hoecker 2007, 38)

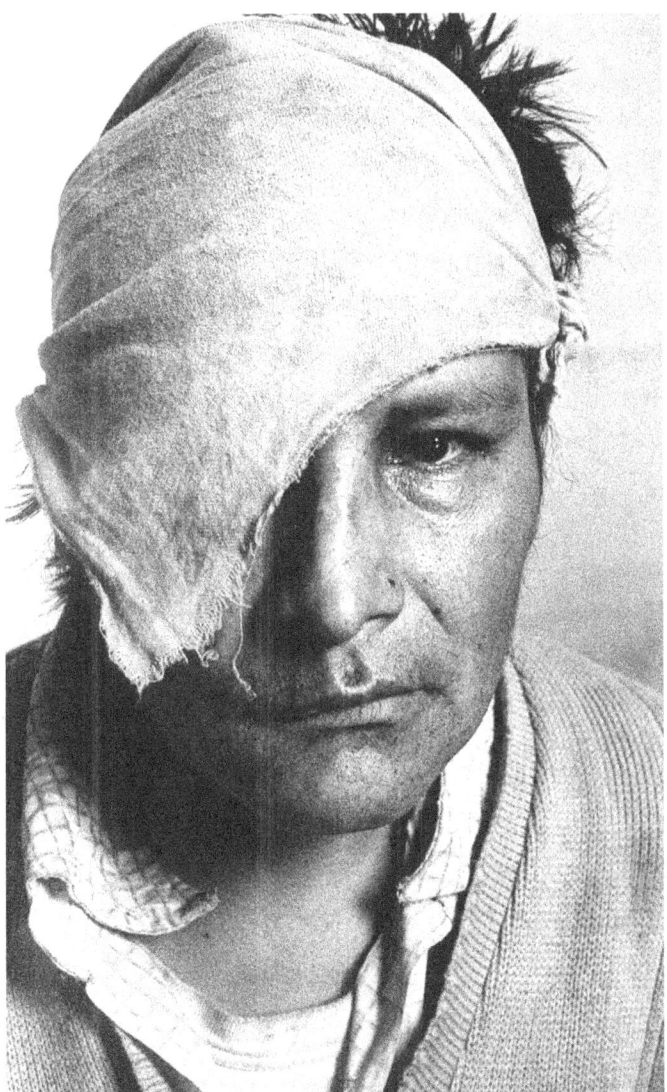

Figure 1 "Celestino Ccente, victima de la violencia politica" Huamanga, Ayacucho, 1983. Fotografo: Oscar Medrano

As someone who experienced the exhibit without previous embodied experience or exposure to historical narratives of the Peruvian conflict, I nevertheless left Yuyanapaq with a deeply set memory of the collective trauma that occurred there. Like the people that Mohanna identified, I will forever associate the photographs I saw at the National Museum of Peru with the activities of Sendero Luminoso and the Peruvian military.

Photography critic and author Vicki Goldberg has identified photographs as "hav[ing] a swifter and more succinct impact than words, an impact that is instantaneous, visceral, and intense" (qtd. in Hoecker 2007, 17). I can attest to the fact that although I remember little of what was written in the exhibit, many of the images have been deeply etched into my memory. Perhaps the images made such a strong impact because I was able to, as Goldberg suggests, "produce responses that closely resemble reactions to actual people and events" (ibid.). Although I felt that I had learned a great deal about what occurred, it is important to note that I did not possess any specific feelings of blame after experiencing the exhibit. It is my assessment that by indiscriminately featuring written, oral, and visual testimonies of victims on all sides of the conflict (as well as those who would be unable to claim any side at all), Yuyanapaq encourages spectators to join and work through the collective experience of suffering rather than reacting to scenes of violence with hate and blame. At the very least, the creators of Yuyanapaq have been successful in contributing to a new historical narrative while having a direct impact on the collective memory of exhibit spectators as well as their potential to engage in a process of reconciliation.

A spectator particularly impacted by Yuyanapaq is Dutch sculptor Lika Mutal. After visiting the exhibit, Mutal was inspired to create a memorial entitled El ojo que llora (The Eye That Cries). Consisting of a large rock in the middle of a pond and surrounded by a labyrinth of circular stones on which the names of tens of thousands of victims are inscribed (see figures 2 and 3), Mutal intended the memorial to commemorate the suffering of Peruvian society overall. In an article encouraging visitation of the memorial, Mario Vargas Llosa describes the site in the following way: "the shapes chosen such as the combination of stones, with minimal filing, cuts and additions on the part of the artist, create an atmosphere impregnated with concentration and alarm, a tense serenity. It's impossible to not feel an enormous sadness before the thousands of names written on the stones by volunteers, among which appear ... uncountable innocents sacrificed by terror without the least bit of hesitation in those years of hate and ideological madness" (2007). Vargas Llosa ultimately identifies El ojo que llora as a valuable site of commemoration and a place where the public has an opportunity to have a physical encounter with individual and collective trauma resulting from decades of social and political turmoil.

Louis Bickford, political scientist and senior associate of the International Center for Transitional Justice, supports Vargas Llosa's understanding of memorials as sites of positive contribution to collective memory of crisis. Using the term "memoryscape" for "memorial," Bickford argues that sites of public commemoration shape the physical landscape of collective memory by "recaptur[ing] public spaces and transform[ing] them into sites of truth-

Figure 2 El ojo que llora (The Eye That Cries)

Figure 3 The names of victims inscribed on stones at El ojo que llora

telling about the authoritarian past" (2005, 96). Where claims of "truth" emerge, however, controversy is never far behind. Mutal did not originally intend for El ojo que llora to serve as a site forum for recounting "truths" about the past. More in line with Vargas Llosa's description of a place of serenity and reflection, she envisioned "a piece of art that would serve as a space contributing to the process of reconciliation in the country" (Vargas Llosa 2007).

Significant controversy surrounded the memorial after judges of the Costa Rica–based Inter-American Court of Human Rights ruled that, as retribution for the Peruvian military's 1992 raid of Miguel Castro penitentiary targeting a cell block housing almost one hundred female inmates convicted of being organizers or militants of Sendero Luminoso, the Peruvian government should add the names of the forty-one deceased inmates to El ojo que llora (Hite 2007, 110). Further controversy emerged when it was soon discovered that many of these names were already inscribed in the memorial because they had been included in the lists of victims produced by the CVR.

Members of civil society began to demand that the names of the deceased from the 1992 raid be removed from the site and even called for destruction of the memorial. Mutal publicly expressed surprise at this outcome, stating that "when someone showed me a newspaper with phrases like 'terrorism now has a monument' it seemed to be the most unbelievable moment of my life. The Eye That Cries was created as a space to awaken the conscience of all Peruvians" (Mella 2007). In an interview published in the popular Peruvian newspaper La República, Mutal goes on to clarify that "I recently realized that the lists of the CVR... had registered all the victims. They gave me the freedom to use the list. It was almost with a mystical attitude that we included all the names" (ibid.).

For his part, Vargas Llosa has publicly criticized the Costa Rican court ruling, stating that "perhaps the most serious error has been to order that the names of the victims of the massacre of 1992 be inscribed on a sculpture that doesn't belong to the State, is in private domain, and regarding the form and content of which neither the Corte nor the government, only the author, can decide" (2007). Vargas Llosa's commentary highlights the fact that much of the debate surrounding the memorial has been rooted in controversy over whether it reflects an official or individual judgment regarding who should be identified as a victim and who should be recorded in history as a perpetrator of violence against the Peruvian state and its citizens.

That such controversy should surround El ojo que llora as a memorial site is unlikely to come as any surprise to Susan Crane, who has written extensively on the nature and implications of memorials and other sites with roots in historical narratives. In an article entitled "Memory, Distortion and History in the Museum," Crane signals that museums are often sites of contention when "official" narratives of history are incompatible with individual memories. Crane proposes that "When members of the public find that their memories of the past or their expectations for museum experiences are not being met, a kind of 'distortion' occurs. The 'distortion' related to memory and history in the museum is not so much of facts or interpretations, but rather a distortion from the lack of congruity between personal experience and expectation, on the one hand, and the institutional representation of the past on the other" (1997b, 44).

Although El ojo que llora is not located in a museum, the artist was granted permission by state officials to install the piece on municipal property. The nature of the memorial's location combined with recognition by an international court is likely to have led many members of the public to draw the conclusion that El ojo que llora reflects an official memory of Peruvian terrorism, a memory that is incompatible with the way they themselves experienced history.

In an article titled "The Eye That Cries: The politics of representing victims in contemporary Peru," Katherine Hite, a political scientist, points out that "international human rights law defines those killed extra judicially, including convicted criminals, as victims. The majority of Peruvians [however] view Senderistas as terrorists" (2007, 113). By inscribing the names of all victims of the Peruvian conflict, Mutal (albeit unwittingly) mirrored the approach of the Yuyanapaq exhibit by blurring the lines between victim and transgressor. Rather than being openly declared and explained to the public through didactic cards, however, spectators who used the memorial as site of mourning were surprised to discover that they had also been unwittingly mourning the passing of those felt to be responsible for the death of their loved ones. This discovery led to exactly the kind of "distortion" that Crane has referred to.

Not all spectators, however, have reported discomfort with the concept of commemorating the deceased regardless of their political affiliation. In 2007 Katherine Hite conducted interviews at the memorial site in order to gauge spectator reactions to the growing controversy. Hite paraphrases spectator Doris Caqui, whose husband was disappeared by security forces, as expressing that El ojo que llora provides her "with a space to mourn because there is no other space" (2007, 123). Caqui is quoted as stating that "El ojo que llora must be seen as a place that unites all families without exception.... Victims are victims, and we are not in favour of excluding anyone" (ibid.). Spectator Mr. Roca, whose son was also disappeared by security forces, echoes this sentiment, affirming that: "They say that we cannot have people who are terrorists here, but when the government killed them like that, they are victims, they are victims! It's as simple as that!" (ibid., 124).

By evoking controversy and inspiring public debate, El ojo que llora has inspired citizens to confront their feelings about the period of national conflict while reconciling the categories of "victim" and "transgressor." Producing a "counter memory" of the conflict, the memorial's creator has ultimately, albeit unwittingly, "force[d] revision of existing histories by supplying new perspectives about the past" (Lipsitz 2001, 213). If spectators are ultimately inspired by the memorial to engage in challenging the "false priorities and hierarchical divisions" that Lipsitz identifies as central components of official histories, El ojo que llora may very well aid the process of reconciling collective memory of victimhood and suffering.

Santiago Roncaglio's novel *Abril rojo* (Red April) also challenges the categories of victimhood and liability in the context of the conflict between Sendero Luminoso and the Peruvian military, while at the same time addressing the myth of the infallible archive. Roncagliolo reports having chosen to address Peruvian socio-political conflict through fiction because he views literature as "a type of deformed mirror that shows us what we don't want to see about ourselves as a country, as a society, as parents and children" (Valenzuela Prado 2006). Various other Latin American authors, such as Gabriel García Márquez, Julio Cortázar, Mario Vargas Llosa, and Carlos Fuentes, have also employed fiction to address terrorism in their own countries. Fuentes identifies the Latin American author as "someone who feels that his exact function consists in denouncing injustice, defending the exploited and documenting the realities of that novelist's country" (qtd. in Vela 2006, 14). Through *Abril rojo* (2006),[1] Roncagliolo provides readers with the opportunity to gain a new perspective on historical narratives surrounding the Peruvian conflict.

Abril rojo is classified by publishers as a detective novel (*una novel negra*). The protagonist, District Fiscal Assistant Félix Chacaltana Saldvídir, is described as a man who "nunca ha hecho nada malo, nunca ha hecho nada bueno, nunca ha hecho nada que no estuviese claramente estipulado en los reglamentos de su institución" [has never done anything bad, never done anything good, never done anything that was not clearly stipulated by the rules of his institution].[2] A steadfast believer in the power of the archive, Chacaltana is first presented as someone who takes great pleasure in composing meticulous reports on the findings of his investigations. Upon filing a report with the corresponding authorities, he is relieved to know that the case is closed and danger has therefore been confined to the past. Having just assumed a new post in the Peruvian town of Ayacucho, the site where Sendero Luminoso initiated the *guerra popular* and maintained the strongest hold throughout the course of the conflict, Chacaltana quickly finds his convictions challenged by ever growing tension between the official position on the status of social and political turmoil in Peru and his own consistent traumatic encounters with remnants of this period of conflict.

The story is set in 2000, the year that Sendero Luminoso was officially reported to have been wiped out by the military. Chacaltana first becomes suspicious that remnants of the conflict have yet to be laid to rest when he is called to document the death of an unidentified man who has been burned to death. From the very beginning of Chacaltana's investigation, the reader is provided with hints that official institutions in Ayacucho do not function as well as one may hope. The detective sets out to obtain the forensic report needed for his work and, upon arrival at the hospital, is made to wait for the doctor. When the doctor finally arrives, he unexpectedly leads Chacaltana to a room hosting the corpse. Chacaltana questions why the body is being held in obstetrics, and is told that the morgue no longer has a freezer because it stopped working during the blackouts. When Chacaltana points out that the blackouts stopped years ago, the doctor responds "not in our morgue" (24). This exchange provides a hint that official narratives, such as those portraying blackouts as a thing of the past, contain hidden realities with significant consequences for those that must grapple with them every day.

Upon learning that the doctor has discarded the possibility of accidental death due to evidence of kerosene covering the body and forced removal of the right arm, it immediately occurs to Chacaltana that the victim died at the hands of terrorists. When he shares this theory with his superior officer, however, the man starts to laugh and responds, "You are paranoid, Señor Fiscal. There is no Sendero Luminoso here" (45). The difficulty of challenging official narratives is highlighted in this scene. Chacaltana describes how a second officer, Pacheco, hesitates for a second and then begins to join in the laughter, followed by "the man in the blue tie, Eléspuru. Behind them, the rest of the room and the universe began to laugh bit by bit, then harder, eventually thundering in the air" (45). It is at this moment that Chacaltana makes his first attempt to challenge official narrative by pointing out, "with the pride of an archivist," that the crime overlaps with the twentieth anniversary of the first terrorist attack (45). To his surprise, however, rather than being praised for drawing on the archive to produce a theory about what may have occurred, Chacaltana immediately faces an onslaught of accusations including that of "screwing around," calling his superior a liar, potentially being a communist and wishing to sabotage the upcoming elections (45–46).

As a means of quelling his suspicions that terrorists may have had a role to play in the victim's death, Chacaltana is reminded by his superior of the violent nature of peasants in the region and it is suggested that the victim is a product of religious fanaticism. Chacaltana admits to himself that he has always simplified the peasants' festivals as "consensual violence committed with religious motives" (46). Nevertheless, he is unconvinced that peasants would take violence to such an extreme. In response, Chacaltana's superior quickly draws on the power of cultural trauma to defend historical narrative by reminding him of the massacre of Uchuraccay: "Chacaltana remembered. He had the sensation that it was a very recent memory. But it was almost 20 years old. The cadavers battered his memory, the pieces of their bodies covered in earth, the unending interrogations in Quechua. He felt relieved that things had changed. He didn't want to say anything. They seemed like far away words that were better off left far away" (47). By invoking feelings of terror tied to historical narrative of cultural trauma in Uchuraccay, Chacaltana's superior is able to convince him, at least temporarily, that such matters are better left to "rest" in the past.

It is not long, however, before memories of the cadaver prevent Chacaltana from simply accepting his superior's command and moving on to the next investigation:

> The words of the commander began to mix in his head with the images of the forensic table until the point of preventing him from concentrating on his duties. Like a mental flash, the face of the corpse appeared to him covered in smoke, the cut at the top of the shoulder, the black skin. The violence. Devotion. The word "terrorist" began to take form again in his mind. They came to him like shocks from electric towers. The sirens of the ambulance. (49)

At this point in the novel the reader is unaware that Chacaltana's mother has also been a victim of arson and that the sirens could either be in reference to the events of her death or that of the cadaver. Nightmares of a woman screaming in the midst of fire prevent him from closing the case even though he is sure that "his work had finished honourably, with the best of efforts" (69). Unable to avoid making a connection between the cadaver's embodied memory of trauma and that of his mother, Chacaltana begins to form a counter memory of the events leading to the victim's death which, as Lipsitz suggests, "starts with the local, the immediate, and the personal... [and] look[s] to the past for the hidden histories excluded from dominant narratives" (2001, 213).

In order to challenge official narratives and to get to the root of the crime, Chacaltana must learn to bend the rules. He acts on his newfound sense that it is more important to uncover the truth than abide by policy when he attempts to gain an interview with a convicted terrorist who is held at the local jail. Chacaltana asks himself "if they could accuse him of failing to respect authority, insubordination and treason" (143) and decides, nonetheless, that he will have to lie to gain entry to the jail. He ultimately chooses to proceed because "suddenly, he felt he was doing something else, maybe something more important, at least for himself, for his dreams" (143). The meeting at the jail proves to shake Chacaltana's confidence in the archive even further, as the convict provides a long list of crimes committed by military officials against members of Sendero Luminoso as well as townspeople, consistently asking "where is that in your archives?" (147), thus challenging Chacaltana to determine who is innocent in these cases (148).

After further investigation Chacaltana comes to the conclusion that "If everything is a lie... nothing is. If one lives in a world of falsehoods, these falsehoods are reality" (202). His disillusionment with the archive is completed when he sits down to write his final report:

> It seemed to him that it was simply a useless paper. The facts weren't enough. The narrated events didn't have anything to do with the assassination, but rather with its discovery. It was as if to describe a fishing session, you provided information regarding how the fish was served for lunch on the table. It didn't have anything to do with what was really important. None of his reports, in reality, had to do with what was important. He thought that the relevant information was just what the report didn't have: who did it, why, what went through their mind. A real report should be written knowing each detail of the life of those involved, their past, their memory, their customs, even their more irrelevant conversations, the perversions that crossed their mind at the moment of executing the crime, all that no one could know. (234)

The detective ultimately determines that an authentic report "could only be written by God, or at least someone that had a thousand eyes and a thousand ears, that could know everything. But if there were people like that... reports wouldn't be necessary" (234). Having established the uselessness of official reports, Chacaltana decides to provide additional functionality to his final report by fudging some of the details, specifically those that may incriminate him for unapproved participation in the investigation.

In an ironic twist, irrefutable evidence is used to convict the detective of a crime he didn't commit. More importantly, however, through the accusation process he discovers that Sendero Luminoso was not in fact responsible for the death of the original victim, causing him to feel "useless [because] this whole time he had been following a tunnel without an end, pursuing ghosts, his own memories, as well as reality that laughed at him" (305). At this moment, although he feels that "a light began to illuminate his mind," Chacaltana is too close to the events to recognize the value of having gained a new perspective on the nature of archive as well as on socio-political conflict in Peru. In effect, by "focus[ing] on localized experiences with oppression, using them to reframe and refocus dominant narratives purporting to represent universal experience" (Lipsitz 2001, 213) he has been successful in developing a counter-memory of cultural trauma in his community. Through Chacaltana's experience, readers are thus provided with the opportunity to develop their own counter-memory by reacting to the darkness of the material, which is emotionally if not historically approximate to the experience of many victims of the conflict.

Mario Vargas Llosa has written that "In the literature that gives testimony to the discovery and the conquest, we also learn about the roots of our problems and the challenges that are still there unanswered," referring to such literature as "half-literary, half-historical pages" (1992). Through *Abril rojo*, Roncagliolo has given testimony to the experience(s) of cultural trauma in Peru, identifying various potential roots of the conflict while highlighting that the "truth" remains a mystery to this day because an authentic report "could only be written by God" (234). At the end of the novel a note from the author is included, emphasising that the work is both literary and historical. Roncagliolo explains that the methods of attack on behalf of Sendero Luminoso as well as the methods of investigation, torture, and disappearance utilized by government officials described in the novel are real. He also reports having taken much of the dialogue from Sendero Luminoso documents as well as from the declarations of government officials and the military. The novel concludes with the statement that "This novel, like all [novels], tells a story that could have happened, but the author doesn't certify that it was this way" (329).

The author's note is an important component of the novel, as it reminds that reader of the historical relevance of the contents while harnessing the emotional high produced by the story. Memory of the novel's contents are thus bound with knowledge that the events also form part of historic narrative. Vargas Llosa has positioned cultural works that are "half-literary, half-historical" as allowing the reader to "perceive—formless, mysterious, fascinating—the promise of something new and formidable, something that if it ever turned into reality would enrich the world and improve civilization" (1992). In the case of *Abril rojo*, the "something new" is a vision of cultural trauma in Peru that focuses on the suffering of all individuals and communities that participated in the conflict rather than assigning and leaving an archive of blame. In fact, the constant confusion of Chacaltana and other characters from all levels of society leaves the impression that the act of laying blame would be senseless.

The central theme of *Abril rojo* provides an interesting context in which to consider the CVR's final report, which was intended to "contribute to finding the truth about the 20 years of political violence experienced in Peru, and thus strengthening constitutional democracy, rule of law and national reconciliation" (CVR website n.d.). In the report, human rights abuses committed by members of Sendero Luminoso and government officials as well as the names of many of the victims were officially archived. If we are to take Roncagliolo's message to heart, although the CVR made an attempt to incorporate a wide range of perspectives on the conflict, the report is inherently flawed because it is impossible to have the "thousand eyes" and "thousand ears" that would be required for true accuracy. Perhaps cultural works such as Yuyanapaq, El ojo que llora, and *Abril rojo* can aid the CVR in "finding the truth," however, by reaching various new eyes and ears, and encouraging the public to embrace new perspectives on socio-political conflict and cultural trauma as well as on how the process of blame laying may impede the path to reconciliation.

By indiscriminately featuring written, oral, and visual testimonies of victims on all sides of the conflict (as well as those who would be unable or unwilling to claim any side at all), Yuyanapaq encourages spectators to both experience and work through a collective memory of human suffering rather than reacting to scenes of violence. The public is thus provided with the opportunity to move forward with reconciliation by sharing in the pain they feel for the victims rather than focusing on feelings of hate and blame. The memorial El ojo que llora has also inspired citizens to confront their feelings about the period of national conflict while reconciling the categories of "victim" and "transgressor" through public debate. Controversy surrounding the memorial has inspired "rejection of its [history's] false priorities and hierarchical divisions" (Lipsitz 2001, 213) among at least some spectators, and it is precisely destruction of divisions that may be necessitated in order to achieve true reconciliation. Roncagliolo's novel *Abril rojo* represents yet another medium of challenging "false priorities and historical divisions" reflected in historical narratives, inspiring readers to engage in their own investigation of the multidimensional truths behind these narratives while reacting to the darkness of the material.

Taylor maintains that "cultural memory is, among other things, a practice, an act of imagination and interconnection" (2003, 82). Crane also takes an embodied and participatory approach to collective memory, which she defines as "lived experience" as opposed to historical memory, marking "the preservation of lived experience, its objectification" (1997a, 1373). Yuyanapaq, El ojo que llora, and *Abril rojo* each provide spectators with the opportunity to undergo an embodied experience of cultural trauma resulting from two decades of internal conflict in Peru, whether through interaction with a physical site of acknowledgement and mourning or emotional responses to intentionally dark literary material. Each of these works ultimately provides a means of "look[ing] to the past for the hidden histories excluded from dominant narratives" (Lipsitz 2001, 213), encouraging spectators to move forward on the path to reconciliation by working through their emotional reactions to these histories. If the CVR and the aforementioned cultural works are successful in inspiring the public to move beyond blame and the question of who and what is deserving of commemoration, Peru might be making a new step toward reconciliation through consolidation of collective memory and healing of cultural trauma.

Notes
1 Subsequent page references are to this edition; translations mine.
2 Text from the jacket cover of Spanish edition; translation mine.

References
Alexander, J., R. Eyerman, B. Giesen, N. Smelser, and P. Sztompka. 2004. *Cultural trauma and collective identity*. Berkeley: Univ. of California Press.
Bickford, L. 2005. Memoryscapes. In *The art of truth-telling about authoritarian rule*, ed. K. Bilbija, J. E. Fair, C. Milton and L. A. Payne, 96–102. Madison: University of Wisconsin Press.
CVR (Comisión de la Verdad y Reconciliación). 2003. *Informe Final*. Lima: CVR.
CVR Website. n.d. http://www.cverdad.org.pe/ingles/lacomision/nlaborlobjetivos.php.
CVR Presentación. *Yuyanapaq: Para recordar*: Testigos de la verdad. n.d. http://www.cverdad.org.pe/apublicas/p-fotografico/discurso.php.
Crane, S. 1997a. Writing the individual back into collective memory. *The American Historical Review* 102(5): 1372–85.
———. 1997b. Memory, distortion, and history in the museum. *History and Theory* 36(4): 44–63.
Ganduglia, N. G., and N. Rebetez Motta. 1994. *El descubrimiento pendiente de América Latina: Diversidad de saberes en diágolo hacia un proyecto integrador*. Montevideo: Imprenta Boscana.
Hite, K. 2007. "The eye that cries": The politics of representing victims in contemporary Peru. *A Contracorriente: Revista de Historia Social y Literatura en América Latina*: 108.
Hoecker, R. 2007. The role of photography in Peru's Truth and Reconciliation Process. Master's thesis. Univ. of Missouri–Columbia.
Lipsitz, G. 2001. *Time passages: Collective memory and American popular culture*. 7th ed. Minneapolis: Univ. of Minnesota Press.
Mella, R. 2007. Entrevista a Lika Mutal escultora del "Ojo que llora." *La República: Lima*, 18 January.
Milton, C. E., and C. Asesor. 2007. Public spaces for the discussion of Peru's recent past. *Antipoda* 5: 143.
Roncagliolo, S. 2006. *Abril rojo*. Mexico D.F.: Alfaguara.

Taylor, D. 2003. *The Archive and the repertoire: Performing cultural memory in the Americas.* Durham, NC: Duke Univ. Press.
UC Davis. 2008. *Yuyanapaq Exhibit Poster.* http://hia.ucdavis.edu/pix/yuyanapaq poster.pdf.
Vargas Llosa, M. 1992. Question of the conquest. *American Educator* Spring: 25–48.
———. 2007. El ojo que llora. *Diario Las Americas: Miami*, 13 January.
Valenzuela Prado, L. 2006. Entrevista a Santiago Roncagliolo. *Sobre Libros*, 31 October. http://www.sobrelibros.cl/content/view/163/6/.
Vela, David. 2006. Terror through the eyes of Latin American novelists. *Peace Review: A Journal of Social Justice* 18: 7–15.

PART THREE

Individualism and Human Rights in Antonio Skármeta's *Match Ball*

Gordana Yovanovich

Antonio Skármeta became an internationally recognized figure when the movie *Il Postino*, based on his novel *Ardiente paciencia*, also called *El cartero de Neruda*, received an Academy Award in 1994; and when popular cinemas brought the story of an Italian mailman who falls in love with the Chilean communist poet Pablo Neruda to millions of people across the globe. Skármeta is a good example of a man who lives and works in the culture of globalization not only because his Chilean novel provided the script for a film directed by an American director, Michael Radford, who made the film in Italy, in the Italian language and with Italian actors, but because Skármeta's life and his work in general are products of cultures in contact. As a grandson of Dalmatian immigrants to the northern Chilean mining city of Antofagasta, he was born into a multicultural environment that was further enriched when his family moved to Argentina, then back to Chile, this time to Santiago. His horizontal contact with different cultures was accompanied by his upward movement in society from an immigrant grandson to a high-level diplomat. He studied philosophy and literature in Chile and later received his master's degree from Columbia University in New York. He taught literature at the University of Chile from 1967 to 1973, when he left, first for Buenos Aires and later for West Berlin. He returned to live in Chile in 1989, after the collapse of Pinochet's military dictatorship, only to return to Europe in 2000, this time not as a refugee but as the Chilean ambassador to Germany.

Writing in the context of two international movements—communism and globalization—which have shaped his generation, Skármeta does not write from a political or theoretical position but from the point of view of migrant, multicultural experience, because, as Jean Franco (2004) observes, human experience and "survival moments" are powerful sources for building individual and cultural identity in Latin America. When, for example, in Argentina the state no longer helped with the day-to-day survival of citizens, Mothers of the Plaza de Mayo acted not according to the ideology of human rights but according to the rights of kinship. Similarly, during the Mexico earthquake, women entered the public sphere not because they were given citizen's rights but because of the need to look after life. Franco observes that in today's Latin American cultural atmosphere in general, chronicles and testimonial literature which are based on women's *experience,* as in Elena Poniatowska's work, for example, show that women's experience has become more important than theoretical feminist issues in the modern Latin American cultural debate.

Skármeta's 1989 novel pretends to be an example of testimonial literature because its fictional author swears to tell a true story as he heard it confessed by the main character, Raymond Papst, while both of them spent time in jail. The anonymous fictional Latin American immigrant author insists in the prologue that he will tell the story as he was instructed: "tal cuál él me la narraba, sin tomar partido ni a favor ni en contra de su conducta o estilo" [in the same way that he narrated it to me, without taking sides for or against his conduct and style] (1989, 19).[1] Thus, it is established from the beginning that the novel's concern with the question of truth based on human experience is more important than questions of aesthetics or stylistic virtuosity as the confession of the principal character and narrator, Raymond Papst, is also contrasted to Vladimir Nabokov's *Lolita.* While the narrator claims that "Nabokov escribía un libro y yo sólo mi vida" [Nabokov wrote a book and I am writing my life], he also recognizes the importance of other literary masterpieces, but views Thomas Mann's *Death in Venice,* for example, as "una novella alemana immortal pero una muerte de mierda" [an immortal German novel, but awfully dead] (176).

While Skármeta's work claims to be a testimony of a true human story, it is different, however, from the testimonial works such as Rigoberta Menchú's and Elizabeth Burgos' *Me llamo Rigoberta Menchú y así me nació la conciencia* (1982), which record Latin American local violations of human rights in order to correct the official version of their story and with the hope that their situation could be improved with the help of the universal human rights politics and international activism.[2] Skármeta's novel is a testimonial work, but it is less trusting than the contemporary testimonial genre initiated by Miguel Barnet's *Biografía de un cimarrón* in 1966 in Cuba and firmly established by Rigoberta Menchu's testimony regarding violence in Guatemala. The work of the Chilean post-Boom writer is written more in the spirit of Spanish picaresque novels such as the anonymous *Lazarillo de Tormes* or José Cela's *La familia de Pascal Duarte,* which caution the reader not to take the world or their stories at their face value. The life stories of picaresque heroes describe social conditions which influence the picaro's life stories, but as the social and the individual elements are meshed together, the aim of the story is not so much to criticize established institutions and politics as it is to warn against naïveté and to argue that an individual must be shrewd and "sharp as a needle," because churches, kings, governments, and today the United Nations are able to provide only some protection for ordinary citizens or the subaltern. As Lazarillo de Tormes says: "solo soy, y pensar, cómo me sepa valer" [I must keep awake because I'm on my own and I've got to look alter myself] (*Lazarillo*, 44).

Written in exile in Germany and published in Argentina in 1989, the year of the beginning of the fall of the Berlin Wall and sixteen years after the fall of the Allende government, which marked a significant change in the spread of communism, the relationship of characters in Skármeta's *Match ball* implies a complex political discussion, despite the fact that the novel is very easy to read. It indirectly questions the new world order which promises better life through the ideology of universal human rights, not because the author disagrees with today's dominant ideology but because its main characters show that old values and practices are not easily changed. Like Néstor García Canclini, Skármeta shows that "As crosscultural contact intensifies through migration, economics, and mass communications, one sees that there is not only fusion, cohesion, osmosis, but confrontation and dialogue" (García Canclini 1995, xxxi). On one level, *Match ball* appears to develop a Hollywood love story, yet the multi-ethnic love affair turns into a dynamic relationship reminiscent of a competition in a tennis game, which serves as a metaphor for modern life. All players are carefully chosen and represent various segments of the "new world order," as George Bush Sr. called the US-dominated world at the outbreak of the Gulf War in 1991. The novel begins when a Chilean illegal immigrant in Germany is saved from deportation by a modern female human rights lawyer: "Cuando estaba a punto de meterme en el avión... se hizo presente en el salón de embarque la prestigiosa abogada Ana Von Bamberg" [When I was about to enter the plane... the prestigious lawyer Ana Von Bamberg appeared in the boarding room] (7). The human rights lawyer is accompanied by her husband Raymond Papst, who co-participates with a medical doctor in the struggle to help refugees by inventing medical reasons why they cannot be repatriated, as in this situation he determines that the Chilean leftist cannot be deported given his medical condition. As the two modern human rights activists save the Chilean refugee from "una celda con carceleros menos corteses que estos alemanes," [a jail cell with prison guards much less polite than the German ones] (7), the introductory pages of the novel recognize that the work of human rights activists is helping improve lives of individuals.

In his book *The rights revolution*, Michael Ignatieff, Canadian writer, historian, and now the Leader of the Opposition, celebrates the results of the modern human rights movement which inspires the work of the German female lawyer and her American husband in Skármeta's novel. Ignatieff explains that in Canada the rights culture is one of the defining national characteristics and that Canada has been active in spreading this "revolution" across the globe. He indicates that Canadians are found in nations "from the Baltic states to Sri Lanka, preaching the virtues of group-rights regimes and federalist devolution as potential solutions to conflicts between ethnic and religious minorities inside nation-states" (2000, 13) and concludes that the rights revolution of the 1960s — "the product of the most sustained period of affluence in the history of the developed world" — has "destroyed the legitimacy of the old virtues and old limits and has created a new force of moral imperatives: new virtues, such as self-cultivation, self-indulgence, and self-development" (2000, 92). In his book, Ignatieff demonstrates how in Canada public policies are designed to protect the rights of its citizens.

In Skármeta's novel, the human rights work of the German–US union represented by Ana Von Bamberg (Germany) and Raymond Papst (United States) is respected, yet it is not sustained in the development of the novel, as young Sophie Mass from an undetermined origin tests this world and shows that the supposed changes of the old limits are artificial and that individualism is more controlled by comfort and materialism than driven by struggle for freedom. In her search for authenticity, which according to another Canadian thinker, Charles Taylor, is "a moral ideal"[3] of the new generation, Sophie builds a case for strong individualism which is developed not through egotistical self-cultivation, self-indulgence, and self-development, as Ignatieff says, but through a dynamic relationship with the Other. The novel ends as she hands a tennis racquet to Raymond Papst and asks him to keep fit, suggesting that the individual must be, as Lazarillo de Tormes said, always on the alert in order to win in a deceiving world defined by "soft despotism," as Charles Taylor calls the reign of modern technology and materialism.

In the rest of the chapter I discuss the Chilean novel as it comments on the dominant human rights and feminist ideology and politics and as it develops a more active and alert individual. Charles Taylor argues that "Two modes of social existence are quite evidently linked with the contemporary culture of self-fulfilment. The first is based on the notion of universal rights: everyone should have the right and capacity to be themselves.... Secondly, this culture puts a great emphasis on relationships in the intimate sphere, especially love relationships. These are seen to be the prime loci of self-exploration and self-discovery and among the most important forms of self-fulfillment. This is also an acknowledgement that our identity requires recognition by others" (1991, 45), Taylor explains.

Writing about the modern relationship between the individual and society in *No such thing as society? Individualism and community*, John Kingdom is more a "knocker" than a "booster" of modernity because he perceives modern society as "masturbatory society" which offers "a solitary view of fulfillment" (1992, 2). When Margaret Thatcher made her imperious declaration that "'there is no such thing as society' she captured the essence of a political mission," Kingdom says. "At one stroke," he continues, "people were to be relieved of any responsibility for one another; the biblical maxim 'love thy neighbour' was exposed as ill-conceived post-war funk" (1992, 4). Thatcher's position was that if each person acts according to naked self-interest, the end result will be the best for society. "Life is a great game of cricket where, if each player scores as many runs as possible, the team will triumph" (1992, 6). "However, in the same selfish society people can relate to one another, like players at the roulette table," Kingdom argues: "The winners would be applauded while the losers could quietly place the loaded pistol in their mouths" (1992, x).

Skármeta's novel explores the question of individual self-fulfillment and also self-interest, and advocates self-fulfillment through the union and "recognition by others," as Charles Taylor suggest, but the Chilean novelist also suggests that an individual must be fit, as Sophie says, in order to participate in the complex modern game of competition and cricket that John Kingdom describes. Both Raymond Papst and his wife Ana are educated individuals who live in modern Germany. Yet, the readers notices that through their marriage the old aristocratic European world is in connection with the modern North American search for wealth. When Raymond Papst, an American-born medical doctor, meets his wife Ana, he immediately notices "que era baronesa, millonaria, culta e inteligente, lo supe antes de cambiar una palabra con ella" [I knew that she was a baroness, a cultured and intelligent woman with money before I exchanged a single word with her] (11). He then tells us that he has been trained to look for such qualities because the leading institutions in the United States orient their students towards money and success: "los años de Harvard crean un sexto sentido para detectar en los seres humanos estos defectos" [Years at Harvard create a sixth sense for detecting these defects in human beings] (11). And when he actually marries and gets closer to his rich father-in-law, he admits: "Sería hipócrita decir que no me interesaba abrir cuanto antes un consultorio, prestigiarme como médico y hacer carrera y fortuna" [It would be unfair to say that I was not interested in opening a medical practice as soon as possible, in gaining prestige as a doctor, in building my career and in making money] (11).

The entrenched world of the moneyed and successful is comfortable, but spiritual only in the amount of spirits it consumes. The young doctor comes to realize that he is nothing but the clothes he wears and whisky he drinks: "smoking suegro, mariposa Harvard, zapato italiano, collera Ana, doble maltés treinta años" [Father-in-law tuxedo, Harvard bow tie, Italian shoes, cufflinks from Ana, and double Maltese scotch thirty years old] (121). His marriage, like the marriage in Carpentier's *Los pasos perdidos* of the narrator to Ruth in New York, is equally reduced to routine, labels, and form: "En las articulaciones de nuestros oficios nos dábamos algunos besos, bebíamos una copa, *consumíamos* una sinfonía. Pero habíamos dejado de inquietarnos entre *el espectáculo* de la existencia" [In the performance of our duties we would give each other a kiss, have a drink, *consume* a symphony. But we had stopped exciting ourselves amid the *spectacle* of our existence] (59, emphasis mine). His work is equally uninspiring. The marriage to a millionaire's daughter leads to a financially successful medical practice. The rich father-in-law's overweight friends are paying patients and a good source of income, but they are hardly a testimony to Papst's professional and personal integrity. They eat as if food could satisfy their hunger for human contact and Papst's professional service to them is simply to lend them his ears. This is hardly a job for a Harvard graduate, who finds himself enslaved by "soft despotism."

The element that injects life into this dull, materialistic modern "soft despotism" is Sophie Mass, a young beauty who takes the doctor out of his comfortable but stuffy setting and makes him find meaning in displacement and becoming. The story that follows in *Match ball* could easily be made into a Hollywood film. When Sophie starts an affair with the married doctor, she also renews her relationship with a rich, romantic Spanish young man, Pablo Braganza, and the suspense in the love triangle brings the whole situation to a boil. The younger Spanish lover complicates the story, but he also keeps the relationship between the young tennis star and the older doctor fresh, so that it does not become stale like the routine the doctor had with his wife. In a jealous rage Raymond Papst shoots the Spanish youth but does not kill him. When this incident uncovers the affair, it ends the marriage and sends the doctor to jail. Sophie Mass does not visit her older lover in jail because she claims that does not have time for "silly things like that." However, unlike the traditional love figure of *La Belle Dame Sans Merci*, or the passive, cold women of romantic or courtly love tradition, she acts as an empowered, intelligent new woman and plans an escape for her man. When the escape fails, she gives the Harvard graduate a tennis racquet and asks him to "keep fit."

Sophie's position in the novel is best related to Aretino's Renaissance motto "live on the alert" ("vivere resolutamente") and Nietzsche's dictum "live dangerously." She also reminds us of Ortega y Gasset's philosophy that "being a man signifies *being a living problem*, an absolute and hazardous adventure" (1963, 25). Her attitude, however, was shaped less by philosophical thinking than by difficult human experience, particularly her mother's experience, which showed her that, in today's society, competition is extremely fierce and only the fittest survive. As a woman who was not of an upper class, Sophie's mother came to understand that money is "un poderoso caballero" [a powerful gentleman], as Francisco de Quevedo observed in sixteenth-century Spain, and that one needs it if he or she is to get out of the population that makes up two-thirds of Latin American countries like Chile.[4] Her mother also knows that structured European society with money has become lifeless and that fresh energy is a source of enrichment. However, as one attempts to improve one's economic situation, it is imperative to avoid routine and other spiritless traps. Hence, as she and her daughter penetrate the establishment, she insists that they remain free: "Queremos ser libres desde la boca hasta los huesos" [We want to be free from our mouths to our bones] (139), because only in this way can they keep their vigour and be a presence in the powerful European business and cultural establishment. In contact with Sophie and spontaneous and instinctive life, Raymond Papst defiantly proclaims from jail: "Más ahora, a punto de terminar mi relato, voy a permitirme una grosería que me sale de corazón: 'Métense su mundo por el culo.' Yo, el doctor Raymond Papst, era de sangre, huesos y sueños, e iba a provocar mi acto, porque no era de celuloide" [And now, at the point of ending my story, I am going to allow myself a rudeness which comes directly from my heart: 'Stick your world up your ass.' I, Dr. Raymond Papst, was of flesh, blood and dreams, and I provoked my act because I am not made of celluloid] (198). This stand is foolish and frightening for the pragmatic modern reader swamped by mortgages, credit cards, and other responsibilities to the establishment, yet the desire to become an individual and to break loose from the rules and regulations of consumer society is not unfamiliar.

"To make a cake you have to break the eggs," Skármeta tells us (160). From a socio-political perspective, *Match ball* suggests that in the new political situation, an individual is a competent player if he or she possesses the human vigour and the courage to "break the eggs." The moneyed class, which intends to hold on to its power and comfort, has opened its doors to skilful and educated players like Sophie Mass and Raymond Papst because they are refreshing and can contribute to their wealth and entertainment. However, the game is complex and has to be played with skill and fitness.

Ana Von Bamberg enjoys the benefits of her social class and education and, as an active player against human rights violations, she is no longer viewed as the "enemy of the people." Papst has genuine love for Ana and for her good work despite the fact that he finds their marriage to be lifeless: "Por cierto que había amado a Ana y de alguna manera... La seguía queriendo" [He certainly had loved Ana and in a way... he still loved her] (125). At the same time, it is clear that Ana is interested in helping the Third World only as long as that world does not pose a threat to the comfort of the elite. When Sophie Mass seduces Ana Von Bamberg's husband and when the interests of new comers and intruders interfere with her interests, Ana stops being good and naive. She divorces her husband and sinks into her father's protective world. Soon after the divorce, she obediently marries a new husband "veinte años menor que yo pero cuarenta veces más ambicioso" [twenty years younger than I and forty times more ambitious] (13), Papst tells us. One of the reasons for such a choice is that the ambitious younger husband can continue the medical practice and the business Baron Von Bamberg helped establish. Ignatieff explains: "One of the strange features of rights talk has been that it makes visible some inequalities—sexual and linguistic inequalities, for example—while obscuring others—such as those based on class and income" (2000, 19). In other words, the dominant ideology of the globalized world gives all citizens the right to speak their language and to preserve their minority cultures, to work where there is employment and to marry the sex of their choice, as long as these rights do not interfere with the structure of the capitalist world. When violations of minority rights occur in parts of the world that are of economic or strategic importance, they become reasons for intervention and for neo-colonial exploitation and control, such as in the "humanitarian bombing" of former Yugoslavia, as Noam Chomsky called it (1999, 3) or the invasion of Iraq. The Middle Eastern war was justified on the grounds of minority rights abuse. According to an interview with Ignatieff, "what Saddam Hussein had done to the Kurds and Shias in Iraq was sufficient justification for the invasion" (Wikipedia). Ignatieff explains that "the key ideas of rights talk are that we are all deliberative equals, that each of us has a right to be heard about the public business of our country, that no one's claims can be silenced and denied simply by the fact of who they are. This ideal of deliberative equality—the commitment to remain in the same room talking until we resolve our disputes, and to do so without violence—is as much unity, as much community, as modern life can afford" (2000, 25).

In Skármeta's novel, Sophie Mass and her mother are not invited into the "deliberating room," nor is a dispute resolved through democratic discussion. Instead, the mother manipulates her way in, while Sophie forces herself on the doctor and the world of the establishment when her mother injects her into the higher society. The mother might be modelled on the Argentinian icon Eva Perón who made changes not by opposing the establishment, but by entering the establishment with a strong general whom she married and used to manipulate changes in Argentina. Like Evita, Sophie's mother leaves her rags when she learns to manipulate the rich. Papst observes that "la técnica de la condesa von Mass, merecería estar en los anales de las relaciones públicas.

Cierto que tenía exceso de rabia acumulada contra la aristocracia, pero sabía administrarla de una manera cautivante y provocadora" [The technique of the countess von Mass deserves to be in the register of public relations. It is true that she had an excess of accumulated rage against the aristocracy, but she knew how to handle them in a captivating and provocative way] (84). The mother enters the aristocratic circle because her daughter is exceptionally beautiful and exceptionally talented in tennis. To play tennis the young girl needs money, and her mother gets sponsors by playing on the elite's desire to preserve their class and to be entertained. In a motherly form of endearment, she calls Sophie a princess and when the old aristocrat Baron Von Bamberg, Ana's father, hears it he eagerly includes the young girl in his circles in order to enlarge and preserve the European aristocracy. He explains that "la señorita Mass no provenía de un anónimo pueblito alemán del seno de una familia anónima" [Miss Mass did not come from an unknown German village and an insignificant family] (18), but that she is a daughter of a respectable woman who had a relationship with a real prince. Sophie's mother exploits the old aristocrat's sentimentality and takes this opportunity to enter the higher social world, and begins to act as if her daughter actually had blue blood.

Sophie's mother knows from experience that reality is not fixed and that opportunities are available for those with the savvy required for social scheming and public relations. The novel echoes and directly refers to the sixteenth-century picaresque work *Lazarillo de Tormes*, in which the pícaro's mother advises her son to look after his individual interests — "válete por ti" (*Lazarillo* 1986, 43) — as she sends him into a world of uncertainty and corruption. She gives him to be the guide of a blind man who teaches the orphan that he must always "keep fit" or that "a blind man's boy has got to be sharper than a needle!"(*Lazarillo* 1986, 27). Following Lazarillo de Tormes' mother's advice, Sophie's mother looks after herself as she gets in tune with the rich. As in the famous picaresque novel: "se arrima a los buenos" [she aligns herself with the wealthy] (43), not to serve them but to attempt to beat them in their own game. Like Lazarillo with the squire, the twentieth-century mother learns about the importance of appearances and deconstructs the new success: "Sophie es un milagro que se lo voy a explicar racionalmente: vestido de Christian Lacroix, cartera de Judith Leiber, collar de Cartier, Lancomes's rouge in red, y zapatos alemanes" [Sophie is a miracle which I will explain rationally: dress by Christian Lacroix, purse by Judith Leiber, necklace by Cartier, Lancomes's red lipstick, and German shoes] (85). With such clothes Sophie is able to enter the upper class and to play her sport and sexual games with men and women from the establishment.

Although Sophie conquers both the old Baron Van Bamberg and Papst by her youth, physical beauty, and fashionable rich-looking appearance, she and her mother are not fully victorious; Skármeta questions their position and comments on the development of women's liberation in the modern world. The mother shares the earlier feminist view that freedom for working class and women is achieved through economic means and through a tactical, intelligent approach rather than through traditional empowerment of women through marriage and, especially, through children. The mother consequently tells Papst that women have gained their rights and independence without men, and that the notion of the communist brotherhood and solidarity is not a part of the equation. As far as the mother is concerned, men are a thing of the past: "Los hombres son anécdotas. Algo que no cumple ninguna función en nuestras vidas y que cuando se nos inflama lo podemos sacar de nuestros cuerpos como un vulgar apéndice" [Men are history. Something that has no function in our lives, like the vulgar appendix we can remove when it starts to act up] (139).

Yet Sophie's mother is forced to admit that individualism and independence cannot be achieved easily; when she recognizes that sexual needs cannot be denied easily, she plans to buy male prostitutes for her daughter: "tras cada trofeo, con un cheque adjunto, una noche de amor" [after each trophy, with a cheque attached, a night of love] (138). But Sophie's mother's arrogance and certainty subside when she recognizes her own errors for which her daughter pays a high price: "He desraizado a Sophie de todo lo que hace la vida normal de una adolescente: no tiene casa, ni amigos, ni padre, y por último tuve que determinar hace dos años que dejara colegio" [I have destroyed for Sophie all that makes life normal for a teenager: she has no home, no friends, no father, and the last thing I had to do is take her out of school two years ago] (79). Sophie's right to participate in the room with the rich and her right to be a self-determined woman have their advantages, and a serious emotional disadvantage. Ignatieff observes that there is indignation towards feminism in the modern human rights culture, and that some critics attribute the long-standing crisis in our family life to the rights revolution. He addresses this criticism by suggesting that "No one seriously supposes that we're going to make family life better by taking away women's rights and the rights of children" (2000, 22). He further explains that the main point in the struggle for women's rights is to acquire agency or the capacity to set goals and accomplish them as a woman sees fit. Sophie certainly becomes a woman with agency, but there is a level of ruthlessness in the struggle of gaining and keeping independence and individual rights, Skármeta observes.

Skármeta's novel questions the human rights ideology which Ignatieff explains in the following way: "The basic intuition of rights talk is that each of us is an end in ourselves, not a means to an end" (2000 24). In the debate regarding family and state rights versus individual rights, Skármeta would agree with Ignatieff that the individual must not be sacrificed for some greater cause. However, in the human rights debate, the Chilean writer would emphasize the adjective *human* (emotional, experiential) as much as the notion of *rights* (rational and legalistic). His novel recognizes that rights are acquired through strong individualism and agency, but individuals are empowered more through love and passion for life than through legalistic means. As Papst listens to popular music in *Match ball*, he realizes that improvisation and human voice are a profound source of individual empowerment. As rules and rights can help societies and individuals, the power of improvisation in music, Papsts finds, is even more invigorating for the individual:

> Me perdí en el último sonido de la trompeta con sordina que semejaba una voz humana en su relajado fraseo. *Fraseo*. Adoro este término favorito de los músicos de jazz para describir la indefinible mezcla de personalidad, originalidad, distorsión y tono emotivo con que un cantante o instrumentista expone un tema. Me detengo en una palabra, pues una vez más quiero detenerme en una persona: Sophie Mass. Sophie fraseaba su belleza con la naturalidad con que un nadador respira. Había en ella estilo y espontaneidad, una fórmula que pocos logran. El exceso de énfasis en el estilo conduce al artificio, [y] demasiado acento en la espontaneidad a la vulgaridad.
>
> [I lost myself in the last sound of the muffled trumpet, which approached a human voice in its relaxed phrasing. *Phrasing*. I adore this favourite term jazz musicians use to describe the indefinable mixture of personality, originality, distortion and the emotional tone with which a singer or an instrument displays a theme. My thoughts linger on a word, and once more I want to linger on a person: Sophie Mass. Sophie phrased her beauty with the same facility with which a swimmer breathes. There was style and spontaneity in her, a formula which few achieve. An excessive emphasis on style leads to artificiality, [and] too much accent on spontaneity becomes vulgar]. (83)

In herself, Sophie combines reason and spontaneity, beauty and ingenuity, or material and the spiritual. She makes on impact on the doctor because her mother had made her into an aesthetically pleasing, rich-appearing object of desire and had taught her to use her intelligence and human spirit. She impresses the doctor with her "phrasing" and improvisation which are impossible without freedom, which she learns to acquire from her romantic Spanish boyfriend, Pablo Braganza, who introduces her to poetry. It is poetry that helps her become a modern woman who is neither artificial nor vulgar.

The Spanish youth is described as someone with "una cierta evocación de una época romántica" [a certain evocation of a romantic epoch] (46), in which literature began to recognize the importance of the individual. Like the Spanish youth, the movement dealt with the idealized world view, which lacked the rational and the instinctive sexual dimensions which Papst later brings into the novel. Pablo Braganza is an important character to the story because when he introduces Bécquer's Romantic poetry to Sophie Mass, she instigates the rebellion against her mother's vulgar materialism and idea of progress and success and recognizes the power of love. She recognizes that her mother's drive for money and success has turned her into a valuable money-making machine without any personal freedom because her mother guards and controls her every step: "Mi madre me trata como si fuera de cristal y en cualquier momento alguien o algo pudiese quebrarme. Ya casi no siento alegría cuando juego tenis. Todo es disciplina, entrenamiento, hoteles, canchas, aviones" [My mother treats me as if I were made of crystal and in any moment someone or something could break me. I already almost do not feel pleasure when I play tennis. It is all discipline, training, hotels, tennis courts, aeroplanes] (88). To escape from her mother's world of discipline and public relations, Sophie responds to Pablo's invitation and frequents lively discotheques with him. Her rebellion is further guided by *Poemas y Milosz*, a book given to her by the romantic Spanish youth. Sophie uses this book to insert the plane ticket for Papst with an invitation to accompany her to Paris. She marks a particular poem in the book by which she declares her love and reveals her sexual desires. Thus, Pablo's literary intervention influences Sophie to rebel against the structured routine which trains her for money and success, and his book sets in motion a chain of events that eventuate in Papst's renunciation of the routine in his professional life and marriage. In his letter to Papst, Pablo explicitly claims credit for his role in converting the formerly "enslaved" girl into a lively, free being, comparable to a work of art: "Sophie posee algo que caracteriza la obra de arte inefable.... De allí que yo haya luchado con el tesón del amante por señalarle la ruta de su libertad. Y no hay otro medio para ser libre que hundirse en los maravillosos vértigos del arte y de la poesía donde la buena metáfora y el sol de la palabra valen más que la vida y el pan" [Sophie possesses something which characterizes the indescribable work of art.... This is the reason why I have struggled with the lover's insistence to show her the road to freedom. And there is no other way to be free but to submerge one's self in the marvellous vertigoes of art and poetry where the good metaphor and the enlightenment from a word are worth more than life and bread] (94).

While poetry and art have a liberating effect, in the modern world very few young people read. Papst says: "Tenía que aceptar mis convicciones de que una chica de quince que leyera a un poeta era un ser irreal o al menos anómalo" [I had to accept my conviction that a fifteen-year-old girl who reads poetry was a surreal being or at least an anomaly] (63). Literature frees Sophie's imagination and she gets into imaginative sexual provocations with her two boyfriends. However, her struggle for greater freedom and personal enrichment is deepened with Papst's intervention, when he confronts her imaginative provocation in which Sophie avoids actual intercourse and sexual penetration:

A medida que el guión se iba cumpliendo según las preguntas efusiones líricas *españolas*,... suspendí mis acciones cuando ella estaba a punto de iniciar el despegue, y apartándome del consabido guión, alcé a la pequeña Sophie de las nalgas, la puse en un operativo relámpago de vuelta en la buena y tradicional cama, y antes de que reiniciase los vericuetos de su defensa, me introduje en ella sin escatimar tosquedad. Si la voluntad nubló mi juicio, si el desatino me hizo siego y sordo a su dolor, el éxtasis me sumergió en la percepción excluyente de mi dicha.

[As the script was developing according to the presumed Spanish lyrical outpouring,... I suspended my activities when she was at the point of starting to take off, and departing from the familiar script, I lifted young Sophie's buttocks, and with the speed of lightning turned her around and threw her on the good old bed, and before she could defend herself, I penetrated her without cutting down the roughness. If desire clouded my judgment, if foolishness made me deaf to her pain, the ecstasy plunged me into the undisturbed perception of happiness]. (131)

As he leads both himself and Sophie into a deeper relationship and greater happiness, Papst puts in question his own and her position in society. But, to make a cake, you have to break the eggs, he says at the beginning of the novel. To be free as individuals and to have happiness there has to be a deeper involvement.

Skármeta's style has been hailed not for its artistic innovations or its philosophical or ideological depth but for, as Poli Délano says, its "ímpetu y desenfado" [impetus and ease] (1978, 35). Donald Shaw praises it for its "instinctive vitality" (1994, 49). In all of Skármeta's works this natural energy stems from his characters' zeal for playful competition and their need to express themselves in love and sexual relationships. In these relationships they instinctively seek the triumph of life over death. But life for them is not something separate from social reality, and this makes Skármeta's works "that much richer," as Shaw says (1994, 64). This is not so much because certain social conditions create specific types of characters (as in naturalism) but because social forces propel characters to either conform to or contest those conditions. Some, like Ana, lose because they do not have the strength — individualism is a difficult sport. Others, like Sophie's mother, play calculated games for material gain, turning themselves into working machines. Papst and Sophie, the protagonists, act in order to find meaning in human contact. The tennis game, which serves in the novel as a metaphor of dynamic relationship, leads Skármeta's characters to dig beyond appearances and to begin to decentralize views held by the establishment, both the literary and the political.

To make a cake, to have a meaningful relationship, or to create a new social reality, one has to break the eggs Antonio Skármeta holds. The necessity of this is seen as Canadian human rights promoters and soldiers Michael Ignatieff describes are changing their roles of peacekeepers to peacemakers. In the world of change where the old order is being destroyed, Antonio Skármeta's

Sophie Mass stands as a prototype of the new woman and a modern individual. The fervour in her life and in the life of those who are involved with her comes from her connection to art, her connection to human experience and alertness that her mother advocates, and from her own ability and courage to play, to be in a love relationship. She is exiled or uprooted from everything traditional, yet she learns to live in the new situation as each one of the characters she comes in contact with teaches her an important lesson. Thus, when looking at this character it is important to understand the relationship of all characters together, because their dialogical interaction paints the image of the new individual.

One has to agree with John Montgomery that to oppose the human rights movement is to oppose "motherhood, or the flag" (1986, 17). One also has to recognize the positive changes that have occurred across the globe in the area of indigenous, minority, children's, and women's rights, as Ignatieff describes. But one also has to recognize the irony that, at a time when the predominant ideology concentrates on individual human rights, both the individual and the human aspect are undermined by routine, the drive for success, and general human disconnectedness.

As Charles Taylor says in his *The malaise of modernity,* modern freedom has been won by our breaking loose from older moral horizons. As a modern youth, Sophie Mass does not see herself as part of any larger order or with any prescribed role. While she is driven by self-interest, and has lost what Taylor calls "the heroic dimension of life," she does not become an egotist, nor does she become a victim of what Alexis de Tocqueville terms the "petits et vulgaires plaisirs" which characterize the democratic age (Taylor 1991, 3) despite her success in tennis and the money that comes with accomplishments in sports. She learned from her mother to keep her survival drive, as mothers of the Plaza de Mayo do, at all times because the modern world created by politicians such as Margaret Thatcher, Ronald Reagan, and Augusto Pinochet is driven by "unrelenting competition — the war of all against all," John Kingdom tells us (15). To play a "match ball" and to keep "love-fifteen" score, as they say at Wimbledon, Sophie has to keep fit, just as her lover Raymond Papst must keep fit in order to maintain a dynamic love relationship. As individuals they have liberated themselves from marriage and old moral restrains, but they must be careful not to fall into new, modern traps. That is why Lazarillo de Tormes never fully trusts his masters and his cunning in his testimony.

Notes

1 Subsequent references to this edition of the novel appear as page numbers in parentheses in the text.
2 For more on this topic see Yúdice (1992).
3 Charles Taylor (1991, 27) argues that the ideal of "moral authenticity" can be achieved if we, as Rousseau said, follow "a voice of nature within us."
4 In his study of the change of events in 1973 in Chile, "Neo-Liberalism and the Chilean model: A forerunner of the new order," Jorge Nef, a Chilean-born Canadian political scientist indicates that the North American mainstream media has viewed the 1973 bloody coup in Chile as a moment of change and improvement. In Machiavellian fashion where the end justifies the means, "mainstream politicians, intellectuals, and media have praised Chile as a political and economic model for Latin America, the Third World, and beyond" (2003, 89). While *The New York Times Magazine* called it "Prosperity Born of Pain," Peruvian Boom writer Mario Vargas Llosa proclaimed that "Chile será muy pronto un país desarrollado" [Chile will soon be a developed country] (Llosa 1991, 10). Nef, on the other hand, is skeptical about the cause for celebration and asks for a deeper analytical approach. He does not deny that there has been economic progress in Chile for some, but he argues that today there are two Chiles. The first Chile, comprising one-third of the population, is made up of "European, affluent, well-educated, well-housed, well-cared-for, consumption-intensive, upper-middle and upper class.... They dwell in neighbourhoods of quality housing comparable to those of ... Toronto, San Francisco, Sydney [or Berlin]." The other Chile, Nef continues, which makes up the other two-thirds of the population, "is largely *métis*, poor or impoverished, unemployed, discriminated against, with limited access to educational, health and mobility opportunities" (2003, 100).

References

Barnet, M. 1968. *Biografía de un cimarrón*. Buenos Aires: Galerna.
Chomsky, N. 1999. *The new military humanism: Lessons from Kosovo*. Monroe, ME: Common Courage Press.
Délano, P. 1978. Antonio Skármeta, un exilio creativo. In *La semana de bellas artes*. Mexico City.
Franco, J. 2004. Going public: Reinhabiting the private. In *The Cambridge companion to modern Latin American culture*, ed. J. King. Cambridge: Cambridge Univ. Press.
García Canclini, Nestor. 1995 [1989]. *Hybrid cultures: Strategies for entering and leaving modernity*. Minneapolis: Univ. of Minnesota Press.
Ignatieff, M. 2000. *The rights revolution*. Berkeley, CA: Publishers Group West.
———. 2006. Canada and the World. *The Globe and Mail*. March 30.
Kingdom, John. 1992. *No such thing as society? Individualism and community*. Buckingham: Open Univ. Press.
Lazarillo de Tormes. 1986. Mexico: Espasa Calpe.
Montgomery, J. W. 1986. *Human rights and human dignity*. Dallas, TX: Probe Books.
Nef, J. 2003. Neo-Liberalism and the Chilean model: A forerunner of the new order. In *The new world order: Corporate agenda and parallel reality*, ed. G. Yovanovich, 89–106. Montreal and Kingston: McGill-Queen's Univ. Press.

Ortega y Gasset, J. 1963. *Man and people*. Trans. W. R. Trask. New York: Norton.
Shaw, D. 1994. *Antonio Skármeta and the Post Boom*. Hanover: Ediciones del Norte.
Skármeta, A. 1989. *Match ball*. Buenos Aires: Editorial Sudamericana.
Taylor, Charles. 1991 *The malaise of modernity.* CBC Massey lecture series. Concord, ON: Anansi Press.
Vargas Llosa, M. 1991. *La época*, April 17.
Yúdice, George. 1992. Testimonio y concientización. *Revista de Crítica Literaria Latinoamericana* 36 (1992): 207–27.

Collective Memory and the Borderlands in Guillermo Verdecchia's *Fronteras Americanas*

Pablo Ramírez

Nations work to create a bounded relation between subjects and national territory, using official histories as both producers and products of borders. As a result, a person's history and sense of self become intelligible through the inside–outside logic of a bounded space; one is either a native or a foreigner, an insider or an outsider. Historical discourse, in other words, helps to constitute what Walter Mignolo calls a "territorial gnoseology" in which knowledge is articulated and legitimated by a nation-building project that works to establish an official language and a national culture (2000, 11). This solidification of space, Kathleen Kirby notes, works to compress "mobile heterogeneities into arrested masses" (1996, 104). Due to the proximity of Latin America and continuous waves of immigration, however, Latino communities and families in North America cannot contain their memories and histories within a single nation's boundaries.[1] Because their memories and histories traverse borders and therefore do not contribute to national formation, they are not sustained by state-mediated forms of remembering and commemoration. Consequently, the imposition of borders can render the memories and histories of the Latino community unintelligible, incomplete, or superfluous.

In the absence of state support, Latina/o cultural producers in North America play a vital role in translating, introducing, and circulating transnational stories and memories into North American culture. For example, Chicana/o artists and writers, influenced by Gloria Anzaldúa's seminal work *Borderlands/La Frontera* have embraced a borderlands subjectivity that encompasses two or more seemingly antithetical cultural frames of reference.

As borderlands subjects, many Latina/o cultural producers work to attain a historical consciousness — which historian Susan Crane defines as the "desire for experiences to be understood historically" — that does not depend on borders for its coherence (1997b, 1373). Consequently, their work often endeavours to sever the tie between a coherent identity and national territory and to create a borderlands no-place space upon which to ground collective memory and foster the Latino community's internecine nature and transnational character. In Canada, playwrights like Carmen Aguirre, Guillermo Verdecchia, Marilo Nuñez, and Latino theatre groups like Alameda Theatre (Toronto) and Latino Theatre Group (Vancouver) have begun to draw on the resources of US Latina/o collective memory to create their own Canadian-specific approach to remembering. Guillermo Verdecchia's *Fronteras Americanas,* influenced by Guillermo Gómez-Peña's performance art and informed by Gloria Anzaldúa's borderlands theory, provides an excellent example of how Canadian Latino theatre can perform the instantiation of a collective memory that will render Canadian Latina/os' memories intelligible both to themselves and to others.[2]

Opening to wide acclaim, even winning the prestigious Canadian Governor General's Award for drama in 1993, Guillermo Verdecchia's *Fronteras Americanas/American Borders* seemed like a timely play about the ever-closer relations between Latin America and North America. With the dawning of the age of NAFTA, one theatre reviewer described "*Fronteras* [as] the perfect play for the age of globalization" (Reid 1999). However, *Fronteras* is not an advertisement praising the benefits of free trade and a united North American market. It is a play about Guillermo Verdecchia, an Argentinean Canadian, who, having traversed borders, finds himself feeling disoriented. In an attempt to explain his disorientation, Verdecchia paraphrases Carlos Fuentes and informs the audience that "a border is more than just a division between countries; it is also the division between cultures and memories" (1993, 21). This explanation is followed by a slide with the question, "Remember the Alamo?" Borders divide memories, and memories — the slide reminds us — create histories. The goal of telling people to remember the Alamo is to give people a common set of memories and thus a national history. But what happens when you traverse borders and your life encompasses two or more national cultures? For Verdecchia, crossing borders and acquiring two or more sets of memories and histories have rendered him incapable of situating himself historically and geographically.[3] Because memory is social and structural and can only be sustained by a community, Verdecchia is traumatized by the fact that his memories have no social meaning and have been reduced to mere individual acts of remembering. As Guillermo Verdecchia explains in his master's thesis, "Staging Memory," without the legitimation of the state and the support of communities Verdecchia's memories in *Fronteras Americanas* "do not 'fit' because... the social spaces in which he tries to retain, organize and understand those memories are all wrong. Because there is no group interested in them, the memories in *Fronteras* float, disconnected and unstable" (2006, 2–3). He wonders how Latina/os in Canada can sustain their identities when "there is no validation, no echo, no correlation forthcoming from the groups in which [they] participate" (ibid.). The inadequacy of historical narrative drives Verdecchia the character to find a space and framework that will render his memories intelligible. This journey of discovery takes him from historical discourse to nostalgia to trauma and finally to the borderlands. In order to ground his floating memories, Guillermo Verdecchia transforms the stage itself into a borderlands space where imagination, desire, and performance can overcome the imposition of borders and allow Verdecchia to place his memories and experiences within the framework of a Latina/o collective memory. Guillermo Verdecchia's play provides invaluable insight into how the stage and performance can "reframe" both official historical discourse and stereotypes in order to create a Canadian Latina/o collective memory that supports the transnational stories, experiences, and memories of the community.

Collective Memory and Stereotypes

Memory is not simply an act of individual remembering; it can be both individual and social. Unlike history, which Pierre Nora defines as a simple reconstruction of the past, memory is constantly evolving in order to create the present (1989, 9). Similarly, Susan Crane does not see memory as a single artifact from the past but as "a production that emerges over time and in the present" (1997a, 49–50). However, memory, Crane insists, is essentially a *historical* process that reconstructs the past in order to create a meaningful present (ibid.). Memories need a framework for their articulation and reproduction, and this framework is known as collective memory (Crane 1997b, 1373). It is important to keep in mind that collective memory does not determine what each individual remembers. As Amos Funkenstein explains, collective memory's relation to individual memory is analogous to Saussure's distinction between *langue* and *parole* (qtd. in Klein 2000, 133). Just as a person may use a shared language to make an individual statement, so can a person use the resources that make up collective memory to create an individual act of remembrance.

While North American Latina/o collective memory may be described as a system that is composed of the signs, customs, languages, official histories, and myths of two or more cultures and countries, it is not simply content. Collective memory is a structure that responds to political and social upheaval and crisis by using memories and history to interpret and create the present. It provides a framework that helps to articulate how and why members of a group remember. As Iwona Irwin-Zarecka explains, collective memory is located not in individuals' memories but in the resources they share (1994, 4). These resources can include official archives, history books, folktales, ads, songs, movies, cartoons, etc. More importantly, collective memory allows a community to "frame" a certain event in order to shape how it is read and remembered by the community (ibid., 5). Collective memory, in other words, is a dynamic process that responds to political and social circumstances in the present by framing and reframing memories (ibid., 7).

Take, for example, the myth of Aztlán, used by Chicano nationalists in the late 1960s and early 1970s to galvanize the community to political action. According to the myth, around the tenth century CE the god Huitzilopochtli told the Aztecs to leave Aztlán and to travel south in order to found an empire. He told them that when they saw an eagle perched on a cactus, devouring a snake, they will have reached the promised land. In 1328, the prophecy is fulfilled, and they establish their empire in Tenochtitlan, the site of present-day Mexico City. It was also prophesied that the Aztecs would once again return to Aztlán, which is believed to be located in the US Southwest. Chicana/o collective memory reframed this story in order to respond to Chicanos' contemporary political and social circumstances as a beleaguered and oppressed racial minority. At the time, the United States was experiencing the largest waves of Mexican immigration it had ever seen. As a result, both Mexicans and Chicana/os were represented as foreigners. Chicana/os responded by reframing the myth of Aztlán in order to posit an Aztec/indigenous origin for Chicana/os, thus establishing a claim to the Southwest that preceded both Mexican and American national territories. The reframed myth changed the representation of Mexican immigration from an invasion to a return to the homeland. Anglos were transformed into foreigners, and Chicana/os and Mexicans were represented as the rightful owners and heirs to the Southwest. This act of reframing gave an intelligibility and legitimacy to borderlands subjects by creating an imaginary indigenous nation that traversed the United States–Mexico border and abolished the divide between Mexicans and Chicanos.

Despite the tremendous political significance of Aztlán to Chicano politics, the myth does not have any inherent political meaning. Its political import depends solely on how a community instantiates collective memory through its framing practices. For example, in response to the immigration rights rallies in 2006 and 2007, American nativists reframed the myth of Aztlán in order to support their claims that Mexican immigrants were engaged in a *reconquista* of the American West. Unlike Chicana/o nationalists, nativists used the myth to cast Mexican immigrants as an invading horde that would transform "proper" Americans into foreigners in their own land. American nativists were able to give the myth of Aztlán a radically different meaning because it is the frame of collective memory that gives memories their historical and political significance.

Guillermo Verdecchia's *Fronteras Americanas* scrutinizes how Latina/os have been framed within North American collective memory by addressing two seemingly unconnected borders: the United States–Canada and United States–Mexico borders. Centuries of contact between the United States and Latin America have produced stereotypes about Latina/os and Latin America that have been deployed again and again, all the while gaining more strength and coherence with each repetition. Guillermo Verdecchia shows how stereotypes are not simply negative representations. Stereotypes are the memories North Americans possess of Latina/os and Latin Americans. Generations of North Americans have grown up with movies, ads, political speeches, cartoons, dime novels, etc., that have stereotyped Latina/os, and they draw upon these stereotypes-as-memories in order to understand their present interactions with Latina/os or Latin America. In other words, stereotyping is a framing practice that instantiates North American collective memories about Latina/os and Latin America. In and of themselves, for example, Latina/o drug dealers and gang members are not stereotypes. Stereotyping unmoors these people from their socio-political context and transforms them into frames that trap, distort, and make Latina/os intelligible in the racist imaginations of North Americans. Stereotyping provides the roles and scenarios available to Latina/os in the North American mediascape, and can force Latina/os to embody the very stereotypes that threaten their individuality and dignity. When Verdecchia auditions for roles, for example, he tells producers that he specializes in "El Salvadorian refugees, Italian bobsledders, Arab horse-thieves and Uruguayan rugby players who are forced to cannibalize their friends when their plane crashes in the Andes" (1993, 64). There is nothing inherently wrong or demeaning about being an El Salvadorian refugee. What is degrading is being condemned to play the same roles over and over again. Stereotyping is especially insidious because it constantly threatens to replace and shape North American Latina/os' understanding of themselves. This is one reason Latina/os in North America must address two or more cultural frames of reference, so they can combat the North American practice of using stereotypes to frame Latinos with a framing practice of their own—one that instantiates their own collective memory.

Unfortunately, due to the prevalence of such stereotypes, North American Latina/os cannot ignore them in any attempt at self-definition. As Frances Aparicio (Aparicio and Chavez-Silverman 1997) asserts in her definition of *latinidad*, most Latina/os do not have the luxury of being able to define themselves without interference from the racial stereotypes and fantasies that circulate around them. Not surprisingly, when Wideload translates the word

"Chicano" to a Canadian audience, he provides a mixture of stereotypes, ethnic slurs, facts and locations:

> Chicano: a person who drives a loud car that sits low to the ground?
> A kind of Mexican?
> A wetback?
> Generic term for a working class Latino?
> A Mexican born in Saxon America? (1993, 26)

This refusal to purge stereotypes from any definition of North American Latino culture illustrates how Latina/os must conceive of themselves within the dynamic of Anglo-Latino contact. As a result, sometimes Latina/os shape their identity as a challenge to these images. Some, as Wideload's mockery of Antonio Banderas's active participation in the creation his Latino Lover persona makes clear, use these fantasies to define themselves in order to gain a visibility or marketability in mainstream culture.

One might object that these racial stereotypes are US-produced and have no power or intelligibility in a Canadian context. After all, the experiences of Canadian Latina/os and US Latina/os are not the same. However, due to the porous nature of the United States–Canada border and the dominance of the US media, Latino communities on both sides of the border do not have the luxury of being able to define themselves without interference from these racial stereotypes and racist fantasies. The furor caused by a poster of a Latino gang posted on the walls of the Bloor-and-Yonge subway station at the very centre of Toronto in the spring of 1999 provides a clear example of how stereotypes affect Canadian Latina/os. The poster was part of an election campaign and urged Torontonians to consider issues of law and safety in the upcoming provincial elections. The poster, paid for by the Toronto Police Association, asked voters to "help fight crime by electing candidates who are prepared to take on the drug pushers, the pimps and the rapists" (Carey 1999, 1).[4] Toronto's offended Latino community immediately protested. As Canadians soon discovered, however, the poster was not produced in Canada. An American ad agency had created it using a Los Angeles-based Chicano gang to represent the dangers of crime and social disorder.

Community leaders complained that this gross misrepresentation of Toronto's Latino community was a geographical mistake. As the president of the Toronto chapter of the Chinese Canadian National Council pointed out, "One fact that the police association does not see is that Toronto is not east L.A." (Carey 1999, 1). This issue of geography is supposed to emphasize the inappropriateness of the poster and its lack of referential power in Toronto. Community leaders characterized these images as foreign products that should have been contained in the United States. What the poster demonstrated, however, is that there is no pure untouched place where stereotypes do not play a role in the constitution of Latino identity in the United States and increasingly in Canada. What community leaders failed to address is that despite the small Latino population in Toronto, these policemen had been exposed to enough stereotypical images of Latino criminals that the American-produced poster was not foreign or incomprehensible—quite the contrary. A mostly white police association saw these young Latinos and decided that they would be the perfect bogeymen for their election-campaign scare tactic. In other words, the stereotype of the Latino criminal was a completely familiar trope and therefore the perfect medium for their alarmist message about crime in a Canadian city.

While stereotypes do distort, *Fronteras Americanas* illustrates how they can also be used to dismantle racist framing practices. Appropriately, it is Wideload, a character who embodies Latino stereotypes, who begins to scrutinize and critique how North Americans view Latina/os. The play alternates between Verdecchia and Facundo Morales Segundo, a.k.a Wideload McKenna, juxtaposing Verdecchia's earnest search for a coherent sense of self against Wideload's comical, fast-talking, energetic scenes. As a character, Wideload has clearly acquired his strength, energy, and intelligibility from a long history of contact between Latin America and North America. While Verdecchia is lost and filled with self-doubt, Wideload is presented as a confident and adept social commentator; he has no identity crisis.[5] However, it would be a mistake to regard Wideload as simple comic relief. Wideload is given a powerful critical voice and plays a vital role in this memory project. While in the first act Verdecchia presents his dilemma to the audience, it is Wideload who begins the process of reframing how Latina/os are read.

Because his energy, confidence, and cultural knowledge are derived from contact zones—not national cultures or histories—Wideload is the perfect translator between Latina/os and Anglos. Wideload establishes a common ground between Latino- and Anglo-Canadians precisely because of the familiarity of the stereotypes and cultural icons that he embodies. He draws upon fantasies and images Anglos have of Latin America in order to explain Latina/os in terms and images that Anglos can understand, only to use these very images and terms to critique North American racism. Stereotypes, in other words, become the medium of translation, making Wideload the ideal locus of enunciation from which to speak with clarity and authority. In a manner, Wideload represents a locus of enunciation that the character of Verdecchia must work to achieve for himself. Wideload's translations, moreover, serve as ethnographic critiques that create what all good translations should according to Stephanos Stephanides: "an interaction of cultures performing and disrupting cultural memory" (2004, 108). Wideload's acts of translation disrupt North Americans' collective memory by calling attention to its framing practices. As an embodiment of Latino stereotypes, Wideload shows how North Americans have constituted their own identities as rational, self-disciplined, advanced, law-abiding people in part through the continual reframing of Latina/os as emotional, lazy, backwards, sexual, and lawless. He then uses their stereotypes of Latinos to frame North Americans themselves by performing an ethnographic study of Anglos that renders the normative into something exotic. He examines what Anglos want and desire: to exoticize, sexualize, and criminalize Latina/os. Suddenly their stereotypes say much more about North Americans than about Latina/os. After conducting his ethnographic study of Anglos, he turns to the audience and asks the Anglos: "So what is it with you people? Who do you think you are? Who do you think we are? Yes, I am calling you you — I am generalizing. I am reducing you all to the lowest common denominator. I am painting you with the same brush. Is it starting to bug you yet?" (1993, 76).

In addition to stereotypes, Guillermo Verdecchia, through Wideload, re-stages and unpacks scenarios of Anglo–Latino contact that have made Latina/os visible and culturally intelligible in the United States and Canada. A scenario, according to Diana Taylor, is a "paradigmatic set-up" that is "structured around a schematic plot with an intended, though adaptable end" and exists as a set of possibilities and represents ways of conceiving conflict, crisis, or resolution (2003, 13). One scenario familiar to most North Americans, for example, is the "frontier scenario in the United States, [which] organizes events as diverse as smoking advertisements and the hunt for Osama bin Laden. Rather than a copy, the scenario constitutes a once-againness" (Taylor 2003, 32). Scenarios, Taylor contends, form part of a cultural repertoire, which produces and reproduces cultural knowledge through participation in a performance. I would also add that scenarios can be performed in such a way that they reframe an event and shape memory and remembrance. In doing so, scenarios are also part of collective memory.

Fronteras demonstrates how such scenarios of Anglo-Latino contact have become marketing tools that represent Latin America as a site of social disorder and backwardness in order to fulfill Anglos' desire for such images and to establish a "once-againness" that makes Anglo North Americans' superiority self-evident. When Wideload pitches the idea to a loan officer of using multiple scenarios to create a theme park for Anglos, he is once again calling attention to stereotyping as a kind of framing practice:

> I want to cash in on de Latino Boom....We are a hot commodity right now. And what I really want to do is get a big chunk of toxic wasteland...and make like a third-world theme park. You know, you drive up to like big-barbed wire gates with

guards carrying machine guns and ... as soon as you're inside somebody steals your purse and a policeman shows up but he's totally incompetent and you have to bribe him to get any action. Den you walk through a slum on the edge of a swamp wif poor people selling tortillas. And ... a drug lord comes along in his hydrofoil and [you] watch a multi-media presentation on drug processing. I figure it would be great—you people love dat kinda shit. (1993, 25)

Wideload strings together a number of scenarios that are performed again and again in various North American media outlets and transfers them to a theme park, an ersatz space near the Trans-Canada Highway. As a Latino attempting to market these scenarios, Wideload points to the nature of his own (in)visibility and coherence in a North American context in order to use these scenarios to read and critique Anglos' collective memories of Latin America. He performs these scenarios, however, with a difference, making it clear that they have little to do with Latin America and more to do with satisfying an Anglo-dominant market. By using stereotypes about Latinos to create an ethnographic portrait of Anglos, Wideload demonstrates how Anglo-produced stereotypes and scenarios can indeed be reframed and adapted for different ends.

Borderlands and Collective Memory
Once these stereotypes-as-memories have been reframed and undermined, the rising action of the play builds towards Verdecchia's entry into the borderlands. The play replaces stereotypes with Latino cultural memories that transcend borders rather than enforce them. In other words, instead of memories and histories becoming the effects of borders, the borderlands becomes both the cause and effect of Latino collective memory. The borderlands comes into being precisely because Latina/os like the character of Verdecchia need it and therefore will it into existence in order to give their history and memories an intelligibility. Without such a borderlands space, Verdecchia is incapable of creating a historical narrative that will ground his transnational memories. For example, in Act 1, he attempts to create a historical narrative by beginning with the Triassic Period of the Mesozoic Era and then jumps forward to Joan of Arc, Christopher Columbus, Beethoven, Beatrix Potter, Ernest Hemingway, *West Side Story*, and the 1969 Stanley Cup. This incoherent historiography, as Kathleen McHugh points out, "exemplifies the seemingly arbitrary character of (any transnational) historical narration divorced from the perspective of a distinct location or nation" (McHugh 2005, 171). Since he cannot ground himself in Canada, he subsequently designates Argentina as his homeland. As the site of a nostalgic return, Argentina comes to represent for Verdecchia the nation that will finally give him the fullness of identity that Canada has failed to provide. Nostalgia, however, is soon transformed into trauma when Verdecchia stops in Chile on his way to Argentina. On his first night there,

he witnesses a murder. Traumatized by what he has seen, Argentina fails to provide Verdecchia with the homeland he seeks and he returns to Canada, feeling ill and disoriented.

Gaspar de Alba argues that Latina/os must discover that identity for diasporic subjects "must be rooted in nonexistence, in the subjunctive netherlands of desire and imagination ('if only I had a homeland'), rather than in the lament for a lost wholeness ('there's no place like home')" (2005, 107). Latina/os, in other words, must abandon their nostalgic desire for an origin, a homeland, and find a way to historicize their memories without territorializing them. One could argue, however, that Argentina as a site of nostalgic return is also an imaginary place. Why can't the Argentina-that-never-existed function as the ground for Verdecchia's memories? After all, there are a number of similarities between nostalgia and historical memory. Both nostalgia and historiography involve, as Michel Serres points out, a movement of return: "History has a fixed point from which it distances itself in order to return to it" (qtd. in Smith 1997, 174). Similarly, historian D. Vance Smith claims that the function of history is to "return to what the self has forgotten [which] is also, in a sense, a return to what the self never could have known" (1997, 175). Both nostalgia and historical memory entail having memories that are not your own — remembering events that never happened to you and people you have never met. The problem with nostalgia and historical memory is that they both deal with a return to an "authentic" past and gain their coherence within one cultural frame of reference. In fact, the reason that Verdecchia's return accomplishes so little is that he simply trades one cultural frame of reference (Canada) for another (Argentina).

To become a borderlands subject, Gloria Anzaldúa explains, one must negotiate between two or more cultural frames of reference. This of course is no easy task, because such a project inevitably produces what Gloria Anzaldúa calls cultural *choques* or cultural clashes and/or shocks. To address these cultural clashes the new *mestiza* "puts history through a sieve, winnows out the lies" and "reinterprets history and, using new symbols, she shapes new myths" (Anzaldúa 1987, 82). Instead of returning to the past of nostalgia or historical memory, borderlands subjects must establish what Michael Hames García, in his reading of Gloria Anzaldúa's *Borderlands,* calls an "original relation to history," which "represents a new way of relating to the past; it responds to the needs of the present and remains dynamic, rather than traditional or custom-bound" (Hames-García 2000, 113). In *Fronteras Americanas,* overcoming trauma necessitates connecting the self and the collective, and the autobiographical with the historical, breaking the link between memory and territory, and thus creating an original relation to history. This borderlands paradigm (the no-place space of desire and imagination) allows Latina/os like

Verdecchia "to create self-representations that address cultural amnesia and trauma by representing both personal and collective meanings of loss" (Velasco 2004, 319).

It is only when Verdecchia goes to see a *brujo* (healer/witch doctor) that he is finally cured of his nostalgia and finds a space upon which to access and articulate a Latino collective memory. Unlike the therapist who asked Verdecchia to remember events from his personal life, the *brujo* asks Verdecchia to remember both the historical and the personal, the individual and the collective. El Brujo tells him, "You have a very bad border wound... and here in Mexico any border wounds or afflictions are easily aggravated." At first Verdecchia is skeptical of the *brujo*, who seems to think the corner of Madison and Bloor is the borderlands (*la frontera*). El brujo then informs Verdecchia that the only way to cure his border wound is to remember both his past and the histories of Latin America. After a failed attempt, Verdecchia begins to remember both:

> I remember the French Invasion of Mexico.... I remember that I had a dream. I was playing the accordion, playing something improvised, which my grandmother recognized after only three notes as a tango from her childhood, playing a tango I had never learned, playing something improvised, not knowing where my fingers were going.... And I remember that I remembered that dream the first time one afternoon in Paris while staring at an accordion in a stall at the flea market and then found 100 francs on the street. As I passed out El Brujo said, "The Border is your Home." I'm not in Canada; I'm not in Argentina. I'm on the Border. I am Home. Mais zooot alors, je comprends maintenant, mais oui, merde! Je suis Argentin-Canadien! I am a post-Porteno, neo-Latino Canadian. I am the Pan-American highway! (1993, 75)

The creation of an original relation to history in *Fronteras Americanas* occurs the moment Verdecchia no longer attempts to make sense of his experiences by applying the inside–outside logic of borders. As Verdecchia explains to the audience: "I am learning to live on the border. I have called off the Border Patrol, I am hyphenated but I am not falling apart, I am putting together. I am building a house on the border. And you?... Will you call off the Border Patrol?" (1993, 78) In other words, Verdecchia's experience of exile and return finally finds expression and coherence when he refuses to allow borders to induce a cultural schizophrenia. Because trauma, like memory, is in part a social construct, it is precisely the meaning (or lack of meaning) one ascribes to events that constitutes trauma (Alexander 2004). Verdecchia realizes that the trauma of crossing borders is the result of the meaninglessness that nationalism has attached to his experiences as a transnational subject. By entering the space of the borderlands, a space that is a no-place, Verdecchia is finally able to subvert the nation's power to impose boundaries on his histories and memories and give his experiences a new coherence.

Conclusion

In order to depart from the "reality" of borders, Guillermo Verdecchia transforms the stage itself into the borderlands—a no-place space where imagination, desire, and performance can overcome the imposition of borders and allow Verdecchia to place his memories and experiences within the framework of a Latina/o collective memory. Because the borderlands does not function like territory, however, it does not exist to serve one ethnic group's memory. It allows for the articulation of a North American–Latin American experience and acknowledges memory as the product of contact zones rather than a national territory. In other words, it is not solely the site of a Latino collective memory. On the contrary, the play encourages North American Anglos to see themselves as already involved in the borderlands. As the first slide in Act 2 informs the audience, "Every North American, before this century is over, will find that he or she has a personal frontier with Latin America. This is a living frontier, which can be nourished... by knowledge.... Or starved by suspicion, ghost stories, arrogance, ignorance, scorn, and violence" (Carlos Fuentes, qtd. in Verdecchia 1993, 54). With the ever-closer ties between Latin America and North America, all North Americans may one day have to call off the border patrol and enter the borderlands to make sense of their own histories and memories.

Notes

1. Canadians use the term "North American" to refer to Canada and the United States but not Mexico. Despite the inaccuracy of the term, it does provide a useful shorthand to discuss the cultural overlaps between Canada and the United States.
2. Verdecchia references Gloria Anzaldúa's theory of the borderlands (n3) and Guillermo Gómez-Pena's *Border Brujo* (n9) in the published version of his play, *Fronteras Americanas* (1993).
3. For the rest of the chapter, I refer to the character in the play as "Verdecchia" and "Guillermo Verdecchia" as the playwright.
4. See also Molony (1999, 1).
5. In the film version of the play, *Crucero/Crossroads*, Wideload's energy stands in even starker contrast to Verdecchia's near somnolent state. In the film version, the first and last time we see Verdecchia, he is getting out of or into bed, respectively. Verdecchia's narration is presented in a voice-over with a silent Verdecchia often sitting down and looking away from the camera. Once Wideload appears on the screen, the pace changes dramatically. Wideload addresses the camera; he is full of action and movement and carries a vitality that Verdecchia's character clearly lacks.

References

Alexander, J. C. 2004. *Cultural trauma and collective identity.* Berkeley: Univ. of California Press.
Anzaldúa, G. 1987. *Borderlands: The new mestiza = la frontera.* San Francisco: Aunt Lute.
Aparicio, F. R., and S. Chavez-Silverman. 1997. *Tropicalizations: Transcultural representations of Latinidad.* Hanover, NH: Univ. Press of New England.
Carey, E. 1999. They are no longer sleeping with their bags packed. *Toronto Star,* 20 June.
Crane, S. A. 1997a. Memory, distortion, and history in the museum. *History and Theory* 36(4): 44–63.
———. 1997b. Writing the individual back into collective memory. *The American Historical Review* 102(5): 1372–85.
Crucero/Crossroads. 1993. Dir. R. Puerta. Toronto: Mongrel Media.
Gaspar de Alba, A. 2005. There's no place like Aztlán: Embodied aesthetics in Chicana art. *CR: The New Centennial Review* 4(2): 103–40.
Hames-García, M. R. 2000. How to tell a mestizo from an enchirito®: Colonialism and national culture in the borderlands. *Diacritics* 30(4): 102–22.
Irwin-Zarecka, I. 1994. *Frames of remembrance: The dynamics of collective memory.* New Brunswick, NJ: Transaction Publishers.
Kirby, K. M. 1996. *Indifferent boundaries: Spatial concepts of human subjectivity.* New York: Guilford Press.
Klein, K. L. 2000. On the emergence of memory in historical discourse *Representations* 69 (Special Issue: Grounds for Remembering, Winter): 127–50.
McHugh, K. 2005. Giving "minor" pasts a future: Narrating history in transnational cinematic autobiography. In *Minor transnationalism,* ed. F. Lionnet and S. Shi. Durham, NC: Duke Univ. Press.
Mignolo, W. 2000. *Local histories, global designs: Coloniality, subaltern knowledges, and border thinking.* Princeton, NJ: Princeton Univ. Press.
Molony, P. 1999. Police union ad incites hatred, ethnic groups say. *Toronto Star,* 2 June.
Nora, P. 1989. Between memory and history: Les lieux de memoire. *Representations* 26 (Special Issue: Memory and Counter-Memory, Spring): 7–24.
Reid, R. 1999. *Fronteras Americanas* fascinating. *Kitchener-Waterloo Record,* 21 October, D20.
Smith, D. V. 1997. Irregular histories: Forgetting ourselves. *New Literary History* 28(2): 161–84.
Stephanides, S. 2004. Translatability of memory in an age of globalization. *Comparative Literature Studies* 41(1): 101–15.
Taylor, D. 2003. *Archive and the repertoire: Performing cultural memory in the Americas.* Durham, NC: Duke Univ. Press.
Velasco, J. 2004. Automitografias: The border paradigm and Chicana/o autobiography. *Biography* 27(2): 313–38.
Verdecchia, G. 2006. Staging memory: Constructing Canadian Latinidad. M.A. thesis, Univ. of Guelph. Dept. of Drama.
———. 1993. *Fronteras Americanas (American borders).* Toronto: Coach House Press.

From Exile to the *Pandilla*: The Construction of the Hispanic-Canadian Masculine Subject in *Cobro Revertido* and *Côte-des-Nègres*

Stephen Henighan

The Hispanic-Canadian masculine subject, as exemplified in two novels by writers born twenty years apart, is perpetually deterritorialized. This suggests a significant contrast between Hispanic-Canadian identity and that of US Latinos, who appropriate and reimagine the United States as a hybridized border territory. The multimedia performance art expression of the US outlook is exemplified by Guillermo Gómez-Peña, who fantasizes about banning the use of English in the southwestern United States in favour of compulsory Spanglish (1996, 28).[1] At the high-art end of the spectrum, Francisco Goldman's *The divine husband* (2004), arguably the most ambitious of all US-Latino novels, painstakingly reconstructs the history of nineteenth-century Guatemala with the purpose, unveiled at the novel's conclusion, of destabilizing traditional readings of New England history by exposing even this northeastern-most corner of the United States as a product of the history of what might be called "Latino"-America. The elaborate intrigues of nineteenth-century Central American politics condense at the novel's close into a cultural sediment that serves as an occluded foundation for a New England community: "When the forest was cleared for new neighborhoods back in the forties and the fifties, strange artifacts were found where the workers' housing in the Aztec Jungle had been: stone pagan idols, circles of black ash, incense burners, little crystals, petrified beans[…]" (Goldman 2004, 453).

US Latino writers who assert the innate linguistic and cultural hybridity of the United States draw on strong historical support. Many Spanish-speaking people in the southwestern United States descend from families whose ancestors did not choose to become Americans but had US identity grafted onto them by the Treaty of Guadalupe Hidalgo in 1848 and the Gadsden Purchase in 1853. Spaniards began exploring the United States in 1513, more than a century before the arrival of British colonists on the *Mayflower* and ninety years before the founding of British colonies in Virginia. Some of the oldest cities in the United States, such as San Agustín, Florida (1565), and Santa Fe, New Mexico (1609), were founded as colonies of Spain; major modern cities, particularly Los Angeles, Miami, and San Antonio, owe their growth, prosperity, and sense of identity to the enterprise and culture of Spanish-speaking people.

The Hispanic-Canadian lacks this historical bedrock. Canada's contacts with the Spanish Empire were glancing. The Basque fishermen who began frequenting the Grand Banks of Newfoundland in the early sixteenth century left traces of the Basque language among the speech of the Native peoples of coastal Newfoundland, but they founded no cities (Brown 1997, 21). On the West Coast, a handful of islands with names such as Cortés and Quadra remain as vestiges of Spanish expeditions which skirted Canada in 1774, 1775, and 1779. During a later expedition in 1789, Esteban José Martínez erected a fort at Nootka Bay which was the first construction built by Europeans on Canada's Pacific Coast (Pathfinders and passageways n.d.). Yet until the rise of the dictatorships in the Southern Cone of South America in the 1970s, the Hispanic population of Canada was probably only about 3000 people; its cultural output was negligible. As Hugh Hazelton has written: "La inmigración masiva latinoamericana de los años setenta marcó el comienzo de un mundo de letras directamente latinocanadiense" (2005, 2). Even today, the most generous estimates calculate Hispanics as being 1.5 per cent of Canada's population, as opposed to at least 13 per cent in the United States. The self-definition of Canadian Hispanics is complicated by the fact that a large proportion of the community's cultural pioneers, the often well-educated Chileans and Argentines who immigrated during the 1970s, settled in Quebec or in nearby Ottawa. Their initial encounter with Canada was with a bilingual society characterized by political tension between the two principal linguistic groups. Originating on the contested ground of the politically turbulent Quebec of the 1970s and 1980s, Hispanic Canadian cultural identity, like Canadian identity in general, emerged as linguistically divided and apprehensive about its appropriate form of self-expression. Hispanic Canadian writing, by definition, was the work of people who regarded themselves as exiles; for this reason, few of these writers relinquished Spanish as their literary language.

One of the most impressive examples of exile fiction is José Leandro Urbina's novel *Cobro revertido* (1992). Urbina, born in Santiago in 1949, studied literature at the Universidad de Chile. In 1974 he fled to Canada, where he lived in Ottawa but spent much time in Montreal. The novel is set in the late 1970s, at a time when the streets of Montreal are dominated by the West Indian festival *Carifête* and the May 1980 referendum on Quebec independence is on the horizon. The protagonist, a Chilean exile who is a graduate student in sociology at the Université de Montréal, learns that his mother has died in Chile. The mother's role as the defining parent is the first in a series of identifications initiated by the women in the Sociologist's life. In Chile his first girlfriend, Magdalena, introduced him to a left-wing political party which, although not named, appears to be the voluntaristic Movimiento de la Izquierda Revolucionaria (MIR), which challenged the social and political orthodoxy of the Chilean Communist Party during the 1960s and 1970s. MIR's appeal to young men lay not only in its insurrectionary politics but also in the MIR leadership's adoption of a "transgressive" style, a self-conscious fusion of the appearance of Che Guevara with styles adopted by 1960s sexual libertines and social rebels known in Chilean slang as *rotos* and *huasos*. Florencia Mallon argues that "such gendered transgression was a particularly effective challenge to the ideal of masculinity deployed by the more traditional organized left, one that emphasized disciplined work habits and responsible family behavior" (2003, 181–82).[2] In *Cobro revertido* the Sociologist's first conflict with his mother arises from his yearning to adopt this style: "Yo también quería tener mi propia radio, escuchar a los Beatles. Dejarme crecer el pelo. No ponerme camisa blanca y corbata y parecer un empleado de oficina de catorce años" (Urbina 1992, 49).[3] Years later, he is unable to refute the theory of his Québécois thesis supervisor, Professor Grenier, that "la extrema izquierda chilena... buscaba representar en la simbología enérgicamente guerrillera aspectos de la cultura juvenil urbana... y crear una realidad alternativa, fuera de la universidad y la familia" (184). The rejection of traditional family roles and patriarchal norms freed the young men of MIR to lead lives in which political radicalism went hand in hand with sexual experimentation. Known only as "el Sociólogo," Urbina's protagonist never reveals the surname that would link him with his father; he remains, in the words of a friend, "un hijito de mamá" (137). The paradoxical outcome of his renunciation of his paternal heritage is that the Sociologist's sexual activity mutates into a form of cultural compliance with his female lovers, permitting them to sculpt his social identity. By fleeing the dictatorship of General Pinochet, who incarnated the stern ideals of the patriarchy and wished to create a Christian civilization defined by traditional family values, the Sociologist renders himself more susceptible to being defined by the women in his life, particularly his English-Canadian wife, Megan, and his Québécoise lover, Marcia. The death of his mother is also the symbolic death of the *madre patria,* the female embrace, both nurturing and suffocating, which has both inspired and tried to suppress his transgressive masculinity. In essence, the *madre patria* has died twice, since Magdalena is presented as an alternate mother figure. She is older than the Sociologist, has been married and separated, and nurtures him, albeit in different values than those advanced by his mother. When the novel opens, she, like the protagonist's mother, is dead, having been murdered by Pinochet's secret police. In the Sociologist's memories of the conflicts between his mother and Magdalena, their identities become blurred: "Cuando pienso en ti, pienso en mi madre, Magdalena" (74).

By following other *miristas* in refusing to assume the responsible *padre de familia* role promoted by both the Communist Party and the military, the Sociologist cements his emotional dependence on his mother. The novel's forward action describes his unsuccessful attempts to make arrangements for the risky flight home to attend his mother's funeral. Sidetracked by friends, memories, insolvency, drunkenness, sex, politics, and *Carifête,* he fails to make the trip. His failure is symbolically consistent, since the implicitly feminized Chile where he consolidated his non-conventional masculinity through the tension between his politically conservative anglophile mother and his revolutionary francophile girlfriend, has been obliterated by the Pinochet patriarchy, "porque el Tata Dios General Augusto cerró la puerta de la madre patria a nuestras espaldas" (45). By going into exile, the Sociologist has abandoned even the *mirista* culture in which his transgressive masculinity was forged. By definition, members of MIR did not go into exile but remained in Chile to wage a clandestine struggle against the Pinochet dictatorship in conformity with their post–11 September 1973 credo: "El MIR no se asila" (Mallon 2003, 207). For the Sociologist, exile is inseparable from an acute crisis in his masculinity. Linguistically divided and threatening to split in two, the Canada of the late 1970s cannot offer the secure embrace of his *madre patria.* The conflict between the mother and Magdalena makes this tension present in the Sociologist's life even prior to his arrival in Quebec. As Norman Cheadle observes, "it appears that Urbina has deliberately set up the central conflicts of his character's life along a dual axis of sex and *langue* (English vs. French)" (2007, 284). The conflict is more persuasive because, as Cheadle points out, it does not follow a fixed pattern. The Sociologist's anglophone wife Megan encourages him to give up his English-language law studies—the fulfillment of his anglophile mother's dream that he is destined to become "un abogado brillante" (26)—in favour of a graduate degree in sociology at a French-language university. Yet even as progressive figures, such as the trilingual Megan, attempt to breach the barriers of language and culture, the divided city deprives the Sociologist of firm ground on which to found the hybridized identity that might rescue him. The final scene confirms the constitution of his masculinity as the merging of his successive responses to the cultures of the women in his life, a process initiated by his relationship with his mother. After his arrival in Canada, the Sociologist's sex drive bypasses Latin American women, concentrating entirely on *canadienses*; where his more decisive fellow refugees choose sides in the English–French debate, the Sociologist moves from his anglophone wife to a francophone lover. This pattern re-enacts the rupture with his mother provoked by his affair with Magdalena. Megan inherits aspects of the maternal role: she feels a rivalry with Magdalena (both Megan and the mother "deseaba[n] que Magdalena estuviera muerta") (150), she provides the Sociologist with the money for the plane ticket to attend his mother's funeral, and she educates him about Canadian society. Her symbolic initiation into this role occurs when, on the night of their first kiss, she picks him up off the Montreal winter ice after a fall. It is to Magdalena that the Sociologist's first-person monologues are directed. In the final scene, drunk and disoriented, the Sociologist symbolically returns to the womb, and to the Inferno of the Pinochet coup, by dancing with an older Chilean woman at a *Carifête* event, provoking the wrath of her Québécois husband, who stabs him and leaves him badly injured and possibly dying. This scene takes place in Parc Lafontaine, the site, during the 1960s and 1970s, of some of the most important demonstrations in support of Quebec independence. The Sociologist's attempt to reintegrate the *madre patria* leads to his death on ground sacred to the independence movement of his adopted "nation," into which the maternal Chilean woman has integrated, and which he has rebuffed by refusing the equivalency, asserted both by his left-wing Chilean friends and by Marcia, of Quebec nationalism with the Chilean struggle, and of Quebec as a "Latin-American" nation.

The Sociologist's family in Chile sees him as a failure because he has not done what is expected of a lower-middle-class Latin American man who gains access to the North American job market: acquire a technical skill and earn dollars. He imagines the judgments they will pass on him: "Si no tienes dinero eres un fracasado, si no tienes esposa quizás seas maricón, si no tienes hijos eres impotente o egoísta y algún día cuando estés viejo y solo te arrepentirás" (147). His non-conformist masculinity remains the object of hostility and suspicion.

While the women in his life guide his cultural decisions, the other side of the Sociologist's adoption of a form of masculinity that rejects the responsibilities of the *padre de familia* is the community of men with whom he pursues the dual goals of "transgressive" sexual relationships with women and political activism. His attempt at domesticity after his marriage to Megan alienates him from this community of males: "ellos comenzaron a considerarme como un perdido para la causa" (152). The Sociologist reconstructs his masculinity, in the aftermath of his divorce, when he becomes the roommate of João Roberto, who was a mathematics teacher in Angola before being forced into an exile which mirrors that of the protagonist. The novel portrays white Angolans, who fled a Marxist revolution in 1975, as the mirror-image of Chileans, who fled a right-wing military coup in 1973. As the Sociologist tells Megan's brother in Toronto, "no podían quedarse en Angola, que ellos consideran su país y que lloran todos los días" (100). In spite of their divergent political stances, the Sociologist and João Roberto share their respective experiences of exile and their constructions of masculine identity. The descriptions of the aquarium which separates their rooms reinforce this point. When the Sociologist looks in the direction of João Roberto's room, "yo veía mi cara reflejada" (13). In their sexual libertinism, in both cases a reaction, with its origins in the 1960s, against the norms of a conservative Catholic society, they find a common definition of self: "se asociaron como solteros que se respetaban con la promesa solemne de nunca dejar entrar el cepillo de dientes de sus amigas en el baño común... Cualquier insinuación de estabilidad, un rostro que apareciera por una tercera mañana en la cocina, alguien que ofreciera café con tostadas y que ya supiera dónde estaba el azúcar, hacía sonar las alarmas y entonces se conferenciaba y se releían los estatuos de la sociedad" (42).

In the end João Roberto breaks their pact by falling in love with a Portuguese girl. In this, as on the political front, the Sociologist is unable to bring his ideals to fruition. Like his *mirista* comrades back in Chile, he finds that an alternative society's rejection of the patriarchal ethos is not on its own enough to bring the patriarchal order to its knees.

One of the most striking features of *Cobro revertido* is its language: a colloquial Chilean Spanish, interspersed with bursts of Québécois slang, English, Portuguese (when João Roberto is speaking), and shards of Greek and other languages. The potpourri language and portmanteau words epitomize the fractured psyche of the exile. By contrast, Mauricio Segura's *Côte-des-Nègres* (1998), published only six years later but expressing the sensibility of a different generation, is written in erudite literary French. In an article published in 1994, Hugh Hazelton suggested that, while "Chilean or other specifically national literatures in the province may die out with the present generation of authors, Latin American literature as a whole in Quebec is almost certain to flourish as long as new immigrant writers continue to arrive" (132). Thirteen years later, few writers have emerged from among the Central American and Mexican migrations of the 1980s and 1990s, or the Colombian and Venezuelan migrations of the new millennium. The future of writing on Hispanic topics seems to rest with the children of immigrants, who write in French or English.

Côte-des-Nègres, which "received a warm reception from the French-language press" (Hazelton 2007, 26), is the most substantial contribution to this tradition in the field of fiction. The novel's dialogue is in colloquial Québécois; Spanish and Haitian Creole phrases appear almost as ornamentation. Segura, like Urbina, arrived in Canada in 1974, the difference being that he immigrated as an infant. Born in Temuco, in central Chile, in 1969, Segura studied economics at the Université de Montréal and later earned a Ph.D. in French literature from McGill University. His second novel, *Bouche-à-bouche* (2003), confirmed him as one of Quebec's most prominent younger novelists; his book-length essay *La Faucille et le Condor: le discours français sur l'Amérique latine, 1950–1985* (2005) helped to establish him as a commentator on Francophone perceptions of Latin American realities.

The title of Segura's first novel is the derogatory slang name for the Côte-des-Neiges area of Montreal, often considered "Canada's most multi-ethnic neighbourhood," since more than 110 languages are spoken in the district (Grescoe 2000, 41). Set in the early and mid-1980s, the novel describes the conflict between two teenage gangs, les Latino Power, who are led by Chileans, and les Bad Boys, who are Haitian. The protagonists, symbolic children of Urbina's Sociologist, are both more detached from and, in a paradoxical way, more identified with, Latin American cultural paradigms than are the exile figures of the earlier novel. In *Côte-des-Nègres,* parents remain in the background. It is life outside the home that shapes the young people's self-definition. Spurning the structures of the traditional Latin American family, the young men construct their masculinity through their public image as "Latinos." This Anglophone-US definition of Hispanic youth, funnelled through Québécois perceptions, becomes, in cultural terms, a void. The characters display no knowledge of US-Latino music or popular culture and have only disregard for the preoccupations of their parents, which revolve around nostalgia for left-wing Chilean politics of the 1970s and foreign sports such as soccer. All the boys, whether of Latin American, Haitian or Asian ancestry, decry the fact that their relatives in their parents' countries of origin, "[ne] savent pas ce que c'est, le hockey" (Segura 1998, 45).[4] Since the Latin American boys share a language—Québécois French—a fascination with hockey, and a residual Catholicism with their Haitian rivals and their Québécois, Italian, and Lebanese Christian classmates, it is only their appearance, the ability to speak Spanish, and a vaguely conceived *machismo* which distinguish them from other young Québécois. The narrator stresses the label applied to the boys by intermittently referring to characters as "le Latino" or "les Latinos" rather than by their names. In terms of the categories of youth gangs identified by the Canadian Research Institute for Law and the Family, les Latino Power are a Type B gang. Such gangs are not formed for criminal purposes, "although criminal activity sometimes occurs spontaneously"; they are given to "gratuitous violence"; they do not exert deep commitment since "many members have other options in life"; and, above all, these gangs are "image-based" (Mellor et al. 2005, 7–8). Les Latino Power are burdened with an imagined Latin Americanness yet have no real experience of Latin American society; they are Québécois obliged to construct their identities outside a Québécois prism.

The novel's structure also relies on Latin American models. The themes, particularly the obsession with the *pandilla,* or gang of teenage boys, like many of the structural techniques, draw heavily on Mario Vargas Llosa's canonical novel about a Peruvian military academy, *La ciudad y los perros* (1962). The two novels share the theme of gang conflict. Both novels open with a theft that sets off a chain of events leading to the murder of a young man. Segura adopts Vargas Llosa's technique of *"vasos comunicantes,"* in which present and past dialogue are intercalated to project the reader directly into flashbacks. As in *La ciudad y los perros,* the identity of a central narrator in *Côte-des-Nègres* remains obscured for most of the novel. Even the name Flaco, which camouflages Marcelo's identity, recalls Flaco Higueras, a character in Vargas Llosa's novel. Where Urbina's free-flowing, emotional, often humorous novel feels influenced by English-language fiction, Segura's work, although written in French, depends on a kind of Latin American formalism that the author seems to have learned by rote. *Côte-des-Nègres* is self-consciously Latin American in a way that *Cobro revertido* is not; while parents are mostly absent in the novel, the shadow of Mario Vargas Llosa, one of the patriarchal giants of Latin American literature, bears down on the careful craftsmanship with which Segura interlocks scenes and temporal settings.

The narrative of *Côte-des-Nègres,* like those of many of Vargas Llosa's novels, employs a contrapuntal structure. One narrative thread follows four boys—one Haitian, one Chilean, one Japanese, one Russian—who are members of the track-and-field team that wins the Quebec relay race championship for ten-year-olds; the second narrative recounts the gang war between Chilean and Haitian sixteen-year-olds who attend the same secondary school. The attentive reader grasps that Cléo, the shy Haitian immigrant who is so innocent that he does not understand what the other boys are talking about when they ask him if he has had a sexual experience, is also CB, the ferocious leader of les Bad Boys in the second narrative; Flaco, the diffident, cerebral leader of les Latino Power, who dreams of being a writer, is revealed at the novel's conclusion to be Marcelo, the Chilean track athlete of the first narrative stream. The first narrative recounts Cléo's integration into the track team, the rise of his friendship with Marcelo, and its eventual collapse; the second narrative, initiated by two Latino Power members' theft from CB's school locker of the condor that his now arch-enemy Marcelo/ Flaco gave him when they were children, describes a spiral of violence that concludes with CB's death in a confrontation with les Latino Power and the police.

Fathers, although remote or absent, become the source of the *machista* code which the boys view as their most tangible cultural inheritance. Even the girls pursued by the Chilean and Haitian youths are from their own communities. Flaco's long-time girlfriend Paulina reflects his integrationist aspirations: she is a Latina who does not look like a Latina: "La première fois qu'il l'a rencontrée... il avait été frappé par son look peu typique pour une Latino-Américaine. Ses cheveux châtain clair sont toujours relevés en queue de cheval, son visage est fin et légèrement basané et elle a toujours un air élancé, sportif" (61). The sexual aesthetic of Urbina's Sociologist is incarnated in Segura's novel by Enrique, an older boy who grew up in Santiago, where, "à cause des filles en mini-jupe, on se promenait bandé toute la journée" (262–63). Enrique, like the older generation of Chilean men, sees the racial diversity of Montreal society as an opportunity for sexual tourism; he boasts of sleeping with girls of many cultures and ridicules Flaco for going out with a Chilean girl. The other boys reject Enrique's tastes (234); yet, in an important paradox, the women from the young men's own cultures have the capacity to save them precisely because they are not afraid to communicate with people who are culturally different from them. Flaco lives and CB dies in the novel's penultimate scene because Paulina is not afraid to communicate with the Montreal police. The pivotal scene in the boys' childhood friendship, delayed to the final pages by the novel's contrapuntal structure, reveals that CB's artistic mother, Carole, committed suicide when he was ten. Carole, like the maternal Paulina, is a figure who bridges cultures. Flaco's parents buy a Haitian mask Carole has made out of a belief that immigrants should help each other; she facilitates Flaco's acceptance into her son's circle of family and friends because, like many educated Haitians, she speaks Spanish: "*Dios mío*, elle parlait ta langue!" (103). Deprived of the female principle, which is portrayed as drawing cultures together, the boys fall back on a deterritorialized male ethos. This outlook values strength, scorns communication, and, for this reason, proves impotent in influencing cross-cultural events in the larger society.

The irony of the *machismo* vaunted by les Latino Power is that the young men reinscribe, in the Canadian context, a male code which young men of the generation of Urbina's Sociologist attempted to subvert through the adoption of transgressive styles. This may also be a question of social class, since the parents of the boys in Segura's novel, although left-wing, are working-class, and back in Chile were more likely to have been rank-and-file members of the Communist Party than MIR rebels. The *machista* code, however, is the sole criterion by which these young men, feeling excluded by their parents' culture and attending an ethnically fragmented school that refutes any notion of a "mainstream" Montreal society, construct their image of themselves as males on the brink of adulthood. The novel opens and closes with the high school's Director haranguing the students against the pitfalls of ethnic identifications: "Quelques individus depuis quelques mois tentent de nous diviser en ghettos.... Au fin fond, nous sommes tous des frères!" (19). Interviewed by Noah Richler for his CBC series on place in contemporary Canadian fiction, Segura said: "For me the novel asks the question 'How can we live together?' or even 'Is it *possible* for us all to live together?'" (qtd. in Richler 2006, 374). The Director's insincere expression of hackneyed sentiments raises serious doubts about this latter question; the doubts, which persist throughout the novel, appear to be confirmed at the conclusion when the Director's second jeremiad against ethnic identification closes with the announcement that the school will be installing metal detectors.

The *machista* code provides the boys with their only articulated aspirations. When Pato, one of the Latinos who robs the condor from CB's locker, is being tortured by the Haitians in reprisal, the reader is told: "Pato ferme les yeux et s'efforce de pleurer en silence. Comme un homme, se dit-il" (41). Flaco, the protagonist, admits to himself: "Il ne veut qu'une chose: qu'on le respecte" (54). This need underlies his loyalty to the *pandilla*, from which he would like to escape, but which he cannot abandon. The other gang members tolerate his love of reading only because he is their leader, voicing their opinion that "les romans étaient juste bons pour les tapettes" (126). The vision of *machismo* as a banner of Latino identity is underlined when Flaco falls back on dictums in Spanish when rallying his followers, to whom he usually speaks in French, for battle: "Il faut toujours être aux aguets. *El que pestañea pierde*.... Celui qui cligne les yeux est fichu, comme dit mon père" (130). Flaco must translate his father's credo into French to ensure that his followers understand it; but the words gain authority from originating in Spanish, as the words of the father. Even so, the relationship between father and son is distant. The father's life revolves around the annual Coupe Allende, a soccer competition among Latino men held in a local park. Combining a foreign sport (soccer) with foreign politics (exemplified by Salvador Allende), the competition confirms the rift between generations. When Flaco passes a Coupe Allende match by chance and catches his father's eye, "il a cru un instant que son vieux détournerait la tête, mais après quelques secondes troubles, celui-ci lui a fait un vague salut de la main. Pourquoi cette hésitation? A-t-il honte de lui?" (239).

Reversing the pattern of *Cobro revertido*, where the Sociologist is brought up to disdain his unsuccessful father, Flaco realizes that his father despises him. In spite of having embraced a code which promotes patriarchal and *machista* Latin American values, the son has offended his father by leading a gang which moves outside the traditional social structures of the Latin American immigrant community. Yet when, after the stabbing of the Haitian youth Mixon by a member of les Latino Power, Flaco tries to defuse the crisis and leave the gang, the two traditional pillars of patriarchal Latin American society, the church and the *padre de familia*, fail him. He attends mass, but when he includes in his confession information about Mixon's stabbing, the priest refuses to listen: "je crois qu'un policier pourrait mieux t'aider que moi" (209). Flaco turns to his father, who, in one of the novel's most striking scenes, refuses to listen to his son's problems, turning the *machista* code into a pretext for abdicating from his parental responsibilities: "Non, Flaco. T'es un adulte maintenant. Tu vas prendre tes décisions tout seul" (246). Failed by both of the institutions in which he professes belief, Flaco turns to violence to resolve his problems; only Paulina's intervention with the police saves him. He lives because his Chilean girlfriend preserves his connection with the *madre patria*; the death of CB's mother Carole has severed this connection, casting him into a deterritorialized void even deeper than that with which Flaco must contend. For this reason it is CB who dies.

Yet fathers do not hold sole responsibility for propelling their sons towards violence. Near the novel's conclusion the reader learns that as Cléo grows up, his mother stops speaking to him: "elle ne lui adressait presque plus la parole: il lui rappelait trop son père, disait-elle" (280). One of the successes of *Côte-des-Nègres* is that the descriptions of the internal dynamics of the Chilean and the Haitian families are equally confident and authoritative. In this sense, Segura writes as a Québécois novelist, grounding himself in the larger society in a way that is available neither to his characters nor to an exiled writer such as Urbina. In light of the revelations of the novel's final chapters, the conflict between les Bad Boys and les Latino Power may be viewed as a struggle between two cultures, one originating in a matriarchal West Indian context and the other in a patriarchal South American context, which resort to hollow forms of self-assertion as a result of having been stripped of their sense of belonging. Cléo's older brother, who defines himself resolutely as Haitian and not Canadian, tells him: "y'a rien au monde de plus triste que quelqu'un qui connaît mal ses origines" (195). The gangs fragment at the novel's close, but the cultural patterns persist. The morning after CB is shot by the police, Ketcia, the sole female member of les Bad Boys, emerges as the heir apparent to his authority. De-Canadianized by violence, she sees her own features in the mirror, "comme si on avait posé un masque haïtien sur son visage... elle s'est juré de poursuivre le combat: l'aventure des Bad Boys ne s'arrêtera pas là" (287). Ketcia's retreat into an identity that is purely Haitian symbolizes les Bad Boys' return to the matriarchal roots of their ancestral culture: the image of her face as a Haitian mask evokes the masks made by CB's mother, Carole. Like Paulina, Ketcia becomes a mother figure. In tandem with Flaco and Paulina's reconciliation and the introduction of metal detectors in the school, Ketcia's vow to continue the gang war presages a hardening of cultural enclaves. Even though the mere existence of a novel such as *Côte-des-Nègres*, with its sympathetic and informed depiction of two different cultures, appears to suggest otherwise, the novel's action and structure insist that the second generation of Latino males, in common with young people from other immigrant groups, are even more severely deterritorialized than the exiles from whom they are descended.

This deterritorialization suggests that future Latino-Canadian writing is likely to continue to diverge from US-Latino literature in significant ways. First, for historical reasons, the dream of a "*reconquista*" of territory that once belonged to Spain or Mexico—an anxiety that animates the work of US-Latino writers as dramatically different from one another as Gómez-Peña and Goldman—is unimaginable in the Canadian context. Even more significantly, Latin American–Canadian cultural identity is blurred by its merging—both in Canadian public discourse, where the term "visible minority" remains a common catch-all, and in its political alliances—with the identities of other marginalized immigrant groups. In contrast to Miami or Los Angeles, where Black and Hispanic residents live in different districts and often regard each other with suspicion, in Canadian cities it is more common for Black and Latin American communities to occupy the same "immigrant neighbourhoods" and, at least in some cases, to recognize their parallel conditions. Nothing illustrates this more clearly than the case of Freddy Villanueva, an 18-year-old Montrealer of Honduran origin who, although unarmed, was shot dead by police in Montréal-Nord on 10 August 2008. The protests sparked by this incident, which included both peaceful demonstrations and a night of violent rioting, saw Black and Latin American youths working together. Black community leaders called for a public enquiry; a Haitian-Québécois rap group recorded a song to honour Villanueva's memory. Black, white, and Latin American residents declared the foundation of "Montréal-Nord Républik," a community organization devoted to "liberating" the neighbourhood from the oppression of the City of Montreal and its police force. The existence of this organization—complete with a website (http://www.montrealnordrepublik.blog spot.com) devoted to documenting the Villanueva case—illustrates that "lateral racism" between Haitian and Latin American youths fades away before the predominant problem of relations with the authority structures of Quebec and Canadian society.[5] Mauricio Segura was invited by the public affairs magazine *L'Actualité* to host a blog dealing with the Villanueva case; on 11 September 2008, he participated in a panel discussion on *BazzoTV*, Marie-France Bazzo's interview show on Télé-Québec, of the riots unleashed by Villanueva's shooting. In her introduction, Bazzo deplored the fact that the riots had occurred in the culturally integrated context of "une communauté noire-latino-catholique parlant français" (BazzoTV). Segura responded by downplaying the racial dimension of the shooting and the subsequent riots. He stated that: "Le fond du problème pour moi c'est vraiment un problème socio-économique" (BazzoTV). It is from the agglomerated contexts of such "noire-latino-catholique" communities, and their variants in other provinces, that future Canadian writing by authors of Latin American origin is most likely to arise, in Canada's two official languages. This development underlines both the integration of the children of Urbina's generation of exiles into one branch of Canadian society, and the persistence of their frustration in being unable to move beyond this fringe status characterized by economic insecurity and enduring identification as "immigrants."

Notes

1 Gómez-Peña's glossary contains the word "Chicanadians," which the author defines as "Second generation Mexicans living in Canada and/or children of Mexican and Canadian parents living in the U.S." (1996, 241). The definition demonstrates that even counterculture US commentators are not immune to the all-American virus of taking for granted that Canadian history is identical to that of the US. Since substantial Mexican immigration to Canada began only in the late 1980s, the number of "second-generation Mexicans living in Canada" at the time of the book's publication in 1996 would have been microscopic (and most of them would have been in diapers). Gómez-Peña displays the same ignorance of Canadian history—in this case of the founding role of Chilean and Argentine immigrants of the 1970s—as US cultural arbiters on the political right. However, it needs to be said that, just as some early popular manifestations of African-Canadian culture consisted of imitations of African-American culture that obscured the distinctive traits of Black Canadian culture, so, too, some of the first Latin American–Canadian writers to use English as their literary language adopt the assumptions of writers such as Gómez-Peña in their struggle to define a Latin American–Canadian identity. Guillermo Verdecchia, a playwright of Argentine descent who spent part of his upbringing in Kitchener, Ontario, cites Gómez-Peña approvingly and imitates his vocabulary: "We can go forward. Towards the centre, towards the border" (Verdecchia 1993, 78). Whether such a vision presages a wholesale absorption of Anglophone Latin American–Canadian culture into US Latino culture, or whether, as in the African-Canadian case, imitation is simply the first step on the road to a vision that is both ethnically particular and particularly Canadian, it is too early to say.
2 The MIR version of masculinity is incarnated in *Cobro revertido* by the figure of Macías, "el representante del pueblo resistente... se largaba una enorme y lírica diarrhea sobre la organización de la insurrección armada... y casi siempre terminaba en la cama de alguna doncella sudorosa que le pedía que dejara la boina puesta" (Urbina 1992, 87). Macías combines a commitment to armed revolution with a "transgressive" masculine personal style.

3 Subsequent references to this novel appear as page numbers in parentheses in the text.
4 Subsequent references to this novel appear as page numbers in parentheses in the text.
5 The author is grateful to Joubert Satyre for discussing the dynamics of interracial interactions in Montreal and "lateral racism" with him.

References

Bazzo.tv. 2008. Télé-Québec, 11 September. http://www.bazzo.tv/occurence.aspx?id=27&rub=1.
Brown, C., ed. 1997. *The illustrated history of Canada.* Toronto: Key Porter.
Cheadle, N. 2007. Canadian counterpoint: Don Latino and Doña Canadiense in José Leandro Urbina's *Collect Call* (1992) and Ann Ireland's *Exile* (2002). In *Canadian cultural exchange/échanges culturels au Canada*, ed. N. Cheadle, and L. Pelletier, 269–304. Waterloo: Wilfrid Laurier Univ. Press.
Goldman, F. 2004. *The divine husband.* New York: Atlantic Monthly Press.
Gómez-Peña, G. 1996. *The new world border: Prophecies, poems and loqueras for the end of the century.* San Francisco: City Lights.
Grescoe, T. 2000. *Sacré blues: An unsentimental journey through Quebec.* Toronto: Macfarlane Walter and Ross.
Hazelton, H. 1994. Quebec Hispánico: Themes of exile and integration in the writing of Latin Americans living in Quebec. *Canadian Literature* 142–43 (Fall): 120–35.
———. 2005. Una literatura nueva: La latinocanadiense. Exposition at Concordia University, Montreal, Québec. February 18. http://www.artsandscience.concordia.ca/cmll/spanish/antonio/Hugh_Hazelton_Nace_nueva_literatura.
———. 2007. *LatinoCanadá. A critical study of ten Latin American writers of Canada.* Montreal and Kingston: McGill-Queen's Univ. Press.
Mallon, F. E. 2003. Barbudos, warriors and rotos: The MIR, masculinity, and power in the Chilean agrarian reform, 1965–1974. In *Changing men and masculinities in Latin America*, ed. M. C. Guttman. Durham and London: Duke Univ. Press.
Mellor, B., L. MacRae, M. Pauls, and J. P. Hornick. 2005. Youth gangs in Canada: A preliminary review of programs and services. Calgary: Canadian Research Institute for Law and the Family. September. http://www.ucalgary.ca/~crilf/publications/Youth_Gang_Report.pdf.
Montréal-Nord Républik. 2009. http://www.montrealnordrepublik.blogspot.com/.
Pathfinders and passageways: The Spanish explore the West Coast. n.d. Library and Archives Canada. http://www.collectionscanada.ca/explorers/h24_1710_e.html.
Richler, N. 2006. *This is my country, what's yours? A literary atlas of Canada.* Toronto: McClelland and Stewart.
Segura, M. 1998. *Côte-des-Nègres.* Montréal: Boréal Express.
Urbina, J. L. 1992. *Cobro revertido.* Santiago, Chile: Editorial Planeta.
Verdecchia, G. 1993. *Fronteras Americanas/American borders.* Toronto: Coach House Press.

Contributors

Norman Cheadle is associate professor in the Department of Modern Languages and Literatures at Laurentian University. Cheadle is the author of *The Ironic Apocalypse in the Novels of Leopoldo Marechal* (2000), co-editor of *Canadian Cultural Exchange: Translation and Transculturation* (2007) published by Wilfrid Laurier UP, and author of refereed articles such as "Twentieth-Century *homo bonaerense*: The Buenos Aires 'Man-in-the-Street,'" "'El Aleph' y *Adán Buenosayres*. El flaco, el gordo y el populismo argentino," "Los intelectuales y el caso Pinochet: ¿canto de cisne de una figura centenaria?" and "Rememorando la historia decimonónica desde *La tierra del fuego* de Sylvia Iparraguirre."

Maria L. Figueredo is associate professor in the Department of Languages, Literatures and Linguistics at York University. Figueredo is already considered a Canadian specialist in the relationships between literature and music in their specific socio-political contexts. Her doctoral dissertation (1999) initiated work in this area and led to the publication of her book, *Poesía y canto popular: Su convergencia en el siglo XX. Uruguay, 1960–1985*. This trained musician and academic has also published articles such as: "Rhythm Nation: Negotiating Notions of Place, Belonging and History in the Process of Setting Poetry to Song," "Latin American Song as an Alternative Voice in the New World Order," "El eterno retorno entre la poesía y la música popular," and "Entre la poesía oral y la escrita: la canción y la cultura literaria."

Jessica Franklin is a Ph.D. candidate in the Department of Political Science at McMaster University and is currently completing her dissertation entitled "Building From and Moving Beyond the State: The National and Transnational Dimensions of Afro-Brazilian Women's Activism." Her research has been supported by the Canada-Latin America and the Caribbean Research Exchange Grant (2007).

Rosario Gómez is associate professor of Spanish linguistics at the University of Guelph. Gómez is a co-author of a book on CD-ROM entitled *El mundo hispano* (Toronto: Canadian Academy of the Arts, 2008), and her doctoral thesis has been adapted into a book that is forthcoming from Iberoamericana / Vervuert

(Frankfurt and Madrid). She is the author of two articles dealing with pedagogy and the history of the Spanish language. She recently published a testing database to accompany the linguistics textbook *An Introduction to Language*, 4th ed. (Nelson Education, 2010). Gómez is also the coordinator of the Corpus of Spoken Spanish of Urban centers of Ecuador, PRESEEA (Proyecto Para Estudio Sociolingüístico del Español de España y América), University of Alcalá in Spain.

Susan Healey received her Ph.D. from the University of Guelph. Her dissertation traces the rise of the MAS in Bolivia through the lenses of counter-hegemony, organized dissent, and alternative notions of development. Healy lived and worked in Bolivia from 1989 to 1995. She has published articles in *Latin American Perspectives* and the *Canadian Journal of Development Studies*, a chapter in *Lifelong Citizenship Learning, Participatory Democracy and Social Change* (OISE/University of Toronto), as well as book reviews and newspaper op-eds on political change in Latin America. In 2004 Healy was awarded the Kari Polanyi-Levitt Prize by the Canadian Association for Studies in International Development (CASID) for the best graduate student essay in international development Studies. Healy has taught courses in political sociology, geography, and international political economy at Wilfrid Laurier University and the University of Waterloo.

Stephen Henighan is a professor of Spanish at the University of Guelph and a recognized Canadian fiction writer. He was a finalist for the Governor General's Literary Award in the category of English Non-Fiction for his debate-provoking book *When Words Deny the World: The Reshaping of Canadian Writing*. Henighan is the author of eleven books and numerous articles, reviews and conference presentations. Some of his books are: *The Streets of Winter*, *Lost Province: Adventures in a Moldovan Family*, *North of Tourism*, and *Assuming the Light: The Parisian Literary Apprenticeship of Miguel Ángel Asturias*. Henighan has also produced the first Canadian textbook for teaching Spanish, and he has translated books from Portuguese to English. His own work has been translated to other languages.

Amy Huras received her B.A. from the University of Guelph, her M.Phil. from the University of Cambridge, and she is a Ph.D. candidate at the University of Toronto. Research for her Ph.D. thesis has been funded by SSHRC.

Janelle Joseph is a Ph.D. candidate at the University of Toronto. In the area of sports, culture, and transnationality, Joseph has published the following articles: "The Logical Paradox of the Cultural Commodity: Selling an *Authentic* Afro-Brazilian Martial Art in Canada," in the *Sociology of Sport Journal*, and "Going to Brazil: Transnational and Corporeal Movement of a Canadian-Brazilian Martial Arts Community," in *Global Networks*. Joseph is the winner of the

Sport Information Resource Centre's 2005 Community Research Award for her essay "A Perfect Match: Brazilian Martial Arts and the Canadian Multiculturalism Act."

Lee L'Clerc is assistant professor at the University of Guelph. He is a mid-career Canadian painter with a Ph.D. in literature from the University of Toronto. He has had a number of solo and group exhibitions both nationally and internationally, and has published "(Homo)Posing the Flesh in Virgilio Piñera's *La carne de René*" in *Revista Canadiense de Estudios Hispánicos* and "Saint Sebastian: A Body Caught Up in Representation" for the Justina M. Barnicke Gallery. L'Clerc is presently working on a book on Cuban art and literature.

Jennifer Martino received her M.A. from the interdisciplinary Latin American and Caribbean graduate program at the University of Guelph. She has worked for different NGOs in Haiti, Nicaragua, Uruguay, and Peru.

Jorge Nef is University Professor Emeritus at the University of Guelph and a Professor of Government and International Affairs at the University of South Florida where he was Director of Latin American and Caribbean Studies. He has published, edited, and co-edited sixteen books and special issues of journals. His most recent publications include: *The Democratic Challenge* (London: Palgrave/Macmillan, 2009), *Capital, Power, and Inequality in Latin America* (Boulder: Rowman and Littlefield, 2008), *Managing Development in a Global Context* (also published by Palgrave/Macmillan of the UK), and *Inter American Relations in an Era of Globalization: Beyond Unilateralism?* (Toronto: De Sitter 2007). Nef is also author or co-author of 115 academic articles in books and journals. Nef's poetry is published in his book, *La región perdida* (Madrid: Betania 1997) and in numerous literary anthologies.

Pablo Ramírez is associate professor at the University of Guelph, where he teaches nineteenth-century American literature and US Latina/o Studies. He received his Ph.D. in American Cultures from the University of Michigan and has published essays and chapters on Chicana/o literature in *The Canadian Review of American Studies*, *Frontieres*, *Journal of American Studies*, and *Questions of Identity in Detective Fiction*. He also has forthcoming articles and chapters in *Aztlán: Journal of Chicana/o Studies* and *Bordered Sexualities*. He is currently working on a project titled, "Consent of the Conquered: Mexican-Anglo Romances and Contractual Freedom in Nineteenth-Century America."

Alejandra Roncallo teaches at York University and at the University of Toronto-Mississauga, and has also taught at the Universities of Western Ontario and Ryerson. She takes an interdisciplinary approach to the study of the Americas, and has published articles in the *Canadian Journal of Development Studies* and

Hechos del Callejón—a journal of the United Nations Development Program of Colombia—and a chapter in *Between the Lines*. She holds an M.A. in Public and International Affairs from the University of Pittsburgh and a Ph.D. in Political Science from York University.

Frans J. Schryer is a professor emeritus in the Department of Sociology and Anthropology at the University of Guelph. Schryer is the author of four books, of which two deal with Mexico: *The Rancheros of Pisaflores* (Univ. of Toronto Press, 1980) and *Ethnicity and Class Conflict in Rural Mexico* (Princeton Univ. Press, 1990). He is also the author of seventeen refereed articles and seven book chapters, including "Native Peoples of Central Mexico since Independence" in *The Cambridge History of the Native Peoples of the Americas*, Vol. 2: Mesoamerica, Part 2 (1999).

Dragan Sekaric Shex received a university degree from the School of Architecture in Sarajevo but drifted from architecture to painting. In Rome he took advanced studies in fine art. After this period of learning and artistic experimentation in Italy, he moved to Montreal. Currently Shex works from his studio in Toronto. He has exhibited across the Mediterranean countries of Europe, in Cuba, the US, and in fine galleries in Montreal and Toronto. He has received numerous professional awards and won first prize in several prestigious art contests.

Adrian Smith is a Ph.D. candidate in the Institute of Comparative Law, Faculty of Law at McGill University. Smith is the author of one scholarly article, "Legal Consciousness and Resistance in Caribbean Seasonal Workers" (*Canadian Journal of Law and Society* 20.2, 2005), two chapters in books: "Transnational Labour Law, Global Governance & the Caribbean" and "A Transnational Turn for/from 'the Worst': Labour Law, Globalization and the Wretched of the Earth," and three book reviews.

Gordana Yovanovich is professor of Latin American literature at the University of Guelph. She is the author of two books: *Play and the Picaresque: Lazarillo de Tormes, Libro de Manuel and Match Ball*, and *Julio Cortázar's Character Mosaic*, both published by the University of Toronto Press, and editor of *The New World Order: Corporate Agenda and Parallel Reality* published by McGill-Queen's University Press. She has also published articles such as: "Intelligence Agenda and the Need for Constructive Intellectual Intervention in the New World Order," "Play as a Mode of Empowerment for Women and as a Model for Poetics in the Early Poetry of Nicolás Guillén," and "The Role of Women in Julio Cortázar's *Rayuela*."

Index

Abbeele, Georges Van Den, 220, 231n6
Abril rojo, xxiii, xxiv, 236, 239, 246–52
Academy Awards, 257
Afro-Brazilian martial art. *See* capoeira
Afro-Brazilian Studies and Research Institute, 101
Afro-Brazilian women, 97–112, 112n1–3; human rights and, 108–11; mobilization of, 101–3
"Afro-Brazilian Women's Identities and Activism," xii
Afro-Caribbean women's network, 106–7
Afro-Latin American women's network, 106–7
agriculture, 16; in Alto Balsas, 54, 57, 66–67; Canadian, 119–20, 123–24, 131
Aguirre, Carmen, 274
Alameda Theatre, 274
Alba, Gaspar de, 281–82
Alcoff, Linda Martin, ix
Alexander, Jeffery, 238
Allende, Isabel, xii
Allende, Salvador, 174, 179, 259, 296
Alliance for Progress, xi, 4, 8
Althusser, Louis, 155
Alto Balsas, xvi, 53–75, 75n11; agriculture in, 54, 57, 66–67; *amate* painting and, 57–59, 62, 68, 72; background and diversity of, 54–57; cargo system of, 54; craft industry and, 57–59; dam project in, 59–61, 62; education in, 56–57; globalization and, 59, 60, 61; global labour market and, 62–71; label of, 61; languages of, 54–55, 65, 66, 70, 71; migrant workers and, 52–53, 56, 62–70; mule skinners of, 55–56; Nuhua migrants to Houston, 67–70; religion in, 55, 71
"Alturas de Machu Picchu," 175–76
Amaru, Tupac, 175
Amazon Basin, 33, 44, 45
"the Americas," xv, 5–7
Ameyaltepec, 54, 57
Ammann, Jean-Christophe, 225
Amura, Tupac, 40
Andean cosmology, xv, 37–41
André, Irving, 128, 131
Andrews, George Reid, 99
Angola, 292
Anzaldúa, Gloria, 273, 274, 282
Aparicio, Frances, 277
Apasa, Julián, 40
Apiaguaiqui, "*El Tumpa*", 41
Appadurai, Arjuu, 146–47
Approaches to World Order, 4
Ardiente paciencia, 257
Aretino, Pietro, 262
Argentina: elections in, xviii; Guillermo Verdecchia and, 281–82; military in, 15; Mothers of the Plaza de Mayo and, 258, 270
Arte de pájaros, 177
Arte Povera, xxiii, 218, 225, 226
astronomy, 38
Ayacucho, Peru, 240, 246, 247
Aymaras, 31, 33, 34, 39–43
Aztecs, 54, 276
Aztlán, 276

Bachelet, Michelle, xviii, 17
Badiou, Alain, 161
baggattaway, 197
Bairros, Luiza, 102

Balcells, Carmen, xi
Banderas, Antonio, 149, 278
Barbet, Miguel, 258
Barral, Carlos, xi
baseball, 199
Basoalto, Ricardo Reyes, 176
Basque language, 288
bateria, 200
Bazzo, Marie-France, 298
BazzoTV, 298
Beauvoir, Simone de, 170
Belén, Ana, 179
Benedetti, Mario, 145, 167
Benítez-Rojo, Antonio, xxv, 145, 161n2
Beres, Derek, 173
Berlin Wall, xx
Bhabha, Homi, 222, 223, 224
Bianchi, Vicente, 178
Bickford, Louis, 242
bin Laden, Osama, 280
Biografía de un cimarrón, 258
Bishop, Claire, 226, 232n15
Bjork, 154
black identity, 99, 100
black militants, 100
Black Women's House of Culture, 98
Bolivia, 27–46; Agrarian Reform, 41–42; Catholic missions in, 36–37; COB in, 42; coca production, 28, 30, 31; Constitution of, 44–45; election (2002), 27–28; election (2005), 27, 28; ethno-ecology of, 29, 32–37; geography of, 32–33; Great Rebellion of, 39–41; identity and class in, 29–32, 46n7; independence of, 37; indigenous peoples of, 27–31; indigenous resistance in, 37–41; labour unions in, 42; language and education in, xviii, 45, 87; Movimiento al Socialismo (MAS), 27, 28, 30, 31; National Revolution in, 33, 41, 175; natural resources of, 28, 29, 33, 34; neoliberalism and, 29; Popular Participation Law, 30; sacred and profane in, 38–39; US power and, 28
Bolland, Nigel, 128
Boom. See Latin American Boom
borderlands, 273–84; collective memory and, 281–83; US–Mexico, 62–71, 74, 276–77
Borderlands/La Frontera, 273, 282
Borges, Jorge Luis, xi–xii, 167
Borja, President, 85
Bouche-à-bouche, 293
bracero program, 62
Brazil: African diaspora in, xviii, 97, 99, 105–8, 111; Bahai and, 201; black women in, 97–112; black women's organizations in, 102, 107, 109; capoeira and (*see* capoeira); Constitution of, 102; democracy in, 100, 110, 201; discrimination in, 98, 101, 109–10; economy of, 100, 170; education in, 101; feminism in (*see* feminism); human rights in (*see* human rights); local women's activism in, 104–5; male organizations in, 102–3; military in, 8, 15, 172–73; music in, xxi, 168, 172–73, 183, 191n13; population census (2000), 101; racial democracy and, 201; racial disparities in, 101–3; racism, 97, 99, 100, 101, 102, 109–11; self-identification in, 101; sexism in, 101, 102, 111; universities in, 101, 103, 110; US power and, 101
Brazilian Duos, 172
Brazilian Network of Black Women's Organizations, 106
Buenavista Social Club, 152, 157
Burgos, Elizabeth, 258
Bush, George (Jr.), 13, 15
Bush, George (Sr.), 259
Byrne, David, 158

CAFTA, 19
Caldwell, Kia Lilly, 100
Camilo, Marcial, 72
campesinos, xv–xvi, 29, 30, 31, 38, 46n5; identity construction and, 41–42; syndicate, 41–42
Canada: African and Afro-Brazilian culture in, 207; blacks in, 211–12; capoeira in (*see* capoeira); discrimi-

INDEX   307

nation in, 211; employment standards in, 121–26; Hispanic immigration and, 288; Hispanic population of, 288; *Immigration and Refugee Protection Act*, 121; immigration to, 117–24, 132–34; imperialism and, 119, 124; Latino stereotypes and, 278–79; Spanish Empire and, 288; SWAP and, 117–34; US border with, 277, 278
Canadian Research Institute for Law and the Family, 293
Canclini, Néstor García, vii, 171, 259
Canto General, 168, 174–76, 178–80, 183
capoeira, xx, xxii, 197–213; in Brazil, 201; Caribbean-Canadians and, 209–12; class, age, gender and, 203–6; commodification and, 206–9; contact zone and, 199–200; Jamaican-Canadians and, 203, 209, 210; martial art, 197; *Mestre* Bimba and, 201; *mestres* and, 203, 205, 206; music and, 200, 202, 210–11, 213n1; *roda* and, 200, 202, 203, 204, 205, 208; rules of, 200–1; *tesoura* and, 205; transculturation and, 198–200, 209, 212
Capoeira Beyond Brazil, 209
capoeira schools, 197
capoeiristas, 197, 200–10
Caqui, Doris, 245
Cardoso, Fernando Henrique, 101
Caribbean sojourners, 117–34
Carifête, 289, 290, 291
Carneiro, Sueli, 104, 105
Carpentier, Alejo, viii, 160, 262
Carter, Jimmy, 10
Castillo, Héctor Antón, 219
Castro, Fidel, xx, 151, 219, 220, 221, 225
Catholic University of Quito, 80, 90
Ccente, Celistino, 240, *241*
Cela, José, 258
Celant, German, 226
Cementerio de barcos, 229–30
Center for Inter-American Relations, xi
Central Obrera Boliviana (COB), 28
Cevasco, Laria Elisa, 104
CFTA-DR, 5

Changing men and masculinities in Latin America, xxvii
Chávez, Hugo, 15
Cheadle, Norman, xx, xxi, xxii, 290
Chicanos, 276–77
Chile, 271n4; Antonio Skármeta and, 257; civil war in, 174; democracy in, 180; elections in, xviii; military in, 15, 179, 291, 292; music in, 162n11, 178; poverty in, 17
Chilean Communist Party, 289
Chinese Canadian National Council, 278
Chomsky, Noam, 264
Choquehuanca, David, 30, 41
CIA, xi
Cien años de soledad, viii
Citizenship and Immigration Canada (CIC), 121
civil wars, 15
Cobro revertido, xxvi, 289, 292, 296–97, 299n2
Cold War, xx, 4, 7, 14, 174
Collins, Patricia Hill, 105
Colombia: elections in, 14; human rights in, 13; military in, 15
colonization, 99
Comisión de la Verdad y Reconciliación (CVR), xxiii, 235–36, 250–51, 252
communism, vii, xiv, 4, 8, 18, 257, 266; Chile and, 259, 289, 290, 296; Peru and, 235
Confederation of Indigenous Nationalities of Ecuador, xviii, 85, 87
Confederation of Indigenous Nations of Ecuador (CONAIE), 43, 85
Congress for Cultural Freedom, xi
Consejo de Pueblos Nahuas del Alto Balsas (CPNAB), 59, 60
Convention for the Elimination of All Forms of Racial Discrimination (CERD), 109
Convention on the Elimination of All Forms of Discrimination Against Women (CEDAW), 109
Cooder, Ry, 152; Cooder–Wenders, 157
corporate elites, 6
Correa, Rafael, 84

corruption, 3, 13
Cortázar, Julio, x, 246
Costa Rica, 14, 244
Côte-des-Nègres, xxvi–xxvii, 292–99
Côte-des-Neiges, 293
Cox, Robert, 4
craft industry, 57–59
Crane, Susan, 236, 237, 244–45, 251, 274, 275
Crenshaw, Kimberle, 105
creolization, xix, 119, 127–28, 136n8, 138n18
cricket, 197
criminal cartels, 69
Criola, 104, 107
Crystal David, 89
Cuba: anti-Castro generation and, 148; culture of, 145–46, 148, 149, 157, 161, 162n7; economy of, 147–48; globalization and, 3, 145–61; health care in, 147; *La regata* and (*see La regata*); Latin American culture and, xi; *los balseros* and, xxiii, 218, 219, 220, 221, 226, 231n7; Miami and, 148–50, 220, 221, 225; Marielitos and, 221, 231n7; music in (*see under* music); rafter crisis and, 217–21, 222, 228; television, the internet and, 149; tourism and, 147; US and, xi, 19, 145, 148–50, 151, 161n4
Cuban Americans, xx, xxiii
Cuban Revolution, vii, x, xi, xx, xxi, 4, 148, 150
Cuevas-Mohr, Hugo, 167

D'Allemand, Patricia, 176
Dario, Rubén, xiii, 184
Dávila, Arlene, 149
Davis, Angela, 104
Death in Venice, 258
de-democratization, 17–21
Délano, Poli, 269
del Prado, Rita, 156, 157, 160
democracy, 12–14; in Brazil, 100, 110, 201; in Chile, 180; dictatorships and, 9; elites and, xv; neoliberalism and,

10; racial, 99, 100, 101; US politics and, 3, 8, 21
Díaz, Clara, 151, 156, 162n6
dictatorships. *See* regimes
Diederichsen, Diedrich, 152–53, 154
"Discovery of the Americas," xiii, xv, 43
The divine husband, 287
Documentation of Endangered Languages, 89
Donoso, José, xi
drug trafficking, 69, 277
Durban Platform for Action, 111

Eastern Europe, 5
Echeverría, González, 175
economic policies: of Brazil, 100; debt crises and, 4, 5, 10–12, 20; financial stability and, 7; free-market, 12; inflation and, 6, 7; neoliberalism and, 8–10, 13–18
Ecuador: demographic shifts in, 81–82; economy of, 92n9; educational reform in, 85–86, 87–88; elites in, 82; indigenous peoples, politics and, 86–87; language and education in, xvii–xviii, 79–81, 83–92; language ideologies in, 83–84; linguistic diversity in, 80–81; Quichua, globalization and, 79–87; socio-cultural displacement in, 82–83; universities in, xviii, 80, 86, 88, 90, 91–92
Ecuadorian Education Plan, 85
El Caimán Barbudo, 151
El cartero de Neruda, 257
elections, xviii, 13–14, 21n8; Bolivia (2005), 27; Brazil, 98; US, 14, 19
El ojo que llora, xxiii, 236, 239, 242–46, 251
El reino de este mundo, viii
El Salvador, 277
Encounter, xi
Endangered Languages Fund, 89
environmental issues, 16
Erlmann, Veit, 147, 152, 156
Escobedo, Gustavo, 184
ethnic identity, 31–32

Ethno-techno: Writings on performance, activism and pedagogy, xxiv
The expediency of culture, xxi, 148
The Eye That Cries, xxiii, 236, 242, *243*, 244

Fagen, Richard, 4, 5
Fala Preta!, 109
La Faucille et le Condor: le discours français sur l'Amérique latine, 293
Feinberg, Joel, xxv
Feliú, Vicente, 158, 160
feminism: Afro-Brazilian women and, 97, 99, 102–5, 108; black, xviii, 97, 99, 103, 104; cultural debate and, 258; intersectionality and, 105; Marxist, 103; US, 103, 104
Fifth Havana Biennial, 217
Figueredo, Maria, xx, xxi, xxii, 151
"Five-Hundred Years of Resistance," xv, 43–44
Flores, Jenaro, 42
football and rugby, 199
Foreign Agricultural Resource Management Services (FARMS), 121
Franco, Jean, 257–58
Franklin, Jessica, xii, xviii, xix
Freyre, Gilberto, 99, 100
Friedman, Milton, 4
Friere, Paulo, 44
Fronteras Americanas, xxv, 273–84, 284n5
FTAA, 6
Fuentes, Carlos, x, xii, 246, 274
Funkenstein, Amos, 275

Gadsden Purchase, 288
Garay, Sindo, 156
García, Michael Hames, 282
Gasset, Ortega y, 262
GBS: Society for Endangered Languages, 89
Geledes, 109
Geledes Black Women's Institute, 98
Gil, Gilberto, 173
Gill, Stephen, 4
Ginga Capoeira (GC), 198, 200, 202–3. *See also* capoeira

Gisbert, Carlos Mesa, 28
Gitlin, Todd, 146
"global culture," 73
globalization, viii, ix, xii, xiv, xvi, xviii, xxi, 3, 7; Alto Balsas and, 59, 60, 61; Antonio Skármeta and, 257; black cultures and, 106; capoeira and, 198; Cuba and, 145, 146, 148; ideology of, 264; *indigenas* and, 51–53, 60; indigenous peoples and, 88–89; inequality and, 51; migrant workers and, 122–23, 124, 131, 135n5; new forms of identity and, 70–71; organized crime and, 69; Quichua and, 79–92; as term, 51
Global Justice Movements, 18
Goldberg, Vicki, 242
Goldman, Francisco, 287
Gómez, Rosario, xvii, xviii
Gómez-Peña, Guillermo, xxiv, 274, 287, 299n1
Gonzalez, Leila, 104
government. *See* regimes
Guatemala: history of, 287; violence in, 258
Guerrero, Mexico, 53, 54, 56, 60, 61, 72
Guevara, Che, 149, 289
Guillén, Nicolás, 169
Gulf War, 259
Guttman, Matthew, xxvii

Hames-García, Michael, x
Hanns Seidel Foundation, 89
Harrington, David, 154, 156
H2-A worker program, xix
Hazelton, Hugh, 288, 292
health issues, 16
Healy, Susan, xiv, xv, xvi, xix
Hegel, G. W. F., viii, 153, 218
"The Heights of Macchu Picchu," 175–76
Helms-Burton law, 147
Hemingway, "Papa," 157
Henighan, Stephen, xxiv, xxv, xxvi, xxvii
Heringer, Rosana, 108–9
"Hispanic American Indians," 51

Hispanic Canadians, 287–99
Hite, Katherine, 245
Hollander, Kurt, 219, 220
"House," 181–82, 185
The House of Spirits, xii
Human Development Index, 6, 22n11
Human Development Index (HDI), 98
human rights, xviii–xix, xxiv–xxv, 13, 15, 17, 45, 83, 88, 89, 259, 266–67, 270; abuses of, 12; Afro-Brazilian women and, 108–11; black feminism and, 97, 99; Brazil's Constitution and, 102; Canada and, 259–60; ideology of, 266; local violations of, 258; memorial and, 244; Mothers of the Plaza de Mayo and, 258, 270; Peru and, 238–39
Hunt, Lynn, xxv
Hurricane Katrina, 16
Hussein, Saddam, 264

Ignatieff, Michael, xxv, 259–60, 264, 266, 269
Iguala (Guerrero), 54, 56
Il Postino, 257
Incas, 33, 35, 40
income disparities, 6, 17, 52
indígenas. *See* indigenous peoples
indigenous peoples: of Bolivia, 27–31; of Ecuador, 79–91; globalization and, 88–89; language and (*see* languages); of Mexico, 51–53, 55, 57, 65, 69, 72, 73, 75n1; rights of, 60
Indigenous Schooling Foundation, 85
Inter-American Court of Human Rights, 244
Inter-American Foundation for the Arts (IAFA), xi
International Center for Transitional Justice, 242
International Clearing House for Endangered Languages, 89
International Covenant on Civil and Political Rights, 88
International Monetary Fund, viii
Inventing human rights: A history, xxv
Irwin-Zarecka, Iwona, 276

"I Will Come Back," 186
Jagan, Cheddy, 13
Jamaica: Bahia, Brazil, and, 210; slavery, maroons and, 210
Jameson, Frederic, 161
Jazz Journalists Association, 172
Jefferson, Thomas, xxv
Jericho Beach Music, 154
Jesuits, 36
Jesús, Nicolás de, 72
Johnson, Lyndon, 8
Jong, Erica, xii
Joseph, Janelle, xx, xxii
Jung, C. G., 153

Kahlo, Frida, xii
kalarippayattu, 199–200
Karl, Terry-Lynn, 4, 5
Katari, Tomás, 40
Katari, Tupac, 40, 41
"katarista-indianism," 41
Kataristas, 41–42, 47n14
Kcho, xxii, xxiii, 217–28
Kennedy, John F., 8
Kerouac, Jack, 152
Keynesian World Order, 4
King, John, ix
Kingdom, John, xxv, 261, 270
The kingdom of this world, viii
Kirby, Kathleen, 273
Kirchner, Cristina, xviii
Kristeva, Julia, 170
Kronos Quartet, 154
Kuitca, Guillermo, 225
Kuspit, Donald, 228

La Belle Dame Sans Merci, 262
labour practices, 6, 7, 8–9
La casa de los espíritus, xii
La ciudad y los perros, 294
lacrosse, 197
L'Actualité, 298
La familia de Pascal Duarte, 258
La isla que se repite, xxv
languages: in Alto Balsas, 54–55; Amerindian, 51, 53; Aymara, 34; in Bolivia, xvii, 36, 45, 46n7; challenges

to indigenous, 89–90; in *Cobro revertido*, 292; in *Côte-des-Nègres*, 292–93; in Ecuador, xvii–xviii, 79–92; in Mexico, 51; migration and, 65, 66; in Peru, xviii; Québécois French, 293; Quichua, xvii, xviii, 79–92; Spanish (*see* Spanish)
La regata, xxii, xxiii, 217–30; Cuban rafter crisis and, 217–21, 228; *los balseros* and, 218, 219, 220, 221, 226
Latin America: history of, 174–75; Miami and, 149–50; music of (*see* music); as term, ix
Latin American Boom, vii–xi, xiii, xxviin1
Latin American identity, ix–x, xii–xiii, xx, 171–72, 277–81, 282; Hispanic Canadians and, 287–99; *machismo/machista* and, xxvii, 293, 295, 296, 297
Latin Grammy Awards, 158, 163n13
"Látino"-America, 287
Latino Canadians: literature of, xxiv, 287–99 (*see also Fronteras Americanas*)
Latin(o)-ness, 149, 158, 171
Latino Power, 293, 294, 295, 297
Latinos, Inc., 149
Latino Theatre Group, 274
La trova en Santiago de Cuba, 156
law and the state, 129–30
Lazarillo de Tormes, 258, 265
L'Clerc, Lee, xx, xxii, xxiii, xxiv
"Leaning into the afternoons," 190
legal creolization, xix, 119, 127–28, 136n8, 138n18
Linguapax Institute, 88
linguistic rights, 88, 91
Linowitz Report, 10
Lipsitz, George, 236, 237, 248
literature, xi, xii; Boom, ix
Llosa, Mario Vargas, ix, x, 242, 244, 246, 250, 294
Lolita, 258
"Loneliness," 188
Lorca, Federico Garcia, 168
los balseros. *See under* Cuba

Los pasos perdidos, 262
Loynaz, Dulce María, 229
Ludwig Museum, 217
Lyotard, Jean-François, viii

Macchu Picchu, 175–76
Machado, Alexis Leiva, xxii. *See also* Kcho
machism/machista, xxvii, 293, 295, 296, 297. *See also* masculinity
The malaise of modernity, xxv, 270
Mallon, Florencia, 289
Managua Declaration, 107
Manducarios Solidario, 83
Manifestos das Mulheres Negras, 109
Mann, Thomas, 258
Manu Chao, 160
Manuel, Victor, 179
maquiladores, 52
Marielitos, 221
Márquez, Gabriel Garcia, viii, x, xii, 174, 246
martial arts, 201, 206; capoeira (*see* capoeira); kalarippayattu, 199–200
Martínez, Esteban José, 288
Martino, Jennifer, xxi, xxiii, xxiv
masculinity, xxiv, xxvi, xxvii, 66, 170, 190, 289–93, 299n2; in Brazil, 205, 210; capoeira and, 205, 206; Hispanic-Canadians and, 287; Latino-Canadians and, xxvi. *See also machismo/machista*
Match ball, xxiv, 257–70
Maxela, 54, 63
Mayflower, 288
McHugh, Kathleen, 281
Me llamo Rigoberta Menchú y así me nació la conciencia, 258
Melo, Alexandre, 229
memory: collective, xxi, xxiii, xxvi; collective, *Fronteras Americanas* and, 273–84; collective, Peru and, 235–46, 251–52; identity and, 236, 237
"Memory," 187–88
"Memory and Identity," 236, 237
Menchu, Rigoberta, 258
MERCOSUR, 14

mestizos: in Alto Balsas, 51; in Ecuador, 82, 83
Mexico, 51–75; Alto Balsas region of (*see* Alto Balsas); earthquake in, 258; globalization and, 51–53; *indígenas and mestizos* in, 51; military in, 15; Nahuatl-speaking region of, 51
Migbolo, Walter, 273
migrant workers, xix, 5, 52–53, 56, 62–75; as "accidental tourists," 130–33; coyotes and, 63, 67, 69; in Houston, Tex., 67–70; law, the state and, 129–30, 135n1; "permanent exceptionalism" and, 119–24, 136n7; race and, 120–24, 126; smuggling of, 69–70; SWAP and, 117–34; US and, 132–33
migration, xvi–xvii, 51, 229, 292; borderlands and, 273–84; criminalizing, 19; in Ecuador, 81–82; Third World, 222; transnational, 199; transnationalism and, 117–19, 133, 134, 138n22
Miguel Castro penitentiary, 244
Milanés, Pablo, 151, 157, 158, 159
military, 7, 8; Brazil, capoeira and, 201; dictatorships and, 4, 8; "Hemispheric Security" and, 15; ideology of, 7; musicians and, 172–73; Peru and, 235, 241, 246, 247, 250, 294; regional structure of, 8; Rio Treaty and, 6; size and cost of, 15, 22n9; Special Forces of, 8; state policies and, xv, 4, 14–16, 18; US, 7, 15–16; US support of, xii, 10, 15
Miller, Paul, 168
Milosevic, Slobodan, xix
minority rights, 264
modernism, vii–viii
modernismo hispano, 184
Mohanna, Mayu, 239, 240
Mohanty, Satya P., xxvii
Mompou, Federico, xxi, 168, 170, 180, 187, 188, 189
Monegal, Rodriguez, xi
Montgomery, John, 270
"Montréal-Nord Républik," 298
Moore, Robin, 149, 151, 157, 159, 160

Morales, Evo, xiii, xvi, 27, 44
Mosquera, Gerardo, 224
Mothers of the Plaza de Mayo, 258, 270
Movimiento Negro Unificado (MNU), 100
Movimiento al Socialismo (MAS), 27, 28, 30, 31, 44, 45
Movimiento de la Izquierda Revolucionaria (MIR), 289, 290
Movimiento Revolucionario Tupac Katari, 42
Moya, Paula, x
mulato women, 99
Mundo Nuevo, xi
music, viii, x, xx, xxi, xxii; Afro-Brazilian, 197; Brazil and, xxi, 168, 172–73, 183; capoeira and, 200, 202, 210–11, 213n1; Chile and, 162n11, 178; Cuba and, xxi, 149–61, 162n8; Cuban Americans and, xx; global and non-globable, 154–58; Inuit, 154, 155–56; by Luciana Souza, 168–72; Miami and, 149–50; Minimalism and, 153; New Age, 154–55; *Portal de Trova* and, 158, 159; *rock en español*, 177; samba, 183, 192n13, 210; silence, language and, 183–91; *tonada*, 178; *Weltmusik*, 153, 155, 161; world, xxi, xxii, 150–54, 155, 156, 157, 158, 160, 161; world beat, 151, 152
Mutal, Lika, xxiii, 242, 244, 245

Nabokov, Vladimir, 258
Nader, Ralph, 17
Nahuatl, 53, 54, 65, 70, 71, 73
Nascimento, Elisa Larkin, 101
National Articulation of Brazilian Women for Beijing, 110
National Confederation of Campesino Workers of Bolivia (CNTCB), 42
National Directorate of Intercultural-Bilingual Education (DINEIB), 85–86, 89, 90
National Human Rights Program, 101
National Museum of Peru, 241
National Organization of Indigenous Peoples of Colombia (ONIC), 43

Nef, Jorge, xiii, xiv, xv, 148, 271n4
neoliberalism, viii, xv, xxi, 3, 8–10, 13–18; Bolivia and, 29
Neruda, Pablo, xx, xxi, xxii, 167–91; in exile, 173–75; *Il Postino* and, 257; Luciana Souza and, 168–72, 180–91; Mikis Theodorakis and, 179–80; Nobel Prize and, 173; Spanish-speaking Americas and, 174–79, 191
Neruda en el Corazón, 168, 179
Neruda song cycle, 168, 170, 171, 172, 178, 180–91
Neruda Songs, 168
Neyret, Juan Pablo, 171
NGOs, viii, xi, xiii, xxiv
Nicaragua, military in, 15
Nicola Noel, 151, 158, 159, 160
Nietzsche, Friedrich, 262
NINA program, 30
Nixon, Richard, 10
Nixon Doctrine, 8
Non-Immigrant Employment Authorization Program (NIEAP), 121–23
Nootka Bay, 288
Nora, Pierre, 275
"North American," 284n1
North American Free Trade Agreement (NAFTA), xvi, 5, 14, 19, 52, 274
North and South, 172
No such thing as society?, 261
novísima trova, 157, 160
nueva canción, 151, 158, 159, 177, 178
nueva trova, xxi, 149–53; "alter-globalization" and, 158–60
Nuñez, Marilo, 274

Oapan, 54, 57, 58, 72
Obama, Barack, 19
Occupational Health and Safety Act (Ontario), 124
oligarchies, 14
One hundred years of solitude, viii
100 Love Sonnets, 184, 185
Ontario Horticultural Advisory Committee, 121
On the road, 152

Organization of American States (OAS), 19
organized crime, 69
Ortega y Gasset, José, xxii
Ortiz, Fernando, 198, 199, 228
Ortiz, Gernando, 146
Otavalo cumminity, 83
Otero, Geraldo, 32
Otras plegarias atendidas, 225

Pachakuti, 33, 47n8
Pachakutik Plurinational Unity Movement–New Nation, 87
padre de familia, 290, 297
Padrón, Frank, 150–51
Paine, Thomas, xxv
Pakari, Nina, 87
Palestine–Israeli wars, 174
Parra, Angel, 177
Parra, Violeta, 177
Partido Comunista de Peru, 235
Partido Indio, 41
Pax Americana, xiii, xiv, xxi, 3–21, 148
Paz, Octavio, xiii
Paz, Senel, 161
"Pentagonism," 8
Peron, Evita, 264
Peru: Ayacuchu, 240, 246, 247; blame and reconciliation in, 235–52; *Comisión de la Verdad y Reconciliación* (CVR), 235–36, 238–39, 250–51, 252; Communist Party of, 235; language and education in, xviii, 87; Macchu Picchu, 175–76; military in, xxiv, 15, 235, 241, 246, 247, 250, 294; *Sendero Luminoso* and, xxi, xxiv, 235, 241, 246, 249, 250; Shining Path and, xxi, 235, 240; terrorism in, 245; Truth and Reconciliation Commission (CVR), 235–36, 238–39
Pinochet, Augusto, xix, 179, 257, 270, 289, 290, 291
Pintado, Maylene Fernández, 225
Plaza de Mayo, 258, 270
plutocracies, 12–14, 17
Poblete, Juan, 176–77
"Poema 20," 190

Poemas y Milosz, 268
"Poetry," 189–90
Polanyi, Karl, 39
The Politics of Aesthetics, 218
Poniatowska, Elena, 258
Portal de Trova, 158, 159, 160, 163n15
Portugese colonizers, 99, 100, 175
postmodernism, x; modernism and, vii–viii
poverty, 5, 6, 16–17
Preto, Gato, 208, 209, 210
public policies: impact of, 16–17; military and, xv, 4, 14–16
Putin, Vladimir, xi

Quebec: Hispanics and, 288–89; Latin American literature and, 292–93
Quechua language, xxiii, 31, 87, 91, 236, 238, 248; Google, Microsoft and, 89; Incas and, 33; and Quichua language, 79; Spanish and, xvii, xxiii, 91; varieties of, 79
Quechua people, xvii, 31, 40, 42, 43; future challenges to, 91–92; speakers of, 79–80, 87
Quevedo, Francisco de, 263
Quichua, xvii, xviii, 79–92; attitudes towards, 83–84; dialects of, 80–81; electronic media and, 89; future challenges to, 91–92; revitalization of, 84, 89; as a second language, 89–90; Spanish and, 79; speakers of, 79–80
Quichua Unificado, 80–81
Quilapayún, 177

Rabassa, Gregory, xi
Radford, Michael, 257
Rama, Angel, vii, 176–77
Ramirez, Pablo, xxiv, xxv, xxvi
Ramirez, Yasmin, 219
Rancière, Jacques, 218, 224, 228, 231n10, 232n16
Reagan, Ronald, 10, 69, 270
Reclaiming Identity, x
reconquista, 276, 298
Red April, xxiii, xxiv, 236, 246–52

re-democratization, 17–21
Red Rider, 177, 179
regata. See *La regata*
regimes: change and continuity of, 12; civil-military, 14; dictator, 4, 8, 172; economic policies and (see economic policies); elites, and, 12, 13; national security, 8–10, 14; oligarchic, 14; plutocratic, 12–14, 17; public policies and (see public policies); stability of, 6, 7
Regional Conference of the Americas against Racism, 107
Reinaga, Fausto, 41
The repeating island, xxv
Retamar, Roberto Fernández, x
Richler, Noah, 296
Rifkin, Jeremy, 153
rights, 266–67; human (see human rights); of indigenous peoples, 60; linguistic, 88, 91; minority, 264; universal, 260
The rights revolution, 259
Rio Treaty (1947), 4, 6
Rivera, Diego, xii
Robbins, James Lawrence, 160
Rockefeller brothers, xi
Rockefeller Report, 8
Rodríguez, Silvio, 151, 158, 159, 160
Roland, Edna, 111
Roldós, Jaime, 83
Roncagliolo, Santiago, xxiii, xxiv, 236, 246, 250, 251
Roncallo, Alejandra, xiii, xiv, xv, 148
Rostagno, Irene, x, xii
Rousseau, Jean-Jacques, xxv

Said, Edward, 174, 222
Sánchez, Pepe, 156
Sánchez de Lozada, Gonzalo, 28
Sansone, Livio, 106
Santa Maria, Haydée, x
Santiago de Cuba, 156
Satzewich, Vic, 120
Saussure, Ferdinad de, 275
Schryer, Frans J., xiv, xvi, xvii
Schulman, Barbara, 108

Seasonal Agricultural Workers Program (SWAP), xix, 117–34; foreign states and, 124–26; law, the state and, 129–30, 135n3–4, 136–37n9–12, 137n17; legal creolization and, 119, 127–28
security, xiv, 3, 4, 7–10, 12, 18; migrant workers and, 64, 67
Segundo, Compay, 156, 157
Segura, Mauricio, xxvi–xxvii, 292–93, 296, 298–99
Sendero Luminoso, xxi, xxiv, 235, 241, 246, 247, 249, 250
Serres, Michel, 282
sexual exploitation, 100
Sharma, Nandita, 120
Shaw, Donald, 269
Shining Path, xxi, 235, 240
Silva, Joselina da, 110
Siqueiros, David, 149
Skármeta, Antonio, xxiv, xxv, 257–70; biography of, 257
slavery, 35, 99, 106; in Argentina, xx; in Brazil, xxii, 103; capoeira and, 201, 210; emancipation and, 100, 128; maroons and, 210, 213n5
Smith, Adrian, xiv, xix
Smith, D. Vance, 282
social reforms, 13
"Sonnet 49," 189
"Sonnet 99," 183–85, 186
Sontag, Susan, xi, xii
Sound Unbound, 168
South American Defense Council, 15
South and Meso American Indian Information Center (SAIIC), 43
Souza, Luciana, xx, xxi, xxii, 168–72, 174, 178, 180–91
Souza, Peter, 168
Spanglish, 287
Spanish: Catholic missions, 36–37; colonies, 288; conquest, 33, 34, 35, 47n12, 56, 175; language education, xvi, xvii, 56, 57; poetry, xxii, 167, 191n2 (*see also* Neruda, Pablo; Souza, Luciana); Quichua and, xviii, 79–84, 91–92

Spivak, Gayatri C., xxiii, 218, 221, 224
Stephanides, Stephanos, 279
stereotypes, 6; collective memory and, 275–81; of Latinos, 149, 278–79, 280; Toronto Police Association and, 278–79
Stockhausen, Karlheinz, 153, 155, 157, 161
structural adjustment packages (SAPs), 10–11
structural changes, 3
Suárez, Hugo Banzer, 42
Sullivan, Rosemary, 170, 184, 185
Summit of the Americas (2009), 19
Suzuki, Ichiro, 199

Tagaq Gillis, Tanya, 154, 155–56
Talking Heads, 158, 163n14
tango, xx
Tapscott, Stephen, 185
Taylor, Charles, xxv, 260–61, 270, 271n3
Taylor, Diana, 236, 240, 251, 280
Telemusik, 153
Terralingua, 89
terrorism, 13, 14, 18, 19; fiction writers and, 246; in Peru, 245
Thatcher, Margaret, 261, 270
Theodorakis, Mikis, 177; Pablo Neruda and, 179–80
Third World countries, xix, 6, 153, 222, 224, 264
Tide, 191
Tiwanaku Manifesto, 42
Tocqueville, Alexis de, 270
Toledo, Viceroy, 33
"Tonada de Manuel Rodríguez," 178, 179
Tormes, Lazarillo de, 259, 260, 270
Toronto Police Association, 278, 279
torture, xv, xxv, 13, 99, 206, 209, 250, 296
tourism, xvii
Training Program in Intercultural-Bilingual Education for Andean Countries (PROEIB), 88, 90
Tranculturación Narrativa en América Latina, 176

transculturation, 176–77; capoeira and, 198–200; sports and, 198–200
Treaty of Guadalupe Hidalgo, 288
Trilateral Commission, 10, 13
Tropicália movement, 173
trova tradicional, 156
Trueba, Estaban, xii
Truth and the Reconciliation Commission (CVR), xxiii, 235–52
Tucker, Eric, 124
Tungurahua Volcano, 82
Tupac Amaru, xvi
Twenty Poems of Love, 190

UNASUR, 15
United Nations, viii, xiii; Brazil and, 109–11; linguistic rights and, 88
United Nations Conference on Racism, 97
United Nations Decade for Women, 109
United Nations Decade of the World's Indigenous Peoples, xiii
United Nations Economic Commission on Latin America and the Caribbean, 6
United Nations Fourth World Conference on Women, 97
United States: border crossing into, 62–71, 74; Cuba and (*see under* Cuba); elections in, 14, 19; Hispanic population of, 6, 21n1, 51; Latin American politics and, ix, xi, xii, 5–10, 12, 18–19; Mexican immigration to, 276; migrant workers and, 132–33; military of (*see under* military); power of, ix, 5–10, 12, 18–19, 101, 259; views of elites of, 6
Universal Declaration of Human Rights, xix, 109
Universal Declaration of Linguistic Rights, 88
universal rights, 260
Universidad Indígena Intercultural, 90
Universidad Intercultural de Nacionalidades y Pueblos Indígenas Amawtay Wasi, xviii, 86
Universidad Politécnica Salesiana, 88
Updike, John, xi

Urbina, José Leandro, xxvi, xxvii, 289, 290, 293, 294, 295, 297, 299
Urrutia, Matilde, 184
Uruguay, xv, 7, 18, 159, 277; "Memory and Identity" and, 236, 237; slaves in, xx

Valenzuela, Luisa, xii
Varela, Carlos, 160
Velasco, General, 87
Veloso, Caetano, 173
Venezuela, xv, 11, 292; military and, 15, 145
Verdecchia, Guillermo, xxv, xxvi, 273–84
Villanueva, Freddy, 298

Walker, Alice, 105
war: civil, 15; national security and, 12; terrorism and, 14
war criminals, xix
"War on Terror," 19
"We Are Many," 182–83, 185, 186
Weber, Max, 31
Weitz, Morris, 228
Werneck, Jurema, 106, 107
white women's identity, 99
Wilka, Pablo Zárate, 41
World Bank, viii
World Conference on Human Rights, 109–10
World Conference on Population and Development, 110
World Conference on Women, 110
World Conferences on Women's Rights and Racism, xviii
World Trade Organization, viii
World War II, xvi, 4, 6, 7, 15, 56

Xalitla, 54, 55, 60, 72
Xavier, Lucia, 104, 107

Yúdice, George, vii, xxi, 148
Yupanqui, Tupac, 33
Yuyanapaq: para recordar, xxiii, 239, 241, 242, 245, 251

Zapatistas, xvi, 52, 60
Žižek, Slavoj, 154–55, 161

www.ingramcontent.com/pod-product-compliance
Lightning Source LLC
Chambersburg PA
CBHW071148070526
44584CB00019B/2702